Guide to Writing Magazine Nonfiction

MICHAEL J. BUGEJA
Ohio University

ALLYN AND BACON
Boston London Toronto Sydney Tokyo Singapore

Vice President, Editor in Chief: Paul Smith
Senior Editor: Joseph Terry
Editorial Assistant: Leila Scott
Marketing Manager: Karen Bowers
Production Administrator: Annette Joseph
Production Coordinator: Susan Freese
Editorial-Production Service: TKM Productions
Text Design and Electronic Composition: Denise Hoffman
Composition Buyer: Linda Cox
Manufacturing Buyer: Suzanne Lareau
Cover Administrator: Suzanne Harbison

Copyright © 1998 by Allyn & Bacon
A Viacom Company
160 Gould Street
Needham Heights, MA 02194
Internet: www.abacon.com
America Online: keyword: College Online

Library of Congress Cataloging-in-Publication Data

Bugeja, Michael J.
    Guide to writing magazine nonfiction / Michael J. Bugeja.
        p.   cm.
    Includes index.
    ISBN 0-205-26113-2 (alk. paper)
        1. Journalism—Authorship.   2. Feature writing.   I. Title.
PN147.B79   1998
808'.06607—dc21   97-7212
                                                                          CIP

Printed in the United States of America
10 9 8 7 6 5 4 3 2   02 01 00 99 98

See permissions credits on pages 325–328, which constitute a continuation of the copyright page.

Guide
to Writing
Magazine
Nonfiction

CONTENTS

CHAPTER SIX

Time
Elements   103

CHAPTER SEVEN

Viewpoint
and Voice   125

CHAPTER EIGHT

Endings   147

PREFACE

Brace yourself for a hard fact: Few, if any, members of a typical magazine workshop or writing class publish their prose. Certainly, publication can be difficult. But that's not the main problem. Unfortunately, too many teachers and workshop leaders believe that good writing cannot be taught. Of course, they won't admit this to aspiring writers, but that's how they feel. So they tell new writers to "discover" their topics, their voices, their endings, and then they mark up the margins of drafts with comments such as "awkward," "trite," or "doesn't flow." These teachers are pointing out problems, sure, but they aren't explaining how to fix them. So beginners sigh and try again until someone says that they got it right or until they lose confidence as writers.

Here's another hard fact: Some people *are* natural-born writers—especially writing teachers. They got their jobs because they could publish in top magazines and literary journals. They're talented folks—so talented that they are capable of envisioning a manuscript without actually outlining it; hence, they "discover" what they already know intimately.

The vast majority of aspiring writers do not fall into this lucky category. They do not envision their stories or know how to fix basic problems with the trusty tools of craft. They get lost during the writing process, taking tangents or trying a hit-and-miss approach. They get impatient or, worse, writer's block, waiting for the muse to come to their rescue. That wastes time, and time is money to a freelance writer.

It turns out, however, that good writing *can* be taught. The problem is that most teachers begin the process at a point already beyond the typical novice. This is only natural. After all, these natural-born writers don't outline their columns or essays; they just sit down and type and then teach that way, immediately telling their workshops to do drafts or assignments. Writing too soon can be the worst thing to do. New writers should learn how to envision their stories the same way Olympic-caliber athletes envision their goals. Beginners have to know the basic elements of nonfiction—title, topic, theme, voice, viewpoint, moment, ending, and so on—and how they complement each other. Otherwise, their teachers will analyze those writing samples and declare them "vague," "confusing," or "contrived."

When writing is vague, confusing, or poorly executed, there is *always* a reason and a solution. That's the focus of *Guide to Writing Magazine Nonfiction*. This is not a typical how-to book that offers hundreds of writing techniques in a hodgepodge of jargon. You may have dozens of such books on your shelf, but after reading this one, you will know how to use those others for the first time, understanding how one technique influences or affects another. In this book, you are going to learn a few *major* concepts—found in every piece of prose, however avant-garde—that have been around for a hundred years or more: topic, theme, titles, moment and occasion of narration, viewpoint, voice, and more. These elements must harmonize, the way instruments do in a symphony—or else your writing will fail. That is why so few beginning writers ever get the freelance process down right.

Here, you will come to appreciate the writing process *as* a process. You will take a step-by-step approach, learning about each basic element and how it functions. You will not only determine why a passage is flawed but also learn how to fix it with universal tools of craft. You'll be writing throughout the process, but as a freelancer writes—logging ideas, isolating themes, researching topics, and more—so that you can envision your feature or article. Before you write a word of it—and you *will* write and revise toward the end of this book, not because you have been given an assignment but because you are going to *want* to write—you will know how basic elements harmonize with each other. Writing will come naturally to you now. You will understand the essence of magazine journalism and will target manuscripts for publication. To keep you on track, you will read magazines on the newsstand and evaluate them as a writer (rather than as a consumer).

To achieve all this, this book contains several layers of instruction. A Guide to Readings section is included at the back of the text, featuring the work of world-class writers who publish in such magazines as *Esquire, Mirabella, New York Times Magazine, The Hudson Review,* and *The New Republic,* along with a variety of consumer, trade, general-interest, and regional publications. In each chapter, excerpts from these articles, as well as others, will illustrate basic functions of nonfiction; you will later read most of these articles in their entirety to see how those elements harmonize to create superior manuscripts. Aspiring and newly published authors will share excerpts from first and second drafts to show how flawed writing can be fixed with the tools of craft. You'll encounter more information at the end of each chapter in The Craft Shop, featuring interviews with writers and editors about essential techniques. This is followed by The Newsstand, exercises that encourage eager freelancers to read and analyze magazines off the racks. Each chapter ends with The Keyboard, assignments that guide you through the freelance process. In sum, you will be immersed in magazine nonfiction. Specifically, you will learn about these nonfiction elements and techniques:

- *Chapter One: Magazine Basics*—People who do not read magazines often want to write for them. That can be a big problem. In this chapter, you learn the basics of magazine journalism—101 craft, freelance, and magazine terms—including common types of magazine nonfiction (column, profile, opinion, interview, essay, feature, and article) and types of approaches (informational, anecdotal, and personal experience). You then investigate magazine writing versus newspaper reporting, the importance of audience (demographics, psychographics), and much more. In The Craft Shop, you encounter the virtual magazine (or *webzine*). At The Newsstand, you envision the reader by analyzing letters, advertising, and contents. You get a jump over competition at The Keyboard, composing audience profiles and soliciting writer's guidelines of your favorite magazines.

- *Chapter Two: Topics and Ideas*—Truth is essential in any magazine piece. But the truth is also subjective and requires *utility*—that is, information or insight that satisfies audience needs. You also discover your own set of truths—epiphanies, peak experiences, turning points in your life—and determine what you know and who, if anyone, would be interested in hearing it. Additionally, you study writing strategies to convey your truths powerfully and effectively. In The Craft Shop, a new author explains the courage it takes to write about personal experience, and a nationally recognized interviewer explains how to brainstorm for story ideas. At The Newsstand, you browse for markets that might be interested in what you know, and at The Keyboard, you compile an inventory of story ideas.

- *Chapter Three: Theme*—Theme is a second, or deeper, layer of meaning related to truth and appealing to reader perceptions. That distinguishes magazine journalism from other media. You learn about thematic breaks and statements. The technical terms *grounding* and *foreshadowing* help distinguish topic from theme. The editor of *Writer's Digest* elaborates about that in The Craft Shop. You scan for themes, or *slants,* at The Newsstand, and you ascertain your own themes at The Keyboard.

- *Chapter Four: Research*—Research is essential in magazine nonfiction, and interviews often are part of that process. In this chapter, you draw a *source box*—a type of outline that identifies who needs to be interviewed before the writing phase begins. The magazine interview differs from the newspaper kind, so you learn how to frame questions to snare thematic quotations from your sources. You also learn about sensory data—to enrich your writing—and research methods to meld topic and theme. Information about library networks and the Internet follows, with a discussion of sidebars in magazines and hot links in webzines. In The Craft Shop, an expert researcher explains information gathering and a book editor discusses the value of research and commitment. At The Newsstand, you research topics and themes to envision your story. You then draw your own source box, determining how much research your ideas may require, at The Keyboard.

- *Chapter Five: Titles*—A magazine title is a handshake with the reader—a kind of contract. It promises to deliver information, and you had better live up to that or face rejection before your first precious word. In this chapter, you examine examples of good and bad titles culled from manuscripts and magazines. Three categories are explained: suspense, descriptive, and label. You see how to mix and match these types and meld them with subtitles. You also discover 21 types of basic titles and how to compose them, and you learn about the special role of subheads. To top it off, a magazine editor discusses the power of titles in The Craft Shop; you scan for titles, subtitles, and subheads at The Newsstand; and you compose working titles for your story ideas at The Keyboard.

- *Chapter Six: Time Elements*—There is real time and then there is *literary* time. The latter is called the *moment of narration,* or the point when the audience "enters" the story. The moment of narration can be close to the action, as if it is happening *now;* removed from the action, as if it has happened in the past, or *then;* and somewhat removed from the action (a combination of both time elements, *now and then*). This is radically different from grammatical and chronological time, also covered extensively. Here, you see how to use time elements to generate tension, drama, comment, and/or perspective. You'll also align a time element with your developing story ideas, helping you outline and envision the structure of your work. You encounter several other concepts related to time element—including flashback and flashforward—with expert comment about the moment of narration in The Craft Shop. At The Newsstand, you analyze moments and magazines, and at The Keyboard, you determine time elements and sketch outlines for your story ideas.

- *Chapter Seven: Viewpoint and Voice*—Voice is the sound you hear on the page. To determine voice, a writer must understand the concept of viewpoint—thoroughly explained—along with key terms such as *narrator* and *persona*. In this chapter, you learn how to align viewpoint with voice to generate proper tones for your piece and increase your chances of acceptance at a target publication. You encounter a dozen of the most common tones used by top-name writers in such magazines as *Esquire, New Woman, Mirabella,* and *Vegetarian Times.* In The Craft Shop, an editor discusses how to capture viewpoint during interviews and a novice writer explains how to hone voice by understanding audience. You note the preferred viewpoints and predominant voices of your target publications at The Newsstand, and you pinpoint your viewpoint and voice at The Keyboard.

- *Chapter Eight: Endings*—Two types of endings are explained in this chapter: open and closed. An *open* ending leaves the audience with a feeling or milieu; a *closed* one reports or shares a final truth. You determine which one suits your type of story. In any case, the ending is a completion of your contract with the readers; it bears your signature, revealing an epiphany or peak experience. The ending is also a destination, representing your journey with the readers. In this chapter, you envision magazine journalism as a journey culminating with a lingering sense of scene or with an enlightening disclosure. You learn common strategies for linking up beginnings with open and closed endings, illustrated with comments and examples by top-name writers. The chapter ends with advice about endings by an esteemed literary critic in The Craft Shop, discoveries about endings and audience at The Newsstand, and assignments about nailing your ending at The Keyboard.

- *Chapter Nine: The Writing Process*—The writing begins! To prepare, you develop a "snapshot" outline of your story idea and analyze other such outlines by top-name writers such as Diane Ackerman and George Plimpton. You discover how to harmonize the basic elements of nonfiction to ensure a workable first draft. Then you view the pitfalls of a typical first draft and see how to overcome them. In The Craft Shop, a versatile writer explains how the revision process led to her publication in the *New York Times Magazine.* A trip to The Newsstand psyches you up. At The Keyboard, you align story elements for one of your developing story ideas, from title to ending, to create a snapshot blueprint. A handy checklist helps you revise initial drafts until you arrive at the final one.

- *Chapter Ten: The Freelance Process*—Here, you find information about standard manuscript format, query and cover letters, and mailing and marketing manuscripts. In The Craft Shop, a new writer explains how the process led to her first publication in *Sassy*. You analyze back issues of potential markets at The Newsstand and log your first submission at The Keyboard.

As you can see, you are going to cover a lot of ground. By breaking down the components of magazine nonfiction and envisioning and revising your prose, you will write naturally and powerfully. You will become skilled as an editor, too, able to decipher and resolve problems in other people's manuscripts. Quicker than you can imagine, you may achieve the ultimate goal of every aspiring writer: a contract for your first freelance work.

Your byline will prove that good writing *can* be taught—and published.

Acknowledgments

This book is a blessing. I could not have written it without the help of some 40 writers who have contributed their works and wisdom. They write in a variety of prose styles and publish in a wide array of magazines. You'll recognize some of their names and periodicals: George Plimpton, *Esquire;* Diane Ackerman, *New Yorker;* Molly Peacock, *Mirabella;* Carol Muske Dukes, *House & Garden;* Patricia Raybon, *USA Weekend;* Catherine Johnson, *New Woman;* Lady Borton, *New York Times Magazine;* Karin Horgan Sullivan, *Vegetarian Times;* Ursula Obst, *New York Woman;* Dana Gioia, *The Hudson Review;* Christina Hoff Sommers, *The New Republic;* Bruce Woods, *BackHome;* Kevin Bezner, *Left Bank;* Kelly Cherry, *Chattahoochee Review;* David Lazar, *Mississippi Valley Review* and *Best American Essays of 1993;* Patricia Westfall, *Esquire;* Bill Brohaugh, *Writer's Digest;* Neal Bowers, *Writer's Yearbook;* Audrey Chapman, *Cleveland Magazine;* Ellen J. Gerl, *Ohio Magazine;* and Michael Burns, *Springfield!*

Up-and-coming writers and the magazines in which their work appears include Bethany Matsko, *Sassy;* Daniel Horn, *Quill;* Peg Dillon, *Southeast Ohio;* Amy Hudson, *Writer's Digest;* and Andrea Tortora and Megan Lane, both in *Editor & Publisher.*

You'll meet some new writers, too, from my workshop at Ohio University. Perhaps more than anyone, *they* know the struggles of trying to master magazine journalism. They include Laura Churchill, Erika Firm, Keith Johns, Susan E. Murphy, Cheryl Powers, Heather Paige Preston, Robin Rauzi, Heidi Reddert, Les Roka, Anna Szymanski, Cathy Twining, and Amy Zaruca.

I also want to thank Tom Clark, my editor at *Writer's Digest*, and Eddith Dashiell, my colleague and friend at Ohio University, for contributing expert comment about writing and research. A special thanks to Polly Tichenor, Anderson Jones, Tom Hodges, and Cathy Twining, who helped me during the research phase of this project, and to Joseph Opiela, Sue Brown, and Karon Bowers of Allyn and Bacon. I also wish to thank those individuals who reviewed this book in its early stages and made useful suggestions, including David Dary (University of Oklahoma); Charles Higginson (University of Kansas, School of Journalism, Adjunct Faculty); and Nancy L. Roberts (University of Minnesota, School of Journalism and Mass Communication).

Finally, I thank my spouse Diane and children Erin and Shane, who inspire me every day with their love, encouragement, and support.

M. J. B.

ABOUT THE AUTHOR

Michael J. Bugeja, a contributing editor for *Writer's Digest,* is a nationally known writer with some 700-plus credits in mass media and literary magazines, including *Harper's, Quill, Journalism Quarterly, Editor & Publisher, Journalism Educator, English Journal, The Georgia Review,* and *The Kenyon Review.* He has authored three textbooks: *Living Ethics: Developing Values in Mass Communication* (Allyn and Bacon); *Poet's Guide* (Story Line Press); and *The Art and Craft of Poetry* (Writer's Digest Books). In addition, he has published two books of social criticism: *Academic Socialism: Merit and Morale in Higher Education* (Orchises) and *Culture's Sleeping Beauty: Essays on Poetry, Prejudice, and Belief* (Whitston). He also has six book-length collections of poems, including *Talk* (University of Arkansas Press) and *Flight from Valhalla* (Livingston University Press), which was nominated for a Pulitzer. Bugeja's collection of prize-winning stories, *Little Dragons,* was published by Negative Capability Press, and his novel, *Family Values,* was published by Sligo Press.

His writing awards include a National Endowment for the Arts fellowship (fiction) and a National Endowment for the Humanities grant (culture). His teaching honors include an AMOCO Foundation Outstanding Teacher Award at Oklahoma State University and the University Professor Award at Ohio University, each bestowed by the student body of the institution.

Bugeja earned a doctorate in creative writing at Oklahoma State University, a master's degree in mass communication at South Dakota State University, and a bachelor's degree in German at Saint Peter's College. He is a professor at the prestigious E. W. Scripps School of Journalism, Ohio University, where he teaches media ethics and magazine writing and serves as an adviser to the President's Office. Before entering academe, he was a state editor for United Press International, operating bureaus in North and South Dakota.

Bugeja lives in Athens, Ohio, with his wife Diane and their children Erin and Shane.

Guide
to Writing
Magazine
Nonfiction

C H A P T E R   O N E

Magazine Basics

Importance of Audience

Magazine journalism is often confused with newspaper journalism. Clearly, both are print mediums, but they are as much alike as television and photography, two visual mediums with obvious differences. In many ways, magazine journalism is closer to advertising and public relations, which target select groups of people, than to newspaper journalism, which targets a geographical base. You can study newspaper writing, television, photography, advertising, and public relations in journalism school, but only a handful of universities—including Missouri, Northwestern, and Ohio Universities—have bonafide magazine programs. And even in schools that offer excellent magazine courses, sometimes "newspaper lingo" creeps in. Teachers might say *headline* when they mean *title, lead* when they mean *introduction,* and *feature* when they mean *article* (or vice versa). And a few instructors still believe the difference between a magazine and a newspaper is the deadline—longer for a magazine, shorter for a newspaper—allowing writers to gather more quotations or compose longer stories.

As you will learn in 101 Basic Terms toward the end of this chapter, a *feature* is a magazine work between 1,000 and 2,000 words. (Length of a filler is 1 to 250 words; a column, 250 to 1,000 words; and an article, over 2,000 words.) Some magazines use slick paper, others use pulp. Some magazines are weekly, biweekly, bimonthly, semiannual, or annual (such as *Writer's Digest Yearbook*). Some magazines come out only once and are called, appropriately, *one-shots,* published because of popular interest about the exploits of a hero, perhaps, or the trials of a celebrity. And while it is true that most magazines are monthly, the deadlines are grueling because the typical editorial staff is small—averaging only four to six people at many specialized business (hobby, craft, technical) and city magazines. Magazines such as *Cosmopolitan, Reader's Digest,* and *Vanity Fair* may have staffs of 50 or more, but their circulations are in the multimillions—requiring lots of in-house coordination between departments—whereas the typical newspaper circulation is in the multi*thousands*. Deadlines, then, do not distinguish magazine from newspaper journalism; the audience for each medium, however, *does*.

A newspaper's circulation may be measured by drawing circles on a map. A local newspaper might reach residents of three counties. That's as far as the delivery trucks can drive. That's as far as the reporters can cover. That's as far as the advertising base extends. So the potential audience for the newspaper is everyone who lives within that circle—women and men of all ages, races, social classes, religions, educations, and interests.

How do you speak to such a diverse group about breaking news? Typically, in one tone of voice—*authoritative*—which sounds like this:

> ATHENS, OH—John Jones, 34, Athens, drove left of center on County Road 17 and was killed in a two-vehicle collision 2½ miles south of the city limits, the Sheriff's Office reported Tuesday.
>
> Jones was northbound at approximately 11:30 p.m. Monday and swerved into the path of a southbound pickup truck driven by Jane Doe, 23, Guysville, authorities said.
>
> Doe was wearing a seat belt, sustained minor injuries and was treated and released at O'Bleness Hospital, according to accident and hospital records. Jones, not wearing a seat belt, was thrown from his vehicle and pronounced dead on arrival at the hospital.
>
> Jones was the fifth person to die this year in a traffic accident on Athens County roads, the Sheriff's Office reported.

Newswriting sounds authoritative because it documents what people do, plan, or announce. "These are the facts," the newspaper implies. "We can't get personal because we have no idea who is reading this report."

The newspaper has an eclectic (or general) audience, so it cannot comment or slant the facts to favor one political, religious, social, or cultural viewpoint. If it does, it will insult or anger readers who hold different or opposing views. That is why editors insist on reporters striving for objectivity—not taking sides on an issue—merely reporting the facts and trusting that truths eventually will be apparent to the public.

Moreover, a newspaper covers *what its editors think readers need*. If the majority of readers believe that they should not have to wear seat belts when driving, an editor might assign a story telling them that they should, citing traffic statistics. If the majority of readers believe that taxes are too high, an editor might assign a story explaining the need for a new school levy, citing high enrollments. If the majority of readers are white Christians, an editor might highlight Kwanza and Hanukah as well as Christmas in December on the religion page.

On some level, newspaper readers appreciate this approach. Unless they are lonely, or stalled in an elevator, few of them will read *everything* in a newspaper. And editors know that. If any story irks a reader who holds a different truth or view, that person will ignore the story and read another news item or wire report or do the crossword puzzle or scan the comics, horoscopes, and classified ads. When a newspaper covers everything, as is usually the case, there is something for everybody.

Only a few regional or city magazines measure their circulations by drawing circles on a map. And even these scrutinize the audience and follow a mission statement or concept when deciding what to print. For instance, a regional magazine might focus on culture, as does *Appalachian Heritage,* and a city magazine might focus on the consumer, as does *Columbus Bride,* an Ohio wedding magazine. In fact, a city magazine with enough general-interest appeal can go national, as did *New York,* competing with rivals such as *Esquire* and *GQ.* Staffs of these and other publications decide what readers have in common and then analyze those commonalties—demographics and psychographics—so that editors can give the audience *what it wants or perceives to need.*

If the editor is a vegetarian, and the readers enjoy red meat, the magazine doesn't run pieces about the dangers of eating or grilling beef. Instead, the editor schedules a rib extravaganza for the July issue and composes titles like "Good Ribbings" or "Firework Tex-Mex Babyback Barbecue!" If the audience thinks it has to diet, the editor knows that doesn't mean readers are necessarily overweight; they may only *perceive* that they are. In that case, the editor orders features with titles like "Low-Fat, No-Frills Diet" or "Cut Calories . . . And This Pound Cake!"

This is why magazines exist. Few people, even family members or loved ones, give you what you want or tell you what you want to hear. Think about it. Say you like astronomy. You wake up your lover at 3 A.M. to see Orion on the horizon. The first time, the lover might think the tryst is romantic and might stumble out to the balcony with a glass of wine to peer in a telescope. The second time, the lover might sigh and spend two minutes on that balcony and then stumble back to bed. The third time, the lover doesn't get up. So the astronomy enthusiast buys *Sky and Telescope* and lets the lover sleep. That's good for the magazine, the enthusiast, *and* the lover.

Do you like poetry but your family and significant other do not? Do they bristle upon hearing the word? Do they think studying it is a waste of your time? Do they think you're foolish for wanting to go to that writing conference in Fairbanks? No problem. Three dollars buys you *Writer's Digest.* The poetry columnist will speak to you the way you wish your loved ones would, in a conversational, compassionate, and informative voice.

> Poetry has a place in your world. It may be the center of your passion, or perhaps your muse has been wounded and dormant for years. If that's the case, you have a responsibility to ask what happened to that passion and to put your feelings about poetry into context. Here's how:
>
> - *Renew your commitment.* Even if you have a passion for poetry, think back. How have you managed to keep it alive? Was there a deciding moment? By remembering, you'll be able to focus on your priorities during dry spells or when you get sidetracked at work or in the home.
> - *Rekindle your muse.* Ask yourself why you stopped writing poetry. By remembering, you'll be able to assess why you're still reading this column and decide whether you'd like to write poetry again.
> - *Heal the hurt.* Some of you have been told that you don't understand poetry or won't succeed as a poet. By recalling your initial love of poetry, you can overcome the pain or disappointment, knowing that thousands like you have had the courage to begin again and publish verse.

This example is downright one sided. The *Writer's Digest* reader who has to hide a love of poetry from family or mate—and there are thousands in that sad situation, lacking moral support—probably also has to hide the magazine. And that "closet poet" will read it, cover to cover, even advertisements selling poetry books or announcing writing conferences in Alaska. That person will devour letters to the editor, realizing for the first time that other people share his or her passions or problems.

In a word, a magazine is *subjective,* appealing to distinct groups. The editor of your favorite magazine knows all about you. Have you ever had a stranger read over your shoulder at a magazine rack or coffee shop and feel your privacy invaded? There are good reasons to pull back and close your magazine. The stranger will have you pegged, depending on the publication and article you are reading. But if you were scanning a newspaper and a stranger read over your shoulder, you might offer a section or discuss an item of interest. Reporters write for everyone, so nothing is at stake. Freelance writers, on the other hand, are *expected* to gear the facts toward the target reader. Magazine editors know that people insulted or angered by a particular slant don't read the publication anyway. They read other periodicals with slants that appeal to their own passions or pursuits, from the *National Enquirer* to *The Atlantic Monthly,* from *Ms.* to *Good House-keeping,* from the *National Review* to *The New Republic,* from the *Atheist* to *Guideposts.*

Again, this approach differs radically from content in newspapers. Basically, a small-town newspaper—the *Centerville Citizen,* say—does the same thing each day as the *New York Times,* only the *Times* does it better because it has more resources or talent. The *Citizen* subscribes to the Associated Press (AP) to cover overseas events; the *Times* sends reporters overseas to cover those events firsthand. The *Citizen* reporter and the AP and *Times* counterparts are *writers for hire,* experts at funneling facts to the newsroom to beat the competition by deadline. In return, these writers receive regular paychecks. Mostly, the writers of hard news cover it in the same tone of voice and in the same inverted pyramid style, putting the most important facts first with a summary or *nut graph* high up, and then the rest of the information in descending order of importance.

Write like that for a magazine, and you'll be rejected time and again. According to educator Eric Freedman in his 1 April 1996 *Folio* article, titled, appropriately enough, "If You're Planning to Hire a J-School Grad . . .": "That each magazine has an individual personality and unique voice is a difficult concept for many students, especially those who are comfortable with the stylistic near-homogeneity of daily newspapers, the Associated Press, syndicates and secondary wire services." Freedman knows that magazine readers want writers to speak to them intimately as friends or compassionately as mentors. To generate an appropriate voice, successful freelancers decipher the special characteristics and perceived needs of the target audience. They do so by analyzing a publication, as you will later in this chapter, or by acquiring a media kit.

A media kit is chock full of data about readers and editorial policies. It is compiled by the advertising and promotional departments and sent to potential customers (usually media planners and buyers) who take out ads in the magazine. The kit is expensive to produce—with glossy folders and slick charts, cards, posters, brochures, and other documents—and is coveted because it contains valuable information about readers and ad rates (information a competing magazine publisher might like to know). Don't lie to get one by calling an advertising representative and pretending you are a customer. Instead, ask a writing teacher to request a kit and explain that it will be on reserve in a school or public library. Knowing its use will be educational, most advertising representatives will be happy to share the information.

Among other items, a media kit contains mission statements, demographics, and psychographics. Let's analyze a few, from a freelance writing standpoint.

The mission statement of *New Woman* asserts that the magazine "is edited for today's contemporary, employed woman, seeking to balance her personal and her professional life. It's about choices and moving toward achievements. It is positive, encouraging, and enthusiastic. . . ." That's a wealth of information in 29 words. The target reader perceives a need to balance her personal and professional life, meaning that she probably has problems meeting obligations to family and career. She wants information from a confidante—someone who understands her concerns—to help her make smart choices so that she can realize her potential. (Remember, she is *moving toward* as opposed to *arriving at* achievements.) Finally, the target reader doesn't want sob stories bemoaning her lot in life or arguments, however level headed, stating that she must sacrifice home life, love life, or work. She probably feels or hears that all the time from family, lovers, and supervisors. So if you want to write for her, you should do so in a "positive, encouraging, and enthusiastic" voice with thematic statements about "balance" and closed endings about "choices."

Family Circle, however, has a somewhat different slant. Its mission statement asserts that the magazine "is written for the way women really live." The magazine offers readers advice "to balance their active lives" and lists several topics of concern, including "the environment, the state of education, care of the elderly and family relationships." It promises to provide information "with an uplifting point of view." Its mission is to "inform, instruct and encourage readers to take charge of their lives." The statement concludes: "That's why *Family Circle* is used over and over again as a sourcebook and a trusted companion."

These readers may be interested in many of the same topics as *New Woman* readers and may seek advice to balance their lives. But they also seem to have made some choices, too, putting home over career. The *Family Circle* reader knows her potential already; the problem is, she has pressing obligations. She's more involved in community affairs than her *New Woman* counterpart ("environment") and has more familial responsibilities ("care of the elderly"). She still wants that uplifting point of view, but a writer can be more candid with this overwhelmed reader who doesn't have time for long and intimate chats ("how women really live"). No kid gloves here, please, or arguments about "women having it all" (no complaining, either!). If you write for this reader, give her plain facts and instruct in the voice of a good neighbor with the focus on "solutions" and an ending urging "action."

The mission statement for *Discover,* a magazine about "emerging ideas in science and technology," asserts that it is "authoritative and accessible"—lots of facts without the technological jargon—and prides itself on being a "lively, entertaining, and compelling" forum. Moreover, it states that its readers "recognize the pervasive influence of science in today's world and the urgency of keeping pace with its progress." So if you want to write for this publication, you had better know your science and deliver it in a "lively, entertaining, and compelling" voice with a theme of "pervasive influence"—showing how your topic will affect society in the near future ("urgency") and reassuring readers that they have an intellectual edge on others.

In promotional literature about *Discover,* its president and editor-in-chief Paul Hoffman says this about his audience: "*Discover* readers are curious, intelligent adults who are passionately interested in science but have no special training in it. The readers are non-scientists who nonetheless recognize the power science has in understanding and transforming the world. They are fascinated by big questions: Where does life come from? Is there life elsewhere in the universe? Will computers ever rival our own intelligence?" Hoffman can speak about the *Discover* audience so definitively because he knows its demographics and psychographics. For starters, 55.7 percent are men and 44.3 percent are women. Their median age is 37.7 years and more than 60 percent of them have attended college. They earn a good salary, more than $46,000 per median household, but only half, 50.2 percent, are married (as opposed to over 66 percent of *Family Circle* readers, for example). Psychographics about *Discover* readers show that some 42 percent qualify as "influential," as opposed to only 10 to 12 percent of the U.S. population. Many, for instance, are officers of clubs or organizations. Other research indicates that they are culturally and socially active—going to museums regularly and attending concerts—in addition to being active in the outdoors, rock climbing, backpacking, and snorkeling. (The overwhelmed *Family Circle* reader doesn't have time for such activities.)

As you can see, magazines spend millions of dollars each year researching and surveying their readers so that they know as much as possible about them. As a writer, you need to know about your target audience, too. Media kits are handy repositories of information about readers, but you can discern as much by analyzing the cover subtitle (a smaller title or slogan heralding the magazine's concept), the editor's introduction (written in the ideal voice—who best than the editor to illustrate tone?), the advertisements (indicating demographics and psychographics), the contents pages (revealing perceived needs), and the letters page (showcasing readers speaking about what matters to them). You will learn how to decipher these components of a magazine at the end of this chapter in The Newsstand section.

Magazines also provide writers with another document almost as useful as a media kit: writer's guidelines. Typically, guidelines explain what editors are looking for, what rights they buy, how much they pay, and how to submit manuscripts and queries. Guidelines are printed inexpensively on a sheet of paper and provided free of charge to writers who request them in a business letter and who enclose a self-addressed stamped envelope for their return.

The following sample guidelines excerpted and reprinted here simply illustrate the type of information that these documents provide. (In other words, don't use them to market your materials; you will learn how to request your own updated, complete guidelines in The Keyboard section at the end of this chapter.)

Guidelines for *Vegetarian Times* detail editorial policies and state, in part:

> Our editorial focus is on vegetarian cooking, nutrition and health. We also cover environmental issues, animal rights, alternative medicine and government policy. The magazine is nationally distributed and has a circulation of 320,000.
>
> We look for articles that are extensively researched and well-written and that provide fresh ideas and new information. It is crucial that articles be from a vegetarian perspective—a diet free of meat, poultry and fish and an outlook that is sensitive to animals and the environment. The tone should be authoritative and engaging. Though we tend to challenge conventional wisdom and mainstream practices, we strive for objectivity, which means incorporating viewpoints that may be different from our own. We have a diverse readership, from vegans who avoid all animal products, to part-time vegetarians looking to cut back on their meat consumption. We don't ostracize those who eat meat. Instead we try to show through lively information and delicious, attractive recipes that a vegetarian lifestyle is preferable. We strongly recommend that you read a few issues of the magazine to get a sense of our tone and focus.

Guidelines for *Writer's Digest* are even more extensive than ones for *Vegetarian Times,* explaining how to submit queries and unsolicited manuscripts along with detailed instructions about writing for each department of the magazine. The magazine's concept is clearly stated at the top of the four-page document:

> *Writer's Digest* is a monthly handbook for writers who want to write better and sell more. Every word we publish must inform, instruct or inspire the freelancer. Our readers want specific ideas and tips that will help them succeed—and success to our readers means getting into print.
>
> Yet that doesn't mean that we don't have a little fun in *WD*. Our style is informal and personal. We try to entertain as well as instruct. We try to speak with the voice of a compassionate colleague, a friend as well as a teacher. And though we don't shy away from explaining the difficulties of getting published today, all of our articles share a certain optimism. *WD* is infused with a belief in anyone's potential to succeed as a writer.

Most writer's guidelines are as succinct as this sample one by *Good Housekeeping:*

> *Good Housekeeping* addresses 24 million married women, most of whom have children (anywhere from newborn to college age) and who work outside the home.
>
> Areas of interest covered include consumer issues, human interest, social issues, health, nutrition, relationships, psychology and work/career.
>
> Several sections are especially well suited to freelancers: Better Way, which is comprised of 300 to 500 word how-to pieces; Profiles, 400 to 600 word features on people involved in inspiring, heroic or fascinating pursuits; and "My Problem and How I Solved It," a first person or as-told-to format, in which a woman (using her real name) relays how she overcame an especially difficult impasse in her life.
>
> It's best to familiarize yourself with the tone and content of *Good Housekeeping* before you query us. (Back issues will likely be available at your local library.) The most successful queries or manuscripts are those that are timely, appropriately researched, engagingly written, freshly angled, and tailored to *Good Housekeeping* readers in particular.
>
> Manuscripts and queries submitted on speculation should be typed, double spaced and when possible, should have clips of previously published articles attached. You must include a SASE to receive a reply. Please allow 2 to 3 months for a response due to the large volume of unsolicited queries we get.

Based on your ability to decode a magazine, as you will learn at The Newsstand, you should be able to compose a target audience profile. Freelancers create such profiles for their own use so that they can fine-tune their prose and target it at readers. Most profiles are one page, like the sample shown in Figure 1.1 created by magazine student Keith Johns, who analyzed components of *Mac Home Journal (MHJ)* according to methods you will learn in The Keyboard section. With a document like this at his disposal, Keith Johns was able to envision the *Mac Home Journal* reader as if he were sitting in the reader's home office.

As you are learning, the quickest way to write for magazines is to read them as a freelancer, rather than as a consumer. In the following section, you will find basic magazine terms. Learn them and you will already be one step ahead of "wanna-be" magazine writers.

101 Basic Terms

To be a freelance writer, you have to understand the language ("lingo") of magazine journalism. As soon as you do, you will graduate from *wanna-be* to *novice*. That's a big step. A wanna-be thinks that he

FIGURE 1.1   Sample Target Audience Profile

Give Your Mac an Interface-Lift
Keith Johns

The *MHJ* reader is a professional adult who either uses a computer at the office (PC or Mac) and has a Mac at home; or works out of her home office and uses a Macintosh system as a part of that work. She believes in the Mac Operating System as the finest and most user-friendly system available; Windows represents "that other system" that still hasn't caught up with the Mac OS. As a Mac owner, she is "a part of something." She will tinker a little, but only if the procedure is simple. Often, the Mac is a toy as well as tool. She loves her Mac, yet she is a certain kind of user. In steps *MHJ*.

MHJ fills the void in the "Macintosh magazine" category left by *MacUser* and *MacWorld* by catering to an audience that is eager to learn, work, and have fun with its Macintosh computers but is not necessarily interested in nor capable of using highly technical information. Many letters to the editor praise the magazine for "being clear and non-technical so that average users can understand," and for "not treating us like we are stupid, nor trying to write for a rocket scientist audience." Letters often complain, "The other Mac magazines (read: *MacUser, MacWorld*) are too technological and hacker-oriented." The *MHJ* reader is intelligent but is not a computer programmer and has no dreams of becoming one. She wants full, productive use of her machine in the simplest, easiest manner possible.

The most noticeable facet of the *MHJ* table of contents is its focus on the New Owner. Not only does it set aside an entire section every issue dedicated to helping the new owner, but also it bullets certain areas of features to draw new owners' attention to information that may have been skipped over for fear it was too technical. For instance, an article titled "Point and Click Publishing" may have been passed over by a novice user; however, a certain paragraph is bulleted with an arrow stating, "For New Owners: Read here for the easiest way to create your own greeting cards!" Now the article is of use to both the experienced user and the novice.

MHJ draws experienced users, too, who are still interested in keeping their relationship to their Mac simple. One letter stated, "I've had Apples . . . dating back to my old IIe . . . I still love reading your New Owners section."

Staples of the monthly magazine include these sections: home/office; education; interactive entertainment; and reviews. The reader is looking for help at home and at work and probably has children whom she hopes to educate using Mac software. An "In the News" section sometimes appears; the reader keeps up on new developments within the Apple business family to see what the future will hold.

Features often focus on choosing hardware (CPUs, printers, scanners), upgrading, performing business tasks and publishing. Often, the features take a "home-y" slant, like using wedding planning software or building a home office computer system.

Advertising in *MHJ* is entirely focused on Mac hardware and software—no cigarette ads, no car ads, no soda ads. Plenty of ads for printers, monitors, and educational and entertainment software. The back 20 or so pages are dedicated to a "Smart Shopper" catalog containing nothing but hardware and software advertisements. Many offer educational discounts, so we might surmise that some readers are teachers or students, both of whom would be primarily concerned with ease-of-use in hardware and software and would look for a down-to-earth magazine like *MHJ* for support.

or she can write for magazines for a number of lame reasons, including "I'll get rich quick!" or "My life is *so* interesting!" or "People will take me seriously!" The problem is, the wanna-be doesn't take writing seriously.

The novice does. He or she is willing to invest time and money into a freelance career before ever seeing a profit. Why? Because the novice has journalistic *zeal,* or an urge to share useful or stimulating ideas with others. Such a person knows that other people's lives are at least as interesting as the writer's. The novice is also eager to learn new concepts, terms, and techniques.

Few, if any, wanna-bes are reading this book. They don't want to learn about freelance writing because they worry that editors' critiques or opinions will crimp their style. Oh, they'll spend hundreds of dollars—sometimes, *thousands*—sending manuscripts to vanity press "editors" (sales people masquerading as publishers who accept everything they receive and charge you to print it). Wanna-bes pay "reading fees" in search of a literary agent who will say, "You'll get rich quick!" or "Your life is *so* interesting!"

You know better. And you will know *more* by becoming familiar with basic magazine terms. These terms will be used in upcoming chapters and will be analyzed later in depth. But a glossary belongs in the beginning of a book so that readers can become familiar with terms *before* they encounter their applications. Otherwise, both levels of learning occur simultaneously—memorization of terms and examination of uses—which might confuse the typical novice.

Let's speak the same language now and worry about applications later.

You'll learn other terms in upcoming chapters along with expanded definitions of these essential ones: *Craft terms* define techniques to hone nonfiction; *Freelance terms* describe formats and marketing concepts; and *Magazine terms* are those that depict a publication.*

Craft Terms

1. *Break.* White space, numbers, asterisks, or some other keyboard symbol separating sections of a work.
2. *Chronological time.* Incidents or events described in a **manuscript** in the same order as they happened in real life.
3. *Closed ending.* The last paragraph of a **manuscript** that summarizes information or action and leaves the audience with a sense of satisfaction or mission.
4. *Epigraph.* A short citation—facts, quotations, excerpts from published works—that usually appears between the **title** and **byline** of a **manuscript.**
5. *Epiphany.* A moment of clarity in which the writer comprehends a universal truth.
6. *Flashback.* A passage in a work that refers to the past and momentarily violates the order of incidents or events as they happened in real life or **chronological time.**
7. *Flashforward.* A passage in a work that refers to the future and momentarily violates the order of incidents or events as they happened in real life or **chronological time.**
8. *Foreshadowing.* A phrase, sentence, or passage—usually related to **theme**—that suggests or hints at a related event or truth coming up later in a work. (See **Thematic statement.**)
9. *Grammatical time.* Verb usage including past, present, future, and **pushed present** tenses.
10. *Grounding.* Basic information the reader needs to understand the **topic** of a work.
11. *Implied author.* The writer as he or she exists at the keyboard, generating what almost always is considered a **lapse** in **voice.**
12. *Implied setting.* A scene or place—never mentioned in a work—in which the writer imagines himself or herself, simply to generate an appropriate **voice** for the audience.
13. *Introduction.* The opening paragraph(s) of a work. (Also known as the *lead* or *lede.*)

---

*Bold terms within these definitions are defined elsewhere in this list.

14. *Lapse.* A writing mistake indicating an uneven, unsustained **voice** or faulty **moment of narration.**
15. *Moment of narration.* The point in time that a writer decides to enter a work, close to the action as if it is happening in **chronological time;** removed from the action, with no reference to events happening in real time; or somewhere in between. (Also known as *literary time.*)
16. *Narrator.* The author uses the first-person pronoun *I;* thus, aspects of **voice** are associated with personality traits of the writer of a work.
17. *Occasion of narration.* An event or circumstance, often associated with the **topic** of a work, that helps generate the **introduction** or that adds another level of meaning.
18. *Open ending.* The last paragraph of a **manuscript** that leaves the audience with a lingering sense of scene or milieu.
19. *Peak experience.* A moment of clarity in which the writer's body senses a universal truth.
20. *Persona.* The author uses a third-person pronoun—*he, she, it,* or *they*—throughout an entire piece, without employing the first-person *I;* thus, aspects of **voice** are not associated with the writer of the work but with some unseen character or storyteller.
21. *Pushed present tense.* A verb form affecting **grammatical time,** changing the past tense to the present and the present tense to the future, thereby adding a sense of immediacy and tension to a work.
22. *Slant.* Another layer of meaning in a work, aligned with the perceived needs of the **target audience.**
23. *Source.* A person interviewed in a work.
24. *Subhead.* A small **title** or headline in the body of a work that introduces new aspects of a **topic** and sections of a **manuscript.**
25. *Subtitle.* A line, phrase, sentence, or even a paragraph that works in tandem with a **title,** either clarifying it or **foreshadowing topic** and/or **theme.**
26. *Target audience.* Readers of a specific publication. (Also known as *target market.*)
27. *Thematic statement.* A phrase, sentence, or paragraph that develops the **theme** of a work.
28. *Theme.* Another level of meaning in a work, developed via **foreshadowing, epiphany,** and/or **peak experience.** (See **Slant.**)
29. *Title.* A word, phrase, or sentence that serves as a contract with the reader, identifying the content of a work. (Also known as *headline* or *hede.*)
30. *Topic.* The person, place, issue, incident, or thing that is the primary focus of a work.
31. *Transition.* A phrase or sentence that propels a work logically and smoothly from one paragraph to another.

32. *Utility.* Aspects or elements of a work that meets the perceived needs of the **target audience.** (Also called *take-away value.*)
33. *Viewpoint.* The world as seen through the eyes of the author or a specific **source** in a work.
34. *Voice.* The sound a reader "hears" on the magazine page.
35. *Working title.* A **title** that helps the writer focus on the **topic** or **theme** during the writing process but that will be changed later.

Freelance Terms

36. *Acceptance.* A letter from an editor offering to publish a work and/or a formal document specifying terms and conditions.
37. *Anecdotal approach.* A work that begins with a first-person anecdote and then expands to include experiences of or information from other **sources.**
38. *Article.* A magazine work longer than 2,000 words.
39. *Assignment.* A work solicited by an editor of a magazine.
40. *Byline.* The author's name.
41. *Clips.* Photocopies of an author's previously published works, often sent to editors with **query letters.**
42. *Column.* A work between 250 and 1,000 words, usually employing a **narrator** and taking a **personal experience approach.**
43. *Contract agreement.* A document stating that a publication is buying **rights** to a work.
44. *Contributor's notes.* Data about the author of a work. (Also known as *bio notes.*)
45. *Copyright.* Ownership of a work.
46. *Cover letter.* A business letter to an editor that introduces an enclosed **manuscript.**
47. *Directory.* A marketing book listing addresses and phone numbers of magazines and describing editorial policies and requirements.
48. *Essay.* A formal or informal work by an author describing a personal experience or presenting an argument, often literary in tone with heavy thematic emphasis.
49. *Exposé.* An investigative work.
50. *Feature.* A magazine work between 1,000 and 2,000 words.
51. *Galleys.* A typeset work, sent to a writer for proofreading before publication.
52. *How-to piece.* A work that presents practical, step-by-step information to readers. (Also known as a *service piece.*)
53. *Informational approach.* A work that conveys data or **research** to an audience via a **persona.**

54. *Interview format.* A work that begins with background about a **source** and then switches to questions and answers.

55. *Kill fee.* Money, usually 25 percent of the typical **pay rate**, that a writer receives if an editor makes an **assignment** and then, for one reason or another, cannot use the work.

56. *Logs.* Informal bookkeeping listing where a writer has sent a **manuscript** and documenting other pertinent information (date sent, editor's decision, etc.)

57. *Manuscript.* A work of magazine nonfiction typed or printed double-spaced on white paper. (Also abbreviated *ms.*)

58. *Multiple submission.* Sending two or more works to the same editor.

59. *On acceptance.* Payment to a writer when he or she signs a **contract agreement** or otherwise is informed of an **acceptance**.

60. *On publication.* Payment to a writer when an accepted work appears in the magazine.

61. *Opinion piece.* Commentary by an author about a political, social, cultural, or moral issue.

62. *Pay rates.* The fee paid to a writer, often associated with the word or page count, as in "10 cents per word" or "$100 per page."

63. *Personal experience approach.* A work employing a **narrator** relating an extraordinarily dramatic or unusual occurrence.

64. *Profile piece.* A work that focuses on the life or accomplishments of a **source.**

65. *Query letter.* A business letter that describes the topic, theme, and approach of a work and that asks the editor for permission to send it to the magazine.

66. *Rejection.* A slip of paper or letter informing a writer that a work is unsuitable for the **target audience.**

67. *Research.* Facts garnered from books, periodicals, or databases (library research) or from on-site visits and interviews (field research).

68. *Response time.* The average number of weeks or months needed by an editor to read a **manuscript** and report back to the writer.

69. *Rights.* What an editor buys to publish a work. Typically, an editor purchases *first rights* (also known as *first serial rights* or *North American rights*) to ensure that his or her publication will be the first to publish a work on the continent. An editor can also buy *reprint rights* for a work whose first rights already have been sold. Sometimes an editor purchases *all rights,* which essentially transfers ownership of a work to the magazine. Both first and reprint rights can be secured via personal correspondence between editor and writer; however, all rights can be secured only via a **contract agreement** that specifies terms and conditions and that is signed by the author and the editor.

70. *Sample issue.* An issue of a magazine that a writer purchases or requests from an editor, to study the **target audience.** (Also known as *back issue.*)
71. *SASE.* An abbreviation for self-addressed stamped envelope, enclosed so that an editor can return a **manuscript** or report on a **query letter.**
72. *Sidebar.* A work, usually between 100 and 500 words (although longer lengths are permissible, depending on content), that provides additional information to accompany an **article.**
73. *Simultaneous submission.* Sending the same work to two or more publications.
74. *Speculation.* An editor's offer to consider a work without any **kill fee** or promise to publish.
75. *Status.* The progress a **submission** has made while under consideration at a magazine.
76. *Submission.* A **manuscript** or **query letter** sent with a **SASE** to an editor.
77. *Unsolicited.* A submission that an editor did not request but that still may be considered, depending on editorial policies.
78. *Writer's guidelines.* A sheet or document describing the target audience and detailing editorial policies, submission requirements, and other pertinent freelance information.

Magazine Terms

79. *Audience profile.* A description of a magazine's readers and their perceived needs, determined by advertisements, **cover subtitle, contents** and **letters pages, editor's introduction,** and other data.
80. *Back-of-the-book essay.* A work (usually a column) that appears near the end of a magazine and often on the last page.
81. *Boldface.* Dark type, **like this.**
82. *Book.* Magazine.
83. *Concept.* A slogan or idea that encapsulates the perceived needs of the **target audience.**
84. *Contents page.* Place reserved for information listing **departments, articles, features,** fillers, and other works appearing in a magazine.
85. *Cover subtitle.* A phrase or slogan on the cover of a magazine, heralding its **concept.**
86. *Cover title.* The name of a magazine.
87. *Demographics.* Facts, figures, and other identifying characteristics (gender, age, household income, etc.) that depict the **target audience.**

88. *Department.* A section of a magazine, such as Beauty, Health, Fashion, Lifestyle, and so on.
89. *Editor's introduction.* Place where the editor previews or otherwise sets the tone of the current issue of a magazine. (Also known as *editor's preface* or *foreword.*)
90. *Filler.* A short work, 25 to 250 words.
91. *Flush left.* Copy aligned with the left margin of the typeset column or type area.
92. *Flush right.* Copy aligned with the right margin of the typeset column or type area.
93. *Font.* An assortment of type in one style, identified by name, such as Times New Roman or Courier New.
94. *Italics.* Slanted type, *like this.*
95. *Letters page.* Place reserved to publish correspondence by readers about contents of previous issues.
96. *Masthead.* A box listing the names and titles of a magazine's staff, along with data about advertising and editorial departments.
97. *Media kit.* An advertising packet with pertinent information about a magazine's audience, including **demographics** and **psychographics.**
98. *Mission statement.* The stated purpose of a magazine and its relationship with its audience, also included in the **media kit.**
99. *Psychographics.* The lifestyle characteristics of readers, including such information as their buying habits, political affiliations, outdoor hobbies, craft interests, and so on.
100. *Roman.* Upright, unslanted type like this.
101. *Standing title.* A title that appears in each issue to identify a regular column or section of a magazine.

These terms, and dozens of others, are used in the magazine industry and in this book. Read over them a few times to become familiar with the lingo. (You'll feel more confident as you tackle assignments at the end of this chapter.) Also, you will learn your first lesson about patience, a real virtue in this business. Soon enough, you will be analyzing markets to target an audience. Most wanna-bes are so eager to publish that they submit any old piece of prose after reading writer's guidelines. You can resist that urge. (You'll learn about submission procedures in the last chapter of this book, after you have mastered each element of craft and envisioned and revised your manuscript.)

So now let's head to the Craft Shop to learn about virtual magazines, to The Newsstand to analyze magazines you might like to write for, and to The Keyboard to solicit writer's guidelines, making your first professional contact with editors.

THE CRAFT SHOP

The Virtual Magazine

Anderson Jones, Associate Writer/Producer, *SPIV* Webzine

Our webzine is geared to 15- to 25-year-olds and is a product of Turner Broadcasting System. We cover pop culture with a specific interest in music, fashion, new technology, movies, and adrenaline-pumping sports.

There are a lot of differences between a real and a virtual magazine. At *SPIV,* we can eliminate the cost of publication in terms of a production and a circulation budget. We can save money because we do not have to worry about printing and distribution costs. Which means we can spend more money on photographers and freelance writers—particularly freelancers.

The Internet is a worldwide source of information. People can tap into your magazine from anywhere, so your webzine has to reflect that you have a variety of voices, commentary, and writers reporting from all over. So if you are a writer, the Internet has some special advantages. Webzine editors can give you all the space you need for your feature. And more freelancers can be published. A publication like *Entertainment Weekly* always has to worry about advertising to determine the number of pages an issue will have. At *SPIV* we don't have to worry about that.

The downfall, of course, is that you can bore your readers. It's tough to read 5,000 words off a computer screen. That's why I think the first few paragraphs of a feature story need to be a lot more interesting in a virtual magazine, or text on line. The World Wide Web encourages a short attention span. Television, in fact, has no claims on the web browser because he can move from page to page and site to site with a click of a mouse. So snagging his eyeballs in those first few seconds (and sentences) become really important. Never has the lead become so important as in the virtual magazine.

THE NEWSSTAND

Method to Picture the Market

1. Browse through the magazine racks at your local or college library. Identify six publications that appeal to you or that you would like to write for because you know or are interested in the contents. Turn

to the masthead in each publication. In a notebook, write down the name of the managing editor and the address of the editorial office.

2. Scan each magazine for a cover subtitle, usually a phrase or sentence that encapsulates the concept, such as *Home Office Computing*'s "Solutions for Today's Small Business" or *Mirabella*'s "a sign of intelligent life." The cover subtitle often appears below or to the side of the magazine's name and occasionally on the magazine's spine (the flat part between the front and back cover), as does *Victoria*'s, whose subtitle is "an intimate journal for you and your home." Some magazines do not carry a subtitle. In such case, study the titles of articles on the cover and invent your own cover subtitle. In a notebook, write a few sentences about the subtitle and what it tells you about the magazine's mission.

3. Translate the items listed on the contents page—departments, articles, features, columns, and so on—and ask yourself why an editor included the work in the magazine or bought it from or assigned it to a freelance writer. What does each item tell you about the perceived needs of the target audience? List at least one observation per item.

4. Turn to the editor's introduction. Here, the editor comments on items included in the current issue. Note the editor's comments about articles or contributors and why he or she thinks they serve the audience. Especially note how the editor is introducing all this, particularly with regard to voice. For instance, is the editor's tone uplifting or candid, inspirational or businesslike? These observations will help you hone your voice to suit a particular readership.

5. Analyze the advertisements in the magazine. What products are the ads selling? Why? Which products are geared toward demographics (toddler toys in a women's magazine, indicating age of children, or luxury car ads in a business magazine, indicating salary) and which toward psychographics (fishing gear in a travel magazine, indicating outdoor hobbies, or concert promotions in a city magazine, indicating interest in the arts)? Make one comment per advertisement.

6. Scan the letters section and determine reader response to specific articles in past issues of each of your select magazines. Note the reader's concern or praise and the tone of voice the reader uses to express it. Note what the reader appreciates or dislikes.

THE KEYBOARD

Targeting the Audience

1. Consult your Newsstand notebook listing of names of managing editors and addresses of your select magazines. Write a short business letter to each one, stating that you are a freelance writer soliciting writer's guidelines. Be sure to enclose a SASE.

2. Review the notes you made about these publications in steps 2 through 6 of The Newsstand assignment and write an audience profile for each publication, based on your observations about the cover title, contents page, editor's introduction, advertisements, and readers' letters.

Topics and Ideas

Utility

Newspaper editors often say that a good news story is like a pane of glass. In other words, reporters should be transparent. Invisible. If so, readers are able to visualize facts pertaining to an issue or event without the taint of subjectivity. Otherwise, reporters "editorialize," smudging the glass with their own relative truths. The copy desk has to window-spray the story, removing the reporter's fingerprints. The utility or "take-away value" of news—what readers anticipate from a story—is topicality: timely newsworthy items of interest. Consumers appreciate that.

But sometimes people consume too much news. They get depressed by the brutalities of fact and realities of record. They seek escape, and creative types provide it. When poets and fiction writers rely too heavily on fact, their compositions go unpublished or are dismissed as "topical." Creative writers have to shatter reality's window so that readers can enter realms of fantasy, intrigue, romance, and occasionally even *enlightenment*. And consumers appreciate that, too. The take-away value of creative writing is stimulation; in a word, the audience wants its imagination *tweaked*.

Fact? Fiction? Can one really speak about magazine journalism this way? Many trade journals, such as *Engineering News Record,* rely on fact, and many pulp magazines, such as *Ellery Queen's Mystery Magazine,* rely on fiction. And some mass magazines—for instance *Good Housekeeping* and *Redbook*—publish fact-based service journalism and fantasy-based popular fiction. (But even fiction is geared toward the perceived needs of the audience.) Again, we're dealing with *subjective truth,* defined as attitudes or beliefs held by significant numbers of people.

Freelance writers do not funnel facts to an audience through a clear pane of glass, the way reporters do on breaking stories or general news.

21

Neither do they shatter that glass, the way creative writers do. The very word *window* is a magazine term meaning the number of readers with similar demographics and psychographics passing through a publication's pages at any given time. It is an element of time and utility. A magazine such as *American Baby* has a *narrow* window, with thousands of women passing through during all three trimesters of pregnancy. The readers want to take away useful information pertaining to childbirth and infant care. Conversely, *Redbook* readers are only mildly interested in the topics of pregnancy and childbirth; their particular window is *wide*, with millions of women between age 22 and 45 passing through in search of service to help them juggle responsibilities. As you can see, utility varies from one publication to another. In any case, a magazine window is made of *stained* glass, colored by the subjectivity of authors whose truths appeal to significant numbers of the target audience.

Patricia Raybon, an ex-newspaper reporter, held some deeply felt beliefs about racism and turned to magazine journalism to express them. As a newspaper reporter, she could not easily do this without being accused of editorializing. Consider her "Neighbors" column in *USA Weekend,* titled "Too Close for Comfort," which begins:

> I am not the maid. My family understands that. One of my neighbors doesn't. But it isn't her fault. She's just a student of time and place and circumstance, and she has been well taught.
>
> So, when she rang my front doorbell one day last winter, she did what comes naturally when somebody who looks like me answers the door in her neighborhood.
>
> She looked startled. Then she coldly issued an order. "Would you get the lady of the house, please?" Her question left me anxious and breathless, too angry to shout a reply.

Here is the same excerpt written in the objective tone of a newspaper, with facts in descending order of importance (also known as *inverted pyramid* form):

> BOULDER, Colorado—An African-American educator who recently moved into her suburban home was mistaken for the maid of that home by a new neighbor paying a visit, area residents confirmed Tuesday.
>
> The neighbor reportedly asked Patricia Raybon, associate professor of journalism at the University of Colorado, "Would you get the lady of the house, please?"

The inverted pyramid form does not allow the narrator's subjective truth to be expressed directly to readers. And without that truth, there is no "story." Now let's recast the introduction as a popular nonfiction:

Patricia was new to the neighborhood, a suburb of Boulder. She taught journal-ism at the state university and sought escape from city smog and hard news. So she and her husband, also a professor, moved across town to a new home nes-tled in a pine-studded acre lot.

Patricia was eager to meet the neighbors, but only after unpacking and getting the house in order. A nationally known writer, she was setting up her home office in the den when the doorbell rang.

A blond woman stood on the stoop, looking startled, looking beyond Patricia and into the house.

Patricia went on alert. She had to endure countless moments like these and sensed what the woman was going to say.

"Would you get the lady of the house, please?"

The fictional tone disregards fact. The scenario is invented. Reality's window is shattered. Words here appeal to emotions rather than the intellect. The format may titillate the imagination, generating a modicum of drama, but readers experience the racial encounter through the filter of a storyteller. As such, they are one step removed from reality—a type of escape.

We need stained glass to appreciate Raybon's subjective, significant truth.

"If I'm honest," Raybon says, "I'm drawn to the personal essay by a need to be heard—and maybe to be seen, too. Certainly, as an African-American woman, I'm desperate to be understood. The personal essay is, therefore, a nearly perfect structure for my writing impulse." Raybon says the best essays are what she calls "conflict narratives," stories in which a problem is solved or at least addressed. "Ideally, that problem has universal interest or appeal. It may be unique to the person writing it, but it repre-sents a problem that most people can appreciate or understand."

Raybon is talking about take-away value—some truth the audience can embrace and put to use in their lives. But how does this relate to her topic, occasion, and target audience (the majority of whom are white)? The target audience for *USA Weekend* has other demographics. First of all, it is a supple-ment distributed mainly by newspapers that lack a Sunday magazine. Read-ers generally remain in their neighborhoods on weekends, preoccupied with recreational, familial, and social concerns. Raybon's "conflict narrative" ap-peals to this audience—regardless of race—because everyone, at one time or another, has been labeled in a confrontation with a neighbor.

Neal Bowers, a creative writing professor at Iowa State University, re-cently turned to nonfiction to confront a plagiarist who was stealing his poems. His feature "The Poetry Thief" begins:

On a miserably cold day in January 1992, I arrived at the office and routinely retrieved my voice mail messages. Among the usual calls from colleagues and students was one from Carrier Etter, a Santa Monica poet then unknown to me, saying that one of my poems had been plagiarized. My first reaction was disbelief, because it had never occurred to me that someone might steal my work. But when I returned Carrie's call and received her fax of the suspicious poem, my disbelief turned into shock and anger. It was my poem, all right, with a different title and someone else's name attached, but otherwise a virtual copy.

The theft of a poem would make a poor news story (although Bowers's efforts to track down the plagiarist eventually attracted worldwide news coverage). Bowers was thoroughly capable of composing a literary fiction about the theft, appealing to reader emotions, describing the possible desperation of the plagiarist and the heartbreak of the artist. But in doing so, he would have escaped reality or, worse, provided the plagiarist with yet another work to steal and pass off as his own! Like Patricia Raybon, Bowers knew that magazine nonfiction was the only medium to convey his personal message. According to Bowers:

> Writing nonfiction is much harder than writing anything else, simply because the facts can be restricting. The fiction writer or poet has much more liberty where "the truth" is concerned and is bound more by the demands of what matters than by the details of what happened. The nonfiction writer is obliged not to make things up, though he still has a responsibility to write imaginatively and to hold the reader's interest.
>
> The more I trusted in the story, the more my own voice came out—the aggrieved concerned voice of a victim—and I began to see that this voice was as important as any of the facts. The annals of plagiarism are replete with anecdotes of assorted thieves of literature and ideas, but their victims are seldom heard even to whimper. Consequently, I gave myself permission to stand near the facts as I presented them, letting the shadow of my injury fall across the page.

Bowers's "shadow" not only falls across the *Writer's Digest* page but also the magazine's window. His topic of plagiarism is of keen interest to freelance writers. And his occasion of narration—an event that sparks a story—depicts his arriving at the office and listening to voice mail, which many *WD* readers do each day. Moreover, Bowers offers information about plagiarism while he shares his feelings about losing his work. Here's a typical passage:

> My poem "Tenth Year Elegy" is a highly personal recollection of my father written on the tenth anniversary of his death. . . . To have the memory of my father appropriated by a stranger and defended as something he believed to be his own is a tremendous violation not only of my poetry, but my privacy.

Utility. Take-away value. Readers of *Writer's Digest* may have understood plagiarism laws before reading "The Poetry Thief," but now they also understand a greater subjective truth: Every writer puts privacy on the line by publishing work based on experience, but when someone steals a manuscript, the writer loses the *experience* along with the work.

Raybon's and Bowers's writings are based on different truths that appeal to distinct readerships. In other words, the audience for *USA Weekend* would have little interest in the emotional well-being of a poet whose verses had been stolen by a literary thief. Sure, some of those readers may dabble in writing on weekends, but mostly they are concerned about neighborhood, community, family, exercise, nutrition, and recreation. Conversely, Raybon's confrontation with her neighbor would be out of place in *Writer's Digest*. True, *WD* readers have neighbors and confront them on occasion, but they would rather hear Raybon, *as a writer,* offer advice about avoiding stereotypes in nonfiction.

As we have seen in Raybon's and Bowers's pieces, topic and occasion are elements of utility. Most manuscripts have clear-cut topics. Raybon's is about racial stereotyping; Bowers's is about plagiarism. Some ideas are powered by occasion alone. Many ideas include topics generated or enhanced by occasions. A neighbor's complaint triggered the topic in the Raybon piece; voice mail was the trigger in the Bowers piece. The occasion is substantial in Raybon's work, less so in Bowers's work. Yet these elements complement each other in both pieces and are aligned with the target audience.

Natural-born writers sense the difference between topic and occasion and easily harmonize the two for readers. Others need to ponder these elements.

Some works do not need an occasion. That is an important consideration, especially when material is targeted at a younger audience. (Save the complexity for *The Atlantic Monthly.*) For instance, magazine student Bethany Matsko published a column in *Sassy* about being the daughter of a teenage mother. Here is a key passage from her manuscript:

> Mom was 15 and Dad was 19 when I was born. They had met two years earlier the way most teenagers meet. Mom and a friend were walking through the gas station that my dad was working at, and he flirted with her.

Most 15-year-olds reading *Sassy* are not pregnant nor do they have teenage mothers. In fact, girls passing through the magazine's window are ages 11 through 17 who worry about being "different." They know *Sassy* will accept them each month, even if their friends (and moms) do not. So the take-away value here is that Matsko, born to a teenage mom—with odds stacked against her—turned out, well, *okay.*

Sometimes the occasion *is* the topic, strong enough to overpower any other angle, as in Dana Gioia's profile titled "Meeting Mr. Cheever"—about the young Gioia meeting the famous fiction writer John Cheever. Gioia's first sentence pivots on occasion: "I was supposed to meet John Cheever in the fall of 1974 when I was a graduate student at Harvard and a tutor at Radcliffe's North House." (Cheever never showed up.) The profile continues until the author finally meets Cheever in another setting. Gioia's piece satisfies the intelligent audience of *The Hudson Review,* eager to know personal tidbits about literary icons. The take-away value in Gioia's profile is not gossip, though; readers want to learn more about Cheever to gain insight into his *New Yorker* fiction.

Typically, freelance writers don't "discover" take-away value during the writing process. (Natural-born writers *intuit* it, of course.) But the typical novice envisions it the same way he or she envisions a target audience. So ask yourself:

- Does my topic appeal to the target audience? How?
- Did something happen—a holiday, a visit, a phone call, a complaint— that triggered the topic? If so, is the occasion able to stand alone as the sole focus of my piece?
- What do my topic and occasion have in common and how can they generate take-away value?

Writers who appreciate take-away value also appreciate readers. The next step is to determine what you know and who, if anyone, would be interested in hearing it.

An Inventory of Ideas

What's the *real* difference between a reporter and a freelancer? Reporters get a steady paycheck. In other words, every time magazine writers sit at their keyboards, they hear a meter running—tick, tock, tick, tock—*How will you pay the rent? Buy food? Order supplies?*—tick, tock, tick, tock—*How will you pay the phone bill? The electric bill? Microsoft?*—tick, tock, tick, tock. . . . You get the idea.

To *get* ideas, writers rely on experience. There's a reason why writing teachers often say, "Write about what you know." Patricia Raybon knows all about racial stereotypes, described in her book *My First White Friend* (Viking). Neal Bowers knows all about plagiarism, described in his book *Words for the Taking* (Norton). Raybon and Bowers were so consumed with their topics that they wrote hundreds of pages about them, beginning with magazine columns and ending with books. What about you? Would you take out several years of your life, spend thousands of dollars on research, and sit in one place for prolonged periods to share your thoughts about stereotypes or plagiarism? Not unless you were the victim of either, as Raybon and Bowers were.

We're talking commitment here. You have to be obsessed about a topic to do it justice. Otherwise, you are not going to do the legwork, research, writing, and revising that magazine journalism entails. You'll start one assignment—tick, tock, tick, tock—and abandon it—tick, tock, tick, tock—when the going gets tough. Instead of fielding calls from editors or sources, you'll hear from landlords and bill collectors. And then the phone company will stop service.

That's no way to live. Or maybe it is. Landing in a soup kitchen when you cannot pay the rent is a valid experience. You can write about that. Things happen if you breathe in and out long enough. Love, death. Cruelty, compassion. Homelessness. You witness something that changes your life. You walk in a daze or on cloud nine, mourning or celebrating beginnings and endings. You can't fathom why something happened or you know all too well. And yes, you will sacrifice time and expense to get to the bottom of *those* things and share them with others whose truths mirror your own. To discover your subject matter:

1. Make a list of the highs, lows, and turning points in your life. A high point can be when you met or married a significant other. A low point might be when you broke up or separated. Maybe the turning point was when you put the relationship into perspective. Here's a typical list:

Lows
- Arrested on prom night for drunk driving
- Breakup with highschool sweetheart
- Parents divorced and married other people

Highs
- Played tuba in the marching band
- Accepted into graduate school
- Paper accepted at writing conference

Turning Points
- Quit newspaper job and enrolled in graduate program
- Went to Europe
- Learned how to fly a plane

2. After you make your list, ask yourself what you learned from the experience:

Lows
- Arrested on prom night for drunk driving. *Alcoholism occurs without warning.*
- Breakup with highschool sweetheart. *Love is a partnership, not a dictatorship.*
- Parents divorced and married other people. *Love may end but it also may renew itself.*

Highs
- Played tuba in the marching band. *Music can be muscular.*
- Accepted into graduate school. *Miracles happen in the classroom.*
- Paper accepted at writing conference. *Excellence matters.*

Turning Points
- Quit newspaper job and enrolled in graduate program. *You can change your life any time you wish.*
- Went to Europe. *You discover yourself when you locate your roots.*
- Learned how to fly a plane. *Your body becomes part of the machine.*

3. Determine a category of magazines whose editors might be interested in your topic and/or occasion. If you have trouble envisioning a market, specify "general interest." (Theme, explained in the next chapter, will help you slant such a topic to an audience.) And don't be surprised if you see one type of category appear several times on your list, indicating a direction your life has taken:

Lows
- Arrested on prom night for drunk driving. *Alcoholism occurs without warning.* **Teen magazines.**
- Breakup with high school sweetheart. *Love is a partnership, not a dictatorship.* **General interest.**
- Parents divorced and married other people. *Love may end but it also may renew itself.* **General interest.**

Highs
- Played tuba in the marching band. *Music can be muscular.* **Arts and entertainment.**
- Accepted into graduate school. *Miracles happen in the classroom.* **Education journals.**
- Paper accepted at writing conference. *Excellence matters.* **Education journals.**

Turning Points
- Quit newspaper job and enrolled in graduate program. *You can change your life any time you wish.* **Education journals.**
- Went to Europe. *You discover yourself when you locate your roots.* **Travel magazines.**
- Learned how to fly a plane. *Your body becomes part of the machine.* **General interest.**

At this stage, you have performed three vital steps: identified a topic that you can commit to, found a kernel of subjective truth, and envisioned an audience that might share that truth. *Truth is defined by degrees, but not by Ph.Ds.* That means you are as wise as anyone else, and substantial numbers of people will share your truths because they also share your experiences. (If you cannot imagine an audience grasping your truth—say, you're really Napoleon Bonaparte—chances are you lack truth.) The fact is, readers know truth when they see it in a magazine because they recognize *epiphanies* or *peak experiences*—universal moments of clarity—illustrated in italics in the preceding lists; in other words, what you learned from a high, low, or turning point.

We're all different, sure. But not *that* different. We wake up in bed at 3 A.M., snap our fingers, and say, "Now I know why I left him (her). He (She) didn't want a partner—but a *parent.*" That's an epiphany, a moment of clarity in which your mind feels at one with the universe. You see things in new light. You reflect. You comprehend. You struggled for that truth about relationships and now you can spare others sleepless nights by writing about reasons for romantic breakups.

A peak experience is when your body is at one with the universe. One day you realize the beauty of marching with a tuba in orderly and intersecting rows as you play orderly and intersecting notes to applauding fans in a football stadium. Music never felt so *muscular.* Or you take flying lessons in a Cessna and finally go solo, realizing that your body is part of the plane. Your body never felt so *birdlike.* You earned your tuba and wings and can share them with others as avid about music or aviation as you.

As you might have guessed by now, epiphanies and peak experiences assure a measure of utility in your work.

Magazine student Susan Murphy made a list of highs, lows, and turning points. A high point was her job as research assistant, gathering information for a professor authoring a book on women, health care, and communication. In her first draft, Murphy criticized the medical establishment without providing much take-away value for her *Redbook* target audience. *Redbook* is a service magazine. Its readers already monitor the medical establishment; what they seek is advice to deal effectively with doctors. So when Murphy focused on epiphany, she found utility. As she puts it:

What my story idea lacked, I soon learned, was take-away value, a fundamental element in a magazine piece. Because of the nature of the problem, my story could offer no solutions. Rather than question the system, I decided to write a piece—"Start Getting Better Treatment From Your OB-GYN"—to help women work within that system. Written for a women's magazine, the rewrite offered advice about how to improve physician-patient communication to get better care from OB-GYNs. This was the take-away value, my gift to the readers.

Use of epiphanies and/or peak experiences enlivens a work, setting it apart from the mediocre arguments and viewpoints that people overhear going about their everyday chores or routines. Epiphanies and peak experiences *elevate* readers out of the doldrums of daily grind. They build bridges of understanding, even on controversial topics.

In his opinion piece "The Hunting Problem," published originally in *BackHome,* an outdoor and garden magazine, Bruce Woods includes an epiphany or peak experience in every other paragraph. Here's a paragraph that contains both elements, identified for you in brackets:

> And then I also hunt for the moment after the shot. Because, and I must face this, too, there is a primitive sort of triumph in having killed; the hand reaches out beyond the body to touch with terrible magic, to *make food* [epiphany]. The war of celebration and regret that defines such moments leaves me awash with emotion, hyper-aware of colors and scents and feeling physically lighter, as after extraordinary sex or a purging cry [peak experience].

The goal of his opinion piece, Woods says, is "taking an abstract issue [hunting] and bringing it down to the individual level, where the reader is faced with a human being in all of his complexities rather than an oversimplified dogma."

You, too, can achieve your goals by focusing on epiphany and peak experience.

Preliminary Approaches

Once you make your list of potential story ideas, you also want to consider which approach might suit your particular items. The three main approaches are informational, anecdotal, and personal experience:

1. The *informational* approach is using a persona (third-person pronoun) instead of a narrator (first-person pronoun) to share knowledge or experience. This is an excellent way to convey service or how-to advice to target readers. This textbook you are reading takes an informational ap-

proach. So does Susan Murphy's feature about getting better treatment from OB-GYNs. In this passage, Murphy shows how poor treatment can lead to tragedy:

> At 28, Cathy was thrilled to be pregnant. She exercised, ate right and enjoyed a model pregnancy—until the end, when she experienced intense pain and noticed she was leaking amniotic fluid. She told her physician, who dismissed her concerns as first pregnancy jitters and said he would see her in a couple of weeks. "The real point is, this was in October. It was during the World Series, and he was a notorious baseball freak," she explains. Dealing with her problem "would've been an inconvenience."
>
> Catherine again experienced the pain and leakage, and she returned to the OB-GYN, who again brushed off her concerns. "Finally, one day I felt the baby kick," she says. "Instantly I knew it was the last kick. I just knew it. And it was." Two days later the physician surgically removed the baby. When he went to break the fluid bag, he discovered there was no fluid. The physician was shocked; Catherine was not.

The third-person approach provides information based on research and legwork. As Murphy's words show, this can be as dramatic and hard hitting as any personal narrative or testimonial.

When considering an informational approach, ask yourself:

- Is my topic and/or occasion strong enough to appeal to the audience without any personal embellishment? (If so, take an informational approach.)
- Is there any compelling reason that my own experience should be mentioned? (If so, consider an anecdotal approach, explained in item 2.)
- Is what happened to me more important than what happened to others? (If so, try a personal experience approach, explained in item 3.)

2. The *anecdotal* approach is using a first-person narrator mostly to begin and/or end a piece—to indicate to readers that the writer has been through the experience—and taking an informational approach in the body of the piece, citing sources, experts, or books. Writers usually take such an approach when discussing sensitive topics relating to gender, race, religion, illness, obsession, or addiction.

Karin Horgan Sullivan, senior editor at *Vegetarian Times,* seldom uses an anecdotal approach because her readers seek information about proper nutrition and vegetarian cuisine. Says Sullivan, "One thing I've found as an editor is that writers often want to use anecdotes from their own lives, even when their experiences aren't that telling. I don't know what it is—ego, or laziness in digging up sources, or a desire to prove their credibility on a topic. Maybe it's just cathartic for them. But as a reader, I don't care about a writer's catharsis; I want to read about her experience only if it's dramatic or if she's skillfully used a device like humor to draw me in."

But one of Sullivan's best articles—"Do You Really Want to Eat This?"—takes an anecdotal approach. Sullivan says she used it only after realizing her anecdotes were compelling and shared by readers. Here's a passage from her introduction: "Of all the editors at *Vegetarian Times,* I was the obvious choice to write an article on sugar. This is not a fact I'm proud of, mind you, but one that's hard to deny, given the well-trodden path between my desk and the pie shop conveniently located across the street from the *VT* office."

The excerpt establishes that, ahem, an editor of *Vegetarian Times* has, well, a sugar addiction. However, Sullivan quickly focuses on information about sugar from an array of sources—books, reports, and medical data—with scant reference to herself in an exceptionally well-researched article.

The strategy was perfect for the target audience. Many of Sullivan's readers have weaknesses, too, trying to maintain a well-balanced vegetarian diet. So her anecdotal approach lets them know that they're not entirely weak-willed if they slice another helping of lemon meringue.

When considering an anecdotal approach, ask yourself:

- Does my idea require a measure of experience to establish my credentials or authority on this matter? (If so, consider this approach but focus on information.)
- What, if anything, is lost by eliminating personal references or anecdotes? (If nothing is lost, consider an informational approach.)
- Are my anecdotes so powerful or compelling that I can focus entirely on them? (If so, consider the personal experience approach in item 3.)

3. The *personal experience* approach is using a narrator to describe an extremely odd or unlikely event or to offer opinion on an important issue or matter, employing compelling anecdotes and/or pertinent insights. Writers usually take this approach when describing bizarre occurrences, as in an angel encounter for *Angels on Earth,* or when providing expert commentary as Bruce Woods does in "The Hunting Problem" for *BackHome.*

Your story idea may emanate out of personal experience, but don't feel you have to take a personal experience approach. (Most beginners use the approach out of ego or creative urge, overwhelming editorial offices with unsuitable material.) Always keep in mind that listing highs, lows, and turning points—based on experience—merely ensures a level of commitment to an idea.

Take the case of a teacher named Bill (not his real name) who was sharing his highs, lows, and turning points in a graduate school workshop. He wanted to write about a low point—getting poor teaching evaluations in which several undergraduates wrote cruel comments—but felt he was too close to the situation to write effectively about it. So he took a purely informational approach, never mentioning his own experience or evaluations. Instead, he interviewed top professors, asking them to share their evaluations with him and to explain the meaning of "bad" ones. Bill discovered that even celebrated teachers get evaluations with cruel, personal comments. So he quoted those professors about how they deal with such evaluations, providing another measure of utility to his target audience: *Journalism Educator*. He published his manuscript there the first try.

The truth is, only a relative few story ideas should be based *solely* on personal experience, without any research or interviews. For instance, you might have been in a jet plane that nearly crashed, but so have hundreds of other passengers. However, if you were in a jet that nearly crashed and, as you were going down, saw your long-dead uncle in the aisle, telling you that everything is going to be all right (as happened to a magazine student who had an "angel" encounter)—well, that rather demands a personal experience approach.

For more about the courage required to take such an approach, read Cheryl Powers's "Not for the Weak-Hearted" in The Craft Shop section at the end of this chapter. Powers wrote about a turning point in a drug rehabilitation center where she was inspired by a counselor named John. True, thousands of people have been inspired by therapists in drug centers. But Cheryl's story was so unusual that it demanded a personal experience approach. Here is a passage:

> I was 12 years old and had been on drugs for two years. During that time I had been raped twice, physically abused by the man I called my boyfriend, and had sold myself for drugs.
>
> Up until that one group session, treatment had been ineffective because I didn't think there was anything in me worth saving. I wanted to go back to my drugs and my "man." The man who had told me repeatedly, while beating me, that I was nothing but a "stupid, ugly bitch" and whom I had believed.
>
> More than anything, I wanted to go back to the streets and die. I wanted to die because I was convinced I was worthless and I also knew that if I died the constant pain from the empty pit inside me would stop.
>
> In a last ditch effort to save me, my parents had sent me to Mercy Hospital in Council Bluffs, Iowa, over 1,000 miles away from my suburban home. I knew I was hurting my parents, but I could not stop my lifestyle. I knew they loved me but thought they had to because, well, that's what parents are supposed to do . . . and because I could not love myself.
>
> All that changed because of John, my counselor. I respected him. In that one group session I realized that if all these other, good people—my parents, friends and teachers—cared about me, there must be something there worth caring about.

That last paragraph of the excerpt is but one of many epiphanies described in Cheryl Powers's powerful work. In other words, her personal experience is not only extremely newsworthy—because so much had happened to her at age 12—but it also provides take-away value to readers concerned about self-worth.

When considering a personal experience approach, ask yourself:

- Is my experience as powerful as the excerpt by Powers? (If not, but nevertheless compelling, consider an anecdotal approach.)
- Are my epiphanies and/or peak experiences useful to the audience? (If not, consider an anecdotal or informational approach to gain such insight from sources or research.)
- Is my expert comment really "expert," or am I overestimating my credentials or experience? (If so, consider an anecdotal or informational approach to add comment by bonafide experts or authorities.)

Consider these final pointers pertaining to topics and ideas:

1. *Narrow your focus.* Each item on your list of highs, lows, and turning points is capable of producing at least 10 story ideas. Don't exhaust each precious vein of experience in one fell swoop. Instead, focus on a narrow moment, incident, or issue related to your epiphany or peak experience. According to freelance writer Kevin Bezner, "The biggest problem beginning writers have is choosing a focus for their articles. They generally try to accomplish too much in their first drafts. Too often they come up with book-length projects when they only have 1,250 words for a feature, for instance."

2. *Sharpen your perspective.* If your personal experience is common, try to make your perspective unusually perceptive. With this in mind, you might decide to write a column instead of a feature story or full-blown article. That's how Bethany Matsko published her piece in the "it happened to me" standing column in *Sassy*. Her experience—being born to a teenage mom—was perhaps ordinary, but her truths were *extra*ordinary. The shorter the work and sharper the perspective, the more you will be forced to excise extraneous material and focus on the epiphany or peak experience.

3. *Seek commonalties in sources.* If you are interested in profiling another person, you might set up a preliminary interview with your source to ask about his or her highs, lows, and turning points. Then focus on one aspect that you and the source have in common, assuring a level of commitment. Again, don't expound on your experience unless doing so is absolutely necessary. Remember, a profile is about *someone else.*

For instance, Michael Burns—an English professor and author in Missouri who shares a passion for truth—wrote about another English professor and author, Katherine Lederer, whose research turned up startling information about lynchings in Springfield, Missouri. Here's an excerpt from his profile, "A Willing Vessel," published in the city magazine *Springfield!*:

> [Lederer] heard about the story of the lynchings. In the fall of 1979, she was assigning research topics to a freshman class at SMSU, and she suggested that someone might want to follow up on some casual references she had heard through the years about some black men being accused of raping a white woman and a subsequent lynching.
>
> Little did that student know that the facts she came up with were to change the direction of her teacher's life.

Burns was especially sensitive to another aspect of Lederer's life. As he tells it:

> As a child in Texas, Lederer came to know very well the two separate worlds that Blacks and whites occupied, and she often found herself at the places where they intersected. Maybe it was this early history that made her role as a witness for Springfield's lost Black history especially fitting. The simple story of Lederer's life mixes with the awful details of the Easter 1906 lynching of three young Black men on Springfield square. . . . [A]s I see it, the events of our childhood often shape us to take on life-enriching roles as adults that we could not have anticipated. Some people call that destiny. As Dr. Lederer discovered, and as the manuscript of her own life story which I quote from makes clear, this richness does not always bring greater happiness. But it brings a depth of character and a sense of purpose, an affirmation that life uses some people, if they are "willing," to hold together what might otherwise just get spilled and seep away.

Burns asks novice writers to be willing vessels, not only of their own stories but also of the stories of others. That is the emphasis you should keep in mind while reading The Craft Shop, The Newsstand, and The Keyboard sections that follow. If you do, you will compile an inventory of ideas with take-away value for readers, as well as experience an epiphany about the role of the writer who, to use Burns's words, "hold[s] together what might otherwise just get spilled and seep away."

THE CRAFT SHOP

Not for the Weak-Hearted

Cheryl Powers, Newspaper Copy Editor

WARNING: Writing about a painful life experience requires that the writer hurt. No matter how far in the past the experience was, in order to convey pain to a reader, you've got to feel it.

It is the nature of human beings that they only grow emotionally and spiritually through adversity. Yesterday's pain becomes today's lesson.

For me, writing the words "I was raped" returned the control stolen from me by my rapists. I was telling the world that this terrible thing happened to me and despite what my rapists may have wanted, I survived, wresting some tiny measure of self-worth in the process.

If you are only a victim of your own mistakes, writing about those failures requires a great deal of maturity and humility. Describing my experiences with drugs allowed me to claim that part of my past. What I found was that claiming my past didn't place blame, but it did make me responsible for learning from my mistakes.

Everybody makes mistakes, not everybody learns from them.

There will probably come a time during the process of writing about a painful life experience when you will wish you had chosen a different topic.

When I chose to write an article about my past, I did so for a lot of the wrong reasons. I was working three jobs and going to school full time and mistakenly thought this article would require little effort on my part. I didn't have to conduct interviews or do any research, but I invested a lot of emotions into that assignment. Since the topic was so much a part of me, criticism became almost unbearable. I gradually learned that my professor and classmates weren't attacking me personally by not liking parts of the article. They actually helped me claim and understand my past.

Writing about a painful experience can be a rewarding and valuable experience for any writer with an open mind and a willingness to learn about himself or herself.

Reading and Writing

Kevin Bezner, Freelance Writer

Many of my ideas come from long months, if not years, of reading. I read and then something emerges from the reading. I think about the topic over and over until it becomes clear in my mind.

I'll read any magazine, if it is around. I will glance at *People* when I find it. Sometimes I look at *The Atlantic, The Washington Monthly*. Sometimes at *Vanity Fair, New Yorker*. I have been known to glance at *US*.

I couldn't imagine writing for magazines without reading them because reading is the only way to write for an audience. Right now, for instance, I have a whole bunch of ideas on parenting that I would like to explore and write about. So I go to the various guide books, such as *Writer's*

Market, that list categories of magazines. I look at what editors expect and try to narrow down my group of magazines to a select few. Then I go to the library and the magazine rack there and start researching these publications.

When I'm thinking about writing an article, I try to find the one essential idea that seems to jump out at me. *What is the essence?* I always try to remember to ask. I often read stories in newspapers and I'm left with a question the reporter hasn't explored. Exploring such questions can make a good article. But that means reading critically, or looking to see how an article is put together or looking for gaps in the article—information it doesn't deliver.

If you're sitting in the dentist's office, reading magazines, you want to be entertained. My problem now is when I look at a magazine I try to think, "Is there anything I can write for this publication?" I wish I could write every story idea that I have. Oddly enough at this point in my life I can't look at a publication without coming up with a story idea. Mainly because I have lived in a lot of different places and done a lot of things and because I have always seen gaps in the writing of others. So I have hundreds of ideas.

To keep track of them, I sit down and try to write out the idea as quickly as possible. I'll write maybe one page and print it out. I might play with it or leave it in a particular computer file or take the printout and put it in a file folder. If the idea really grabs me, I'll go back to it quickly. Right now I'm trying to write short, bright pieces between 750 and 1200 words that might be of interest to a wide audience. I try to figure out what type of readers my ideas might appeal to.

That starts the process again, and I head back to the library.

 ## THE   NEWSSTAND

Deciphering Truths

1. Now that you are realizing what you know and who might want to hear it, return to the magazine rack at your local or college library and check out at least six more publications. Turn to the masthead of each. In your notebook, take down names of magazine editors and addresses of these select publications.

2. Read your select magazines. Photocopy any column, feature, or article that captures your interest. Keep these in a personal file labeled Story Samples for later consultation or inspiration.

3. Reread your photocopies of columns, features, and articles in these magazines and note:

   ■ The type of approach employed (informational, anecdotal, personal experience)

   ■ Any paragraphs containing subjective truth (epiphanies or peak experiences)

   ■ Any paragraphs providing insight or service to readers (take-away value)

T H E   K E Y B O A R D

Compiling Story Ideas

1. Consult your Newsstand notebook that lists names of managing editors and addresses of your newly selected magazines. Write a short business letter to each one, stating that you are a freelance writer soliciting writer's guidelines. Be sure to enclose a SASE.

2. Reread columns, features, and articles that you photocopied in item 3 of The Newsstand section. Note any gaps that you can fill via research or personal experience. Type your observations about what these stories lack and how you might fill those gaps in your own column, feature, or article. Put these observations in a separate file labeled Story Ideas.

3. Compile a list of highs, lows, and turning points of your life, noting lessons and potential markets, as described earlier in this chapter. Determine what you know and who might like to hear it. Decide which approach might best suit your topic and/or occasion. In about 100 to 150 words, document such information for each item on your list. Add these to your Story Ideas file.

CHAPTER THREE

Theme

Distinguishing Topic from Theme

The reporting of hard news is transparent, or it should be. Such news is as clear as a pane of glass. An article about a traffic fatality is *really* about a traffic fatality. A feature about the divorce rate is *really* about the divorce rate. Note the word *really*. Author and educator Patricia Westfall, whose work is featured later in this book, has a nifty way to distinguish topic from theme. She asks, "What is your story about?" (That's the topic.) Then she asks, "What is your story about *really?*" (That's the theme.)

No one has ever defined theme as easily as that. Better still, you can test your story idea by asking the same questions. Question: "What's your story about?" Answer: "The divorce rate." Question: "What's it about really?" Answer: "The divorce rate." If your answers to both questions are the same, you're probably writing for newspapers instead of magazines. The phrase *slanting the facts* is a sin in newspaper writing; it means tampering with the truth or presenting only one side of an argument or issue, and by doing so, misinforming the public. The phrase *slanting the theme* is a virtue in magazine journalism; it means highlighting one facet of a truth that interests the reader, and by doing so, meeting the expectations of your target audience. When you see the word *slant* in this book, or hear it from a magazine editor, it means *gearing theme to audience*. As Westfall has said, "Even the recipe for pound cake in *McCall's* has a theme: Cake baking is easy!"

If you want to write for magazines, master theme. It's the most important concept in this book, and for good reason: *Editors buy themes, not topics.*

A good editor can put a spin on any topic and slant it to readers. A good freelance writer can do the same thing and, in the process, increase sales dramatically.

Consider this illustration: Remember reading about this low point from the sample list in the last chapter: "Parents divorced and married other people"? The epiphany was: *"Love may end but it also may renew itself."* And the target market was murky: **General interest.** Ask those Westfall questions now. "What's the story about?" Answer: Divorce. "What's it about really?" Answer: Renewal. Voila! You got topic and theme. If you ask another question, you might get a target market, too: What readers are interested in both the topic of divorce and the theme of renewal? Answer: *New Woman.*

You should be able to describe your theme in a word or phrase and aim it at a target market. Celebrated poet Molly Peacock wrote about her grandmother's garden for the standing column "State of Grace" in *Mirabella.* Her introduction describes the garden:

> Orange poppies lolled in a great pride, like lionesses, beside the apple trees. Huge and real, they leapt to life from a book I had stowed in my suitcase that summer, the *Lilac Fairy Book.* I'd finally come to visit my grandmother by myself, old enough to be sent the mere hundred miles that separated my prim suburbia from her ramshackle house. She'd placed the perennial beds in a remnant of an apple orchard that still had a few gnarled trees, just to make her garden even more of a fairy tale. Forces I felt responsible for but did not understand were the cause of my prolonged visit: the death throes of my parents' marriage, and my grandmother's insistence that I go to summer Bible school. But the religion she gave me was her garden.

Neat writing, full of poetic imagery, insight, and basic information (called *grounding*). The topic is a garden, and the occasion is a visit prompted by parental strife. Peacock's sophisticated writing appeals to the audience. *Mirabella's* cover subtitle is: "A sign of intelligent life." Peacock provides evidence thereof.

So far, so good. Peacock's second paragraph begins:

> It was a place of grace, a sanctuary I spent hours in, where flowers had personalities, including the queen, a recalcitrant French lilac who had gotten her seasons turned around and insisted on producing blossoms in September.

"A place of grace." Now you know why Peacock's manuscript was accepted at *Mirabella.* Her well-penned introduction may capture reader interest, but the opening phrase of the second paragraph was responsible for the sale. That's the theme, of course. *Grace.* It jibes with the column's standing title: "State of Grace" (which alludes to Grace Mirabella, one of New York's finest editors, who founded the magazine). A beginning writer would have pegged grace as the topic, analyzing that philosophical concept. Peacock realizes that *theme,* not topic, is the route to a reader's soul because theme is associated with epiphany or peak experience.

Every time you change the theme, you target a new market. That's how freelancers keep generating story ideas based on *one* item from their list of highs, lows, and turning points. After all, they earned that truth with blood, sweat, and tears. Was it only worth one article? Hardly. Freelancers slant their truths at different groups of readers, simply by changing the theme. Look at this example:

Topic: **Divorce**

Theme: Obsession	*Market: Cosmopolitan*
Theme: Celebrity excess	*Market: National Enquirer*
Theme: Commitment	*Market: Guideposts*
Theme: Forgiveness	*Market: Harper's*
Theme: Stress	*Market: Men's Health*
Theme: Healing	*Market: Parents Magazine*
Theme: Values	*Market: Reader's Digest*
Theme: TV values	*Market: TV Guide*
Theme: Custody (as in "Who gets the children?")	*Market: Good Housekeeping*
Theme: Custody (as in "Who gets the season tickets?")	*Market: Sports Illustrated*

As you can see, readers demand strong themes. Take a moment to review the relationship between topic, theme, utility, and target audience. *Topic* is what a story is about. *Theme* is what a story is about really. Theme encapsulates an epiphany or a peak experience—elements of *utility*—and adds another layer of meaning to a work.

To ensure that your manuscript has two levels of meaning, you have to distinguish your topic from your theme. You do this by *grounding* your topic. Grounding provides basic information so that the audience can identify your topic and separate it from occasion (if there is one) and theme. Depending on length and approach, you can ground your topic with a sentence or two or even a paragraph or two. You have to keep reminding readers about your topic throughout your piece, defining terms, explaining issues, and depicting scenes and situations. That is grounding, too. (This paragraph, by the way, is grounding about *grounding.*)

Beginning writers don't like to ground. They like to set mood, waxing poetic about rainbows, geese, lovers, and dark and stormy nights. They think grounding is boring—facts, definitions, situations—so they omit them. Sometimes they don't even realize that they are omitting them because those facts, definitions, and situations are absolutely obvious to the writer. But they may not be to the reader, and your first reader is the editorial assistant who opens the mail at a magazine. He or she has the power to reject you (but not to accept you); so if this person likes your writing, he or she will pass it along to a supervisor. But if the editorial assistant reads your introduction and still doesn't know what your story is about, he or she is not going to keep reading, as your mother would out of obligation; that editorial assistant is going to stuff your manuscript like a turkey in your SASE.

So make certain that everyone knows what the topic is, from the first page to the last page. The danger is, you may think you have a topic when you actually don't. Heather Paige Preston, a member of a magazine workshop, thought everyone would know what she was writing about in this introduction:

> "Why do you like the Beatles?" my husband asked me as we packed the car on a rainy afternoon. "I, well, their music has a good beat and I can dance to it," I replied as I checked my cassette holder to make sure the choice between Beatles albums and solo Paul McCartney work was balanced. The truth was, just as I couldn't predict which songs I'd want to hear on our trip, I really couldn't explain to him why I'm such a Beatles fan.

Hey, you may say, she *has* a topic. Her piece is about being a Beatles fan. Oh, yeah? What about that husband? Why are they packing the car? Where are they going in the rain? The writer keeps referring to this spouse, car, and trip throughout her piece—without providing any answers. Somehow the reader was supposed to know that Preston and her husband were packing the car to attend a concert and that she was hoping that her husband liked the Beatles as much as she did. The situation was so apparent to the writer that she didn't bother to explain it—until the second draft. Here's her new introduction, showcasing the occasion of her column:

> The rain pelting the windshield did nothing to dampen my mood on July 20, 1990. As my husband and I drove to our second Paul McCartney concert in seven months, the dreaded, yet familiar, question was asked of me once again: "Why do you like the Beatles?"

Incidentally, Preston's piece is not about being a Beatles fan. It's about marriage. She grounds that point, too, on every page of her rewrite so that readers are able to distinguish her topic from her occasion (a concert) and her theme: *passion*. Preston has a passion for the Beatles but her husband does not. Her theme has take-away value when targeted at women's magazines whose readers might not like the Beatles but understand how it feels when spouses don't share passions—be it a hobby, skill, or lifestyle.

Preston skillfully grounds the topic with brief but effective comments. In one scene, the narrator is singing along with the soundtrack of "A Hard

Day's Night" and notices her husband sleeping. She stops singing and tells the audience:

> I listen carefully for any signs of my husband stirring. He has his own passions in life and although he says I'm one of them, the Beatles are not.

Readers are hooked. They don't have to appreciate the Beatles to appreciate Preston's topic. (How many times do you wish that your spouse, lover, or best friend would partake in your hobbies and interests?) Because Preston grounds basic information, her ending fuses topic, occasion, and theme as her spouse finally understands her passion and dances with her at the concert:

> My husband turns to me after Paul takes the stage and plays a few songs. "This is terrific!" he yells as I dance around, singing. "I'd forgotten he'd written so many good songs."
>   I smile. I know it's catching. My husband and I are on our own mystery tour, waiting to take us away.

Talk about take-away value! (Did you notice the ending actually includes those words?)

General rule: Do not set mood (otherwise known as a *purple patch* or *purple prose;* that is, dense, overly descriptive, artificial language that proclaims "I am a '*wry*-tah!'"). Instead, ground your topic and/or occasion. Then introduce theme so that readers realize that your work has at least two levels of meaning.

When a piece has a strong "occasion," you have to juggle three levels of meaning: topic, occasion, and theme. You separate those elements as early and as efficiently as possible. Grounding becomes essential. Bill Brohaugh, the editorial director of Writer's Digest Books, accomplishes this in a back-of-the-book column for *Writer's Digest,* "Talking to the River," grounding his topic (a stream) and his occasion (meeting a deadline) and suggesting his theme (control) in a 19-word introduction:

> Halfway into the biggest writing project I have ever tackled, I decided to change the course of a river.

That sentence packs punch. A beginner might have set mood with a purple patch:

> The stream becomes a river. The river floods the yard, a wetland of mud-hued buffalo grass and dirty dandelions, sloping, ever so ominously, toward the sawdust shell of the house. In the flood plain, a home becomes a house, wetland, endangered as heron in Ohio spring, the downpour heavy as fruit. Cherry becomes apple-hail, but trees do not blossom.

Say what?

Brohaugh resists the *"wry-*tah" urge. In his second paragraph, he grounds the stream so that readers can envision it, comprehending why the narrator wants to alter its flow in the middle of a writing project:

> The poetically correct would call it a river, anyway. The real-estate agent who sold us the six acres two years back had called it a stream, and indeed by each mid-summer, it settles down to a trickled rivulet over the rock bed it has bared over the years. But in its annual spring resurrection, the "stream" rain-swells to about 25 feet across, rushing downstream to take its assured time in eating away the base of the hill where construction has begun on our house.

Topic and theme are clear. Now Brohaugh grounds the occasion—meeting a deadline—again, so that readers can track each layer of meaning:

> I'll finish writing *The Chronology of the English Language* in that eventually existent house. The book was begun a year before the bulldozer touched topsoil, and will be done, if my projections are right, six months after we step over the finished threshold. I conceived *Chronology* as a fun project, a couple hundred pages long and a few months in the compilation. A reference book chronicling the approximate dates of words' entry into the language, a fun project? I soon found out just how crazy I was: Now, a full year after I started *Chronology,* and about a month before my original deadline to have the book completed, I find myself only halfway through the research.

Three opening paragraphs, all devoted to grounding. Only now, in the fourth paragraph, does Brohaugh begin his story:

> So much writing work to do, and yet I stand at the side of the stream, about to ask it to move.

Writers like Brohaugh know that grounding is an *art,* not an obligation. You do it out of *discipline,* not out of habit. And you do it for your *audience,* not for your ego.

Keep in mind that what is *in your mind* might not be apparent to your readers. To assure that it is, ask yourself:

- Am I leaving out details that are obvious to me but not to my readers?
- Do I have enough grounding in my introduction so that readers can clearly distinguish topic and/or occasion from theme?
- Where in my manuscript can I provide particulars so that readers know exactly what I am discussing, from the first page to the last?

Grounding topic and/or occasion to distinguish them from theme is only half the battle. You also *develop* theme throughout a work and guide readers to your epiphany or peak experience.

Thematic Development

To derive theme, analyze your epiphany or peak experience and boil it down to a word or short phrase. It helps if the word is abstract, such as *betrayal* or *greed,* because an open concept is easier to relate to the specifics of any topic. But you can employ a more concrete theme, too: *the writing life,* for instance, or *mother-daughter relationships.* In any case, a theme has certain criteria:

- The theme works in tandem with, deepens the meaning of, and yet is distinct from the topic and the occasion.
- The theme should be stated or implied repeatedly throughout the manuscript, revealing something new each time.
- The theme leads to an epiphany or peak experience.

When you list your highs, lows, and turning points, you may assume that your epiphany or peak moment is related to topic. It's probably not. You can leapfrog from topic to truth only because you know both intimately or have experienced them personally. So think of theme as puzzle pieces that, when connected, fill the blanks between topic and truth, enabling the audience to envision what the writer or the writer's sources did. That's why magazine journalism is an art as much as a medium. If the writing is good enough—containing a theme that leads to the truth—target readers experience another person's life *as if it were their own.*

To show that, let's make an assumption: You are a freelancer or an aspiring one because you are reading this book. You want information about writing. Yet only a small percentage of you have ever had, say, an eating disorder. You do not want information about anorexia nervosa. But what about an essay that describes the disorder that also appeals to you as writer?

Amy Hudson, now a psychologist, used theme to accomplish that objective. Several years ago, Hudson was a graduate student in a magazine workshop. As a teen in Oklahoma, she had suffered from anorexia nervosa and wanted to write about that. But she didn't want to target *Seventeen;* she wanted to publish an essay about it in *Writer's Digest* (and eventually did). In other words, she was aiming at readers whose profiles contain demographics and psychographics similar to your own.

Like Bill Brohaugh, Hudson chose a theme of control—freelancers are big on control—over the writing process, schedules, book tours, rejections, ambitions. Rivers. Once Hudson pegged the theme, she developed it from start to finish via *thematic statements,* a type of foreshadowing, or preparing the reader for what is to come in a work.

Theme *develops,* statement by statement, puzzle piece by puzzle piece. As the pieces connect and accumulate in a work, readers sense an epiphany or a peak experience arriving near the ending. That's called a *convention*—a device so common that readers anticipate it instinctively (just as TV viewers anticipate a plot being resolved within a network time-slot). With each statement, readers distinguish theme from the topic and follow the trail, awaiting an ending payoff.

Grounding is to topic as statement is to theme. Grounding separates topic from theme and statement separates theme from topic. A writer needs both elements to establish two distinct levels of meaning in a manuscript. Like grounding, thematic statements are usually found in the introduction of a work and elsewhere as appropriate, ranging in length from a word or phrase to one or several full-blown paragraphs.

Amy Hudson relied on grounding to explain circumstances that led to her eating disorder, recounting an anecdote in elementary school. "Every day I took a spanking in front of the class for not paying attention," she wrote. "The message in Miss File's Fly-Back paddle stuck: Forget about the self. *Give people what they want.*" Hudson then proceeded to another anecdote about lugging a Hitler biography to her room to copy a sketch, letting her family believe that a young girl was reading dense literature.

Interesting, maybe, but not thematic. So between those anecdotes, Hudson inserted this statement:

> Ironically, the same experience taught me that words could be a refuge. I skipped over the intimidation children can feel in grappling with verbal skills and moved straight to appreciation for the security and escape reading offers. And I took up writing, partly due to my perception that it fit the image of a child who likes to read, and partly out of genuine enjoyment in playing with words. Making up poems and rhymes was, on the one hand, an honest kind of construction and, on the other, manipulation.
>
> The family gave encouragement and support.

Writing is *manipulation,* Hudson states. That's an aspect of control. (Anorexia is all about control.) Knowing this, the reader can anticipate how theme is going to harmonize with topic later in the essay and so reads with a hightened sense of expectation. In other sections of "Invictus under Glass," Hudson adds these statements:

- A sentence in a paragraph about siblings:

  > Juggling the calories and meals was sort of fun, like playing with words in poems.

- A paragraph about reading an article on anorexia in *Seventeen,* including these comments:

  > But the article's main focus, as with most of the anorexia literature then, was on ballerinas and gymnasts who placed high priority on thinness. My image was more literary. The whole thing just didn't apply.

- Back-to-back paragraphs about control and poetry, including these key sentences:

  I took a crash course in great poets, from Wordsworth to Eliot to Whitman. I liked Whitman's imagery; I couldn't understand his joy. . . . I felt more like the embodiment of William Ernest Henley's ubiquitous contribution to hoary English verse anthologies: 'Invictus,' unconquered, master of my fate, captain of my soul. Nothing wrong with the airtight-structure; but the content was an unconvincing farce.

- A paragraph about writing poetry, including these sentiments:

  But it was all joyless. . . . Writing was no longer fun word-juggling, or even cathartic self-expression. It was a chore, a duty. A penance.

- A paragraph about family upheaval, including this observation:

  I kept writing anyway, out of force of habit, convinced that it was all drivel, yet unable to stop.

- A paragraph about refusing counseling, including these remarks:

  The problem, I thought, was not my structured world; it was the very prospect of losing it. It was like an intricate, deranged sestina I had trapped myself in.

- A sentence in a paragraph about going to the hospital for treatment:

  Control started to splinter.

- A paragraph about suicide, including this passage:

  I could never regain the quality of self-control I had before, but I could take a kind of ultimate power over my destiny in one violent step. . . . I was still writing—mostly self-absorbed litanies on the meaningless of life, or at least of my own.

Hudson's thematic statements make up a small part of her 4,105-word essay. But they remind readers about writing and control, leading them step by step to the narrator's lowest point: contemplation of her own death out of fear of losing control.

Because of convention, readers realize that Hudson is not going to kill herself and will explain why near the ending. That's the payoff. So readers are ready for the epiphany or peak experience. Hudson's truth is powerful, too: Writing is as much a liberation as a manipulation. Toward the end of her essay, she describes composing a poem about the death of an infant in her neighborhood—helping friends and family mourn its passing—and glimpses honesty in her elegy. Her piece ends with this epiphany:

Writing, for the first time in my life, was liberation. It had become a chance to see the real self inside the shell. And more important, it had become an answer to loneliness, rather than the source of loneliness. Once, writing was a barrier I built between me and a world I thought shouldn't accept me because I couldn't accept myself. Now it had become a channel through which to reach and share those feelings and experiences that are common to all of us, that bring us out of isolation if we choose to come.

Because the fact is, we are bound, inextricably, to the nature that produced us all, to all humanity, to the very human capacity to love and accept. The only separation for me was in the persona I had contrived out of fear and doubt. And it was gone, released by some part of the self that was apparently wiser than the conscious mind. "The frost makes a flower," Plath wrote in "Death & Co." "The dew makes a star."

The dead bell./The dead bell.

Somebody's done for.

This time it didn't look like it was going to be me.

Consider how Hudson's thematic statements led to such insight:

- Narrator makes an analogy:

  Calories are to food as words are to poems; you can control them.

- Narrator makes an assumption:

  Anorexia concerns ballerinas and gymnasts, not writers.

- Narrator makes another assumption:

  Poetry has structure, but content is a farce.

- Narrator experiences a low point:

  When poetry cannot be controlled, it is a type of penance.

- Narrator sinks lower:

  When poetry is unstoppable, it becomes drivel.

- Narrator sinks lower still:

  When poetry is uncontrollable, it becomes a trap.

- Narrator realizes her plight:

  Control splinters.

- Narrator reaches lowest point:

  When poetry fails, you kill yourself.

Readers are entranced. They sense that the narrator survives because of an important truth related to writing. And now they want to know that truth because, they suspect, it contains utility. They also comprehend the theme of control and so are experiencing the terrors of anorexia for the first time *without ever having had the eating disorder.* As Hudson snaps each puzzle piece into place in a suicidal jigsaw, readers anticipate an upbeat ending.

(After all, the author did not kill herself but is writing about her experience.) Her thematic statements are elements of foreshadowing, predicting a turn of events. When Hudson reveals her epiphany—writing as liberation, as *savior,* almost—readers relive her recovery in a few paragraphs. Theme set that up, too.

But theme does not have to be as intricate or complex as in the Hudson example, especially in shorter works. (The fewer the statements in a work, the shorter the work should be.)

In a "Hers" column in the *New York Times Magazine,* freelancer Lady Borton needed only three thematic statements about forgiveness in "A Forgiving Land." During the Viet Nam War, Borton worked for the American Friends Service Committee and returned to Viet Nam in the 1980s, chronicling postwar life in the Mekong delta and marveling at the beauty of landscape—chortling frogs, fruit-laden milk trees, and perfumed frangipani flowers. Her first thematic statement occurs after her introduction:

> Amazing, I thought: The earth has forgiven us.

Borton continues, grounding topic. By now she is living and working among the Vietnamese and has a confrontation with her main character, a woman-friend and former Viet Cong commander named Second Treasure. The narrator realizes that she has been insensitive and rude to the woman. Borton inserts her second thematic statement in the middle of her column:

> "Forgive me," I said in Vietnamese.

Borton's last statement occurs before her ending. Second Treasure's father gives the narrator a picture of himself and tells Borton to deliver it to her own father, offering to take care of him in his old age. The narrator asserts:

> It's even more amazing, I thought: The people have forgiven us.

Now we are ready for the epiphany. Borton returns to the natural beauty of peacetime Viet Nam, describing breadfruit trees scenting the air and an owl coo-cooing in the distance. The scene has been foreshadowed. Readers recall the descriptive introduction and feel as if they have been on a journey with Borton, who allows Second Treasure to articulate the epiphany in the final paragraph:

> "Don't you understand, Little Sister?" Second Treasure said. "This is all we wanted."

Thematic development can be as easy to execute as that. As promised in her title, Borton depicts "A Forgiving Land" in which Viet Nam forgives the war and the Americans (including Borton) for mistaking their intentions. All they wanted was harmony, peace of mind.

When determining how your theme will develop and lead to epiphany or peak experience, ask yourself:

- What aspects or elements of my theme are associated with my epiphany or peak experience? Can each aspect or element serve as a thematic statement in my work?
- Does each statement deepen the theme in a logical or natural way? If not, can I rearrange the order of statements or change or add a few for more impact?
- Do my statements complete a puzzle and help readers relive my (or my sources') experience as if it were their own? If not, should I add, delete, or revise my statements to attain that goal?

Finally, you need to know about a tool to help you execute those objectives.

Thematic Breaks

Magazine journalism is a *visual* print medium. A little white space, a punctuation mark, or a drop letter goes a long way, as does a subhead, which is a small title within the body of a work, separating it into sections. These are known as *breaks* and are as important as fade-outs or cuts are in film.

Let's examine that metaphor. Have you ever watched an amateur home video in which the camera operator focuses on, say, a person sitting at a table, and then fades to black, only to return to that person in the same pose sitting at the table. Something is unsettling about that (again because of *convention*). You've seen countless movies in which a scene fades to black and then cuts to another setting. The fade conveys a message, telling viewers to recall the last shot because it foreshadows the next segment. A detective in a crime drama ponders an autopsy report and says to the coroner, "Agatha killed her husband, but I don't know where she is." *Fade. Camera opens on Agatha on a Maui beach, sipping a daiquiri.* Viewers understand the cut and anticipate the next sequence. Occasionally, the screen fades to black and words appear before the next sequence. That means something, too. It tells viewers to keep the last segment in mind because the plot is going in a new direction. A detective in a crime drama ponders an autopsy report and says to the coroner, "Agatha killed her husband, and I'll spend my whole life finding her." *Fade. Words appear on a black screen: "Twenty years later, Maui."* Agatha has assumed an alias and is mayoral candidate and a model citizen, making an appearance at a tourist hotel. Who's in the lobby? You guessed it. The detective. Because of the cut, viewers anticipate the next turn of events.

Magazine breaks function the same way. When a writer drops four to six lines, leaving a white space, that also conveys something to the reader: *Keep that last statement in mind because it foreshadows something in the next section.* This is called a *space break*—a simple fade-out. When a writer uses a subhead or a keyboard symbol—usually an asterisk (*), number sign (#), or number (1 or I, and 2 or II, etc.)—that means: *Remember that because the topic takes a new direction.* This is called a *section break.* (When a writer uses a drop letter—which will be discussed later—that can herald either a space break or a section break, depending on the manuscript.)

Four to six lines of white space can dramatically improve a work. In a magazine workshop, Heidi Reddert's first draft described a common college practice called *shacking,* or sleeping with a prospective lover but not necessarily having sex. She wrote:

> It all has to do with the risk involved. Usually if two people leave a bar together the feelings are obviously mutual and there is no fear of rejection on either side. On the other hand, if he calls her and she calls him for a date, neither knows what the other will say.
>
> Soon the time came when I, too, found myself in the potential "shacking" situation. "Last call!" screamed my friend Bridgette from behind the bar. "Do you want to go?" he asked. . . .

Here's the same excerpt from Reddert's second draft, with an improved voice, more research and, most importantly, a space break:

> Unfortunately shacking can have damaging outcomes (with or without contacts). Although STDs and date rape are well-publicized campus issues, shacking hasn't decreased. But many students did say that they wait to have sex. Still, no one could really give reasons for this bizarre way to "date," so I satisfied my curiosity and did what everyone else was doing.
>
> I shacked.
>
> "Last call!" screamed a sorority sister, Bridgette, from behind the bar at The Crystal. It was the usual Thursday-night crowd, packed in like sardines. I was sipping a warm Bud Light and talking to my friend Zach.

The space break foreshadows what is going to occur as soon as Reddert mentions the name Zach. Moves like that are exciting because—bingo!—readers envision what is about to happen next in one fell swoop. Magazine editors even have a name for it: *hook.* The writer hooks readers with a thematic statement or other element of foreshadowing, drawing in the audience the way an angler does a walleye.

A section break can indicate a new direction in a number of ways, via an asterisk, symbol, or numeral. But the subhead is the most popular form. (Subheads will be discussed further in Chapter 5.) In his feature about the world-class orchestra in Adrian, Michigan, magazine workshopper Les Roka turned in a first draft with poorly executed breaks. This first-draft excerpt describes director David Katz's arrival and how he transformed the orchestra:

> Asked about his first perception of Adrian, Katz recalls, "People feel very strongly about having good schools or good city services, so why shouldn't they feel the same about having a good symphony orchestra?" His flair for public relations would let everyone know that Adrian has, as its letterhead claims, "quite possibly the finest symphony orchestra in America for a city of its size."
>
> The orchestra started broadening its membership base, drawing players not only from Adrian and surrounding communities, but from Toledo, Ann Arbor, Jackson and Detroit. Some now travel as much as 100 miles for a rehearsal.

Here's the same excerpt in section-break format:

> Asked about his first perception of Adrian, Katz recalls, "People feel very strongly about having good schools or good city services, so why shouldn't they feel the same about having a good symphony orchestra?" His flair for public relations would let everyone know that Adrian has, as its letterhead claims, "quite possibly the finest symphony orchestra in America for a city of its size."
>
> The reputation is living up to its billing.

Transformation

> Changes came but only with community approval. The orchestra started broadening its membership base, drawing players not only from Adrian and surrounding communities, but from Toledo, Ann Arbor, Jackson and Detroit. Some now travel as much as 100 miles for a rehearsal.

Roka's section break was executed with these minor but essential elements:

- An exit: A transitional or thematic sentence that leads the reader out of the section and into four lines of white space:

  The reputation is living up to its billing.

- A subhead: A thematic word or phrase that foreshadows what is contained in the new section:

  Transformation.

■ An entrance: A transitional or thematic sentence that guides the reader from the subhead to the new section:

Changes came but only with community approval.

A *drop letter,* a letter cast in bold and in larger point size than the text, is more versatile than a space or section break. It combines elements of both with the design feature of a subhead. In her article about a Gulf War veteran named David, who suffers from chemical warfare symptoms, Audrey Chapman, senior editor at *Cleveland Magazine,* employed both functions at different junctures of her article, "And Justice for All?" Chapman's theme was misplaced trust, stated in a paragraph before her drop-letter break:

David was trained to believe that hundreds of camels could die at the same time, in the same place, of thirst or hunger in the desert if his commanding officer said so. David was trained to believe *everything* he said.

Nearly five years later, as David McGee sits in his Lisbon home and recalls that day in the desert, he stops speaking momentarily to tend to his 2-year-old daughter, Desiree. She wants a bear that sits just beyond his feet.
Unable to reach it, the 27-year-old father pins it down with his cane. . . .

The paragraph before the drop letter foreshadows symptoms depicted in the next section when David is unable to fetch a toy bear and uses his cane. The drop letter functions as a space break.

In this excerpt quoting an officer of a veterans' group, Chapman uses the drop-letter break as a section break so she can take a new direction, flashing back to David's war:

"We will not give up the fight because we're right," says Vic Silvester, president of the national Operation Desert Storm Association and co-chair of the Yellow Ribbon Commission. "All we want is what this country promised. . . . We will win."

As the orange glow of the sun started to creep over the horizon in Mashawb one early morning in late January 1991, the distant sounds of a soldier running woke David McGee up. The soldier bounded into his tent wearing Mopp 4 gear—the highest level of suit, gas mask, rubber boots and rubber gloves designed to protect a soldier during a chemical or biological attack.

To envision what type of break will serve your piece, determine the number of thematic statements you need to convey your epiphany or peak experience, as you learned earlier in this chapter. Then analyze your statements and ask yourself:

- Do my statements flow smoothly from one issue or scene to the next? (If so, envision your work with space breaks.)
- Do my statements take new directions, jumping from one issue or scene to another related issue or scene? (If so, envision your work with section breaks.)
- Do my statements combine elements of both? (If so, envision your work with drop letters.)

In sum, theme is at the heart of magazine journalism. It appeals to the audience directly. If you change your theme, you usually change the target audience. Theme adds another layer of meaning and utility to a work, developing page by page, hooking readers, and elevating them out of their lives and into yours or—as evidenced in excerpts from "And Justice for All" by Audrey Chapman—into the lives of your sources. Thematic breaks help achieve all this.

Now let's learn about another tool in The Craft Shop and about methods to analyze theme at The Newsstand and infuse theme in your work at The Keyboard.

T H E   C R A F T   S H O P

The Billboard Paragraph

Tom Clark, Editor, *Writer's Digest*

The billboard paragraph (a type of grounding) lends itself nicely to how-to and service magazines. It keeps the focus on what you mean to accomplish in an article. In fact, the subtitle of a magazine is a little billboard explaining the content of a specific publication. For instance, the subtitle of *Writer's Digest* is "Your Monthly Guide To Getting Published." Without that phrase, the reader might not know what our magazine is about. Same thing with an article. The billboard lets the reader know what is coming up in a piece.

Typically, the billboard paragraph immediately follows the introduction, or lead. The lead hooks readers, but the billboard keeps them reading. It says in almost so many words: "This is what I am going to tell you." Well, maybe a little subtler than that. But it lets the reader know what the writer's point is. It says, "When you're done reading this, you will know 'how to build a great deck' or, maybe, 'how to control children's temper tantrums.'"

The billboard works best in a how-to piece, but grounding is found in all types of magazine articles. At writer's conferences, I like to use a *Sports Il-*

lustrated article about spandex. It's a wonderful piece that covers that topic fully, with a lead that goes on for six or seven paragraphs. Then the billboard immediately follows, discussing how spandex has changed fashion radically. It promises to tell readers everything they never knew they needed to know about this particular fabric.

The lead is going to tell the reader a couple of things, too. It's going to indicate the tone of the article. The voice will explain that this is going to be a happy, sad, dramatic, or traumatic piece, depending on the writer's purposes. But it's the billboard paragraph that tells the reader what is going to happen in Act Three.

Foreshadowing, for the most part, is an element of transition from paragraph to paragraph. My favorite way to describe a transition is "an echo of what went before." In a good magazine article, those transitions will carry a reader's interest all the way through, to the conclusion, reminding people about your theme or slant—even if it is "Ten things you need to know." The writer will use an occasional transition—"This is the tenth and most important element"—and that will remind the reader, "Oh, yes. We're talking about ten things. Now we're getting ready to conclude."

And in the conclusion the reader remembers the promise that the writer made in the lead, solidified in the billboard.

T H E   N E W S S T A N D

Reading the Slants

1. Continue to visit your library and read magazines that you would like to write for and photocopy any columns, features, and articles that appeal to you. Add them to the photocopies in your personal file labeled Story Samples.

2. Analyze the photocopies in your Story Samples file and note:
   - Grounding that distinguishes topic from theme
   - Statements that distinguish theme from topic
   - The number of thematic statements and how they progress in a piece, leading to epiphany or peak experience
   - The type of break, if any, employed in the piece—space, section, or drop letter—and how these enhance theme or foreshadow other elements in the work

T H E   K E Y B O A R D

Identifying Your Theme

1. Reread your magazine photocopies, this time for ideas. If you discover gaps in a particular piece—something the author omitted and on which you can base a new idea—note it on a page or in a file at the keyboard. If you conceive a new idea based on thematic statements in your photocopies, note them, too. Determine what approach might best suit each idea and document it, as you learned to do in The Keyboard assignments in the previous chapter. Add these new ideas to your Story Ideas file.

2. Take out each item in your Story Ideas file and, according to the methods explained in this chapter, enhance your ideas in the following ways:

   - *Identify the topic and the theme.* In a few sentences or paragraphs, describe what elements of your topic require grounding. Encapsulate your epiphany or peak experience with a word or phrase to serve as a theme and target that theme at a potential market.

   - *Focus again on epiphany or peak experience.* Analyze your theme and write down statements that will guide the audience, step by step, to your epiphany or peak experience.

   - *Study your statements to determine breaks.* Note which kind of break you might employ—space, section, or drop letter—to develop your theme.

CHAPTER FOUR

Research

The Magazine Interview

"Write what you know!" That magazine journalism cliché is good advice, as long as what you know has take-away value. So the saying really should read "Write what you know . . . only if you know what others have written about it, too."

That requires *research*, defined as acquiring facts, quotations, citations, and data—from sources and personal observation—about topics, occasions, and themes. Research will reveal:

- *Whether your truth is significant and shared by thousands of others.* If you can't find any information on "Ten Surefire Ways to Conceal Arson," chances are that no one is interested in your insight (except, perhaps, the District Attorney).
- *Other opinions about your truth, enhancing your perception.* If sources cannot add any insight to your topic—"Sooner or Later, Everyone Croaks"—your truth might be a fact of life and obvious to everyone.
- *Different thematic slants, helping you target the right market.* Your "War and Peace" column might suit *Soldier of Fortune* or *Mother Earth News,* depending on which concept—war or peace—is the topic and which is the theme.

Before you start hitting the books, determine who you need to interview. That's how you test the utility of your truth. Almost all story ideas, even personal columns, require quotations or background from other people. You may decide not to use that information but you will benefit knowing it during the writing process, lending an air of authority to epiphanies or peak experiences.

To identify your sources, make a source box. Type your information on a sheet of paper and use a ruler to frame it, or open a text box and symbol—circle, ellipse, square—on a computer. (Do create a frame around your information; it helps you envision the sources that your story should contain.) At the top left corner of the box, note your target audience. In the middle of the box, note your topic, theme, and truth. All around your topic, theme, and truth, name experts and others you need to interview. Ask yourself:

- When I experienced my high, low, or turning point, who else was involved in or affected by the experience?
- With whom did I consult to celebrate, mourn, or otherwise put the experience into perspective?
- What experts specialize in aspects associated with my experience?

An example of how your source box should look may be found in Figure 4.1.

A source box is a playbill for your story idea. It contains a cast of good and bad characters with distinct motives and viewpoints, as in a morality play. You'll know many sources personally or professionally, of course. They may play a role in your truth. But if you are targeting a national publication such as *New Woman,* some of your sources should be newsworthy or nationally known experts. (Later in this chapter you'll learn how to locate them.) At the moment, you need to envision who you should contact and how you should question them in a magazine interview, which differs significantly from the newspaper kind.

When you are on general assignment for a newspaper, an editor usually assigns stories. One day you report on a prison riot and the next day on center pivot irrigation systems. Chances are the U.S. Justice and Agriculture departments do not figure in your list of highs, lows, and turning points. So your research commitment is going to be light, especially when facing a daily deadline. True, some reporters working on special projects or investigations have longer deadlines and do meticulous research. But even here, strong themes are discouraged in newspapering. (Remember the two definitions of *slant* in Chapter 3.) So a newspaper reporter covering a breaking story or an important issue emphasizes facts and attempts to gather them as accurately and as quickly as possible.

The magazine interview emphasizes theme. There are two formats: question and answer (Q&A) and story.

F I G U R E   4 . 1   Sample Source Box

Target Audience: *New Woman*

Judges

Lawyers   Bankers   Accountants

Real Estate Agents   Employers   Marriage Counselors

Divorce

Renewal

Love may end but it also may renew itself.

Clergy   Children   Family

In-Laws   Friends   Partners

Women

The Q&A format begins with a research section. It showcases your interviewee's newsworthiness and/or accomplishments. It's called the *introduction* and is cast in italicized type to distinguish it from the body of quotations in the Q&A segment that follows. Here is an excerpt from the introduction of an interview by Kevin Bezner with environmentalist-poet Gary Snyder, originally published in the small-press magazine *Left Bank:*

At Kitkitdizze in the Yuba Watershed, Snyder carries on what he calls "the real work." This means knowing where your food and water come from so that you can actively participate in the decisions that affect the region in which you live; it requires hands-on work and living interdependently with the natural world. While Snyder teaches at the University of California at Davis and gives lectures and poetry readings to earn a wage, his aim is to avoid what he has called (in an interview with Peter Barry Chowkra in The Real Work) *the "triple alienation" of contemporary life—alienation from energy and resources, the body, and the mind. This is why he is involved in all aspects of work at his home, why all members of his family are engaged in such work, why he has taught his daughter how to change the oil on the generators at Kitkitdizze, and why he has a deep love and respect for tools and knowing when to use the right tool.*

Note the background that Bezner provides about Snyder who, as in typical Q&A interviews, is also the topic of the piece. Bezner grounds the key term, *the real work*, and provides thematic focus about resources, body, mind, and even tools. A portion of the Q&A segment of his interview follows. Typically, interviewers employ a space or an asterisk break, switch to upright type, and spell out the name of the interviewer and the interviewee in boldface type:

> **Kevin Bezner:** How do you define the word "work," which in our culture seems to have taken on the definition of something you do to do something else?
>
> **Gary Snyder:** You mean like "work" as occupation. That you have to do to support yourself. Yeah. That's actually called wage work, or wage earning, and as Ivan Illich points out in his very useful book called *Shadow Work*, working for wages is a very recent thing in history, and it's part of the rise of industrialism, the destruction of rural agriculture, and the creation of a working class. . . .

After the first question and answer, you may abbreviate names:

> **KB:** One of your poems that I admire the most is "The Bath." What you're doing there, in that poem, is the real work of showing your son Kai how one cleans oneself and how one lives in a family.
>
> **GS:** Well, that's what you have to do with your kids no matter what. If you don't prove a leader to your own children and take time to show them each of the little things they have to do, and then take time out to help them learn to cook or help them learn to handle tools and involve them in the things that you do around the place, how are they ever going to learn?

Bezner says that his interview with Snyder "focuses in on a theme that he's spoken about many times, 'work.' But because I had read all I could of what he said on this topic, I asked questions that were different from what he had been asked before. I tie in a reference to the past by asking him about his poem 'The Bath,' and I ask him about a subject that he himself had only started writing about, 'the Yuba Watershed Institute.'" Bezner shows up prepared for an interview, knowing his topic and theme, with questions already sketched out. "I had, by the way, only twenty minutes for this interview, and we didn't go beyond twenty minutes, which meant that I had to be very focused to get the information I needed."

Bezner calls Q&A interviews "essays in conversation." That reminds him to focus on theme. "The interviewer arranges, essentially, for the interviewee to say the words that make up the article or essay," he adds, "but it is the interviewer who has created the piece."

In the same manner, freelance writers also create the interview employing a story format—typically a feature or an article relying in part on interviews to convey information to the audience. In a masterwork of magazine journalism, "Anna's Tangled Destiny" (formerly titled "Acts of Kindness"), Ursula Obst profiled a bag lady named Anna Podobna for the premiere issue of *New York Woman*. Obst quickly establishes a theme of "uncompromising pride" in her article-length profile, citing this as a reason why Podobna wanders New York City following a harrowing experience as a "lice feeder" to make typhus vaccine in a Nazi medical facility in occupied Poland. In the following scene, set in New York City, a minister named Laura Jacobs tries to get Anna to sign Social Security papers:

> Despite Laura's efforts, Anna would not sign the Social Security disability application. Perhaps it was pride, perhaps she would not admit to being disabled, Laura is not sure.
>
> It took a long time for Anna to trust Laura enough to admit her into her room, but once she did, she welcomed Laura's visits. On one such visit Laura asked her about the war. "Joe told me he believed she must have been in a concentration camp, so I was kind of on the lookout for something that created this way she coped with life." Laura had wanted more information, but when Anna began to talk about it she was unprepared—shocked and moved, she could not ask for details. "She told me there were boxes, I didn't understand about the lice. She showed me a scar. She pulled back her skirt and there it was on the inside of her right thigh. That conversation was clearly the most intimate moment we shared."
>
> Their relationship changed after Laura, frustrated over another fruitless attempt to get Anna to sign, lost her temper and spoke harshly to her. "It seems to me, after that, she didn't give me access to her room or to her thoughts. I think I hurt her pride."

In this excerpt, Obst makes a thematic statement: "Perhaps it was pride, perhaps she would not admit to being disabled, Laura is not sure." That foreshadows a quotation in her interview with Laura: "I think I hurt her pride." As in the Kevin Bezner example, Obst as an interviewer sustains thematic focus throughout her 6,057-word article.

Anna Podobna was reluctant to speak to Obst, so her profile was compiled via meticulous research, including interviews with people who knew the bag lady. (Obst explains the process in The Craft Shop at the end of this chapter.)

Another scenario may occur, involving quotations. Sometimes, sources perceive writers as unfriendly and do not grant interviews. Writers, then—again, knowing the importance of theme—quote from sources' speeches or public presentations. This was the case in an exposé, "Sister Soldiers," published in *The New Republic* by philosopher and author Christina Hoff Sommers. "I tried to let the subjects—in this case, radical feminists at the highly charged gathering in Austin, Texas—speak for themselves. Much of what I was hearing could be described as 'off the wall.' But I never say that in the piece. I simply quoted what I was hearing, allowing readers to react."

The opening paragraphs of her exposé illustrate her method. Sommers explains the occasion—a conference—in the first paragraph, quoting a stray complaint by a participant. Then she states the theme in the first sentence of her second paragraph, quoting speakers who reinforce that assertion:

> The Hyatt Regency in Austin, Texas, is a pleasant hotel, but not all of the 500 participants in this year's National Women's Studies Association Conference [NWSA] were happy with it. One woman from a well-known Southern college complained about the weddings held there throughout the weekend. "Why have they put us in a setting where *that* sort of thing is going on?" she demanded.
>
> Dissatisfaction was a conference motif. The keynote speaker, Annette Kolodny, a feminist literary scholar and until recently dean of the humanities faculty at the University of Arizona, opened the proceedings with a brief history of the "narratives of pain" within the NWSA. She reported that ten years ago the organization "almost came apart over outcries by our lesbian sisters that we had failed adequately to listen to their many voices." Five years ago sisters in the Jewish Caucus had wept at their own "sense of invisibility." Three years later the Disability Caucus threatened to quit, and the next year the women of color walked out. A pernicious bigotry, Kolodny confessed, persisted in the NWSA. "Our litanies of outrage . . . overcame our fragile consensus of shared commitment, and the center would no longer hold."

When conducting interviews with reluctant sources, or excerpting their presentations, fairness is a primary concern. The writer focuses on the theme, but the theme also should be reflected in coverage; otherwise, the writer will be accused of quoting "out of context," misrepresenting the speech or presentation. In her opening thematic statement, Sommers asserts that dissatisfaction was a conference "motif." That word implies she will provide several more quotations to back up her claim. (And she does.) To ensure a measure of fairness, Sommers says she tries to sympathize with those she criticizes. But, she adds, "you need to show whom they are hurting."

Balancing theme with fairness is a concern in most magazine interviews, especially ones about sensitive topics, such as divorce. There's as much pain as renewal in a typical divorce, and you should acknowledge that when questioning certain sources. You should also try to *serve* your readers as much as possible—guaranteeing take-away value—by asking experts for advice.

Let's illustrate that, referring back to the people in the source box (Figure 4.1) for a *New Woman* piece about divorce. They included judges, lawyers, bankers, accountants, real estate agents, employers, marriage counselors, clergy, children, family, in-laws, friends, partners, and women. In researching such a piece, you would try to interview nationally known judges, lawyers, and other experts—as you will learn in the upcoming Research Methods section—and an array of others who have experienced divorce and renewal. You would ask each source thematic questions, keeping fairness and service in mind—for example:

- *To a judge:* "Judges often grant divorces because of irreconcilable differences. In cases like these, do you ever see divorce as a chance for one or both spouses to renew their dreams or ambitions? What advice can you give women about dealing with the courts, emphasizing their concerns to a judge?"
- *To a lawyer:* "I'm sure you have handled plenty of contested divorces. But what about friendly ones in which one or both partners thrived after parting ways, renewing dreams or ambitions? What advice can you give to women about parting amicably?"
- *To a banker:* "More and more women are opening small businesses, especially after a divorce. What procedures do such women typically go through, obtaining loans to renew their dreams or ambitions?"
- *To an accountant:* "What tax or credit advice can you give women who recently divorced so that they can renew a comfortable lifestyle?"
- *To a real estate agent:* "Many women going through a divorce are trying to sell jointly held property. How do they recoup equity so that they have adequate funds to renew their dreams or ambitions?"
- *To an employer:* "What policies does your company have for a worker going through a divorce, and how effective have those policies been in renewing the worker's commitment to the company? What employment advice can you give to women who might need time off or support during a personal upheaval such as divorce?"
- *To a marriage counselor:* "Certainly, divorce is painful. But tell me about women you have counseled who have gone on to renew their dreams and ambitions. What were their special qualities? How can other women nurture those qualities in themselves to thrive after a divorce?"
- *To a clergy member:* "Marriage is an important commitment, of course. And churches consider that sacred. But divorce happens. When it does, how can women renew their faith—especially after a betrayal by a spouse?"

- *To a child* (after receiving parental permission to interview him or her): "Your mom says you're excited about her opening an office downtown. How have you felt about your mom, seeing her renew her dreams or ambitions?"
- *To a family member:* "Divorce can be tough on everyone, especially families. But how have you felt, watching your daughter survive her divorce and then go on to renew her dreams and ambitions? How can mothers nurture their daughters when they are going through a divorce?"
- *To an in-law:* "You seem to have a special friendship with your former daughter-in-law. How have you been able to renew your relationship and what advice can you to other ex-mothers-in-law in your situation?"
- *To a friend:* "How has your friendship been renewed or enhanced, following your best friend's divorce? What role should friends play when women are going through a divorce?"
- *To a partner:* "What special qualities attracted you to your lover? What can boyfriends do to help women renew their dreams and ambitions, following a divorce?"
- *To a woman:* "How have you been able to renew your own dreams and ambitions following your divorce? Get a loan to start a new business? Establish credit? Sell property? Keep your job? Cope with stress? Keep your faith? Bond with children? Maintain relationships with family, in-laws, friends? Renew romance?"

Except for the child, sources were asked to share advice because *New Woman* emphasizes service to readers. To ensure fairness, many other questions were prefaced by acknowledging the pain and upheaval of divorce. Notice that the word *divorce* is not even mentioned in the question to the child. Every question, however, contains the phrase *renew dreams and ambitions* or the word *renew*. This will help generate thematic statements that lead to the epiphany: *Love may end but it also may renew itself.* Better still, you should be able to combine similar statements into groups—maybe ones about the legal/emotional process (judge, lawyer, counselor, and clergy); money (banker, accountant, real estate agent, and employer); and relationships (children, in-law, mother, friend, and partner). Those suggest specific sections of a manuscript.

Slowly you are becoming able to visualize this story. That's the goal. Before you schedule interviews or compose a piece without any interviews—focusing on sensory data, say, to describe a place—you need to bone up on issues or sharpen your perspective.

Sensory Data

Talk about research, and the typical novice bristles. Magazine writing is personal and creative, isn't it? Wait a second. What the heck does *personal* and *creative* mean? Most people think that a Shakespearean sonnet is exceptionally personal and creative. What it is, is exceptionally *numerical:* five metric feet of iambic pentameter per line according to a predetermined rhyme scheme—abab cdcd efef gg—with each four-line stanza (or quatrain) developing a theme and the ending two-line stanza (couplet) stating a truth. You learned all that in high school. Then you purged. The point is, when done well, a sonnet seems as seamless as the epiphany or peak experience that spawned it. When done poorly, a sonnet is as artificial as saccharine. The same goes for magazine journalism. The goal of a good sonnet is the same as a good prose work. *You say something significant while transcending the limits of the form.* When you do, readers forget about their own lives and enter yours or your sources'.

Nothing is more personal than a mother's memoir. And few writers are more creative than Kelly Cherry, prize-winning poet, short story writer, and celebrated author. Yet, research plays a key role in anything that Cherry writes, even a profile of her grandfather titled after him: "Mr. Allen Dewey Spooner." As Cherry tells it, "In her seventies my mother wrote an unpublished memoir. Worried that she might not have time to finish, she rushed her material. It was marvelous material. She gave me a copy of the manuscript and said I could do with it whatever I liked. I proceeded to steal from it." Then Cherry realized that the memoir needed more detail. "That meant I had to do research even when working from a personal history. There will be a reference to 'pirogues,'" Cherry says, "and I have to find out what a pirogue is."

Cherry also had to depict the era in which the memoir was set, verifying dates, proper nouns, names, songs, and even cuisine, as this excerpt shows:

> The conversation in the parlor turned to the war. It was 1917, and the day before, a trainload of soldiers from nearby Gertsner Field had pulled out of town to the accompaniment of cheers and waving banners, and the town band, in which Allen played clarinet. Grandma LaBesse expressed displeasure with the neighborhood children for mocking poor old Professor Schultz and shouting "German spy! German spy!" as he shuffled along the sidewalk. Flags draped front porches; women rolled bandages for the Red Cross; and Mr. Cloony, the choir director, organized community "sings," flailing his arms enthusiastically while belting out the words to "It's a Long, Long Way to Tipperary" and "I'm Forever Blowing Bubbles." Everyone ridiculed the Kaiser and boasted of self-im-

posed privations. Mrs. Beardsley told the assemblage in the parlor how she had carried a case of railroad salvage pork and beans all the way from the depot to the house in South Ryan Street, and Hattie explained, to their daughters' lasting horror, that the "scrambled eggs" they had eaten for supper the night before had really been *brains*.

Such writing not only contains historical detail but also *sensory data*, defined as words or phrases depicting one or more of the five senses—sight, touch, taste, smell, and sound—or size and motion. In the preceding excerpt, Cherry evokes a sense of sound (conversation, band, cheers, song); sight and motion (banners, pedestrians); sound and motion (train, taunting children); taste and motion (carrying pork and beans); touch (rolled bandages); and taste (brains.) These observations are also functions of research. Without them, the reader could not time-travel to 1917.

Sensory data also transports readers to new places. Without such data, the audience stays put. To illustrate, here is an excerpt about a windmill on an Iowa farm:

The windmill was big. It worked when the weather kicked up. But we loved the farm because of that windmill. It didn't generate much power, except in my relationship. It brought my husband Jeff and me together in ways we had only dreamed about when we dated. Because of the windmill, I think, Jeff bought me wind chimes. Somehow that gift made me think about the frogs in our pond and the birds in our grove. We were city kids, after all, who had only worked in gardens, not farms. Now we had our neighbors' sheep, hogs, and cows to contend with. The cows were especially animated when calving, and at first we didn't understand the commotion. Then Bird, one of our goats, kidded for the first time. The connection was clear.

Now read that same passage with sensory data from an excerpt from Patricia Westfall's essay, "An American Dream," which originally appeared in *Esquire:*

The windmill was a lyrical detail in the classic sense of the word—that is, exuberant, almost pure sound. The windmill had a marvelous sound whenever it pumped, not quite like a cricket, not quite like a heartbeat. It was distinctive, and it set the tone—very literally—for us in the months that followed the move. Jeff instinctively understood the importance of sound—or seemed to. He bought me a wind chime for the porch, but a very special one, tuned to a Grecian tonal scale, he said. It was beautiful, producing rich notes and pure melody in endlessly intriguing variety. I never tired of it and thought it an exceptionally appropriate gift for the farm because, of course, the discovery process in this place would be sensory and sound should be dominant.

In spring, for example, there would be a night when all at once all the frogs began bellowing; it would sound as if there were more frogs on the pond than stars above it. And yet the sound of a single whippoorwill, which always followed a few nights later, was more strident than the noise of those millions. The call was a mixture of surprise and urgency, made strange by the fact that it came at night, so rare among birds. Decoding the sounds became a major adventure for us, both still basically city kids despite the gardens behind us. Our training taught us to distinguish bus from dump truck, not oriole from goldfinch. We learned most sounds simply by freezing in place in woods or pasture, hoping for a glimpse of the bird or animal that made the noise. We also mastered farm sounds, such as the cry of a sheep separated from the flock (it was infuriating how the flock never answered the lost one) or the screams of hogs being loaded into trucks for the one-way trip to market. One sound defied decoding by us for a long time. It was a sound cattle made, a roar of rage or pain, similar to the screams of hogs but always from one animal at a time. Then Bird, one of our goats, kidded for the first time. Her bellows were different, but even so the connection was clear. We felt foolish not to have realized sooner we were hearing cows calving.

Most people think sight is the sense of discovery; they think what is lyrical must be something seen, but that is not true. Seeing was very difficult in this place; too many distractions, too many changes.

Because of sensory data, readers feel they are at Westfall's farm; she has transported them from their loveseats and La-Z-boys so that they can experience what she did in Iowa. Lacking such research, the earlier description of her farm was flat. (Few readers would dub it "creative.") Westfall's excerpt, on the other hand, sparkles. You *hear* the windmill, the frogs, the wind chimes. But, hey—she must be one of those natural-born writers. Sensory data has to come easy for her. Not so. As she puts it:

I am by nature dense. Everyone on the earth may have bought brown plastic combs to hold up their hairdos or be walking their dogs on retractable leashes and I will not notice. Yet paradoxically I am told that one of the strengths of my writing is wealth of detail.

Having rich detail at my command is not something that comes easily to me. Thus, when I write, I do not struggle with words. My hurdle is never with the language, but with the seeing. I miss so much. To compensate I research to crazy excess. My voice has power because I father data, not because I'm deft with a phrase. I'm truly methodical about research. I'm almost embarrassed to tell you how methodical. I set out to sense on purpose, to perceive with a will.

My method? I box reality into tidy categories. I start with visual details, and I divide them further into two groups, light and space. Next I study sounds, again of two styles; one set I call the "chirp-chirp" category, or sound for sound's sake; next, but more important, is the sound of speech—not quotes, maybe not even dialogue, but the sense of speech. Next I hunt for motion—again of two types in my ordered, overly deliberate process: I examine motion in time (action) and motion in space (change). Next I hunt for measurements—not literal inches and miles, but a sense of size when measured against bodies or space. A chicken yard might be as big as my living room or a dog as chunky as rototiller, say. Last I gather what the other senses offer: touch, smell, taste.

I gather such details as deliberately as I would phrase questions in an interview. I run through each category in turn, now look, next listen, now wait for time to pass, next gauge, now touch. Mechanistic? Yes. I hope the final product sounds as if I were a natural observer. But the truth is I'm not. If I seem so, it's because I work at it and I work harder at seeing than I have ever worked at phrasing a sentence.

Some topics, such as an Iowa farm, require more sensory data than others. But even in a service piece, you should be able to include sensory data. As you interview each source, note how your senses are stimulated by what you hear, see, or otherwise experience. Let's return to that list of sources in the divorce story for *New Woman*—Westfall's essay, by the way, is about a divorce—and cite examples of sensory data (especially ones symbolizing renewal) that you can document during an interview:

- *Judge:* Describe his or her chambers. Note the desk. Any family pictures? How about the view from the window? Does it overlook a bustling downtown? River? Park?
- *Lawyer:* Describe clientele in the waiting room, especially women. Are they drinking coffee? Wearing wedding bands?
- *Banker:* Describe loan applicants awaiting appointments. Any women? How are they dressed? Do they walk confidently to the loan officer when they are called?
- *Accountant:* Describe the surroundings. Sound of adding machines? Rustle of papers? Crack of file drawers?
- *Real estate agent:* Describe a house being sold due to divorce—the garden, the bedroom, the den—emphasizing anything associated with the senses: scent of lilacs, big screen TV, candy bowls.
- *Employer:* Describe the document containing corporate policy and how it feels in your hand. Note any illustrations or pictures on the document.
- *Marriage counselor:* Note any personal touches meant to soothe during sessions. Color of walls? Type of artwork? Posters? Slogans? Background music?
- *Clergy member:* Describe the symbols of faith and renewal in the church, synagogue, or temple, from stained glass to pillars.
- *Child:* Describe the sounds you hear on the playground or in the house, from the whiz of jump rope to the whir of video games.
- *Family member:* Describe the daughter's bedroom and note trophies, certificates, or other symbolic objects of past dreams or ambitions.

- *In-law:* Note any gift or memento from an ex-daughter-in-law.
- *Friend:* Note photos or souvenirs that symbolize good times with a woman-friend going through a divorce.
- *Partner:* Take in the bachelor digs and describe the lover's fashion sense or cologne.
- *Woman:* Note objects in her hope chest or predictions in her year-book.

Recording sensory data while doing interviews with sources can put the reader at the scene with you and showcase theme as well. Author and educator Carol Muske Dukes does both in "Farrah Fawcett Up Close," profiling the star's redecorated home for *House and Garden:*

> There's a ruckus outside in the hall. A worried little boy with platinum hair and zebra-striped pants hurries into the living room, gesturing and murmuring to himself like the White Rabbit. He's lost his wand, he tells the room at large, then throws himself disconsolately into his mother's lap. She whispers in his ear, he nods and trots off happy—she turns back to me, magically transformed from Mom to Farrah Fawcett.
>
> The house, which Farrah shares with actor Ryan O'Neal and their five-year-old son, Redmond, appears to be the product of a wand with an enlightened personal touch.

A beginner, eager to interview a famous actor, might have been upset at the little boy's interruption. Instead, Dukes describes the ruckus, the color of the boy's hair and pants, the motion of his gestures, the texture of held-back tears, the intimacy of whispers, and the boy trotting off—and then uses the wand as a symbol to introduce a redecorating theme: magical transformation. All in about 100 words.

Research Methods

Diane Ackerman, one of the world's best writers, focuses so intently on research that she can title her natural history articles with names of species. Discovery, or rediscovery, is usually her theme enhanced with epiphanies about and peak experiences in nature. A case in point is "Bats," which originally appeared in *New Yorker* and which is based on an extensive interview with bat expert Merlin D. Tuttle. Ackerman accompanied him to the Texas hill county to observe the creatures. Most writers would read a few bat books before meeting Tuttle or simply quote Tuttle as "expert"; Ackerman does that, of course. But she is also known for making the *unknown* familiar, in poetry and prose, relying on (1) *field research,* going to the scene to generate sensory data (and peak experience); and (2) *library research,* reading extensively on a subject to provide perspective (and epiphany).

Here's a typical passage from "Bats" featuring both kinds of research—from observations about bat guano smelling like "stale crackers" to citations from an array of books, including "Macbeth" and the Bible—presented conversationally, as if Ackerman were speaking to a friend:

Bats are extremely tidy: they comb themselves thoroughly, and don't gather a mess of nesting materials for their homes, as birds do. Their guano smells like stale crackers, and sometimes insects invade it, so that it appears to be bubbling, but the bats themselves live high above, in penthouse roosts, and keep their bodies well groomed. Since they don't build nests, they take shelter in a wide range of secluded places appropriate to the unique needs of each species: spider webs, unfurling leaves, animal burrows, eaves, caves, open brickwork, hollow trees. Seldom a belfry, despite the saying; belfries are more often occupied by birds. Perhaps it was bats darting around church belfries at twilight in their normal pursuit of insects that made people think they lived there. Or perhaps it was the image of the Devil, traditionally drawn with bat wings, and the sermons that warned of his being always in the vicinity. People also think that bats have a penchant for bedrooms, and a wayward bat might indeed be tempted to stray in through an open window at night, but bats much prefer the gables of a house, or a chimney, or even the space behind a window shutter. Most American bats roost wherever there's a good supply of insects nearby, and that often means in forests or parks, along rivers, lakes, or marshes, in churchyards (another possible source of the bats-in-the-belfry myth), or even near city street lamps that insects circle. Drawn to the free lunch at searchlights, they frequent baseball parks and even airports, along with starlings, finches, and many other winged things; since they spend their lives in a barrage of sound, they may not be bothered much by the engine noise.

A single small insect-eating bat can eat a thousand insects each night, so these bats are a good investment for a homeowner. Bat Conservation International, or B.C.I., sells "official bat houses" for homeowners to hang in their yards, and emphasizes what good citizens bats are. They are gluttons, and gorge themselves on offensive nocturnal insects. Little brown bats, the most common of the North American species, can catch six hundred or more mosquitoes in an hour. And as many as thirty bats may live in a single bat house. Of course, bats do change their homes, depending on the time of year. When the females are giving birth and raising their young, they prefer warm places, but for hibernating a cold cave or mine is better.

Bat houses look nothing like bird houses. For one thing, they don't have cutesy roofs made to look like Swiss chalets. (I don't know why, or when, people decided that birds preferred to live in human-style houses, and just because desperate birds do live in them doesn't mean they like them. I much prefer the eighteenth-century-style bird bottle, still used in Colonial Williamsburg, Virginia—a swollen earthenware cylinder, glazed brown, that looks like a vase lying on its side.) An "official bat house" is made of red cedar, is squarish, and suggests an old-fashioned mailbox of the type that used to hang on a householder's front door. On the front is B.C.I.'s logo, an abstract drawing of the *wu fu,* a decorative emblem that the Chinese have traditionally used as a talisman. The *wu fu* shows the tree of life encircled by five bats, whose wingtips touch or sometimes interlock. The bats symbolize the five elements of good fortune: health, happiness, long life, contentment, and prosperity. Indeed, the Chinese word for happiness, *fu,* though it is written differently, is the same as the word for bat. So bats occur often in Chinese conversation—especially during marriage ceremonies and other celebrations.

Inside the bat house, movable dividers, "to allow for different bat preferences," create crevices of varying widths where bats can roost in privacy. There is a solid roof and sides but no floor; thus squirrels and birds won't be able to nest there, while bats can get in and out easily. If you have given some thought to the preferences of different sorts of bats, then you are probably already a bat fancier, and have decided whether you would prefer to attract "mother" bats or "bachelor" bats, as the positioning guidelines in the instructions suggest.

There must originally have been some confusion about what a bat was. This isn't really surprising. Many people still think bats are a sort of mouse, and the word for bat in various languages reflects this misconception. In Mexico, bats are sometimes called *ratones voladores,* or flying mice; in Germany, a bat is the operatic *Fledermaus,* or flying mouse; and in France it is a *chauve-souris,* or bald mouse. Then there's the confusion between birds and bats—the simple facts are that a bird is a bird and, as Bela Lugosi indignantly points out to the police inspector in the 1941 film "The Devil Bat" (a.k.a. "Killer Bats"), a bat is a mammal. Except that both have wings, they look very different. Birds have beaks, for example, and bats have teeth. Baby bats are born with milk teeth, which are hooked, to help them hold on to the mother; they grow their permanent teeth a few weeks later. Yet such obvious differences didn't stop people from confusing birds and bats for an extraordinarily long time. In both Leviticus and Deuteronomy, where the injunctions about eating clean and unclean meats occur, bats are identified as unclean birds: "among the fowls, they shall not be eaten, they are an abomination: the eagle, and the ossifrage, and the osprey . . . and the stork, the heron . . . and the bat" (Leviticus 11). Aesop has a fable in which a weasel snares a bat and pauses before devouring it to explain that he preys exclusively on birds. No fool, the bat quickly informs the weasel that it's a mouse, and is let go. Later in the story, the bat meets another weasel, who feeds only on mice, and the bat swears to this weasel that it's a bird, and escapes again. Various Greek, Roman, and Chinese stories try to explain why the bat flies at night, and they all have to do with a confused self-image: the bat is not sure whether it's a bird or a mouse or something else, and as a result it acts with cowardice or treachery or indecision, and is banished to the night-time world. In "Macbeth," the three witches season their pot with "wool of bat," and in "A Midsummer Night's Dream" bat wings are used to make elves' coats. "Witches' birds," bats were called in the Middle Ages. They were always associated with witches, devils, and other no-goods, and it was far from lucky to have them roosting in your house, whether they were birds or not. Some people knew all along that bats weren't really birds but, rather, some sort of mouselike mammal that could fly, even if, as John Swan noted in a rather prosaic poem in 1635, "this creature thus mungrell-like, cannot look very lovely." In the East, where bats tend to be large and prominent, instead of small and secretive, they figure as heroes in myths and legends. And in this country there's a Hopi story in which a bat created out of dust and spirit saves a maiden from being raped. . . .

This excerpt continues for several more pages and is only one of many research sections in Ackerman's 18,450-word article. She shares her "discovery" theme with readers, as if arriving at their doorsteps with snapshots of bats from her Texas trip, along with bat-house brochures and photocopies of citations. That's personal. That's creative. That's what Ackerman, researcher extraordinaire, does better than almost anyone else writing today.

Chances are, you won't be writing an article as long as Ackerman's or one requiring as much research. (*General rule:* The simpler the topic [e.g., bats, sugar], the more extensive the research.) In any case, topic is only one aspect of magazine research. You have to investigate theme as well, often in conjunction with topic.

In precomputer days, magazine research was grueling. You yanked out small wooden boxes in libraries and looked up topics and themes on poorly typed 3" × 5" cards. Then you went to places the cards said the research was. Sometimes you'd find it. Sometimes you'd find it missing. Now libraries are on line. Even small-town ones are linked by computer network. Research is a cinch. You can find in a minute what would have taken days—even weeks—the old-fashioned way.

Time is money to a writer. That's why they buy computers with modems. They no longer have to work at the library to do library work, accessing a network from their home computers and downloading and printing information. They save travel time, car expense, and photocopy costs. Still, most writers love the serene atmosphere of working in a personal nook surrounded by walls of books and racks of magazines. If you can't afford a computer, you usually can use one in the local library, especially to do research.

Computers, though, are a necessary tool for every writer. To understand why, you need to ponder the information explosion that began in the 1980s and will continue for the rest of your life. Set some research priorities. Books are important, of course, and you should consult them to gain insight or depth when content pertains to your topic or theme. But books, even this one, usually have a lifespan—one of the reasons why only basic information about the Internet and library networks are going to be covered momentarily in this chapter. Otherwise, a new edition of this chapter will have to be produced every six months or so. A webzine (on-line magazine) research book should be published on, well, the *web*.

Technology is moving as fast as a comet. Philosopher and writer John Marks Templeton, quoting researchers in his 1995 book *The Humble Approach* (Continuum), notes that the amount of information in the world doubles every 30 months. "At such rate the quantity may be 1000 times as great in only 25 years," Templeton reports.

That should humble you somewhat. But the practical matter is time. A book may be wise philosophically, but usually it is the most outdated repository of information—especially with regard to scientific or technological subjects. A conference paper is more up to date. So is a recently published magazine or journal article. But electronic information—a library network or web site—is the most current in our Information Age world.

Most writers prefer library networks to web sites on the Internet, again because of cost and time. Certainly, the web contains a wealth of information, but it is also a home-page vanity press. Along with gems, you can find misleading, inaccurate, unedited, otherwise unpublishable text. Worse, you usually have to pay per hour to get on line with the rest of America. The *web* is aptly named, too. It can entangle you as easily as a spider can a fly, surfing from home page to home page, downloading pictures and real audio, clicking all over the world, site to site—and forgetting, exactly, what it was three hours ago you meant to research. The web is useful, too, especially when you need addresses or phone numbers of agencies or the latest news reports about specific topics. You can find that kind of data by keyword or concept via one of several search engines such as Yahoo (whose menus will help guide you through the researching process). The web is a quick and efficient tool if the user is disciplined.

A library network is also fast and efficient. To show that, let's return to the divorce story for *New Woman.* The theme was renewal. If you did a keyword search using a network database called Periodical Abstracts—summaries of magazine articles—you would come up with half a dozen documents that included the words *divorce* and *renewal,* including this one:

AUTHOR: Ehrler, June A.
TITLE: "Rediscovery after divorce."
APPEARS IN: *Single Parent* 1994, v37n2, Summer p. 14-15.
ABSTRACT: Divorce will seem less distressing if one knows what emotional changes are customary. Most people experience four stages of loss: shock and numbness, denial, acceptance and renewal.
SUBJECT: Divorce.
            Personal development.
            Emotions.

This is an important abstract, verifying that renewal has take-away value. But the most important piece of information is in the subject category: personal development. That means when librarians see words such as *renewal,* they catalogue it under *personal development.* Therefore, a new keyword search using that term with *divorce* should yield more results—in this case, 60 of them—including these 5 documents:

1. **AUTHOR:**   Shapiro, Dani.
   TITLE: "Second marriage."
   APPEARS IN: *Glamour* 1995, v93n11, Nov p. 238.
   ABSTRACT: Shapiro offers her reflections on her divorce as she plans her second marriage. Her divorce taught her that she was capable of ignoring her best instincts, but it also taught her to trust herself.

2. **AUTHOR:**   Nathanson, Irene G.
   TITLE: "Divorce and women's spirituality."
   APPEARS IN: *Journal of Divorce & Remarriage* 1995, v22n3-4, p. 179-188.
   ABSTRACT: A study found that for all subjects, the divorce experience affected spirituality. For the majority, spirituality facilitated healing, a finding with profound implications for social work intervention.

3. **AUTHOR:**   Hayes, Christopher L.
   TITLE: "Happily divorced."
   APPEARS IN: *New Woman* 1993, v23n7, Jul p. 130-135 (4 pages)
   ABSTRACT: An excerpt from the book "Our Turn" is presented. A discussion of the reasons why some women seem to be so vibrant, confident and exciting following a divorce is offered.

4. **AUTHOR:**   Davidson, Joy.
   TITLE: "After the split."
   APPEARS IN: *Muscle & Fitness* 1992, v53n9, Sep p. 38.
   ABSTRACT: Breaking up with a spouse doesn't mean one can't enjoy and fill the time void by going out with friends and those one used to see with an ex. Ways to renew life after a relationship fails are offered.

5. **AUTHOR:**   Safran, Claire.
   TITLE: "The winners : Women who beat the odds."
   APPEARS IN: *Ladies' Home Journal* 1994, vIIIn5, May p. 164-165+
   ABSTRACT: Resilient adults—people who are able to bounce back from such traumas as abuse, divorce or job loss—are discussed. Hope, a person who offers unconditional love and acceptance and a sense of faith in oneself are essential ingredients for success despite one's setbacks.

Bingo. *New Woman* is even mentioned as a market for divorce and re-newal. Research shows that the magazine has not covered the topic and theme in several years, and when it did, editors reprinted a book excerpt. An article on the topic is due. More importantly, this document list provides names of national-caliber researchers discussing rediscovery, trust, spiritual-ity, confidence, friendship, and hope. Some will be associated with universi-ties, some with businesses, some with publishers. Each magazine may pro-vide more data about authors in contributors' notes: residence, job title, place of employment. That means that sources should be easy to contact by dialing telephone directory information or by matching names and/or busi-nesses with phone numbers via a library network database such as First Search (also available on the web). You also can use network databases or the Internet to access "white pages," locating your source's electronic mail address. A *white page directory,* simply, is a list of e-mail addresses classified by university, institution, country, or some other classification. Services such as CompuServe or America Online have *proprietary white pages,* only al-lowing customers to identify e-mail addresses of people who subscribe to the same service.

When you are researching topics, pay special attention to sidebars in magazines and hot links in webzines. Typically, a sidebar is a filler- or col-umn-length research piece that accompanies a feature or article in a maga-zine, often providing research summaries, addresses of associations, and even warnings, as does the following sidebar to Karin Horgan Sullivan's arti-cle "Do You Really Want to Eat This?" in *Vegetarian Times:*

When Sugar Is a Problem

When consumed in moderation, sugar doesn't appear to be a problem for someone in good health. However, there *are* medical conditions in which sugar should be strictly limited, including diabetes, candida overgrowth and heart disease. And though studies indicate that sugar doesn't cause hyperactivity, hy-poglycemia, headaches or myriad other problems popularly attributed to sweeteners, science doesn't always account for individual variation. You may very well notice a sugar sensitivity in yourself or other family members, in which case you'd be wise to cut back or eliminate sugar altogether.

Finally, another reason to consider whether white sugar belongs in your diet: The end of the refining process often involves filtering crystallized sugar through charred animal bones to remove remaining impurities from the prod-uct.—*K.H.S.*

In a very general sense, a sidebar is to a magazine as a hot link is to a webzine. There are important similarities and a few key differences. The term *hot link* is defined as a word, phrase, or reference highlighted in an-other color (usually blue) from the basic text color (usually black). It is an accompaniment to the feature or article in a webzine. A hot link takes a pre-Internet data-accessing idea called *hypertext*—again, a different-colored word, phrase, or reference—and enhances the idea on the web: *hypertext transfer protocol*. (That's the *http* abbreviation on web-site addresses.) Tom Hodges, computer specialist and educator, says,

> Hypertext transfer protocol [or hot links to other web sites] not only lets you access information on a disk or a network. You can get information, videos, pictures, and audio anywhere in the world where your hot-link data exist.
>
> Essentially, the sidebar in a magazine stops where the writer stopped thinking. Hypertext transfer protocol goes to where one writer stopped thinking to a site where another writer stopped thinking to a site where another writer stopped thinking and so on. Each time you click to a new web page you encounter more hot links. So you can continue site to site as long as you want, all over the world.

To prepare yourself for research, read interviews in The Craft Shop. To get you going—to the library, to the photocopier, into cyberspace—turn to The Newsstand. To enhance your story ideas with research, click to The Keyboard.

THE   CRAFT   SHOP

Information Gathering

Eddith Dashiell, Journalism Educator

In a democracy, information is power. A trite, overused expression, but a cliché that holds quite a bit of truth. Historically in the United States, a faction or party can stay in power by being militarily or financially stronger than the opposing side. That faction or party, however, stays in power by keeping control over the information.

My favorite example is the institution of slavery in the United States. When slavery was legal in the U.S., it was illegal to teach slaves how to read or write. Why? Because enslaved but educated African-Americans were a threat to preserving the institution of slavery in the United States. If the power structure was to remain white and the slave culture was to remain black, the slaves had to be remain ignorant. They had to be denied access to information. To keep slaves from accessing the information necessary to secure their freedom, they had to remain uneducated. Hence, giving slaves the tools to access information via education was against the law. Slavery has been abolished in the United States, but the strategy of maintaining control by controlling the information is still very much a part of American society.

Today, Americans are not separated by chains and laws barring an education, but the new advances in accessing information via computers has created a gulf between the "information haves" and the "information have nots." Journalists can help bridge that gap by developing their computer skills to access information stored electronically and disseminating that information to their reading or viewing audiences. Many older journalists, however, tend to view electronically stored information with distrust and fear.

Journalists should not fear computers. By becoming familiar with electronic databases, journalists are able to access a variety of different information sources in a fraction of the time. Writers, using computers, can access dozens of databases around the world to get the necessary sources to write a thorough, accurate news report without having to leave the office. A journalist could gather in days—or even hours—information that would have taken weeks or months to gather if that person had to physically travel to each distant location to collect the data.

Database-analysis and computerized reporting are becoming a valuable commodity to the news gathering operations in print, broadcast and cable. The journalist who can master the skills to access these variety of electronic databases will have an advantage in the job market over the computer-shy applicant.

Research & Commitment

Ursula Obst, Freelance Writer

EDITOR'S NOTE: Ursula Obst, freelance writer and book editor, published an article titled "Anna's Tangled Destiny" about a Polish-born New York City bag lady named Anna Podobna. The profile is a meticulously researched touchstone of magazine journalism. I had read the original piece in the now-defunct *New York Woman,* a women's general-interest magazine, and used it for five years in my magazine writing workshop to illustrate the freelancer's commitment to a story. I did some meticulous research trying to track down Obst. Editors at several magazines in New York City did not know her. (Ironically, I did *not* check with my own publishers for whom Obst has worked as an outside book editor.) Nonetheless, her name was not listed in New York City-area phone directories. Using several databases, I compiled a list of some two dozen people named Ursula Obst who had listed telephone numbers.

Each night I called six of them and asked the person who answered if she was the writer who had composed "Anna's Tangled Destiny." No luck. I worked from the East to West Coast and on the last night of calling left a message on the next-to-last person's answering machine, heartened by the fact that the recorded announcement mentioned a fax number, indicating the person might be a freelance writer. Later that evening, Ursula Obst telephoned me and agreed to discuss research and commitment.

In doing so, Obst describes the plight of Anna Podobna, who was jailed by Nazis in her occupied Poland because of an act of kindness—Obst's original title was "Acts of Kindness," changed by editors to "Anna's Tangled Destiny"—and who later became a human host for lice in an inhumane Nazi laboratory producing a typhus vaccine. Here, she describes the patience and persistence of a writer—"The piece took two years to research and another four to get into print," she says—and also explains her personal connection to Anna's story.

First: It was an obsession. I think every memorable story must be one. It is the extra effort that in the end shows through. I knew for a long time that there was a great story in Anna's life. I had heard about her from people who had tried to help her, and in turn had tried to interest reporter friends of mine, who, unlike me, were really great writers and investigators and who could put a magazine story together in a way I could not. But after some successes in newspaper journalism, I decided I'd do it. Perhaps it was my successes (I had been nominated for a Pulitzer by then and had my own column with the *Philadelphia Daily News)* that made me think that there, for the grace of God, go I. In the newspaper business, you are only as good as your last story if you fail to deliver once too often, and if you lose your job to someone younger and tougher—well, it could be you on the street pushing a cart. Some time after I embarked on the Anna story, I read a HERS column in the *New York Times* by a young woman lawyer that said exactly that—single women all have a deep-seated fear inside of them; they feel that what separates them from the bag ladies on the street is just a bit a luck and a couple of paychecks. But I digress—

Second: I had wonderful mentors. If you want to do something well, you can't do it on your own. You have to have mentors, and I have to tell you about one of mine. He was Bill Marimow, the two-time Pulitzer-prize winner (formerly of the *Philadelphia Inquirer* and now the managing editor of the *Baltimore Sun).* Bill taught me that "God is in the details." If you do your research right (by which he meant if you accumulate about ten times the amount of information you can use in the story), you will pick up little rich bits and pieces that you will inadvertently weave in here and there. They will seem innocuous but they will make the reader trust you—to recognize that you have the real goods, that you know what you are talking about. Translated another way: The writer talks to the reader between the lines as well as with the words and the reader trusts the writer based on what is communicated soul to soul. Which also means—you can't bullshit, they'll know it.

Following Bill's advice, I did all the research. Anna was in one of her phases when she wouldn't talk to people, but that did not stop me. I interviewed everyone I could track down that had had contact with her over the course of her entire life. One person led me to another. I called her sister in Poland. I wrote letters. I was inexhaustible. But I could not get a handle on the most fascinating thing about her, this time in her life when she was a victim of some sort of Nazi experiment, which, I believed, eventually drove her to distrust people, to paranoia, and finally to her particular brand of madness. How did she get those scars from the lice? What sick Nazi thing was this? I could not find out.

Third: I had lots of luck. On that subject, I came across this great quote in a book by Harold T. P. Hayes. (He was the editor of *Esquire* in the 1960s and is credited by many as being the inventor or instigator of New Journalism.) He says luck comes to those who are committed (in my case, *obsessed*):

> Until one is committed there is always hesitancy, the chance to draw back; always ineffectiveness. Concerning all acts of initiative (and creation) there is one elementary truth—the ignorance of which kills countless ideas and splendid plans—that the moment one definitely commits oneself, then Providence moves, too. All sorts of things occur to help one that would never have occurred. A whole stream of events issue from the decision, raising in one's favor all manner of unforeseen incidents and meetings and material assistance, which no man could have dreamt would have come his way.

So I got this Providential assistance. And this is just such a great bit that I had to tell you about it. I had spent days in the Blaustein Library in New York, which is the best place I have found for Holocaust research. I had to go to the bathroom with dry heaves once, but I found nothing to help me. I started reading the transcripts of the Nuremberg Trials—the case against the doctors. Nothing. But maybe one little thing. The evidence transcripts included the diary of one of the mad doctors and there was one entry that caught my eye: "Received today a package of lice from Dr. Weil in Krakow." That's all—"lice" and "Krakow" were the only things that matched up to Anna's story. In the end, a year later, when I still didn't know anything more about the lice thing and had exhausted all leads, I remembered that Melania Kulik (one of my sources) told me that she had taken Anna to some sort of exhibit of accomplished Poles, and that Anna had pointed to one portrait and said, "He is the doctor I worked for in Krakow."

(Of course, Melania had told me that story as an illustration of Anna's delusions.) I tracked down the exhibit to a Polish heritage society in Miami. Yes, there was a section that featured accomplished Polish scientists. Who? I was given a list of names, and the third one was Dr. Weil, the inventor of the typhus vaccine. A connection at last! Then, I went to a medical library and found old articles by Dr. Weil describing his invention and how the vaccine was made—all in French. But from then on, it was easy; that is, I knew now specifically what I was after. I contacted typhus experts—in the U.S. Army—and learned that one of the great secrets we kept in World War II was that you could make the vaccine in egg embryos; you didn't need to feed the lice on human beings. But we didn't want the Nazis to know that. We wanted them to make it in this excruciating process, so that more of them would die of the disease on the Russian front. If they knew what we knew, perhaps Anna would not have suffered. But then maybe, not having a job as a lice feeder, she might not have survived. And maybe the Nazis would have taken Moscow after all. All this is a tiny footnote to history.

Fourth, and I'll take credit here: I had patience. Once I wrote the story, I could not sell it. I was told it was too long, it was too sad, successful women didn't want to read this sort of stuff. The editors were wrong, of course, and I knew it; the HERS column validated what I knew. But everyone who read the story somehow became a friend of it; I got other assignments as a result. I was by then working at *Esquire.* Three years to the day that I showed the story to the then-owner of *Esquire,* Phillip Moffitt, he called me in and asked to see it again. He was putting out a new magazine, *New York Woman,* and was unhappy that there was no hard journalism for the premiere issue. He still remembered that story.

All that was a long time ago. I went on to edit books (which is what I still do) for Simon & Schuster (primarily) and others. Oddly enough, in 1989, I was asked to finish a book because the author had died. He was Harold T. P. Hayes and the book was *The Dark Romance of Dian Fossey,* which was made into a movie, *Gorillas in the Mist.*

T H E   N E W S S T A N D

Researching Topics and Themes

1. Take your Story Idea file to the library and, according to methods explained in this chapter, do a network search of periodical abstracts—for each story idea—using keywords for topic and theme. (If you have

access to a library network via home computer, do the topic-theme search by modem.)

2. By now, some ideas in your Story Idea file should seem incomplete or otherwise problematic. That's normal. Some ideas just don't pan out. Feel free to eliminate ideas, but do keep developing at least six. For each one, locate material generated by your network search, photocopy those works, and put them in your Story Samples file.

3. Analyze the photocopies in your Story Samples file and note:

   ■ Evidence of field research and sensory data

   ■ Evidence of library research and citations from books, reports, brochures, newsletters, and so on

   ■ Quotations from sources that support the theme of a work

4. Determine which of your developing story ideas will require interviews. Scan your research material for names of possible sources. Note titles, employers, and hometowns, and check contributors' notes for more identifying information. According to the methods explained earlier in this chapter, use a library network database to match names with telephone numbers, or e-mail addresses of people you might like to interview, or call directory assistance for phone numbers. (If you have access to the Internet, log on to the appropriate search engine, scanning appropriate sites or home pages for phone numbers and addresses.)

T H E   K E Y B O A R D

The Source Box

1. Your Story Idea file must be getting bulky by now. Make a separate file for each developing story idea. (Keep incomplete or problematic ideas in your Story Idea file in case you want to develop them in the future.) Label your new folders Project #1, Project #2, Project #3, and so on. Feel free to add a working title, of course, so that you can easily identify specific story folders, such as Project #1: Divorce and Renewal.

2. According to the methods explained earlier in the chapter, do a source box for each idea in your project folders.

3. List the names, addresses, and phone numbers of potential sources that you identified for each story idea in item 4 of The Newsstand assignment. List other potential sources for each idea from the source box exercises. (Identify them later via library network or Internet access.) According to the methods explained earlier in the chapter, draft at least three thematic questions for each source in each project folder.

Titles

Titles and Subtitles

Some beginning writers compose the title first because, they posit, a title is the first thing that a reader sees on a page. That's faulty logic. Assembling a manuscript is a lot like assembling a house, only the blueprint is in the writer's mind rather than in the builder's pocket. The writer starts with a little excavation (highs, lows, turning points), adds a solid foundation (topic), nails down floors (grounding), erects rooms (thematic statements), and then wires it (research). Only then does a contractor begin thinking about the front door, although that's the first thing that a visitor sees when strolling up the promenade to the split level. In sum, a builder cannot begin with a door because there is nothing to attach it to; the same goes for the title.

Other beginning writers see no need to write a title because, they reason, editors change them anyway. That's faulty logic, too. Imagine if a builder felt that way about the house, finishing the project down to the woodwork, trim, and carpeting but forgetting about the door. "Homeowners end up changing them anyway," the builder might complain, wondering why nobody is making any offers. Editors might not bid on your manuscript, either, if it lacks a title. Editors don't think this when they stuff your work in the SASE, of course; and yes, in nearly every case, they are going to change your title anyway—for a number of newsroom reasons, almost all related to design. Nonetheless, an editor is apt to reject a manuscript when it lacks a title because the writer has missed the chance to open doors in the editor's head.

Do you know how much junk an editor sees "over the transom" (magazine talk for unsolicited submissions)? At some mass magazines, such as *Cosmopolitan*, thousands of pieces each month. And, of course, much of it is inappropriate: articles on onionskin, crumpling like gift wrapping out of the envelope; tomes about the Spanish American War sent to a women's magazine whose readers are concerned about beauty, health, fashion, travel, careers, horoscopes, and romance; psycho-fiction (or worse, nonfiction) describing in detail what the sicko is going to do to the editor if she rejects him *one more time;* essays from prisoners claiming "I didn't do it" and seeking—what else?—pen pals; postcards from good Christian God-fearing Daughters of the American Revolution obsessing over the whereabouts of grandmother's memoir, sent to the editor without a SASE or an explanation; and more, much more. After dealing with unsolicited mail by writer wannabes for a few hours, any editor starts going brain dead. She's going to reject you at the slightest infraction. And she's not interested in reading a wordy cover letter that explains what your manuscript is about. Or, if she *does* read your cover letter, she's looking for you to botch up early—maybe misspell a word or brag about what you can do for her. She has a saying—the editor's mantra—"You don't have to eat the whole apple to know it's rotten." Don't mess with this woman. It's Thursday night, her supervisor has bought her a pizza, and she's catching up on the mail. You have about 30 seconds to catch her interest.

Now imagine her taking your envelope from one of three stacks on her desk. She pulls out a manuscript on crisp bond paper and reads a title and subtitle in her magazine's style and voice. That communicates something. She's dealing with a writer who actually *reads* her publication—who maybe even mimics how she writes titles when she's not eating pizza and rejecting the wanna-bes. Better still, your title introduces the topic. Your subtitle heralds the theme and sends the editor to magazine heaven. She remembers why she used to look forward to opening mail and discovering writers like you.

Titles are that important. In most pieces, title and subtitle work in tandem to set up an epiphany or peak experience. So, you should think about a title only after identifying and researching your topic, theme, and truth. A title and subtitle foreshadow those key components of a manuscript, promising the editor that you will deliver information, service, inspiration, entertainment—you name it. And you name it in three basic ways:

1. A *descriptive title* is a phrase, statement, or question that identifies the topic for the reader, as in "Covering the Rape of a Child," or "Start Getting Better Treatment from Your OB-GYN," or "What Is Your Heirloom Worth?"

2. A *suspense title* is a phrase, statement, or question that appeals to the reader's curiosity without identifying the topic, as in "Talking to the River," or "And Then I Met Matthew," or "And Justice for All?"

3. A *label title* is a word or brief phrase, descriptive or suspenseful, as in "Crop Circles" or "Circles," and which also may be cast as a statement or question, as in "Serve!" or "Tennis, Anyone?"

A descriptive title is used to *ground* the topic, making sure the audience knows your focus. That gives you some freedom. You can digress a while and tell an anecdote or address theme or emphasize voice, baiting readers with a provocative introduction. Andrea Tortora, now a reporter for the *Cincinnati Enquirer,* wrote this introduction for an essay in *Editor & Publisher,* a trade magazine for the newspaper business:

> For the past 10 months, I've been racist, homophobic, sexist, biased and stupid. I've been exploitative and insensitive.
>
> I've been a college newspaper editor.
>
> At 22, I'm burned out, hardened and exasperated. As the editor of the *Post,* the independent daily student newspaper at Ohio University, I've defended my writers, my editors, and my newspaper to its patrons, many who do not understand journalism and its principles.
>
> Often I'm at a loss about how to explain the tenets under which we operate. The E. W. Scripps School of Journalism doesn't offer a class in "Damage Control: How to Explain Journalism to Readers Without Losing Your Temper and Their Advertising."

Tortora's piece is not about explaining editorial decisions. As her title asserts, it is about "What J-Profs Should Be Teaching You." That description grounds the topic of her piece, allowing her to focus on voice and to sound off in the opening paragraphs. After sharing anecdotes depicting the frustration of student editors in professional settings, Tortora recommends changes in specific courses:

- Journalism classes can't cover everything students need to know to be good editors—the experience itself provides the bulk of the education—but professors can prepare students for what's coming.
- Newswriting classes should teach future editors that mistakes happen and can and should be corrected. Professors need to have a deft teaching hand, being sure not to instill shame, especially when grilling student reporters about their mistakes in the newspaper.
- Editing class must prepare editors for the public response to stories and how to handle it. Role-playing, rather than journalism theory, may help editors deal with angry readers. Editing other students' copy and explaining the changes in

class will give editors the personnel skills they need to command respect and articulate their views. . . .

Tortora continues in this manner, making recommendations for Public Affairs Reporting, Media Law, Ethics, and other journalism courses. Make no mistake. Her bold, descriptive title is meant to provoke educators and professionals who read *Editor & Publisher*. As they scan her introduction, she baits them with a frank, explosive tone of voice. They read on. Yet the topic, grounded by her title, is always in the readers' minds. As she shares anecdotes about shortcomings of current journalism courses, they think, "All right, smarty pants, what *should* j-profs be teaching?" Tortora, of course, is ready for that question with an entire curriculum, fulfilling the contract promised in her title.

As Tortora's title indicates, descriptive titles don't have to be boring— in fact, the wittier, the better. Few writers possess George Plimpton's wit. A title in his *Esquire* column, "Bonding with the Grateful Dead," describes what occurred between him and his son at a concert featuring the classic rock band. But it relates to Plimpton, too—who tried to join the band as a tambourine player, years earlier—light-heartedly coming to terms with his past. In another *Esquire* piece, featuring one of his famous interviews, Plimpton invited artist Larry Rivers—nearly shot during civil unrest in Nigeria— out to lunch. That occasion seemed odd to Plimpton, who wondered, "How often does one have lunch with a man who has survived the firing squad?" Plimpton used that phrase to generate this witty descriptive title with a "service journalism" ring:

How to Face a Firing Squad

A suspense title has only one goal: to intrigue. When such titles are used without subtitles, they usually are tied to themes, as in Lady Borton's "A Forgiving Land," mentioned in Chapter 3. Her title, in fact, is the first thematic statement in her column for the *New York Times Magazine*. But most suspense titles—no matter how interesting or innovative—take a subtitle: a descriptive word, phrase, sentence, or even paragraph to clarify the content of a work.

The title and subtitle operate in tandem to distinguish topic from theme. This is especially vital when a suspense title cannot stand alone. In such a case, a descriptive subtitle not only explains content but also suggests or states the theme. Here are examples from Ursula Obst's profile of Anna Podobna with a theme of uncompromising pride in *New York Woman;* Catherine Johnson's article about autism with a theme of mother-love in

New Woman; and Amy Hudson's article about anorexia nervosa with a theme of control in *Writer's Digest:*

Anna's Tangled Destiny

A Woman's Uncompromising Pride Defines Her Own Harsh Existence

The Broken Child

A True Story about Loving and Living with an Autistic Son

Invictus under Glass

A Writer Discovers Her Own Balance of Life and Art
through Her Battle with a Modern-Day Disorder of Control

If you eliminated subtitles from these examples, you would have to read for several paragraphs beyond the introduction to know, precisely, what each manuscript is about and *really* about. Watch what happens when Heather Paige Preston, former student writer, violates this basic rule. You remember her meditation on the Beatles and her marriage, described in Chapter 3. In her first draft, Preston missed opportunities to ground her work so that readers could distinguish topic from theme. Titles and subtitles can accomplish that goal, too. But in her second draft, Preston missed another chance to ground her work, using a suspense title *and* a suspense epigraph (a type of subtitle, in this case, based on song lyrics):

A Magical Mystery Tour

It's an invitation to make a reservation.
We've got everything you need, satisfaction guaranteed.
The Magical Mystery Tour is waiting to take you away.

The suspense title—"A Magical Mystery Tour"—is fine, suggesting the occasion of Preston's piece, a Beatles concert, and alluding to her topic, marriage. But note how a descriptive subtitle would have grounded the work while introducing her theme of passion:

A Magical Mystery Tour

A Woman's Love for the Beatles Finally Reignites Her Marriage

Descriptive subtitles come in handy when you juggle three levels of meaning in a manuscript: occasion, topic, and theme. This was the case with Patricia Raybon's column in *USA Weekend.* She needed a suspense title to suggest a confrontation—the occasion of her piece—and then a descriptive subtitle to distinguish the topic of stereotypes from the theme of pride:

Too Close for Comfort

A racial stereotype ruined their first meeting.
Now stubborn pride keeps neighbors apart.

The ideal suspense title intrigues as it introduces a theme—especially important in a profile—because the topic is also the source. Lisa Frydman, writing for *Vogue*, profiled Leah Rabin, the spouse of assassinated Israeli prime minister Yitzhak Rabin. The theme is strength of character, elicited in quotations throughout Frydman's piece. Her profile uses a suspense title to suggest the theme and a descriptive subtitle to ground the topic:

His Legacy, Her Way

Leah Rabin was never the typical political wife. Now that her husband
of 47 years, Israeli prime minister Yitzhak Rabin, has been assassinated,
she refuses to be the typical political widow.

Subtitles do not have to come below titles. You can begin with the subtitle, called a *bleed-in*, as in this descriptive one leading into a suspense title to introduce Audrey Chapman's exposé in *Cleveland Magazine*:

As we approach the five-year anniversary of Iraq's invasion of Kuwait,
local Gulf War veterans are fighting their toughest battle yet.
Here, they talk about chemical warfare, their debilitating illnesses
and how their own government is failing to help.
For these men and women, is the war really over?
Or has it just begun?

And Justice for All?

Label titles can be suspenseful *or* descriptive and often take subtitles or epigraphs. A good label and subtitle/epigraph combination should intrigue and suggest or state the theme, as seen in the following suspense label and descriptive subtitle from Christina Hoff Sommers's exposé in *The New Republic* and in the descriptive label and thematic epigraph from Bruce Woods's opinion piece in *BackHome:*

Sister Soldiers

Life from a Women's Studies Conference

The Hunting Problem

"The beauty of hunting lies in the fact that it is always problematic."
—*Jose Ortega y Gasset*

A label title is short—only one or two words—but it also must be memorable. As noted earlier, George Plimpton is a master at writing titles, able to make descriptive titles sound positively suspenseful, as in "Bonding with the Grateful Dead" or "How to Face a Firing Squad." But his best-known title is a descriptive label that graces his sportswriting classic, *Paper Lion.*

Paper Lion? Descriptive? You bet your Detroit Lion football jersey it is. But the label may need a little explaining after so many years. Plimpton popularized "participatory journalism," trying to play tambourine for the Grateful Dead so he can describe what it feels to be a rock star, for instance. In the 1960s, Plimpton was trying to share how it feels to be a quarterback in the National Football League. As his title indicates, he was a *Lion* on *paper,* not part of the team (although the coach allowed Plimpton to play during spring training).

In *Paper Lion,* Plimpton tells an anecdote about the importance of titles. This awful one is what his publisher preferred: *Where Are You, Dink Stover?* Right. Plimpton wasn't impressed, either. As he explains in the preface of his book, "I knew who Dink Stover was—the all-around hero of Owen Johnson's boys' books, Stover at Lawrenceville, Stover at Yale, and so forth, very popular in my father's day—but it didn't seem to me . . . to be what is referred to as a 'selling title.'" So Plimpton, in desperation, tried to come up with a catchy title to replace the Dinky one. "I was staring at a pad in a telephone booth in a midtown athletic club, fussing with a slew of words in my mind while waiting for a call, when almost as if by divine guidance I saw my pencil form the words *Paper Lion* on the paper. Catchy, simple, with all the proper allusions—'paper tiger' and so forth—it seemed absolutely on the button." Excited, Plimpton put in a call to his publisher:

"Buz, I've got it!" and I told him.

After quite a pause he said, "You mean you don't like *Dink Stover, Where Are You?*"

Plimpton's book, still in print, would probably not be with the Dinky title. *Paper Lion* illustrates the essence of a stand-alone label title. If you use one, your work has to be so meaningful or complete that readers will never again view your label in quite the same way. You may use the word *bats* to describe your mental state or the pipistrelle in the belfry, for example, but if you read Diane Ackerman's masterwork by that title in *New Yorker,* you will never again see bats in the same light (or lack thereof).

Now that you know the various types of magazine titles and how to use them, you should learn how to write them.

Composing Titles and Subtitles

The most common type of title in consumer and trade magazines is the *how to*. Magazine editors give readers what they want, so readers trust them to give good advice in service and information pieces, which nearly every publication carries. So you see a lot of how-tos, from "How to Boost Your Sexual Confidence" in *Cosmopolitan* to "How to Boost Your Sales" in *Business Week*.

How-to titles are easy to write. Just jot down what your story is about and add *your* to personalize it. Editors love *your*. It connects with readers, as in "*Your* How-To Title." Now think of a snappy verb in the infinitive case, as in *to hone*—editors adore snappy verbs in the infinitive—and put *how* in front of it, as in "How to Hone." Snap the two halves together:

How to Hone Your How-To Title

The big problem with how-to titles is that editors see (and use) too many of them. They are the chocolate cake of title making in the typical magazine newsroom. So editors often hone how-to titles by changing the verb infinitive to the gerund form and cutting the fat from the how to, as in:

Honing Your How-To Title

Sometimes editors hone the gerund case a wee more by changing the verb to the command form and adding an exclamation:

Hone Your How-To Title!

And when editors are really pressed for space, or feeling stingy as a production deadline nears, they come full circle and drop the verb entirely:

Your How-To Title!

Now you know the basic elements of descriptive, suspense, and label titles. You also can mix and match them, as in this combination of a suspense label with a descriptive title and subtitle:

Head Trip

How to Hone Your How-To Title

Editors cut them like calories. Here are 3 "low-fat" variations on the chocolate cake of titles.

Editors appreciate good titles. Apart from design, title writing is about as creative as some editorial jobs get. Think about it. Editors give readers what they want month after month—same topic, same concept. But they have to present it as if the information was as new as a top quark. To do so, they use "generating devices" to refresh themselves and their readers. Here are 21 common ones, along with methods to compose similar titles:

1. *Alliterative*

Definition: Using words that begin with the same letter, as in this descriptive title with descriptive subtitle from *Sassy:*

Going from Gawky to Gorgeous

How Growing Up Feels

Method: Use words that begin with the same letter and that also depict your topic. Then read the title out loud. You may have created a tongue twister. (If you can't say it, you can't use it.)

2. *Allusion-Based*

Definition: Revising a phrase from a famous book, song, or film title; a quote or slogan; a play; a poem—even a TV show—as in this suspense title introducing content of a family newsletter, harkening the TV classic *All in the Family,* from *New Age Journal:*

All on the Family

Method: Think of a title or phrase from a well-known book, song, film, quote, slogan, play, poem, or TV show that relates to your topic, occasion, theme, or truth. Then revise it slightly so that it depicts your title while alluding to the original source.

3. *Alphabet-Based*

Definition: Mentioning *ABCs* or *A to Z,* as in this descriptive title from *New Woman:*

The ABCs of Great-Looking Skin

Method: Combine *ABCs* or *A to Z* with a phrase based on your topic. There's one catch here: Give your readers basic or comprehensive content. In other words, don't use *ABCs* if your content is complex or *A to Z* if it is incomplete.

4. *Homonym-Based*

Definition: Using a word that is spelled and pronounced the same way but has two or more meanings, as in *lie*—to recline or fib—suggesting both meanings, as does this title about bed buying and commitment, from a feature in *Cosmopolitan:*

Make Your Bed and Lie in It

Method: Determine whether your topic, theme, or occasion uses any homonyms. If it does, determine the different meanings and whether you can combine them in a phrase to suggest both, creating an optical illusion, as does the preceding title. In general, *homophones*—words that sound alike but that have different spellings, as in *banned* and *band*—are less effective and more confusing than homonyms. (But they *can* make excellent word plays or puns, described later.) Avoid *heteronyms*—words with the same spelling but different pronunciations and meanings, as in *minute* (60 seconds) and *minute* (tiny). Readers generally find them confusing. (If you have to say "Get it?" you can forget it.)

5. *Long Title*

Definition: Stringing out a phrase or sentence so that the title contains more than a dozen words in a humorous or cunning tone of voice, as in this descriptive title from *Cosmopolitan:*

What Men (Still) Don't Know about Sex Because No Woman Ever Told Them

Method: Determine your topic and lengthen it by using a humorous or cunning tone, as if you had to convey everything your story contains in one breath. If your voice or content isn't humorous or cunning, don't use this title, because it can offend, given sensitive subject matter (such as rape or suicide).

6. *Name-Based*

Definition: Using a source's name as part of the title, as in this suspense title with descriptive subtitle introducing a photospread of TV star Teri Hatcher, from *TV Guide:*

The Elemental Teri

The Lois & Clark *Star conquers earth, air, fire, and water*

Method: This type of title is used in profiles or photospreads. The source's name must mean or suggest a key or thematic word. For example, "Teri" suggests "terra," meaning "earth" and implying "earthy"—perfect for a photospread of Teri Hatcher in nature. But don't force a name to conform to your subject or theme, as in *"Teri-ible Times for Lois & Clark"* or use a name inappropriately, as in "Hatcher Job."

7. *Number-Based*

Definition: Using numbers to depict components of a story, as in this descriptive title from *McCall's:*

Three Mistakes Even Good Doctors Make

Method: Determine if your topic, occasion, theme, or truth has steps or specific pieces of advice which, taken together, complete a picture or investigation. If so, count them. Then combine that number with key words that depict your topic, occasion, theme, or truth.

8. *Onomatopoetic*

Definition: A real or invented word that sounds like some aspect of your topic, as in this suspense label with descriptive subtitle from *People:*

Rat-a-Tat Tap

*Dance phenom Savion Glover's furious feet
raise an exhilarating racket on Broadway*

Method: Determine whether your story idea will employ sensory data related to sound and whether these data are a key component. If so, use or invent a suspenseful sound-effect label title (but be sure to add a descriptive subtitle to explain the content).

9. *Paradox-Based*

Definition: Combining variations of the same word in an ironic way, as in this descriptive label with descriptive title from *Time:*

Tolerating Intolerance

*A silly G.O.P. debate masks the real
problem with the party's pro-life plank*

Method: This type of title relates more to theme than topic. Analyze your theme word or concept and determine whether the root word (in all its noun, adjectival, adverbial, and verb forms) can be altered to make a paradox, as in *obedience* and *disobedience* and the paradox, "Obeying the Laws of Civil Disobedience."

10. *Parallel-Based*

Definition: Resembling the paradox-based title but using two phrases with different meanings in the same grammatical structure, as in this descriptive title from *Cosmopolitan:*

Can't Live with Him, Can't Live without Him

Method: This type of title is good for stories that promise solutions to dilemmas or mysteries. Determine whether your story idea or truth has an element of irony or paradox that can be captured in two parallel phrases with a slight change in one or two words of that phrase, as in "More than a Mate, Less than a Lover."

11. *Pun-Based*

Definition: Changing the spelling of a word so that it is close in pronunciation but suggestive of another definition, or using a heteronym (see item 4 of this list) to allude to a common phrase while introducing humorous, witty, or wry content, as in this suspense title and descriptive subtitle from *Mirabella:*

Living in Blondage

Betsy Israel exposes the darker roots of the cult of blondness

Method: Determine whether your material lends itself to humorous, witty, or wry treatment and whether a common phrase or saying is associated with your topic, theme, occasion, or truth. If so, analyze the operative word in the phrase "down the *shore*" and pun it, say, for a travel magazine: "Romance Is a Shore Thing." When writing this type of title, always gauge the "groan" factor (the louder the groan, the lamer the pun).

12. *Question-Based*

Definition: Casting the topic, occasion, theme, or truth in question form, as in this descriptive title from *Time:*

Can Your Faith Make You Whole?

Method: This type of title is used in issue- or opinion-oriented stories. If you're writing one of these, simply cast your topic into a question.

13. *Quotation-Based*

Definition: Highlighting a quote from a source or yourself, as in this descriptive title from *YM:*

"My Mother Died"

Method: This type of title is often used in personal columns and in interview and profile pieces. The quote has to sum up the experience in a personal piece or depict the essence of the source in an interview or profile. Avoid sensationalism—using a quotation out of context or in a false light—just to create an attention-grabbing title.

14. *Resurrected Cliché*

Definition: Taking an overused phrase and making it new again, as in this suspense title with descriptive subtitle from *Ladies Home Journal:*

Up in Arms

Millions of women own guns—and millions of other women think that's wrong. Read this report, and decide for yourself.

Method: Think of a word that depicts your topic, occasion, theme, or truth and determine whether that word is a homonym, such as *title* (pertaining to headlines, documents, or peerage). Then think of a common phrase using a *different* meaning of your homonym, in this case *document: clear title,* as in the cliché, "You have clear title to this land." Finally, use the cliché to introduce your real topic, a how-to feature, say, about title writing for *Writer's Digest:* "Clear Title to Your First Sale." (See item 19 in this list if your cliché is colloquial.)

15. *Rhyme*

Definition: Using like-sounding words, as in this suspense title about prayer beads from *New Age Journal:*

Hope on a Rope

Method: Consult a rhyming dictionary. Locate the operative word in your topic, theme, occasion, or truth and rhyme it. (If you can't rhyme it, refine it with a *near*-sounding word or two, such as *rhyme it* and *refine it.*)

16. *Riddle-Based*

Definition: Using a suspense title as the riddle and a descriptive subtitle as the answer, as in these examples from *The Lutheran:*

Like Mushrooms After a Rain Storm

Young Slovak Christians breathe new life into a repressed church

Method: This type of title often foreshadows an epiphany or peak experience. Analyze yours. If you are not good at riddles, use a simile to make one. For instantce, revise the epiphany "Love may end but it also may renew itself" so that it reads "Love Like Tulips Long Dormant." That's the riddle. The answer is your theme: renewal. Write a descriptive subtitle using or suggesting that word: "How Romance Blossoms After Divorce."

17. *Satire-Based*

Definition: Using a term that exaggerates a grain of truth, as in this suspense title with descriptive subtitle from *Fortune:*

Rambos in Pinstripes

Why are so many CEOs lousy leaders? Research shows
they tend to be impatient, impulsive, manipulative,
dominating, self-important, and critical of others.

Method: Make sure satire is appropriate for your target audience and that the term you use has a grain of truth in it. There is a fine line between satire and sarcasm (mocking with no grain of truth). Tread carefully, here. Mock a public figure, and you invite a libel suit; satirize a private person, and you solicit one, too.

18. *Statement-Based*

Definition: Introducing your topic with a declaration, as in this descriptive title from *Time:*

Free Speech Comes to the Net

Method: This type of title is good for news or announcements. Simply cast your topic, occasion, or truth in sentence form. (The more concise, the better.)

19. *Vernacular-Based*

Definition: Using common speech or a colloquialism to depict the essence of a work, as in this suspense label with descriptive subtitle from *College Sports:*

Oh, Brother!

Virginia Tech's Cornell Brown Draws Raves from Big Brother Ruben
in Buffalo and Comparisons to Another Bill—All-Pro Bruce Smith

Method: This type of title is similar to the resurrected cliché, differing only in that the common phrase is associated with speech. In other words, you have to make it new again, relying on homonyms, puns, and word play. Moreover, the vernacular has to depict or imply the topic *and* be associated with a source, as in the colloquial "Well, Shoot!"—conveying light-hearted dissatisfaction—used to profile a West Virginia sharpshooter who failed to qualify for the Olympics.

20. *Word Play*

Definition: Inventing new words to describe content, as in this suspense label introducing books about television, from *New Age Journal:*

Tele-Visionaries

Method: Find the keyword in your topic and combine it with another word or term to invent a concept in keeping with your content. Magazine student Keith Johns did this for a feature targeted at *Mac Home Journal,* coming up with this descriptive title: "Give Your Mac an *Interface-Lift.*" (If no one can cipher your word play—"D-lete" for "Decathlon Athlete"—delete it.)

21. *Multiple Combinations*

Using several generating devices operating in a title or in a title and subtitle, as in these examples:

- Alphabet-based, rhymed descriptive title with alliterative descriptive subtitle from *Mademoiselle:*

Allergies from A to Z

Everything you wanted to know about sneezing, sniffling and spots

- Alliterative, rhymed word play, descriptive title from *New Age Journal:*

Mix Up Some Sublime Slime

- Vernacular resurrected cliché, homonym-based descriptive title from *Smithsonian:*

En Garde! We Seem to Be Getting the Point of Fencing

A Word about Subheads

Subheads are titles that introduce new sections within the body of a work, using the same generating devices as just discussed. But subheads have another more important function: providing transitions from one section to the next. In fact, when you view your subheads along with your title and/or subtitle, you should be able to envision an outline of your entire piece. Try it. You might get a sense of structure, especially if your subheads are composed in parallel fashion.

Megan Lane, former magazine student, wanted to write about the emotions she felt covering the trial of a child-rapist. Because Lane was close to the topic emotionally and planned to use different time elements in each section of her piece, she was having trouble envisioning it in the early stages. Her target publication was *Editor & Publisher,* whose style is to use subheads, even in its back-of-the-book column called Shop Talk. So Lane studied those subheads and jotted down a few of her own, making them parallel so that she could depict her personal experience:

Covering the Rape of a Child

> **The Student World**
> **The Real World**
> **My Own World**

As her title and parallel subheads indicate, Lane covered the rape of a child from a student, professional, and personal perspective. And she published her column in *E&P* the first time out.

Ideally, subheads should be parallel but not to the point of wrenching and distorting meaning. When that happens, subheads no longer serve their main purpose as transitions in a sectioned work. Nonetheless, subheads should be as close in voice and style as possible. Following are titles and/or subtitles of three articles using subheads. Analyze them for style. Try to imagine, based on titles and subtitles alone, the structure and content of these articles:

Health Scares Real or Not?

> **The Water We Drink**
> **The Air We Breathe**
> **The Sun We Worship**
> **The Air Inside Our Home**
> **The Smoke from Other People's Cigarettes**
> **The Pesticides on the Food We Eat**
> **The "Rare" Burger We Savor**
> **The Critters We Encounter**
> —Laurie Tarkan, *Woman's Day,* April 23, 1996

I Am Marc Twight.

Feel My Pain.

He climbs. He writes. And all the while he is hurting.
The life and hard times of mountaineering's king of angst.

　　I.　Go to Europe

　　II.　Get Famous

　　III.　Come Home

　　IV.　Capitalize

—Craig Vetter, *Outside,* February 1996

Changing the Face of the Magazine Industry

Were it not for black publishers, African Americans
would be almost nonexistent in the magazine business.
Here's the ugly reality behind the glossy cover.

　　"Lily White and Read All Over"

　　Getting into the Club

　　Wanted: A Staff That Looks Like America

　　Climbing the Brick Wall and Breaking the Glass Ceiling

　　Trickle-Down Policy Is Not Enough

—Carolyn M. Brown, *Black Enterprise,* August 1995

As you can see, good titles and subheads not only are contracts with your readers but also blueprints from which you can structure a story. You'll learn more about the importance of titles in The Craft Shop, analyze more titles at The Newsstand, and compose working ones for your story ideas at The Keyboard.

THE CRAFT SHOP

The Power of a Title

Audrey Chapman, Senior Editor, *Cleveland Magazine*

The power of a title. A bad one will sell a great article short, while the best ones entice readers to dive into stories they may have otherwise passed up. The marriage between the title and the subtitle, beautifully packaged with art design, is especially underestimated by many writers. If the title and subtitle have no impact, the reader you've catered to with riveting prose may not even get to your words. The title and subtitle seduce the reader. They lure him in.

It's important, then, to invest as much passion and energy into writing your title and subtitle as you did throughout the painstaking process of writing your piece. Why would you toil over each syllable in your story, crafting every paragraph to perfection, without taking ownership of these elements—two of your article's most important selling tools? Don't leave it up to your editor. Write a compelling title and subtitle that hooks your readers and never lets go.

Writing titles and subtitles also helps focus your story. When you're lost in the maze of information you've gathered for an article and don't know where to begin, write and rewrite your subtitle: It will force you to see what your story is *really* about, which will help you shape the piece. As the theme of your article, the subtitle includes the storyline (Why are we telling this story now?) and your article's most provocative details. These tidbits tease your audience into poring through each paragraph on a mission to know more.

Catchy titles also mean the difference between your query letter ending up in an editor's wastebasket or turning into a sale. Look at a magazine's title style as a gateway into the editor's mind. If you're pitching a piece on the latest medical treatment for AIDS, for example, there's little chance that a magazine brimming with sensational stories heralded by racy titles will bite. Send that query to *Health* magazine instead, or change your slant to suit the book you're pitching. Otherwise, those rejection letters will never stop coming.

Subheads and story breaks are other tools that some beginning writers find intrusive, but experienced writers and editors know are essential. Beginners will learn that subheads—short headlines inside the article that break up the copy—do not detract from poetic prose. They organize your story and, if written with punch, keep your readers interested. Subheads and story breaks also give the reader a chance to breathe. And they're a wonderful opportunity for a journalist to kick off a new section with fresh, anecdotal writing that's as alive as your heart-stopping lead.

Your efforts in writing titles may also propel you to the top of an editor's freelance-writer list. Study the way magazine editors use these elements in their publications and show them that you've taken the time to think like them. Whether you're writing a groundbreaking cover story for a national magazine or an intimate profile for a city magazine, go the extra mile. You'll see the results—in your articles and your pocketbook.

THE NEWSSTAND
Scanning for Titles and Subheads

1. Head out to the library. Research several back issues of each of your select publications, targeted in your project files containing active story ideas. Go through each magazine, analyzing titles and noting:

   ■ *Descriptive, suspenseful, or label titles.* Which ones do editors favor? Jot down titles that intrigue or interest you. Photocopy articles using subheads for future reference.

   ■ *Generating devices.* Which ones do editors favor, according to types listed earlier in this chapter? Jot down favorite ones for future reference.

   ■ *Combinations of title types (descriptive, suspenseful, label)* and *generating devices.* Jot these down, too, for future reference.

2. Return to the photocopies of the articles using subheads and note:

   ■ The subtitle style and generating device

   ■ How each introduces information and provides transition

   ■ Any parallelism in structure

   ■ How title, subtitle, and subheads combine to outline content

THE KEYBOARD
Generating Titles

1. Refer to your notes and photocopies compiled during The Newsstand exercises. Analyze the types of titles and generating devices for each target publication in your project files. According to the methods explained in this chapter, and in the style of your select magazine, compose at least three working titles for *each* of your story ideas.

2. Determine whether any of your story ideas will require subheads. Because you already have done thematic and research assignments at the keyboard, you should have a rough idea of how sections of your story will evolve. Organize information in these project files—according to

events, issues, sources, data, and so on—for each section that you envision. Write a working subhead for each section in the style of the target magazine listed in each project file. Finally, jot down the title and/or subtitle and all subheads, making them parallel if possible and envisioning a structure for your piece.

Time
Elements

Moments of Narration

At this point, you might be wishing you were a newspaper reporter rather than a magazine writer. Don't. Reporters are foot soldiers of truth, risking their lives and nerves to report tragic or vital events. Like you, they have clear story forms and general themes, such as community business is good or federal taxes affect you, and they gather facts. But someone else writes their headlines. And "time element" to them means the name of the day, as in:

The state of the union is good, the president said *Monday*.

That's it. Apart from deadline, this is about all reporters need to know about time to satisfy copy editors.

The same can't be said for the magazine business. Of course, "time element" can mean the name of the day, but it also can mean verb tense, as in *grammatical time,* or a sequence of events, as in *chronological time*. It can mean the point in time that a writer chooses to enter a story: close to the action, so that events transpire before the reader's eyes (called *now*); far from the action, so that events go unmentioned (called *then*); or somewhere between those two points (called *now and then*). These last three zones are known as *moments of narration,* also dubbed *literary time*. Finally, there are five major transitional moments related to grammatical, chronological, and literary time or combinations of all three time elements.

Magazine writers need all the time they can get—not only to meet deadlines but also to convey to readers the *reality* of an experience. If a subjective truth is significant, narrating it via the elements of grammatical, chronological, and literary time enchants or engages the audience, allowing readers to immerse themselves in a work. That's why magazines are visually powerful. The medium was interactive long before webzines on the Internet.

To interact with your readers, to make them feel your joy or pain—even to serve or inform them—you have to pinpoint the right moment of narration. Time is *paramount* in magazine journalism, so much so that this book omits a chapter on structure. Time provides structure, especially in conjunction with epiphany and peak experience. Time shapes a story the same way that it shapes your life, allowing you to relive an incident from your list of highs, lows, and turning points; to look back and contemplate meaning; to glimpse the future and gauge impact; and to share current news or advice and inform or enlighten others.

Think of it this way: Writers have time machines at their disposal. Equipped with a keyboard, you, as a writer, can time-travel to the precise moment when something significant happened in your life. Better yet, you can transport readers there. You can put them on the spot, sharing the drama of what you or a source felt during an epiphany or peak experience. You can serve them, sharing life lessons without ever mentioning the incident that spawned them. Or you can do both, but to lesser extent, depicting action and commenting on it.

Of all concepts that you will have learned in this book, literary time may be the most important with respect to writing (because it shapes writing). *Now is the time to ponder time.* In a few chapters, you will be writing your first draft. Knowing the time element will give you a frame of reference to envision your developing work.

You enter a story strategically. You use a moment of narration to pinpoint a time to relate what you know. Because you know different things, depending on when you opt to share an event or idea, the moment determines:

- *Content.* Will you share your own or a source's personal experience? Or will you or your source speak as expert without mentioning the personal experience at all? Or will you do both, sharing the impact of experience and the insight of expertise?
- *Expression of content.* Will you put the readers on the scene, recounting events chronologically as if they were happening before the readers' eyes? Or will you articulate your truths without any sense of plot (time line) or chronology, as if you were conversing with readers or sharing your opinions? Or will you do both, recounting events so readers can envision them first and analyze them later?
- *Structure.* By answering the preceding questions, you can outline a story according to events associated with it or insights emanating out of it—step by step, point by point.

Let's analyze the three time elements. Once you know them, you will start to visualize your first draft.

Grammatical time is easy to determine—past, present, and future tense—and is second nature to most writers. Usually, most people write in the past tense because teachers have trained them to do so from preschool to Princeton. Many magazine editors also prefer that mode. Some editors argue that grammatical time has little effect whatsoever on prose, whereas others believe that the present tense may be personal and immediate. (See The Pushed Present Tense in the upcoming section Transitional Moments.) In any case, composing in one or another verb tense does not really affect basic information conveyed to readers. Consider this excerpt from George Plimpton's "How to Face a Firing Squad," which originally appeared in *Esquire,* presented as he wrote it, in the past tense, and then shown in the present and future tenses:

Past Tense

In the early hours of December 22, 1849, Fyodor Dostoyevsky was led out to the Semyonovsky parade ground in St. Petersburg to be executed by a firing squad. He was twenty-seven at the time. The crime he had committed was the "attempt to disseminate writings against the government by means of a hand printing press." Twenty others—poets, teachers, officers, journalists had been sentenced with him. The procedure was that they would die in groups of three. Dostoyevsky was in the second group.

It was a monstrous hoax, of course, initiated by Nicholas I, known with good reason as the Iron Czar. Just as the adjutant in charge of the firing squad was to lower his saber and shout "Fire!" one of the czar's aides-de-camp galloped across the parade ground and handed the officer a sealed packet that contained commutations of sentence. According to a historian friend of mine, these were read out at agonizing length by an officer known as the worst stutterer in the Russian army. Dostoyevsky was sentenced to four years of penal servitude.

I looked all this up the other day because I had a luncheon date with Larry Rivers, the well-known painter, who during the civil unrest in Nigeria some time ago went through a similar, if not quite as dramatic, experience. How often does one have lunch with a man who has survived the firing squad?

Present Tense

In the early hours of December 22, 1849, Fyodor Dostoyevsky is led out to the Semyonovsky parade ground in St. Petersburg to be executed by a firing squad. He is twenty-seven at the time. The crime he has committed is the "attempt to disseminate writings against the government by means of a hand printing press." Twenty others—poets, teachers, officers, journalists have been sentenced with him. The procedure is that they will die in groups of three. Dostoyevsky is in the second group.

It is a monstrous hoax, of course, initiated by Nicholas I, known with good reason as the Iron Czar. Just as the adjutant in charge of the firing squad is to lower his saber and shout "Fire!" one of the czar's aides-de-camp gallops across the parade ground and hands the officer a sealed packet that contains commutations of sentence. According to a historian friend of mine, these are read out at agonizing length by an officer known as the worst stutterer in the Russian army. Dostoyevsky is sentenced to four years of penal servitude.

I look all this up because I have a luncheon date with Larry Rivers, the well-known painter, who during the civil unrest in Nigeria some time ago went through a similar, if not quire as dramatic, experience. How often does one have lunch with a man who has survived the firing squad?

Future Tense

In the early hours of December 22, 1849, Fyodor Dostoyevsky will be led out to the Semyonovsky parade ground in St. Petersburg to be executed by a firing squad. He will be twenty-seven at the time. The crime he will have committed is the "attempt to disseminate writings against the government by means of a hand printing press." Twenty others—poets, teachers, officers, journalists will have been sentenced with him. The procedure will be that they die in groups of three. Dostoyevsky will be in the second group.

It will be a monstrous hoax, of course, initiated by Nicholas I, known with good reason as the Iron Czar. Just as the adjutant in charge of the firing squad is to lower his saber and shout "Fire!" one of the czar's aides-de-camp will have galloped across the parade ground and handed the officer a sealed packet that contained commutations of sentence. According to a historian friend of mine, these will be read out at agonizing length by an officer known as the worst stutterer in the Russian army. Dostoyevsky will be sentenced to four years of penal servitude.

I will have looked all this up because I have a luncheon date with Larry Rivers, the well-known painter, who during the civil unrest in Nigeria some time ago goes through a similar, if not quire as dramatic, experience. How often will one have lunch with a man who has survived the firing squad?

As you can see, basic information does not really change. Plimpton's original past tense is the correct one because the present and past versions alter voice. The future tense one sounds weird. But the overall style remains the same, and you get the exact chronology of events.

Chronological time has a slightly greater impact on prose but again comes naturally for most writers. People usually tell stories in fairy-tale form: with a beginning (once upon a time), middle (and it happened then), and end (happily ever after). Some magazine editors argue that such a form makes the prose easier to follow because readers are so accustomed to traditional story telling. Others maintain that switching the order—putting the end or middle first—mimics the mind because human beings do not remember events chronologically.

For instance, if you have experienced a fire, you probably do not immediately recall the first wisp of smoke but your belongings in debris (end) or your house engulfed in flames (middle). Again, however, the effect of chronological order (or disorder!) is not powerful enough to dash or salvage a magazine work. To see why, analyze the excerpt below from "The Broken Child"—a personal experience article about infant twins and an older autistic son—by Catherine Johnson, contributing editor for *New Woman*. The original excerpt features events as Johnson had experienced them in real time. The revised version rearranges those events in random order:

Original

We all were sitting in the kitchen together—babies, Jimmy, Martine the nanny, and me. I was dutifully rehearsing Jimmy on his speech, saying, "Jimmy, how many babies do we have?"

He'd been able to answer this query correctly once before: "Two," he'd said. In the midst of all the misery, his and mine, it had been a happy moment, since whether or not Jimmy will ever be able to learn numbers is, at this point, an open question.

So I was saying, in my loud and cheery pay-attention-to-me voice, "Jimmy, how many babies do we have?"

No answer. I did get some eye contact, which, for me, always sparks hope; I always assume when Jimmy looks at me as I speak that he's trying.

Of course, I could be wrong.

Nevertheless, right or wrong, I gave Jimmy his "prompt": "Jimmy, how many babies do we have? *We have . . .*"

Again, no answer. Now he was looking back down at his snack.

So I went back to the prompt, extending it this time. "Jimmy, how many babies do we have? We have t—" Exaggerating the *t*.

By now I was just going through the motions, not expecting much more than an autistic echo: "we-have-two-babies" intoned lifelessly, expressionlessly, when suddenly Jimmy looked me in the eye and came out with it: "We have too many babies." *That* was a Moment!

Jimmy was transcending the autism, was breaking through, telling me exactly what he thought. I looked across the table at him, and I felt my heart stir; if I had fallen out of love with Jimmy after the babies, suddenly, here and now, I remembered the passion that had held me fast to my son and his future for so long.

Revised

I was just going through the motions, asking—"Jimmy, how many babies do we have?"—and not expecting much more than an autistic echo: "we-have-two-babies" intoned lifelessly, expressionlessly, when suddenly Jimmy looked me in the eye and came out with the right answer.

That was a Moment! Capturing it, though, took about ten minutes.

We all were sitting in the kitchen together—babies, Jimmy, Martine the nanny, and me. I was dutifully rehearsing Jimmy on his speech.

When I first asked the question, I got some eye contact, which, for me always sparks hope; I always assume when Jimmy looks at me as I speak that he's trying.

Of course, I could be wrong.

So I was saying, in my loud and cheery pay-attention-to-me voice, "Jimmy, how many babies do we have?"

No answer.

Jimmy had been able to answer this query correctly once before: "Two," he'd said. In the midst of all the misery, his and mine, it had been a happy moment, since whether or not Jimmy will ever be able to learn numbers is, at this point, an open question.

This day, however, Jimmy was transcending the autism, was breaking through, telling me exactly what he thought. I looked across the table at him, and I felt my heart stir; if I had fallen out of love with Jimmy after the babies, suddenly, here and now, I remembered the passion that had held me fast to my son and his future for so long.

Nevertheless, right or wrong, I gave Jimmy his "prompt": "Jimmy, how many babies do we have? *We have . . .*"

Again, no answer. Now he was looking back down at his snack.

So I went back to the prompt, extending it this time. "Jimmy, how many babies do we have? We have t—" Exaggerating the *t*—when he said it: "We have too many babies."

Several events in the revised anecdote are out of order, and yet, the voice is able to smooth over these wrinkles in time and make sense of the exchange between narrator and son. (As you will learn in the next chapter, voice is a kind of glue that holds the structure together.) So even violating chronological time usually does not affect interest or readability, as long as the writer sustains voice and viewpoint (also discussed in the next chapter).

Far and away, *literary time* is the most important element to master. It structures stories from top to bottom. As such, the moment of narration is a visual tool. To picture your story, you imagine content being expressed from one of three distinct moments:

1. ***Now.*** The *now* moment is when you relive an event or a problem so that the work is close to the action, with no commentary but heavy emphasis on plot (chronological sequence of events in a work). Theme is implied by actions or quotations from sources. There is a distinct sense of time passage in the *now* moment: a beginning, a middle, and an end. You are generating drama and tension, referring to an event or a problem that appears on your (or your source's) list of highs, lows, and turning points. For example, if you were robbed at gunpoint at an automatic teller machine (ATM), you depict that with plenty of sensory data as if the incident were happening *now*, before the reader's eyes. But you cannot offer service or advice on security measures at ATMs, informing readers how to stave off a robbery. The

now moment won't allow it, and if you try, you will commit a voice lapse—a jarring mistake that so flagrantly interrupts the rhythm of a story that the editor stops reading and writes you a rejection.

2. Now and Then. When you look back somewhat on an event or a problem so that the work is a mixture of plot and commentary, you are in the *now and then* moment. The focus now is on a balance of action and theme. There is a subtle sense of time passage. Thus, you might mention an event drawn from your (or your source's) list of highs, lows, and turning points but not dwell on it. You place the reader at the ATM where you were robbed, commenting on actions during that incident and emphasizing the need for consumers to know security measures. You share expert advice and field and library research with readers. As such, you convey a sense of drama and provide consumer information, though not as much drama as an article in the *now* and not as much information as an article in the final category, *then*. Try to do one or both, and you commit another voice lapse. The editor stuffs your manuscript into an SASE like Michael Jordan stuffs a ball into a basket.

3. Then. The *then* moment is when you look back on an event or a problem so that the work is far from the action, emphasizing commentary without much of a plot. The focus is on theme. There is no sense of time passage in the *then* moment. You are providing service, opinion, and/or information without referring to an event or a problem that might appear on your (or your source's) list of highs, lows, and turning points. If you were robbed at gunpoint at an ATM, you might write a piece about security measures that consumers can take to stave off such an assault. You share library research and expert interviews with your readers but never mention what happened to you. If you do, your voice lapses. The editor spills coffee on your piece and doesn't apologize on the rejection slip.

Moments of narration are elusive at first. The more you read work in each time zone, the more you can distinguish between action and comment. *Jack and Jill go up the hill* is an example of action; *Jack and Jill never learned to hike uphill* is an example of a comment. Let's illustrate moment of narration with excerpts from three published works.

Then

This passage from Catherine Johnson's article "The Broken Child" employs a moment far from the action with heavy emphasis on comment and perspective:

> And autism is not a particularly lovable condition. With autism you have a child who is spinning and flapping and hooting away at the top of his lungs; a child making eye contact only to demand food; an enraged child biting and

scratching his parents or himself; a child whose idea of play is to pull out a pitcher of juice from the refrigerator and dump it out on the living room carpet. It's the bottle of shampoo dumped on the sofa; the bucket of green paint dumped in the hot tub. It is hundreds of dollars spent each month replacing and repairing the latest toll of household destruction.

And the Kodak moments are few and far between, not least because an autistic child will refuse—violently refuse—to pose for a snapshot: with autism you have a child who doesn't comprehend Christmas, or birthday parties, or toys; a child who is impervious to the "magic" of childhood; a child who doesn't sing songs or draw pictures; a child who, at age 7, has yet to have his first conversation with his parents, except in our dreams at night. And yet . . . and yet . . . my seven years as Jimmy's mom and no one else's are now years that I miss. Because despite his disability, Jimmy and I, we were a team. We had that Oedipal magic of mother and son alone together, with no other children to get in the way. I worked part-time, and at home, so when the bus pulled up after school I was all his, and he was all mine. We baked bread together, we tooled around in the car, we ran errands, we got lollipops at the dry cleaner. We had a life. And having no other children to compare him with, I often experienced his disability as being not that . . . different.

Now and Then

This excerpt from Ellen Gerl's "Tradition" in *Ohio Magazine* describes her mother's potica recipe, providing a balance of action and information:

To watch a potica being made is to believe in evolution. The art of shaping the sweet Slovenia pastry didn't happen overnight. Nor is it for the weak of muscle. My mother wrestles flour, butter, yeast and 12 egg yolks into an elastic dough the color of a young goldfinch.

"When I was a kid, we always used brown eggs. Made it richer," she says, her voice admonishing a society that prefers its eggs white.

She throws the dough on the formica table and kneads it, fingers and palms performing a dance choreographed generations ago. "Just poke a finger in the dough, and if it pops up right away, you're done," she says. You suspect that's like a composer telling you to quit when the symphony sounds right.

As the dough rises, a cast-iron pot on the stove simmers with a mix of walnuts, honey and just a little rum. Was it this forbidden adult substance that made stealing fingerfuls so irresistible?

Now

This excerpt from Lady Borton's "A Forgiving Land" in the *New York Times Magazine* describes action with the author's friend, a former Viet Cong commander named Second Treasure:

"Hands up, American!" Second Treasure said in Vietnamese. She poked my ribs. "You're under arrest!"

I lifted my sandals over my head. In the moonlight, the tiger cactuses along the rice paddy loomed like phantoms with prickly limbs.

"Forward!" Second Treasure said in a teasing voice. She was leading me into Ban Long, a village of 4,000 people in the Mekong delta southwest of Ho Chi Minh City. Throughout the war, Ban Long had been a Viet Cong base. American B-52's had bombed the village, turning houses into craters, families into corpses. Agent Orange had stripped the earth of green.

Now, 15 years after the war, foliage obscured the moon. Milk trees hung heavy with fruit. Frogs chortled. Frangipani flowers like tiny trumpets broadcast their insistent perfume.

Amazing, I thought: The earth has forgiven us.

As you can see from the selections, the closer you move from the *then* zone to the *now*, the more you inch toward the moment of truth and the less you may say about the matter (apart from grounding). To illustrate, let's rewrite Lady Borton's *now*-moment introduction in the *now and then* and in the *then*, showing how drama diffuses as perspective rises.

Revision in the *Now and Then*

Visiting with my Vietnamese friend, Second Treasure, I always appreciate her sense of humor and the irony that accompanies it. Especially for me, an American. On our last outing, she poked my ribs and said, "Hands up, American! You're under arrest!"

We're role-playing, of course. She the Viet Cong commander—and she *was* one during the war—and I, the enemy (though I was *not* during the war). I'd worked in Viet Nam with the Quakers as a health administrator. Ten years later, in 1980, I lived in Malaysia's largest refugee camp for Boat People who'd fled Viet Nam. Now, I wanted to know Vietnamese who had chosen to stay.

Second Treasure was (and is) a patriot. Our friendship would allow for some teasing. So on our outing, I lifted my sandals over my head. In the moonlight, the tiger cactuses along the rice paddy loomed like phantoms with prickly limbs.

"Forward!" Second Treasure said. She was leading me into Ban Long, a village of 4,000 people in the Mekong delta southwest of Ho Chi Minh City. Throughout the war, Ban Long had been a Viet Cong base. American B-52's had bombed the village, turning houses into craters, families into corpses. Agent Orange had stripped the earth of green.

Now, 15 years after the war, foliage obscured the moon. Milk trees hung heavy with fruit. Frogs chortled. Frangipani flowers like tiny trumpets broadcast their insistent perfume.

Amazing, I thought: The earth has forgiven us.

Revision in the *Then*

I appreciate Second Treasure's sense of humor, and the irony always accompanying it. So I role-play with her, imagining we are back in the war: enemies instead of friends. Second Treasure was, in fact, a Viet Cong commander. I'd worked in Viet Nam with the Quakers as a health administrator. Ten years later, in 1980, I lived in Malaysia's largest refugee camp for Boat People who'd fled Viet Nam. Now, I wanted to know Vietnamese who had chosen to stay.

Second Treasure was a patriot. I, an expatriate.

As friends everywhere, we have a lot in common. Both of us love the land and villages like Ban Long, where 4,000 people dwell in the Mekong delta southwest of Ho Chi Minh City. Throughout the war, Ban Long had been a Viet Cong base. American B-52's had bombed the village, turning houses into craters, families into corpses. Agent Orange had stripped the earth of green.

Now, 15 years after the war, the flora and fauna have returned—milk trees, frangipani flowers. Frogs.

Amazing, I thought: The earth has forgiven us.

By now you should sense how choosing the right moment of narration also structures your entire manuscript. Mess up the moment, and you're looking at an entire rewrite. To show how fatal the wrong moment of narration can be, let's analyze two excerpts by student writers—written in the *right* time zone and then recast in the *wrong* ones (given their approaches, topics, and themes).

Writing far from the action, in the *then,* Anna Szymanski waxes philosophic about children:

> I have never liked kids. They whine. They drool. They smell. I see no joy in changing a diaper, little fun in playing hide and seek. Until recently, every moment spent with a child would leave me irritable and intolerant. My old definition of children? They are dirty, small creatures with no respect for others and no ability to comprehend basic rules in life, such as no rustling my hair or tugging on my earrings. I envisioned myself childless and content for the rest of my life. Then I met Matthew.

Writing close to the action, Megan Lane composed a dramatic introduction about covering the rape of a child:

> I gripped the reporter's pad, as if it might fly away, as if I might throw it at the next passerby. Half-running, I could hardly feel the sidewalk under my feet. When I finally stopped, I found myself in the last five minutes of my magazine editing class. Breathless, I tried to decipher the white chalk words on the blackboard in front of me.

Here are the excerpts in the *opposite* moment, beginning with Anna Szymanski's in the *now* and following with Megan Lane's in the *then:*

> I watch a kid whine in the park. He drools. He smells. He wants to rustle my hair and tug on my earrings. I hide behind a tree, as if I want to play hide and seek. This way, I can run away from him. When he spots me, I bolt, hurdling the low end of a teeter-totter.

I was so upset after covering the rape of a child that I felt like throwing away my notebook at the next passerby. They never train you in Journalism School to handle these stories. "Objectivity," professors cry. That rape victim cried in court, I can tell you, when she testified about her ordeal.

As you can see, action in the rewrite of the Szymanski excerpt is awkward and misleading. (She comes off as child hater, when hers is a story about love.) The perspective in the rewrite of the Lane excerpt isn't as powerful as the on-the-spot drama in the original. (She comes off as a disgruntled beginner, berating professors even though a magazine professor showed her compassion.) These are jarring mistakes. An editor will stop reading after the first paragraph, tasting a rotten apple.

When determining the right moment for your story idea, ask yourself:

- Is my goal to let the reader experience what I or a source did (requiring the *now* moment)? Or to help readers learn from my or my source's experience, sharing information (requiring the *then*)? Or a little of both (requiring the *now and then*)?
- What is more important in my piece—comment, perspective, interviews, and library research (taking a *then* moment) or tension, drama, and sensory data (taking a *now* moment)? Or some of both (taking a *now and then* moment)?
- What type of approach do I envision for my work? Informational, usually far from the action with the focus on expert advice (employing a *then* moment)? Personal experience, usually close to the action with the focus on an emotional incident (employing a *now* moment)? Or an anecdotal piece, in which expert advice and personal experience blend (requiring a *now and then* moment)?

If you ask those questions and get the same moment of narration each time, no sweat. That's the right moment for your story idea. But if you get a different answer with each question, then you probably need to consider varying the moment according to the techniques described next.

Transitional Moments

The term *transitional moment* refers to variations of grammatical, chronological, and literary time. Some manuscripts need only one transitional moment to solidify structure; others need a few or several. Because each manuscript is different, you have to become familiar with each transitional moment and determine whether it will help solve your writing problem.

Here are the most common transitional moments, with excerpts to illustrate how they operate and advice about when and how to employ them in your work:

1. *Flashback*

Definition: Related to literary and chronological time; an incident or event that occurred earlier than the point in which it appears in the particular time line of a manuscript.

When to Use: The device is especially effective in a work close to the action to provide context or motive, or in a work far from the action to enhance characterization or theme.

Example: In "Jorma Kaukonen's Organic Odyssey," a profile in *Southeast Ohio* about the former lead guitarist for the 1960s rock band Jefferson Airplane and cofounder of the contemporary group Hot Tuna, author Peggy Dillon inserts a flashback noting how Jorma Kaukonen met his wife and business manager Vanessa. The flashback characterizes Kaukonen and augments an "organic" (synchronicity) theme:

> His chance meeting with Vanessa six years ago seems equally fateful. He and Hot Tuna were playing at a club in Key West. She was working as an interior designer there and went to hear music that night. During that July evening in 1988, the two began talking backstage, ended up going sailing the next day, and fell in love on the trip. A compressed courtship followed: constant phone calls, a midwest rendezvous, and the discovery of shared interests ranging from motorcycles to animals to a passion for life. Fourteen days after they stepped onto the sailboat, as they drove along the northbound lane of the New York State Thruway, Jorma proposed. Vanessa accepted, and the rest, as they say, is history.
>
> They tell the story in tandem, filling in each other's sentences as they recall the proposal and describe what they have in common. "We both liked to sing blues," Jorma says.
>
> "We're into the same actors," Vanessa adds.
>
> "Same books," Jorma says.
>
> ". . . and we just *liked* each other," Vanessa says, adding that even if they hadn't become a couple, she believes they would have been friends.
>
> "And we still are friends, which is kind of nice," Jorma adds, smiling at her.
>
> As the story unfolds, however, it becomes clear that the odds of their paths crossing were miniscule. Jorma says he almost skipped that fateful gig, it being far away and squeezed into an already busy schedule. Vanessa admits that when she suggested they go sailing, she didn't even know where she'd get the boat. (She ultimately borrowed it from a sympathetic friend.) Jorma chalks their union up to synchronicity. "Yeah," Vanessa agrees, "it all just clicked."
>
> His career, too, has progressed organically. . . .

Method: Identify where you need a flashback in your work. Insert it. Then make transition back to the main story via thematic quotations or statements, as Dillon does after the preceding flashback in quotations and a summary paragraph.

2. *Flashforward*

Definition: Related to literary, grammatical, and chronological time; referring to an incident or event that has yet to occur in the particular time line of a manuscript.

When to Use: The device is especially effective in a work close to the action to provide a sense of closure, or in a work somewhat removed from the action to foreshadow a theme or scene.

Example: In the following excerpt, Patricia Westfall discusses the marital influence of "the forester," a character in her *Esquire* essay "An American Dream." Westfall uses a flashforward to foreshadow how she and her husband will discover, through the forester, that their once-shared perception (theme) no longer extends to actions or people. The flashforward is not italicized in the original but appears in italics here so you can spot it toward the end of this excerpt:

> The idea that we plant those two thousand trees was the forester's. In fact, the forester thought we should become tree farmers. And he had sketched us a map, charted symbols, filled out forms, and mailed off "our" forestry plan to the state nursery before either of us could contemplate what the forester was, or think about what his impact upon us might be. The issue would not be trees, of course, but perception. Jeff had not changed since the day on the rock; he still saw perception as absolute; I was willing to allow for some confusion. *Even if our perceptions on sounds and sights were the same, we would discover through the forester, that our shared sense of lyric did not extend to actions or people.* Jeff saw the forester as the embodiment of the lyrical life-style. I did not. I saw him as a living myth.

Method: Locate the spot in your manuscript where you need to foreshadow a scene, especially one associated with theme (as in Westfall's example). Use *would* to imply the future in a manuscript written in the past tense and *will* to do so in a manuscript written in the present tense. Then provide a quick transition out of the flashforward and back to the chronology, using phrases such as *At the moment, though* or *And yet now* or making a thematic statement, as Westfall does.

3. *Pushed Present Tense*

Definition: Related to grammatical and literary time; recasting thoughts in a work set far from the action from the past tense to the present tense, intensifying "interior monologue" (a conversation one has with one's self); or recasting events in a work set close to the action from the past tense to the present tense, adding a sense of urgency.

When to Use: The device is effective when the writer uses a *then* moment in a personal essay, sharing intimate thoughts; or when the goal is to place the reader on the spot in a story told in the *now*, focusing on a life-altering event.

Example: In the following excerpt, magazine journalist Erika Firm uses the pushed present tense to describe how it feels to have survived Hurricane Hugo, whose winds were clocked at 138 mph:

> The wind sounds like a freight train crashing through the building. Car windows explode and my ears pop as the storm screams by. Mom and Dad are in the other room. I don't know how they can possibly sleep. Every dog in South Carolina must be howling. A row of pine trees snap. Rain seems to be pouring from every direction, even up from the ground. Then an eerie stillness settles. Birds chirp, confused. Cautiously I open the front door and tiptoe outside in my bare feet. I can hear a woman sniffling and a baby sobbing in another apartment. I look around. Can it be over? The wind starts to pick up again and horizontal sheets of rain hit my back as I struggle to re-open the door. I huddle by the window and brace myself for round two. Hugo screams a greeting into the chimney, as if I don't already know he's here.

Method: Here are some guidelines for changing verb tense from past to pushed perfect.

- *Past progressive tense* is cast as *present progressive tense:*

  I was trying to keep a black woman writer from strangling a white male one in my magazine workshop at Ohio University.

  I *am* trying to keep a black woman writer from strangling a white male one in my magazine workshop at Ohio University.

- *Past perfect tense* takes *present perfect tense:*

  He had written a flawed popular fiction from a black male viewpoint.

  He *has* written a flawed popular fiction from a black male viewpoint.

- *Past tense* becomes *present tense:*

  His apparent middle class isolationism resulted in a few misconceptions.

  His apparent middle class isolationism *results* in a few misconceptions.

- *Present tense* becomes *future tense:*

  We meet in my office, heal, and go to work.

  We *will* meet in my office, heal, and go to work.

■ *Present perfect* becomes *future perfect:*

They have learned a lesson about stereotypes.

They *will* have learned a lesson about stereotypes.

■ *Past subjunctive mood* becomes *present subjunctive mood:*

If I had been argumentative, I would have shortchanged myself as a teacher.

If I *were* argumentative, I would shortchange myself as a teacher.

4. *Moment Shift*

Definition: Related to literary time; a gradual move within the *now and then* moment of narration, closer to or farther from the action, to highlight drama or commentary as needed in a work.

When to Use: The shift usually succeeds in a piece that begins somewhat removed from the action, foreshadows one event, and slowly moves closer to the action and that event, building in intensity—with or without any space or asterisk breaks.

Example: In the following three excerpts, taken from "Mr. Allen Dewey Spooner" and published in *The Chattahoochee Review,* essayist Kelly Cherry describes her grandfather having lunch with her mother Mary, foreboding a hurricane with the symbols of windchimes and a scarf. The piece shifts closer to the *now* as the hurricane nears, and closer still as the hurricane hits. These transitional moments happen gradually (and without numbers) in Cherry's essay but are excerpted here with numbers to designate the moment shifts:

[1] He was a saw filer, keeping the teeth of the giant saw impressively and precisely sharp, and they ate lunch on a tablecloth Mary spread over a broad, flat rock near the mill. He was the foremost filer in the business, it was said in that part of the country. This was a strange and beautiful part of the country, where huge cypresses immodestly revealed their roots, and hanging moss swayed back and forth like silent wind chimes, and a heavy aroma of sulfur lay on top of the still day, smothering it, clinging to people's throats like a scarf. . . .

[2] By morning, frenzied gusts of wind were slinging rain against the windows so hard that the panes shuddered and threatened to collapse. My mother crept downstairs to the kitchen, where oatmeal had been steaming all night in the "fireless cooker"—a double-welled cabinet with hot round slabs of stone at the bottoms of the wells. Allen motioned for her to sit down at the breakfast table while he read the scripture aloud, as he did every morning. Then Hattie read a prayer from a familiar booklet titled *Our Daily Bread.* It didn't matter that my mother didn't fully understand the scripture passages: Just the fact that her parents were seated there, so inseparable in their faith, lent stability to her small world.

But today, the ritual seemed somehow perfunctory, as if her parents were really thinking about something else. There was an impatience, an urgency in the room. . . .

[3] Windows were blown in as easily as if they'd been made of cellophane, the chimney crumpled as if it had been made of tissue paper, and the servants' house in the back yard toppled over. The mailman, conscientiously trying to make his rounds in the horse-drawn cart that had a little step on the back, where he stood, gave up just has he reached the Spooner residence. He brought his pouch into the parlor, spread the wet letters all over the imitation Persian rug, and carefully patted them dry. Every time a window blew in, Hattie and her daughters and the mailman would push a heavy piece of furniture up against the opening. Just when Hattie determined that they should all make a dash for the school building, a tin roof came hurtling past the house and she decided they'd better stay where they were.

Method: Determine the movement of your work with respect to action (somewhat close to or far from within the *now and then* moment). Be sure to foreshadow the event or incident with symbols, imagery, or thematic statements as you gradually make the shift.

5. *Multiple Moments*

Definition: Related to literary time; an abrupt move from one moment of narration to another, highlighting tension and commentary as needed in a work.

When to Use: Two or more moments of narration enhance a work that depicts an event close to the action, allowing the reader to experience tension, and then discusses the event far from the action, allowing the reader to analyze it—typically with distinct space and asterisk breaks.

Example: In the first excerpt, from "Covering the Rape of a Child," Megan Lane conveys drama close to the action as she hurries to class after covering testimony in the trial. In the body and ending of her piece, Lane discusses the impact of the trial, far from any action. The second excerpt is taken from her ending, when she puts her experience into perspective. Again, numbers do not appear in Lane's original manuscript but are used here to help you identify excerpts:

[1] When the class was dismissed a few minutes later, my professor, Patricia Westfall, called me to the front to explain my late appearance. I answered by sobbing.
    She hurried me down the hall to her office while I tried to release all the anger and fear that had tormented me for the previous three hours. Eventually, I was able to tell her the facts.
    Each one hit me like a brick. . . .

[2] As difficult as it was to do, I'm glad I covered that trial. It taught me things about myself, and about journalism, that I never would have known otherwise. I know what to expect from trials now. I know I can wait until I get home to be upset. I know I could make it in the real world on any big-time newspaper.

I also know that journalism and emotions do mix. Objectivity is a tone of voice, not a state of mind.

Method: Before writing a work, determine whether it hinges on depiction and discussion of an event. If so, use a moment close to the action so the reader can experience the event and then a moment far from the action so the reader can analyze ramifications of the event. Typically, such a piece employs space or asterisk breaks to herald the new moment of narration. Often, the piece begins with the event in the *now* moment, discusses the event in the *then* moment, and returns to the event in the *now* moment before ending. (This is known as a *bookend* story.)

Breaking the Time Barrier

Magazine writing pivots on grammatical, chronological, and literary time, as well as transitional moments. Each time element has specific uses and risks. Some see risks as barriers and find innovative ways to break them. For instance, a sophisticated writer such as David Lazar, Director of Creative Writing at Ohio University, can vary time elements and seemingly break rules in his award-winning essay "The Coat," which originally appeared in the small-press magazine *Mississippi Valley Review* and was reprinted in *Best American Essays, 1993*. The piece is about buying a second-hand coat in Dublin. Lazar uses an abrupt moment of narration to jar the reader, as he was jarred, writing an essay about his secondhand coat when he witnessed from his window a child on a bike being struck by a mail truck. Lazar's narrator changes perspective and topic without warning or any space or asterisk break, as one might find in a work using multiple moments; neither does he employ a gradual moment shift. Instead, he moves from musing about coats to describing a car accident outside his window. The accident occurs in *real writing time*—a time element that readers do not acknowledge because they "suspend disbelief" when paging through a magazine. (In other words, on some level, readers know that a writer—unshaven or needing a shower, swilling cold coffee—actually is at the keyboard typing details of an issue or event, a concept known as *implied author*.) The move in Lazar's piece is so abrupt that readers sense the implied author, which usually results in a voice lapse, or the breaking down of rhythm and tone. That's exactly what Lazar wants so readers can experience how the writing process can be jarred by sudden tragedy. In sum, Lazar breaks the basic rules of time and structures a unique award-winning essay. Here is the ending of "The Coat," where Lazar breaks the time barrier:

I tried one more shop: "Rose's" (second-hand implied). Their specialty was clearly coats; they had a dazzling array. In addition, there was a floor mirror, but it was standing upright. A middle-aged man with a sagging face full of flagging hope flared out of it from an unlovely wonderland. I tried on a black cashmere: too long. Then a salt and pepper wool and acrylic: the sleeves would have hit China if they hadn't been stopped by the linoleum floor. On the third try came luck, buyer's kismet: a blue calf-length coat of coarse material, perfect sleeves, and it hung loosely, but fashionably, like a cape. It cost seventeen pounds. The figure in the mirror, a dashing modern highwayman, turned to the man at the cash register: I'll give you twelve pounds and this—

Thirty minutes ago I was about to type the word "coat." I looked up from my desk and saw a child on a bicycle slammed into by a mail truck. He or she flew fifteen, maybe twenty feet. He or she started spinning around, shrieking in pain, a wounded banshee. I ran out. There were already half a dozen people there. Two boys were running to the news agent's to call for help, running with commitment and care in their speed. I didn't need to get closer, did not need to look at a broken child. I have the twisted little thing firmly in mind. The ambulance just arrived. The crowd is larger, flashing blue lights. The familiar European siren sound changes its pitch as it approaches.

I wonder about writing this, if whoever reads it will feel tricked, annoyed by the intrusion. I wonder if I should just say "coat." I didn't have much more to say. I left the store with two coats. I was going to say that no self-respecting person should be caught dead with two coats, that that made me more self-conscious than before, that a couple of women smiled broadly at me on my way back to Connelly Station and at first I felt my sense of attractiveness regenerate, followed by the frightening possibility that they were laughing with the divined knowledge that my new coat was worse than the old coat, which pulled me up short. I was going to say (the ambulance has gone and there is only a police car with smaller flashing lights) that I was determined to rid myself of that albatross of a coat, that I wanted to give it to a beggar, a busker, in a saintly gesture, a convenient self-apotheosis, but I didn't see any, a feat in Dublin. I left the coat hanging in a toilet stall in Connelly Station. And though I'm sure some poor unknowing soul has claimed it, not knowing what he was getting into, I think of it there, a desultory image. I was going to comment about my vanity.

Some men are pointing to the spot where the child landed. It is very close to the Chalk Farm tube station, and I'm hoping there will not be an outline in chalk. How heavy that coincidence would seem. But things just come together that way sometimes; they clash, they collide, creating new intersections. This intrusion wasn't my intention. I may have ruined the rhythm of a story, but at times it can be desperately hard to care. I have nothing else to say except that the street has resumed its normal, sullen flux.

Lazar discusses the risks involved in such a move in "Moment and Meaning" in The Craft Shop. Megan Lane also makes an appearance in The

Craft Shop, discussing multiple moments. Make a stop at The Newsstand to analyze moments and magazines and then stop at The Keyboard to determine moments for your stories in progress.

THE CRAFT SHOP

Moment and Meaning

David Lazar, Essayist

I want to discuss time in my essay for several reasons, most prominent of which was my decision to break the narrative near the end and introduce a present sequence. This was a painful decision, and one that I received far from unanimous support for before I published it. The decision to break the narrative rested on several assumptions: (1) that the violation of the narrative was honestly introduced and not a fictional ploy; (2) that the violation took the essay to a deeper inner chamber, that it deepened and added to what came before it; and (3) that continuing the essay to its "natural" narrative conclusion was in some sense already performed by the voice and sequencing in the essay. In short, I had to decide whether I was being honest with myself as both the persona in and of the essay, and whether I was unduly manipulating the reader for effect.

The inclusion of the break of the narrative was not, in fact, mere effect. The accident certainly happened. Of course, I had worked on the essay many times before that. The reader senses a single narrative experience with an interruption, as though the essay were written in one sitting during which a child happened to be hit by a lorry, but that is the usual narrative experience of reading, be it essay, novel, or poem. I might add that it was a rather desultory experience having an essay I felt was charming, perhaps too charming, rescued as it were by disaster, but it is that sorry fact of the coincidental I tried to inscribe. And the reader, I believe, is pulled up short, as I was.

Whether we want to or not, nonfiction sometimes challenges us to describe what seems so fictive that it would be fictively unbelievable.

Multiple Moments

Megan Lane, Former Student Writer

When I first walked into Michael Bugeja's magazine feature writing workshop, I had no idea what the moment of narration was and I wasn't sure why it was so important. I'm not even sure I knew I was manipulating the moment of narration to heighten the drama of my story when I was writing

"Covering the Rape of a Child." But I understood what I had done by the end of the workshop and realized I could use the moment of narration to create drama or to avoid it. I wanted the readers of "Covering the Rape of a Child" to feel the same kind of awful tension I felt as I sat through the trial of a 32-year-old man accused of assaulting a 13-year-old girl. I wanted readers to feel the sensation of losing control so completely that you begin to question everything you thought you knew up to that point.

In the body of the article, much of the emotion is excluded, but the tension is still present in the opening paragraph where I race down the street away from the courtroom. I had to use multiple moments, moving from the *now* to the *then,* to incorporate interviews with practicing journalists about their experiences covering sensitive topics.

I started the story in the *now:* "I gripped the reporter's pad, as if it might fly away, as if I might throw it at the next passerby. Half-running, I could hardly feel the sidewalk under my feet." It would have been ridiculous and melodramatic to continue writing in the same moment in the body of the piece: "My heart pounded as I picked up the phone to call Pulitzer Prize-winning photographer John Kaplan." So I moved the story to the *then* and wrote in a natural, calm voice, simply quoting Kaplan and other journalists.

In this way, multiple moments can create tension or provide information.

THE NEWSSTAND

Taking a Moment

1. Analyze at least 12 back issues of each of your select publications, targeted in your project files containing active story ideas. Go through each magazine, analyzing time elements and noting:

   - *Literary time.* Which moment of narration (*now, now and then,* or *then*) do editors favor in each specific section of the book (departments, back essays, fillers, columns, features, articles, etc.)?

   - *Grammatical and chronological time.* Which verb tense is the most popular in each piece: past or present? Do you have any examples in the pushed present tense?

   - *Transitional moments.* Which magazine pieces include flashbacks, flashforwards, moment shifts, or multiple moments? Do any of the pieces use combinations?

2. You have been researching each of your target publications. By now, you may have spotted work that resembles one or more of your developing story ideas. If so, you should:

   - Temporarily abandon the story idea, placing it in your Story Idea file.

   - Change the title and theme of the story idea in question, shifting focus enough to interest the editor of your target publication.

   - Consult a directory such as *Writer's Market* for another magazine with a similar audience and analyze back issues to determine whether your final draft is appropriate for this publication.

THE KEYBOARD

Picking Your Moments

1. According to methods outlined earlier in this chapter, envision the proper moment of narration for each idea in your project files. Select a moment close to the action (or *now*) for stories that pivot on drama or tension. Choose a moment far from the action (or *then*) for stories that pivot on commentary or opinion. Pick a moment between both points (or *now and then*) for stories with a beginning, middle, and end requiring a modicum of drama and commentary.

2. Determine whether any ideas in your project files require transitional moments, such as flashbacks, flashforwards, gradual moment shifts, and/or multiple moments of narration. If so, type a note to yourself to include these time elements according to methods outlined in this chapter. Typically, profiles employing a moment far from the action (or *then*) will require flashbacks. Narratives close to the action (told in the *now* moment) may need flashforwards. Essays, features, and articles (in the *now and then* moment) may improve with a moment shift. Stories with distinct sections may be enhanced via multiple moments, especially ones recounting a dramatic experience in one or more sections, and then explaining or commenting on it in others.

3. After you have determined the moment of narration, and any transitional moments for each story idea in your project files, sketch a rough outline for each idea, taking into account:

- *Approach.* Note whether you are writing a personal experience, anecdotal, or informational piece and describe what you hope to convey to the readers (drama or perspective or both) in the beginning, middle, and end of your piece.

- *Content.* Determine what specific events or issues (along with sensory data, interviews, or library research) you intend to treat in the beginning, middle, and end of your piece.

- *Expression of content.* Plan how you intend to depict events or discuss issues (close to, somewhat removed from, or far from the action) in the beginning, middle, and end of your piece.

CHAPTER SEVEN

Viewpoint and Voice

Points of View

Viewpoint and voice rely on and harmonize with each other. Think of them as two parts that snap together into one larger part in the assembly of a magazine work. You have been aligning components all along and have even sketched some rough outlines to imagine your developing story ideas. You might be itching to write, but resist the urge a bit longer. Remember, the goal of this book is to help you envision a manuscript *before* you write it—just like natural-born writers do. You're making a film in the mind so that you can replay it at the keyboard when all the basic story components are in place. And in your film, viewpoint is the camera and voice is the microphone, determining what your readers see and hear.

Voice relies on viewpoint, so you have to decide viewpoint first. If you're planning to appear in your "film" via the first-person pronoun *I,* you will be using a *narrator.* Voice tones will be aspects of your personality—not the source's—even if you are writing a profile about a source's life. The following excerpt, from Dana Gioia's "Meeting Mr. Cheever," employs a narrator (Gioia) who observes the famous author John Cheever through the filter of viewpoint:

> Although Cheever looked almost exactly like his many dust jacket photographs, I was initially surprised by three things about him. First, he was so small. For some reason, probably not unconnected with my mental images of his fictional protagonists, I had expected a magisterially tall Yankee gentleman instead of this slight, almost boyish man who stood only a few inches over five feet. Second, Cheever was the most perfectly poised man I had ever met. Every gesture was so gracefully conceived and executed that he scarcely seemed part

125

of the clumsy everyday world. Even the way he sat still seemed as carefully composed as a professional portrait. Not that his presence was domineering or dramatic; just the opposite was true. His manner was relaxed, understated, and self-assured, but he nevertheless had a style that captivated one's attention the way a great actor can steal a scene on stage without speaking a word. Finally, I was stunned by his voice. Cheever spoke a brand of patrician Massachusetts English which I now suspect he invented, for I have never heard anyone else speak quite like it. Nevertheless, he used this suave, fictional dialect so convincingly that in his mouth it seemed to have the force of ancient authority, as if he were some New England Homer standing at the apex of a long oral tradition.

As you can see, readers view Cheever through the lens of Gioia's eyes. That's viewpoint. As you can hear, the writing contains certain tones: sophisticated, observant, gracious. That's voice, and those tones are aspects of Gioia's personality because he is using a first-person narrator.

A writer can profile John Cheever without using the first person, by employing a third-person *persona,* an "unseen" character who views the world through nobody's eyes in particular (one type of magazine piece) or through a source's eyes (another type of piece). To imagine a persona, think of a storyteller around a campfire. That person uses certain tones—ominous, terse, and descriptive—because he or she is trying to frighten campers. The storyteller might experience plot through no character, simply relating events, or through a main character, usually an individual with whom the campers can relate. (In other words, the main character is *not* the chainsaw murderer but the teenager who witnesses the killings; the teen is called *the viewpoint source.*) The persona's sole purpose is to generate the right voice tones for target listeners. (That's what *persona* means—someone who wears a mask.) As such, the voice tones are aspects of the *storyteller's* personality—not yours and not the viewpoint source's.

In the earlier excerpt from "Meeting Mr. Cheever," Dana Gioia was writing for the literary readers of *The Hudson Review.* Let's rewrite that excerpt using a persona without a viewpoint source for a less sophisticated crowd, to illustrate how persona generates voice:

Cheever looked like the dude on his dust jacket, but minuscule, man. You guess God Xeroxed him smaller. Cheever may be a giant in the lit annals, but boyish up close—barely over five feet—like a jockey without the silk suit. Poised as a jockey, too. He waves at you in the cafeteria, or asks you to pass the salt, and you wonder why he is even *in* a cafeteria or *uses* salt. Dude rises above routine. Dude sits at your table and poses, as if Picasso is due soon to cube a portrait. Cheever's above it all, but ain't uppity. Self-assured maybe. Relaxed, humble. He has style, too. *Panache.* When he speaks, you heed that nasal twang and think black and white flick on HBO: Cary Grant in a Connecticut court.

This persona speaks in a hip, clipped, and awe-struck voice. Those tones are not aspects of the writer's personality. In real life, the implied author might be as sophisticated, observant, or gracious as Dana Gioia in the original excerpt but you do not see the implied author (although you hear him). The implied author simply is inventing a storyteller with whom target readers might feel comfortable.

You might feel comfortable using the first person if you plan on offering opinions in the *then* moment of narration or recounting events in the *now* or doing both in the *now and then*. However, remember that you align story components in magazine journalism according to editorial preferences at your target publication. Editors know their readers better than writers do. In general, mass market magazines such as *New Woman* or *Esquire* use more narrators than personae, especially in columns, because the writing is intimate and personal.

You might use a third-person viewpoint if you are taking a how-to or informational approach. If so, voice tones reflect personality traits of *an invented storyteller aligned with target readers* who views the world through a source's eyes or through nobody's eyes in particular. In general, many trade magazines such as *Writer's Digest* or *Business Week* prefer personae because the writing is service oriented.

Most magazines use content that is a mix of intimate and informational musings. Few editors demand a persona or narrator exclusively. Of course, a lot depends on what section of the book you are writing for, what format you are writing in, and what approach you are taking. For instance, in trade magazines, editors typically prefer personae in opinion and interview pieces and narrators in back-of-the-book personal columns. In mass market magazines, editors usually allow narrators or personae in profiles and articles, but prefer personae in fillers and narrators in anecdotal features. Each magazine will have a different mix. To illustrate, here are three types of viewpoint and tones for three distinct readerships:

1. *Narrator.* In his first attempt at magazine journalism, Dan Horn, now a professional reporter, wrote an anecdotal article in the *then* moment about journalism-student burnout, titled "The Superman Syndrome" for the trade magazine *Quill.* Horn chose the anecdotal approach because he was establishing expertise—he was a student reporter at the time of his submission—and was interviewing friends suffering from burnout. The viewpoint was his. The voice tones (conversational, self-effacing, informed) were aspects of Horn's personality:

> Like many kids who grew up in conservative, middle-class homes, I went to college on my parents' money and became a liberal. Naturally I was attracted to journalism school because of the caped crusader image. I wanted to be one of the superheroes. I wanted to be Bob Woodward. I guess I really wanted to be Robert Redford, but at the time I couldn't distinguish one from the other.

2. *Persona and viewpoint source.* In her first attempt at magazine journalism, student Amy Zaruca targeted *Seventeen* and composed a feature in the *now* moment about teen domestic violence, "Dangerous Games." Zaruca chose a persona and depicted events through a source named Michele so that readers could experience the intensity of a car chase between Michele and her abusive boyfriend Chris. Viewpoint was that of the persona, an unseen character who knew about obsession and abuse. Voice tones (tense, ominous, reportorial) were generated by the storyteller and were not personality traits of the viewpoint source Michele:

> The cars raced through the winding streets of the suburban neighborhood—60, 65, 70 miles per hour—the needle rose on the speedometer. The familiar fear overcame Michele again as she sped to her friend's house to avoid Chris's rage at just about three o'clock on a Tuesday afternoon. *Jessica will help me,* Michele thought to herself. Chris's car tailed hers, not letting her violet-colored Neon— a seventeenth birthday present from her father—out of sight. She swerved into Jessica's driveway and jumped out of her car, barely making it to the front door before Chris screeched to a halt in his car and caught up with her, yanking her by the arm off the porch and screaming at her the whole time. Jessica threatened to call the police as Michele shook uncontrollably, tears streaming down her face. Chris let her go, evidently scared away by Jessica's threat.

3. *Persona and no viewpoint source.* In his service piece in the *then* moment, titled "Give Your Mac an Interface-Lift," Keith Johns didn't need a narrator. Like many trade magazines, his target market, *Mac Home Journal,* tended to shy away from narrated how-to pieces. Neither did Johns need a viewpoint source because he was taking an informational approach. Nonetheless, Johns spoke to readers in a hip, informational, and user-friendly voice. Those are not aspects of Johns's personality. Simply, he employed an unseen storyteller to generate the proper tones for the audience:

> Sure, system 7.5 lets you change the pattern of your desktop, the color and font of the clock, the color of the text highlighter and the color that tints the window borders. You've played around with those a few times, even given the clock a new font and a color to complement your favorite desktop pattern.
>   But so has everyone else. And although your screen looks okay, you're ready for a fresh interface that's uniquely you. Here are some eye-candy shareware products you can acquire off the World Wide Web. Download 'em, drop 'em in your system folder, and give your Mac the interface-lift it needs.

Viewpoint not only generates the right voice for your target audience but it also helps fine-tune the structure of a story. Structure can be a subtle thing. You can view events via the filter of a narrator, for instance, but focus on a theme that relates to a source's truth (typically in profiles). In "Mr. Allen Dewey Spooner," Kelly Cherry employed a narrator to profile her mother's father with a theme of loving memory. Kelly could not have written the profile without a narrator, because the piece is based on her family's history. Because she was also basing her piece in part on her mother's memoir, the mother's truth was paramount. As Cherry tells it, "In the piece presented here, my subversive intent was not to 'characterize' her father as much as it was to illuminate *her* feelings *about* him. Imagining her world is not only a way of returning to it but a way of returning to her, to all those evenings when we all sat around the kitchen table, swapping stories."

Here is the introduction from her profile, grounding the viewpoint and introducing the theme:

> I can barely remember him, but I will never forget him. He was my mother's father. He died when I was seven. He died in Gulfport, Mississippi, at one end of the country, while I was a child in upstate New York at the far other end. We lived in a railway flat in a tenement apartment three flights above a grocery store on a busy, dirty street. My mother typed dissertations for Cornell students at a nickel a page. When she heard the news, she "sat down and typed for forty-eight hours straight," she told me, "just as if my heart had not been broken forever."

Note that Cherry does not say "my grandfather" but "my mother's father." Neither does she quote her mother as if she was privy to all her mother's thoughts. She documents the quotation in the excerpt with the attribution, "she told me."

Viewpoint is seldom omniscient, or all knowing, in magazine journalism. When you choose one viewpoint—your own via a narrator or someone else's via a source—you need to sustain it throughout the entire piece. That creates a modicum of suspense. Knowing what everyone is thinking might seem clever at first, but when you employ more than one viewpoint in a work, readers lose interest in and do not empathize with the concerns of your narrator or viewpoint source.

In this excerpt from "Invictus under Glass" by Amy Hudson, the narrator relates an anecdote from her personal history. Hudson is remembering a visit to an Oklahoma City psychiatrist treating her for anorexia nervosa. Note how the narrator depicts a girl in the waiting room, through a distinct filter, and then has a brief exchange with her—unable to access the girl's mind or motive:

> One afternoon I stood in the office waiting for my mother to schedule the next appointment with my Oklahoma City psychiatrist; considering that I was undergoing therapy for my folks' benefit, not mine, I let them handle the particulars. A girl, about my age, sat next to me in the lobby, dressed in surgical scrubs, like I often wore because they were loose-fitting. Her hair was in a French braid, the style I adopted when my hair got so dry that it was unmanageable. She wore running shoes. She looked like a normal-weight version of me on any given day. She looked up and spoke.

> "How much do you weigh?"
>
> I was startled. "Excuse me?"
>
> She repeated the question slowly, as if speaking to a mildly retarded child.
>
> I told her 90 pounds, padding it by 15 or so.
>
> "I used to weigh less than you," she said, "but I started gaining and now I can't stop." She was talking fast, in a secretive voice, but urgent. "I wish I could get back down. I keep trying, but I can't stop gaining. I just can't."
>
> What a weird girl, I thought.

In this case, readers understand what the narrator doesn't at this stage in the waiting room. Hudson is in denial, conversing with an anorexic girl but overlooking symptoms that both share. When the narrator states "What a weird girl," readers well up with compassion, comprehending the severity of the narrator's illness.

Now let's rewrite the exchange with multiple viewpoints, tapping into both the narrator's and the girl's heads:

> "How much do you weigh?" the girl asked, knowing I was anorexic. She would observe each patient in the room and ponder our lives. Her mind was a video that she could rewind or fast forward at will.
>
> I was startled. "Excuse me?"
>
> She repeated the question slowly, as if speaking to a mildly retarded child. She knew what phase of the disease I was in: *denial.* And she was toying with me the same way she toyed with her mother at the kitchen table. Once her mother begged her to eat turkey at Thanksgiving, and the girl spoke in a singsong voice, asking, "Have you stepped on a scale recently, Mother?" Now the girl was asking me about scales. "How much do you weigh?" she inquired again.
>
> I told her 90 pounds, padding it by 15 or so.
>
> "I used to weigh less than you," she said, "but I started gaining and now I can't stop." She was talking fast, in a secretive voice, but urgent—thinking about how she needed to cut back on her food intake as soon as she got home. "I wish I could get back down," she said. "I keep trying, but I can't stop gaining. I just can't."
>
> What a weird girl, I thought.

What's weird is how the narrator knows all about the girl's life when she has yet to learn her name. And how, exactly, does she have access to the girl's thoughts, especially if she is a stranger? True, the narrator might have gotten to know the girl later. True, the girl could have shared a few anecdotes which, curiously, the writer omitted from the manuscript. But the point is, readers no longer empathize with the narrator. The suspense of Hudson's original version is lost—a mistake called a *viewpoint lapse,* which occurs when the following criteria exist:

1. The narrator has mysterious access into another person's mind (as in the preceding Hudson example).

2. The first-person narrator mode changes into a third-person persona mode, or vice versa, simply to solve a writing problem. (Say you are writing about how you were arrested for drunk driving, using a moment close to the action. A cop asks you to get out of the car and, when you do, you pass out. Oops. What now? So you switch from the narrator mode to the persona mode, using a storyteller and viewing events from the cop's perspective: "The trooper gazed at my crumpled gin-soaked body and wondered why he ever joined the state patrol." This writing problem has nothing to do with viewpoint; you resolve it via chronological time, using a space or asterisk break and continuing with the narrator in jail: "I woke up in a cell, smelling of gin. Later, a deputy told me I had crumpled in a heap when the trooper ordered me out of the car.")

3. The persona switches from one viewpoint source to another, again to solve a writing problem. (Say you are writing about crack from the viewpoint of a girl named Mindy who dies two-thirds into the story in front of best friend Beth in the emergency room. You can't possess Beth's body because Mindy overdosed: "Mindy closed her eyes, seemingly entering a tunnel instead of a crack house, spiraling toward the Light in an aura of forgiveness. Beth looked at Mindy on the gurney and wondered whether to call her mother." A writing problem like this has to do with chronological, literary, and transitional time elements. You have to wrap up your piece with Mindy in the forgiving light, because the *now* moment cannot continue the time line without violating viewpoint, and flashforward while sustaining viewpoint: "Mindy would never learn of the call Beth placed to her mother, or hear her mother's gasp and wail, although both women would also forgive Mindy in the months following her death.")

As long as you sustain viewpoint, you can use a persona to see the world through your source's eyes. You don't have to remind readers that the writing is based on an anecdote garnered during an interview session in somebody's living room. (You are documenting truth for magazine readers, not recording facts for newspaper ones.) Viewpoint is a powerful writing tool. It can place the audience on the spot in someone else's shoes in an intense or dramatic situation, as Audrey Chapman does in her exposé "And Justice for All?" Here is her introduction, depicting the aftermath of chemical warfare in the Gulf War:

> At first they saw one, in the middle of the road, dead. Perhaps it was shot. Perhaps it just died. But then they saw more.

As Marine Sgt. David McGee and his partner maneuvered their Humvee over the silky mass of Saudi Arabia's desert, they didn't think much of the dead camel.

It was war, after all. But as they plowed their vehicle through the sand and climbed up and over a dune, a patchwork quilt of death lay before them, made up of hundreds of dead camels. The herd's migration across the desert was interrupted by something—something that caused them to drop, one by one, hitting the sand with a sequence of thuds that continued for minutes.

This horrific sight was something their commanding officers had warned them about. Something that signified chemical warfare. They radioed communication.

Ignore it, they were told of the warning they came across. *Pile them up and start burying them.*

With their bare hands, they grabbed the animals' thick, smelly coats and pulled them, one after the other, into a pile. As sweat poured down their skin in the 120-degree heat, they followed orders: *Examine them for gunshot wounds.*

They turned the camels over, haunted by the stunned expressions in their wide-open eyes, and examined their skulls, their backs, their bellies, their chests. There were no bloody masses, only dead flies that rained off the camels' coats onto their feet.

When the rear unit caught up to them, they were ordered to stop. Bulldozers were called in. The animals were plowed into a big pile. Some were buried. Others were burned. . . .

That introduction was based on an interview that Chapman conducted with Gulf War veteran David McGee. For more information about her interview and the power of memorable anecdotes, see Chapman's "Capturing Viewpoint" in The Craft Shop.

Here are general guidelines summarizing viewpoint:

- Use a narrator if your own experience or expertise will enhance the work or if you are taking a personal experience or anecdotal approach. Remember, voice tones will be aspects of *your* personality and must also suit the topic, occasion, theme, moment, and truth of your work.
- Use a persona without a viewpoint source if you are writing a news filler or a how-to/service piece or are taking an informational approach. Voice tones are aspects of the storyteller's personality who speaks the lingo and knows the jargon of the target publication.
- Use a persona with a viewpoint source if you are recounting an extraordinary event or dramatic experience from his or her life or if commenting on such an event or experience. Voice tones are aspects of the storyteller's personality—aligned with the lingo or jargon of the target publication—but also distinct from aspects of the source's personality. In other words, your unseen storyteller should not sound like your source but should see the world through the source's eyes, from start to finish, without any lapses.

Tones of Voice

Once you know the right viewpoint for your piece, voice should come easily and naturally. You don't have to labor for years to discover your voice; you have one. Each day you speak to people in different settings and situations about sensitive or significant topics.

You arrive at work in the morning only to find the boss by your desk, asking when you will finish your latest report. "I'll have it to you by noon. I have to check a few sources—some of them may not be reliable—and print it out," you say in an efficient, professional voice. But your boss is not impressed. "When I hired you," he replies, "I told you that time is money, but you still don't seem to get it." He wants the report by 10 A.M. You nod and say, "I'll get started right away."

At lunch, you eat with your best friend in the cafeteria. "My boss is a snake," you tell her in a candid, frustrated voice. "No matter how hard I try to meet deadlines, or what I do to impress him, he complains. You won't believe what he said to me this morning. 'You still don't seem to get it.' He waltzed up to my desk, sneered at me, and quipped, 'When I hired you, I told you that time is money.' Can you believe that? This guy rushed my report so I didn't have enough time to do a fact-check. If he finds a mistake, he'll belittle me. Or fire me."

You leave the office promptly at 5 P.M., eager to get home. Your bad day follows you. You are driving in your car and see the flashing lights of a state trooper. She pulls you over and saunters to your car, asking to see license and registration. "Officer," you whine, "I was driving behind an 18-wheeler and couldn't see the road so I tried to pass him. The rig sped up. And I did pass him on that hill a few miles back and, well, just *forgot* to slow down," you say in a respectful, reportorial voice. The trooper appreciates the truth and gives you a warning rather than a ticket.

Each time you switch the setting and the situation, you naturally hone your voice to suit your topic, occasion, theme, moment of narration, truth, and viewpoint. In the office, confronted by a boss, you sound efficient and professional. That's a natural voice, given the setting. Your topic is a report; your occasion, a deadline; your theme, accuracy; your moment, *then* (to state your case); your epiphany, *Accuracy takes time in the short term but saves time in the long term*—all expressed via your viewpoint. Your boss has an entirely different viewpoint and truth—*Time is money!*—and speaks to you in an authoritative, angry tone that may be permissible in the office but actionable as harassment at the mall. In the cafeteria, your topic is the boss; your occasion, lunch with a best friend; your theme, dissatisfaction; your moment, *now and then* (to comment on his actions); your epiphany, *Bosses create problems and then blame you for them*—again, told via your viewpoint in a candid, frustrated voice. Speak that way to the state trooper, and she'll write you a whopping ticket. So you used a respectful, reportorial voice to express your viewpoint. Your topic is speeding; your occasion, a speeding ticket; your theme, innocence; your moment, *now* (to describe action); and your truth universal: *Break the law, ask for a break, and get it.*

Voice is style. Voice is smart. Voice is natural. It has attitude. It marks you as a writer who can target readers and not only know their truths but also speak their truths as friends, advisers, teachers, peers, colleagues—whatever the magazine concept requires. You have requirements, too. Before you write a word of your piece, you have to know:

- ■ *The reader.* Ask yourself: To whom am I speaking? What is my relationship with the reader—friend, adviser, teacher, peer, colleague? How should I speak to that person, given my topic, occasion, theme, and moment of narration? What would the person want to learn from me? Would the person rather learn it from someone else—a source with more experience or expertise?
- ■ *The situation.* Ask yourself: What problem, issue, motive, incident, or person sparks my conversation with the reader? Would the reader like me to resolve the problem, explain the issue, imply or peg the motive, describe the incident, or introduce the person from my viewpoint or someone else's?
- ■ *The implied setting.* Ask yourself: Where would such a conversation take place? Outdoors? In the office? On a subway? At a kitchen table?

The *implied* setting is not real, of course. Don't confuse it with the real setting (you in the den at the keyboard in your pajamas or sweats, needing a bath and spilling coffee on your notebook). Don't confuse it with the source setting, either. You may interview a psychiatrist at her office, but the office setting—professional, efficient—might not generate the appropriate voice for your work. Neither should you ever refer to the implied setting. It's imaginary—a device to generate the right voice, reminding you how natural writing can be. After all, you already know how to speak outdoors or in an office or on a subway or at the kitchen table as a friend, adviser, teacher, peer, or colleague about problem, issue, motive, or person.

This is a gem of an epiphany for most beginning writers. They realize that writing is not blood, sweat, or tears—struggling for and earning each precious word of a manuscript, waiting years to discover you have or lack "style"—but natural human communication. It just occurs on paper or in cyberspace. Speech flows freely as the First Amendment. You don't have to struggle learning the rules of lead writing, the grade levels of diction, or the forms and formulas for magazine features. You just have to envision your work at the keyboard the way the pros do.

But if you don't know the reader, the situation, or the implied setting, you can rewrite and polish your prose umpteen times with the same result:

You are still going to be rejected. Editors will tell you that the most common errors in manuscripts concern voice. Tones are wrong for the target audience. Tones are inappropriate, given the topic, occasion, theme, truth, and viewpoint. Tones lapse when presenting research or change so often and abruptly that the author seems to be suffering from multiple personality disorder.

In her first draft, former magazine student Laura Churchill did not consider the audience, situation, or implied setting when writing about friendship at the yearbook office of Ohio University. Her feature tells about befriending a student journalist, Amy, and traveling with her on a class trip to Europe. Following are three excerpts from the introduction, body, and ending of her untitled piece, numbered here so that you can compare them later with her revisions:

[1] The first time I met Amy I didn't know her. I knew her credentials. I met her when she came to the Athena Yearbook office to drop off her application for copy editor. The job I wanted. Sherry, the editor in chief, told me not to look at the applications, but I looked anyway. Amy had more experience than I did. She was a copy editor for *The Post* and *Keeping Touch,* the College of Communication's alumni magazine. I was doomed. She would be the Athena's next copy editor. What would I do?

[2] The two most important characteristics of a friendship are intimacy and trust. These factors are used to judge the closeness of a friendship. According to Altman and Taylor in *Social Penetration: The Development of Interpersonal Relations,* "Our closest or best friends tend to be those whom we trust implicitly, and to whom we reveal most of ourselves."

[3] This is where I lost faith in Amy. In London I felt she no longer considered our relationship important. But by ignoring her, I showed her I had no faith in our friendship. As a result, she thought I no longer considered our friendship important. My lack of trust and commitment undermined our relationship. Even though we left London as friends, we would have to rebuild the trust we once had. That was the hard part.

The voice problems here should be obvious. The introduction is wordy, clipped, and whiny. The author fails to ground her topic, assuming that readers know all about Ohio University publications. The voice also lapses as soon as it tries to share research, changing from wordy, clipped, and whiny to authoritative. The ending reverts to the original voice, but lacks take-away value. Worse, the author is employing a moment far from any action, emphasizing comment and perspective and putting the focus on her ineffective voice.

Laura Churchill learned about these shortcomings during a critique session in a magazine workshop. Highly motivated, she wanted to generate an appropriate voice by envisioning readers (high school yearbookers), the situation (maintaining friendships in a stressful work environment), and the implied setting (the newsroom after hours). Knowing these factors, she grounded her introduction and distinguished topic from theme. She depicted friendship in the newsroom instead of citing it from a book but still quoted a brochure without suffering a research-related voice lapse. She moved the moment from the *then* to the *now and then* to depict an act of friendship in her ending epiphany. Finally, she created a title ("Yearbooks and Friendships") to herald her topic and theme and a subtitle ("They Can Last a Lifetime") to foreshadow her epiphany. The following revised excerpts are from the same sections of her original draft, numbered again so you can compare them:

[1] The *Athena* Yearbook offices at Ohio University appear ordinary. We have an office, a workroom and a darkroom. We use computers to process all of our copy and layouts. The photographers shoot, process and print all the film. Our thirty-six staff members work to complete 184 pages of the *Athena* as it follows the life of students. Coverage includes campus, community, state, national and international events; sports; academics; seniors; organizations and Greeks. The *Athena* records Ohio University for posterity. In addition, it makes an impact on every staff member. The *Athena* is part of who I am and what I do—it has my heart. So much of what is important in my life has happened there. It is the place I learned how to make something last a lifetime. One was a yearbook, the other a friendship.

[2] Our fun continued in and out of workshop sessions. We learned how to put together a "complete, contemporary, appealing" yearbook. (At least that's what the brochure told us we'd learn.) More importantly Amy and I became friends. She asked me a lot of questions about the *Athena*. She wanted to know exactly what we did and how we did it. It amazed me how much she valued my opinion. This helped me realize that we both wanted the same thing—for the *Athena* to be a great yearbook.

[3] My chance [to rekindle trust] came sooner than I thought. After I got off the phone with my editor Sherry, I got ready for dinner with my cousin Stephanie, her husband Mike and their 3-month-old baby, Rachel. They had driven up from New Orleans to visit family. I was excited, since I'd never seen Rachel. Everyone at the *Athena* knew how much I wanted to see the baby. Amy even mentioned she'd like to see her.

Before we went to dinner I asked Stephanie and Mike if they would mind going to the *Athena* to meet Amy. I wanted to share my happiness with her.

Stephanie, Mike, Rachel and I visited the *Athena* and surprised her. Amy loved holding little Rachel in the otherwise barren newsroom, proving that journalism isn't all facts . . . but feelings, too.

I learned many important lessons at the yearbook office. How to edit. How to design. How to make and *keep* friendships.

This informed, descriptive, and compassionate voice was appropriate for the publication that Churchill had targeted: *Scholastic Editor.* Churchill struggled in the first draft, earning each word with no prospect of a sale to a magazine. Her rewrite might seem more sophisticated or complex, but it was *natural* and easier to write once she focused on the issue of friendship at the workplace and imagined speaking to high school yearbookers after hours in the implied setting of a newsroom.

Voice is the easiest route to publication—not structure, not formula, not even language usage. What earns an A in a Freshman English Composition class earns a rejection in *English Journal.* You might spell every word correctly, use proper grammar and punctuation, follow essay format, and heed the *MLA Handbook* style (rather than your own), but that's not going to impress the editor, as magazine student Heidi Reddert learned in an essay titled like an academic paper: "Fast Forward: My Introduction to College Dating." Here is her introduction:

> A few months ago I began experiencing college life as a junior. Although my freshman and sophomore year I lived in the dorms, went to bars, and hung out with friends like everyone else, I excluded myself from one of the most educating, exciting, and frustrating aspects of college life: dating.

The ho-hum voice here may be appropriate in the classroom but not in a teen magazine, where Reddert had hoped to place her piece. Like Laura Churchill, Reddert had to endure a tough critique session. Afterward, she realized that good writing contains correct spelling, grammar, punctuation, syntax, structure, consistent style, and something else—a relationship with the reader. Appreciating that relationship can help you hone voice. Reddert, a busy public relations major, was writing for magazines *without reading magazines*—an all-too-common beginner's problem. So she headed for the newsstand (as you will do later) and revised and retitled her piece, "Shackin'," describing the campus craze of sleeping with a date but not necessarily having sex. Here is Reddert's jazzy rewrite:

> I heard the word "shacking" from a girlfriend who went to college a year before me. Nikki told me that her sorority sister at the University of Kentucky "shacked." Translation: She spent the night with a guy. An innocent senior in high school, I thought, "What kind of *sorority* is she in?"

Reddert sustains her conversational, innocent, witty voice throughout her column-length piece. She learned valuable lessons about voice and, within a few months, knew so much about freelance writing that she was able to intern at F&W Publications, a magazine corporation in Cincinnati. As she tells it:

Mastering voice in writing is a key factor in the success of your essay, feature, or article. I learned this while trying to write a column about college dating for a magazine feature writing class.

My intentions were to write a somewhat comical piece illustrating the absurdity of "shacking," a practice many college students equate with dating. I wanted my audience (college students) to laugh at my shacking experiences and reflect on their own. But I knew I had a problem with my first draft when my classmates seemed concerned that I was advocating one-night stands—the exact opposite of my original purpose! After careful analysis and some constructive criticism, I realized that the column lacked a uniform, satirical voice needed to convey the truth. My voice fluctuated from serious to sarcastic, confusing my audience and distorting my message.

To rescue the piece, I read other magazine articles that had a humorous, slightly sarcastic tone, learning how successful writers maintain voice. Then I set out to rewrite the article as if I were recounting my dating experiences to an intimate friend. By visualizing this "conversation," as I was writing, I was able to keep my thoughts focused and my voice consistent.

The best way to learn about voice is to analyze it in your target publication. (You'll be doing that at The Newsstand.) And of course, there are as many tones in magazine journalism as there are in real life, because magazines reflect life and relationships. As in life, some tones of voice in magazines are more common than others. Here are 12 for you to consider:

1. *Contemplative*. The contemplative voice suggests that the writer has mulled over material in a story. This contemplative passage is from Bill Brohaugh's column, "Talking to the River," originally published in *Writer's Digest:*

> That night I close my eyes in bed and see quicksilver geology in front of me. All the rocks I picked up, pried up, dug up, then chunked to the other side of the stream: I see images of all those rocks piled together, swirling, rearranging themselves, stifling then creating gnawing eddies of water. Such imaging is familiar to me. After a few hours playing computer games, I'll close my eyes and watch aliens and their spaceships exploring my mental darkness and asking me why I killed the electron streams that gave them life. After I've completed a long night drive, closing my eyes launches a flow of white lines stabbing me in the left shoulder.

2. *Conversational*. The conversational voice suggests that the reader and writer are talking to each other as friends. This chatty passage is from Bethany Matsko's "it happened to me" column in *Sassy:*

> Friends and relatives tried to convince my parents to give me up to an older, more responsible couple who could raise me in a soft and comfy atmosphere. But they didn't listen. They got married in March 1972 in a courthouse. Mom

wore an orange and blue flowered polyester dress, which she gave away about eight years later. (I'm still mad at her for that.) Dad wore a dark suit and platform shoes. I was born five months later in Cleveland, and they named me after a character on a soap opera my mom watched.

3. *Descriptive.* The descriptive voice conveys sensory data or depicts a setting or scene. In this excerpt from "Farrah Fawcett Up Close," Carol Muske Dukes profiles the celebrity for *House and Garden,* describing the room where the interview is taking place:

> The room we're sitting in, done in alternating shades of creamy white, sandy brown, and darker earth tones (except for the jewel box Warhol), reflects Farrah's love of eloquent restraint: clean lines, simple statements. A delicately curving Japanese roof tile reclines on a shelf-like maverick haiku; there is a Byzantine crucifix on a table, an El Grecoesque bust by the fire.

4. *Experienced.* The experienced voice suggests that the writer knows the topic because he or she has lived or survived it. In this excerpt from "The Broken Child" in *New Woman,* Catherine Johnson relates how it feels to be the mother of an autistic son:

> And autism is not a particularly lovable condition. With autism you have a child who is spinning and flapping and hooting away at the top of his lungs; a child making eye contact only to demand food; an enraged child biting and scratching his parents or himself; a child whose idea of play is to pull out a pitcher of juice from the refrigerator and dump it out on the living room carpet. It's the bottle of shampoo dumped on the sofa; the bucket of green paint dumped in the hot tub. It is hundreds of dollars spent each month replacing and repairing the latest toll of household destruction.

5. *Informative.* The informative voice is meant to serve the audience, providing facts, advice, or instruction. In this informative passage about sugar consumption from "Do You Really Want to Eat This?" in *Vegetarian Times,* Karin Horgan Sullivan shares research without a voice lapse:

> Somewhere along the way, though, this inborn preference becomes an out-of-control habit for a lot of folks, including me. Seems like the inner child just won't let go. According to a 1986 report from the U.S. Food and Drug Administration's Sugars Task Force, a panel convened to interpret the scientific literature on the health effects of sugar; sugar consumption is at a high. In the United States, the average per-capita intake of added sugars (as opposed to naturally occurring sugar, such as that in fruit) is 53 grams per day—which equals 48 pounds per year—or 11 percent of daily caloric intake. Now, admittedly, some of us are making up for others who eat only a fraction of that average, but the fact remains that as a whole, Americans eat an awful lot of sugar. Why do we have such a desire to belly up to the sugar bowl?

6. *Informed.* The informed voice establishes an authority base and suggests that the writer can be trusted because he or she has done meticulous research. The goal, however, is not to serve readers via research, as Karin Horgan Sullivan does in the previous item. In this informed passage, Ursula Obst chronicles the life of a bag lady in "Anna's Tangled Destiny," published in *New York Woman:*

> Born May 27, 1923, Anna was the youngest (her sister Lesia was seven years older, her brother Stanislaw, now deceased, eleven) in a Catholic family that had endured many hardships. From the time Anna was three, when her father, Jan, a train conductor, died, the family had lived on his small pension and on what Marianna, her mother, could eke out of a hectare of land behind the small house they owned in Grodzisk (a town located about fifty kilometers from the city of Poznan). The house on Polwiejska street, number 4, near the railroad, was modest. Stuccoed gray like many country houses, it contained only two rooms, one in front and one in back, with a shed added on for a kitchen and an outhouse in the yard.

7. *Introspective.* The introspective voice suggests that the writer is looking inward for deep truths. In this excerpt from her column "Where You'll Find Me" in *Mirabella,* Molly Peacock reflects on how she felt in her grandmother's garden:

> A Buddhist might call it mindfulness. A Quaker might call it connecting with the light inside you. To be able to look an orange poppy in its chartreuse eye and simply be doing nothing other than looking at that blowzy-headed flower, feeling only one experience without competing subsidiary ones, is my idea of grace. To be fully inside the looking moment is to be fully in your true self, not the one you have created for others' demands. This grace is a kind of blooming.

8. *Observant.* The observant voice is similar to the descriptive voice but related again to the authority base, leaving readers with the impression that nothing escapes the keen eye of the writer. In his excerpt from "Anna's Tangled Destiny" in *New York Woman,* Ursula Obst remembers her first encounter with bag lady Anna Podobna:

> I could see the network of bluish veins through the skin of her bony hands. Her arms were twigs. Above the neckline of her blouse, the collar bones stuck out sharply. Her gray hair was swept back neatly and coiled at the back of her head. Her face was pale and drawn—eye sockets defined by dark circles, prominent cheekbones, concave cheeks, flesh collapsing into a toothless mouth. The corners of her lips frequently curled into a half-smile as she talked, responding with shy courtesy to my polite remarks, while her eyes studied me with intense interest.

9. *Plaintive.* The plaintive voice, perhaps the most difficult of tones, is a combination of descriptive and introspective (with an overlay of resignation or desire). This plaintive passage appears in Patricia Westfall's "An American Dream" in *Esquire:*

> One spring, our second spring on the farm, we bought two thousand tree seedlings to fill in our woods and recruited a small army of friends to help us. We began work on planting day, all of us chatting, but as the rhythm of the work took hold of each person he fell silent. Soon the only sound was a thumping as we closed each planting slit. I found myself working alone as again and again I sank a shovel, rocked it, slipped in a seedling, closed the slit. It took only seconds per seedling, but I did it over and over and over. The rhythm of fixing slits for trees set my thoughts wandering for a time. Then the rhythm emptied my mind entirely so there was only the work of it, so simple, but over and over and over. Then in the rhythm I began seeing the ground. There were ferns curled in whorls, wild flowers emerging, tiny may-apples, miniature goldenrod, tiny Virginia creeper—hundreds of things I seemed able to see only when they were large and unavoidably evident. I stopped work to look, the ground became invisible again, still late-winter brown. But if I kept the rhythm going, I saw unmerged things in their April beginnings. This had become our woods; we owned it, walked it, cut firewood from it, made payments on it, fixed fences around it, lived by it; how little of it we saw. That night neither aspirin nor brandy would relieve the soreness I felt from planting, but neither would the soreness cloud the pleasant clarity planting our woods had brought me. This is the only moment of vision I can claim here, though. Because vision was so rare, Jeff and I rarely discussed sights, but we found words for sounds.

10. *Reportorial.* The reportorial voice suggests that the writer is covering an event from a distinct viewpoint (unlike the objective viewpoint of newspapers). In this passage from "Sister Soldiers" in *The New Republic,* Christina Hoff Sommers covers a Women's Studies conference and reports about happenings from a skeptical viewpoint:

> Eleanor Smeal, the former president of NOW, was scheduled to be the first speaker on the NWSA "Empowerment Panel," but her plane had been held up in Memphis. To pass the time, we were introduced to an array of panelists who were touted as being experienced in conflict resolution. One woman was introduced as a member of the Mohawk nation who "facilitates anti-bias training." Another who had training as a holistic health practitioner, headed workshops that "creatively optimize human capacity."

11. *Self-Effacing.* The self-effacing voice is an excellent tone to evoke humor, poking fun at one's self, as George Plimpton does in this excerpt from "Bonding with the Grateful Dead" in *Esquire:*

Years ago, practicing participatory journalism, I made a halfhearted attempt to join a rock group as a tambourine thumper or whatever to get a brief sense of what that world was about: the travel, the fans, what it was like to gyrate on the stage with a sea of faces out front . . . Three Dog Night, Led Zeppelin, the Rolling Stones. The Grateful Dead—Jerry Garcia, Bob Weir, Pigpen, et al.—were on the list. None of them had been anxious to take on a part-time tambourine player. Perhaps it was just as well.

I remembered that one of the Dead, in the clarity of an overdose, had seen great lobster claws in the sky and pterodactyls in the garden. I went on to try other professions.

12. **Sophisticated.** The sophisticated voice suggests that the writer is educated in the arts, sciences, and/or humanities. In this passage from "Meeting Mr. Cheever" in *The Hudson Review,* appropriately set at a university, Dana Gioia describes and comments on a reading by the late literary icon John Cheever:

John appeared to improvise his program, but actually his first two selections that evening were a set program from which I never subsequently heard him depart. He began with "The Death of Justina," one of his best but least celebrated stories, followed by "The Swimmer" (introduced with anecdotes about its filming in Hollywood), and ended with a brief sketch he called "The Death of the Short Story" (it was actually the conclusion to "A Miscellany of Characters That Will Not Appear") which suffered in comparison with its two bewitching predecessors.

One or more of the preceding voice tones may be appropriate for your developing story ideas, depending on your topic, occasion, theme, moment, viewpoint, and truth. You are in the process of aligning these basic elements so that you can envision your work before you write it. In The Craft Shop, you'll find more information about viewpoint and voice. You'll discover more viewpoints and voices at The Newsstand and you will enhance your story ideas with viewpoint and voice at The Keyboard.

THE CRAFT SHOP

Capturing Viewpoint

Audrey Chapman, Senior Editor, *Cleveland Magazine*

Some of the most compelling magazine writing occurs when a writer draws the reader into the heart and mind and emotions of a person via viewpoint. Anecdotes can trigger a crucial memory during an interview. A memory like this often defines a piece; it carries the reader from paragraph to paragraph through to the end of the story and remains. Memories like these speak to the reader; they reach out and grab him and may never let go. Memories like these make your piece stand out among many. They make your story have impact. Most of all, they make your story *memorable.*

But anecdotes are rarely handed to you. A writer must be aware of their importance and must search for them as he interviews. When he hears it he will know, and from there, he must shape it through questions, pulling the thoughts and feelings and memories out of the person who experienced it.

In "And Justice For All?" a piece I wrote about Gulf War Syndrome for *Cleveland Magazine* in August 1995, I distinctly remember hearing David McGee—a soft-spoken, 27-year-old ex-Marine who had become seriously ill after the war—simply, quietly, casually mention something that was so alarming it caused me to gasp.

"And then," he plainly said when describing a journey he took with another soldier, "we saw a herd of dead camels."

Based on my research, I knew how important this was. Dead animals within the reach of Saddam Hussein were not simply "dead animals." They were possible signs of chemical warfare, signs our soldiers were told to watch for in the Gulf.

A man of few words, David was not an eloquent speaker. But he was patient and kind and very, very honest. I needed to tap into his memories of the incident so I could paint a picture of his thoughts in my story. I needed to see what he saw, to feel what he felt. In short, I needed his viewpoint.

What thoughts came to your mind when you saw the first camel? What did you think it died of? What did you think when you saw more? Were you scared? About how many camels were there? What did the scene look like? What did you and the soldier say to each other at that moment? Did you want to turn and run? When you followed orders and checked the camels for gunshot wounds, where did you look? Were the camels heavy? Did they smell? Were their eyes opened or closed? Were their bodies stiff? Were there any dead flies or insects on the camels? What did your commanding officer think killed the camels? Did you believe him?

David answered each question, providing me with the color and detail I needed to put the reader in the heat of the desert, on top of that dune, next to those camels. Research was of utmost importance at this time. Had I not prepared the way I did, I would not have known, for example, to ask about the flies. Chemical warfare not only kills animals; it kills the insects on the animals as well. David had not only noticed the flies, he actually remembered watching them tumble to the ground on that hot, dreaded day. This grisly memory enabled me to write the anecdote's most gruesome yet impactful detail.

Through this anecdote, I was also able to demonstrate the kind of soldier David McGee was. He *believed* his commanding officer's explanation of why the camels died. No matter which way I asked, no matter how much I pushed, the answer was always the same. It was important to illustrate David McGee's faith in his government and devotion to his country. But the anecdote also provided exactly what I needed to open my story. This perfect yet haunting image suggested something wasn't right in the desert—something that killed those camels and flies may have caused 70,000 veterans to become ill.

It's tough to forget that patchwork quilt of death. This is the power of capturing an anecdote, along with a source's viewpoint.

Keying Voice

Cathy Twining, Former Student Writer

When I wrote the first draft of my article, "First-Love Breakups," I made a typical beginning voice mistake. It is too easy to fall right into the "just the facts, ma'am" mentality. In my case, I knew better, but my compulsive journalistic personality can make me put too much focus on getting down the facts. This resulted in a dry, reportlike and boring voice:

> The death of a loved one is a well-known and well-documented loss. But little attention is given to the loss felt by young adults after the break-up of a long-term relationship. Yet second only to the death of a loved one, the end of a romantic relationship is the most frequently occurring loss reported by young adults. Seventy-four percent of young adults who experienced a break-up reported feelings of depression that are intensified by the closeness and length of a relationship. Thus, although it is unrecognized, the loss of a romantic relationship and the resulting feelings of depression are an unfortunate and significant part of young adult life.

In the second draft, I tried to make my voice more personal and friendly. I knew I had some important information to share with my target audience, *Mademoiselle*. I needed to tone down my voice but also maintain my authority. It wasn't as hard to do as it sounds, because I just followed Michael Bugeja's advice. I tried to remember the breakups that I had been through and how they made me feel. I tried to filter this empathy and emotion through my voice as if I were talking to a friend (magazine reader) in the same situation. Yet I also had to remain detached from the subject, because my article had no real viewpoint. Here's how the revision sounds:

> You've just broken up with your boyfriend of five years. Barely alert, you drag yourself to work, knowing that your boss won't understand that all you want to do is collapse on the nearest couch and cry. Your well-meaning mother calls to check on you and tries to cheer you up by saying, "You can do better. Your

father and I never really liked him anyway." But your best friend is the clincher. She shows up after work with a pint of your favorite flavor of Hagen Daas, complete with two *really* big spoons, and patiently listens while you describe in detail, every time you and *he* ate Hagen Daas.

This change in voice came almost subconsciously. It is really important to read as many magazine articles, poems, and books as you can. My voice change was greatly influenced by the writing of Diane Ackerman [whose writing is included in this book]. I had been reading her wonderful book, *A Natural History of the Senses* (Random House), for a poetry class. Diane Ackerman has the ability to take complicated subjects and put them into a context that not only helps you understand but also lets you see the world in a new, more poetic way. So when I was writing my second draft, I kept her style in the back of my mind, and the result is a voice that is much more friendly, open, and empathetic.

T H E   N E W S S T A N D

Preferred Viewpoints, Predominant Voices

1. At the library, analyze the most recent issue of your target publications for each developing story in your project file. Consider all items (columns, features, and articles) in each target magazine. On a sheet of paper, note the approach (personal experience, anecdotal, informational) of the column, feature, or article. Also note the viewpoint for each item (narrator, persona with viewpoint, persona with no viewpoint). For each magazine, analyze the data to determine:

   - The preferred viewpoint for columns, features, and articles

   - The preferred viewpoint for personal experience, anecdotal, and informational approaches

2. Analyze the tones in each of the columns, features, and articles for each target publication in your project file. Look for at least three tones for each piece and assign an adjective to identify them. Circle such tones as *descriptive* or *conversational* or *informational* that recur repeatedly in a magazine. Then, for each target publication, determine:

   - The predominant tones for columns, features, and articles

   - The predominant tones for personal experience, anecdotal, and informational approaches

T H E　K E Y B O A R D

Pinpointing Your Viewpoint and Voice

1. Review the data from the Preferred Viewpoints, Predominant Voices assignments at The Newsstand. In each of your project files, revise your outline to include the preferred viewpoint for each item (column, feature, article) and approach (personal experience, anecdotal, informational). Typically, you will use:

   - A narrator if your own experience or expertise will enhance the work or if you are taking a personal experience or anecdotal approach

   - A persona without a viewpoint source if you are writing a news filler or a how-to/service piece or are taking an informational approach

   - A persona with a viewpoint source if you are recounting an extraordinary event or dramatic experience from his or her life or if commenting on such an event or experience

   As a final check, write a paragraph introducing your topic/occasion and theme to target readers, using each of the viewpoint options. Choose the viewpoint that best serves your topic, theme, occasion, moment, and truth.

2. Review the data from the Preferred Viewpoints, Predominant Voices assignments at The Newsstand. In each of your project files, revise your outline to include one predominant tone that matches your item (column, feature, article) and approach (personal experience, anecdotal, informational). Determine your two remaining voice tones by:

   - Answering questions about the reader (To whom I speaking? What is my relationship with the reader—friend, adviser, teacher, peer, colleague? How should I speak to that person, given my topic, occasion, theme, and moment of narration?)

   - Pegging the implied setting (Where would such a conversation take place? Outdoors? In the office? On a subway? At a kitchen table?)

   - Choosing one of the common tones discussed earlier in this chapter, as long as it harmonizes with your topic, occasion, theme, moment, and truth

3. Using the preferred viewpoint (from item 1), rewrite your introduction for each of your developing story ideas, enhancing the voice with your three select tones (from item 2).

Endings

Closed and Open Endings

The ending of a magazine work may seem easy or incidental, especially to beginners, journalism students, or reporters. Yet the ending represents the last piece in the jigsaw puzzle depicting your peak experience or epiphany. Force it, and other pieces dislodge. Omit it, and everyone notices the missing gap in your mosaic of truth.

Magazines are *oracles* of truth. But typical beginning writers lack the discipline to reach inside for one more culminating scene or powerful comment reflecting or stating the peak experience or epiphany. Their stories end abruptly because they hesitate to share their subjective truths, unsure that others will recognize lessons or profit from the take-away value. Or beginners marvel at how theme, moment, viewpoint, and voice harmonize with each other. They're impressed so much that they quickly summarize events or arguments, committing voice and moment lapses. At the most critical points in their stories, when they should be making one last push toward truth and utility, these writers are wrapping up and disappointing readers.

Newspapers, on the other hand, are mostly fonts of fact. When beginning newswriting students and reporters try to write for magazines, they usually flub the ending. (Later, they get better as they write more newspaper feature stories.) But starting out, the poor dears have had the endings drummed out of them, thanks to the inverted pyramid form—a useful hard news structure. However, when facts are presented in descending order of importance, the ending is the *least* interesting component of the news story. Worse, reporters are trained to include a *nut graph,* a paragraph appearing shortly after the lead and summing up the impact of a story, so that subscribers can stop reading whenever they like. True, nut graphs may be socially responsible, ensuring that even the slackest citizen is still informed, but they also undermine the importance of an ending.

In sum, a news story takes a direct route to the truth. It's an "interstate" of fact, A to Z. There is a good reason for that kind of economy. A reporter should be able to dictate hard news from the scene to an assistant in the newsroom, as many wire-service reporters or foreign correspondents do. The form is easy to keep in mind because there is only one level of meaning: topic. If you depicted such a story, it would look like Figure 8.1.

A good magazine story takes a scenic route, presenting the same facts, perhaps, but with more levels of content and truth, more thorough research and observation, more drama or perspective, clearer focus, and deeper tones and textures. There are at least two levels of meaning: topic and theme (and often occasion). Unless these levels of meaning are clearly distinguished from each other, via grounding and foreshadowing, readers are going to get lost in the maze. Scenic routes may be beautiful—presented through the filter of viewpoint and voice (the total shaded area of the graph in Figure 8.2)—but they also take tangents. If you can envision a good road map, readers will follow, wending via the moment of narration toward an epiphany or peak experience.

If you depicted the structure of a typical magazine story, it might look like Figure 8.2. As you can see from the "*You are here*" designation, you only have a little more road to travel in this book. Don't run out of gas, patience, courage, stamina, insight—or paper and supplies. You're going to be writing soon. And if you have followed the guidelines for each concept in the key of

F I G U R E   8 . 1   Inverted Pyramid Structure

Key:

☐ = Introduction

A–Z = Facts in descending order of importance

⇨ = Nut graph, summarizing remainder of story

■ = Ending

F I G U R E   8 . 2   Magazine Story Structure

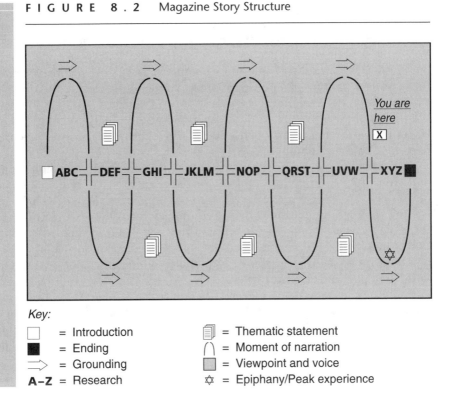

Key:

☐ = Introduction

■ = Ending

⇒ = Grounding

A–Z = Research

▤ = Thematic statement

⋂ = Moment of narration

☐ = Viewpoint and voice

✡ = Epiphany/Peak experience

Figure 8.2, you will have no trouble determining the correct ending for your work. An ending has these basic requirements:

- It echoes or answers the introduction, fulfilling the contract promised in the title of your work.
- It has been prepared for, or foreshadowed, via preceding thematic statements.
- It is the last and often most memorable segment of time line in a work employing the *now* moment of narration; the most memorable segment or significant comment in a work in *the now and then* moment; or the most significant comment in a work in the *then* moment.
- It contains a final epiphany or peak experience for take-away value.
- The epiphany is expressed in an open or a closed manner, depending on the piece.

The decision to use an open or closed ending can dictate the success or failure of a work. As in joke telling, endings have to be foreshadowed throughout a magazine piece. If you skip the punchline, readers get angry. You have wasted their time (as you would if you told a joke without a punchline). Magazine works are more complex than jokes, of course. Sometimes readers want to linger or luxuriate in your ending, closing their magazines and sighing. Sometimes they want to be satisfied or affirmed, flipping their magazines to the next article, eager to read on. That lingering, luxuriating feeling occurs in an open ending. The satisfied or affirmed feeling happens in a closed ending.

An *open ending* suggests rather than states a conclusion, echoing topic, or theme, often by implying epiphany or peak experience in one final scene or thought. Use an open ending if your goal is to leave the reader sighing, craving, pondering, guessing, living vicariously, or otherwise yearning to see, experience, or imagine your truths. Typically, you find such endings in stories employing the *now* moment of narration or using other time elements in travel, cuisine, romance, supernatural, suspense, horror, humor, satire, outdoor, and adventure pieces.

A *closed ending* states rather than suggests a conclusion, resolving topic, or theme, often by referring to epiphany or peak experience in one all-encompassing depiction or disclosure. Use a closed ending if your goal is to satisfy the reader or otherwise entice him or her to act or think a certain way. Typically, you find such endings in stories using the *then* moment of narration or using other time elements in detective, science, religious, business, medical, psychological, news-oriented, service, consumer, and inspirational articles.

Empowered by epiphany or peak experience, you echo or resolve your topic or theme in the ending. That ensures take-away value, which should have been foreshadowed earlier in your piece. Here are four types of open and closed endings, echoing or resolving topic and theme:

1. *Open ending, echoing topic or occasion.* Diane Ackerman concluded her topic of "Bats" with this hauntingly beautiful paragraph, leaving *New Yorker* readers with a medieval epiphany about life and a peak experience about bats against an urban landscape:

> In a metaphor of the Venerable Bede's, from the Dark Ages, life is a beautiful and strange winged creature that appears at a window, flies swiftly through the half-lit banquet hall, and is gone. That seems about right for a vision of creation as beautiful as this one, which now includes the city lights, the sunset doing a shadow dance over the water, and the four columns of bats undulating across the sky.

2. *Open ending, echoing theme.* In his long profile "Meeting Mr. Cheever," Dana Gioia employs a theme of surprising impressions. From beginning to end, Gioia's expectations are either mistaken or surpassed in each scene—an intentional strategy so that *The Hudson Review* readers feel that they are meeting Mr. Cheever, too. In this last symbolic scene, Gioia does not anticipate the specter of an aging, ailing Cheever; nonetheless, he implies an epiphany that the writer would rise, posthumously, above other more celebrated literary icons:

> The last time I saw John was by accident. In late September 1981 my wife and I went to hear Eudora Welty speak at the Katonah Library. It was a crisp autumn day when the leaves in Westchester were just beginning to turn, the sort of day John so frequently celebrated in his work. Outside the library a long, noisy line of people waited for the doors to open. Walking to the end of the line, we passed Robert Penn Warren, William Maxwell, and, my old teacher, Robert Fitzgerald. Everyone seemed hale and happy. A waterfall of conversations filled the air. Then suddenly I saw John and his wife, Mary, standing quietly near the end of the line. He looked thin, ashen, and painfully frail next to her. When he coughed, he shook with pain. That afternoon he seemed half a century older than the quick, boyish man I had met only six years before. I stopped to say hello, but as we talked, he sounded so tired that I quickly excused myself. After the reading Mary led him gently through the packed room towards the door, and I watched them over the bobbing heads and shoulders of the crowd until his tiny, shuffling frame disappeared into the early evening.

3. *Closed ending, resolving topic or occasion.* Bethany Matsko closed the topic of her parents' marriage with this final paragraph, containing an epiphany about teen marriages and including the word *happen* (alluding to *Sassy's* standing title "it happened to me"):

> Despite their naiveté and relative inexperience with life, my parents have managed to stay together (they just celebrated 21 years of marriage) and raise four great kids. The classic argument is that young parents—mothers especially—who aren't financially secure will fall into poverty, giving birth to children who will eventually do the same, creating a vicious cycle. In my case, this is wrong. I'm a senior in college who's putting herself through school by working two jobs. I get good grades too, and scholarships. My goal is to become a fashion editor of a magazine. It could happen. I know it will.

4. *Closed ending, resolving theme.* In her *New Woman* article "The Broken Child," Catherine Johnson sets up her ending by telling an anecdote. She and her friends are laughing at a rap song whose operative line is "I like big butts and I cannot lie." All the while, Johnson's autistic son is studying his mother, in hysterics over the line. Johnson then states her epiphany in the next to last paragraph and resolves the theme of mother love with a final disclosure:

> And suddenly, he gets it: "Mama *waughs* at me!" he exclaims, beaming with pride. In his little-boy mind, his little-boy-mind-with-autism, he is the source of all this fun.
>
> I look at him in astonishment. How can he be coming up with this completely original, completely nonechoed and nonmemorized sentence? A perfect sentence; the only thing missing, the *I*. Of course, he has the meaning of the scene all wrong . . . but the *sentence!* It is priceless.
>
> And I have to conclude that this is one of those small miracles that happen while we're busy doing other things. As I sit there in the quiet kitchen in the spring light, my heart floods with mother-love for Jimmy, new babies or no. And I feel some small measure of forgiveness for myself, too. Because whatever my failings as Jimmy's mother, whatever my faltering will, I have raised a boy who thinks, when he sees me cracking up in laughter on a sunny day, that he is the source of his mother's joy.
>
> And that much, he has just right.

After reading Catherine Johnson's article, readers feel a sense of hope or mission in their own lives. The ending comment has a lot to do with that. "In terms of technical approach," she says, "part of what makes 'The Broken Child' satisfying, I think, is its sin-and-redemption structure. The mother starts out in love with her severely handicapped child, then falls from grace after her new babies are born and she contemplates sending the older boy away. Then in the end she is redeemed by love and she stays. Mother and son find their way: a happy ending!"

To determine which type of ending suits your story, ask yourself:

- Do I want to leave my readers with a lingering sense of subject or scene, so that they can appreciate the utility of my topic? If so, set up the ending with an epiphany or peak experience related to topic (or occasion) and use an open ending to echo it.
- Do I want to leave my readers with a lingering stab of emotion or tweak of imagination, so that they can experience the universality of my theme? If so, set up the ending with an epiphany or peak experience related to theme and use an open ending to echo it.
- Do I want to leave my readers with a sense of satisfaction, so that they can appreciate the take-away value of my topic? If so, set up the ending with an epiphany or peak experience related to topic (or occasion) and use a closed ending to resolve it.

- Do I want to leave my readers with a catharsis or emotional sense of completion, so that they can experience the universality of my theme? If so, set up the ending with an epiphany or peak experience related to theme and use a closed ending to resolve it.

Beginnings and Endings

The ending is often indicated in the introduction, a natural place. Usually, you know where you are headed if you embark in a car on a road trip. Only natural-born navigators are able to hop in the Chevy in Maine and end up in San Diego, without a map or a prayer. Likewise, only natural-born writers can "discover" their endings without preparing for them at the very start.

Dan Horn, now a reporter for the *Cincinnati Post,* learned to write for magazines by envisioning the ending of "The Superman Syndrome," a piece about journalism-student burnout, published in the trade magazine *Quill.* Horn begins his piece by sharing an anecdote:

> A few weeks before I graduated from journalism school in 1988, a friend told me he wanted to spend his career writing stories about Siamese twins who explode on operating room tables and aliens who rape nuns.
>
> The friend—Steve—had a resume that looked like the front page of The Weekly World News with a headline proclaiming: "Scientists Confirm Amazing Discovery: The News Needs Steve." Since few professors were willing to attach their names to such a production, Steve placed a carefully doctored photo of himself and Elvis arm-in-arm beneath the heading "references."
>
> The resume was an inspired work. Most of the people who saw it chuckled, but those of us who knew Steve well realized he wasn't kidding. He had made a decision. He wanted to be the most famous reporter to work for a tabloid sold next to the nail clippers, Bic pens, and Tic-Tac rack.

After the introduction, Horn focuses on issues pertaining to journalism-student burnout. Then, in the closed ending, he alludes to the anecdote about Steve and uses him to make a transition to deeper truths, resolving the topic foreshadowed in his title:

> I talked to Steve about a month ago. He still has a copy of his tabloid-style resume, but he's now writing and editing a weekly newspaper in Ohio. He tells me he likes the creative freedom. . . .
>
> I don't know what the future holds for me, but I'm beginning to get a better idea of what I want to do in journalism five or ten years down the road.

> I've learned, like most other recent graduates, that it's sometimes necessary to put dreams on hold. The trick, I think, is not giving up on them.
>
> I've also found that the difficult transition from journalism school to the first job is less painful when you're doing the kind of work you enjoy, not the kind of work others say you should enjoy.
>
> It's important for new reporters to remind themselves every now and then that sometimes being happy is more important than being Superman.

Discussing his piece, Horn notes that the goal of his introduction was to make his manuscript stand out a bit from the other, more academic advice columns in *Quill*. "I figured one way to do that was to mention exploding twins and rampaging aliens in the same sentence," he says. "More important, though, is the rest of the introduction, which suggests my friends and I are as confused about career issues as many other young journalists. Steve and his resume are symbols of that uncertainty. This approach, I think, lets the reader know that instead of preaching about the subject, I'll be writing from personal experience."

Horn adds that the ending of his piece revisits Steve and shares with readers "some of the things we've learned in the years after graduation. Since the essay is something of a personal journey, it's necessary to show how we've changed and where we are now. In this way, readers see some resolution to the big questions outlined in the introduction. The ending epiphany doesn't presume to answer all of those questions, but it does offer hope that we can grow and learn from our experience."

This is known as the *pivotal anecdote,* the most common of beginning-ending strategies. It is used in an open or closed manner to echo or resolve topic or theme, depending on the piece. Typically, the writer starts with a memorable anecdote in the introduction, uses it to provide transition to related concerns in the middle of the work, and then pivots to the anecdote again in the ending to provide yet another transition to a deeper truth and closure.

Although other types of beginning-ending combinations are possible, depending on the topic and theme of a particular piece, here are four other common strategies:

1. *The answered argument.* The writer introduces a problem or issue in the introduction, investigates all sides or opinions in the body of the work, and then resolves the problem or issue with a closed ending. Bruce Woods's feature in *BackHome*, "The Hunting Problem," begins with a statement concerning the morality of hunting:

> The killing bothers me.
>
> Oh, I haven't stopped hunting. Killing is, after all, the only way to make meat, and I enjoy meat. Raising grain kills, too. Every additional acre in culti-

vation is an acre not available as wildlife habitat, an acre lost to indigenous flora, an acre that loads another chamber in humanity's slow game of pesticide roulette.

But that's the stuff of rationalization, of apologia; I'm after more elusive game here. If the killing bothers me, what exactly is there about hunting that I like (or need) enough to cause me to tolerate the resulting deaths. What return do I get for my discomfort?

Woods proceeds to answer that question, contemplating all issues related to hunting. Then he resolves the argument with this ending allusion and epiphany:

Sure the killing bothers me.

It's supposed to.

And if it ever stops bothering me I pray I'll be big enough to let go of hunting forever. Because to hunt and not despise the killing would be to become not an animal, but a form of human that I shudder to even imagine.

2. *The humorous allusion.* The writer begins the piece with an unanticipated image or reference associated with the topic or theme, goes on to investigate concerns or elaborate on issues, and then alludes to the beginning image or reference—now as a kind of punchline—to create a satisfying upbeat closed ending. In her *Vegetarian Times* article, "Do You Really Want to Eat This?" Karin Horgan Sullivan uses the unanticipated image of a pie shop in the introduction of her article about sugar consumption:

Of all the editors at *Vegetarian Times,* I was the obvious choice to write an article on sugar. This is not a fact I'm proud of, mind you, but one that's hard to deny, given the well-trodden path between my desk and the pie shop conveniently located across the street from the *VT* office.

After sharing extensive research in the middle section of her piece, Sullivan puns the image of the pie shop to resolve her topic with a satisfying closed ending:

In the course of doing this story, I realized that all too often what I eat to satisfy a sweet craving is something awfully high in fat. I'm trying to be more disciplined about jettisoning such junk food from my diet—but I refuse to spurn my old love. On those days when I've eaten at least five fruits and vegetables, kept my fat intake low and still feel a desire for dessert, I reflect on the perspective of George Blackburn, M.D., head of the Center to Study Nutrition and Medicine at New England Deaconess Hospital in Boston: "The belief that sugar is bad is based on our Puritan background, that we're not put here to enjoy life, that something must be a sin to taste so good. Sugar eaten in moderation is okay." I find this excellent food for thought on my way to the pie shop.

3. *The resurrected symbol.* The writer begins with an introduction containing an image or reference and then resurrects it with new meaning in the open ending, echoing theme or topic. Patricia Westfall's *Esquire* essay, "An American Dream," is a complex, metaphoric work with a theme of perception. Westfall sets up her ending with two symbols, one occurring in the middle of her piece about her husband Jeff discovering that his poem about owls also predicts the death of a beloved professor (who would sell the couple his farm). In her introduction, however, Westfall focuses on the variations and meanings of her first name:

> I used to ask to be called Patricia. To me, Patricia was a pretty word, unlike Pat, which seemed abrupt, or Patty, which seemed too silly and girlish for a woman nearly six feet tall. Of course I asked Jeff, shortly after we met, to call me Patricia, and to my surprise he firmly refused. No friend had ever refused this harmless request before, but he argued that names are external, something others use, something my parents and friends choose for me. To attempt to control my name was to block intimacy, because, in part, it is through the names we give one another that we carve paths to one another. Those were not his words, I'm sure—he always spoke in a rapid avalanche of metaphor that I find impossible to capture or mimic—but those were the ideas. Over the years he called me many names, even the dreaded Patty. In fact, in the word Patty especially there were many doors.

The word *Patty* spoken by the husband Jeff at a critical moment in the open ending echoes the theme of perception and, along with the other resurrected symbol of the owl, implies the death of their marriage:

> He was staring at me. It wasn't like me to be silent, ever. I felt if I said I would do the research I'd destroy myself, because I was truly exhausted. Life here had become untenable chaos. If we did not pause to recover, I would break. But if I said I'd not do the research, I'd destroy his vision of me. He would begin to see me as expedient, not committed, perhaps not lyrical. Lyric and myth seemed to be the same to him. His perception of me would change, perhaps slowly, perhaps quickly. I would become something silent and songless in his mind, a dot firmly attached to a line that measures realities like time, money and skill. I wouldn't be what I seemed to be.
> "Patty?" he said. He sounded frightened too. The night was filled with its usual sounds, the windmill, the wind chimes, the crickets, the frogs, and a sound new to this house, the soft sound of owls whooing on the roof.

4. *The bookend moment.* The writer begins with a scene or situation in one time element and then proceeds to another time element in the body of the work, returning to the original scene or situation and time element in the open ending. In the introduction of her profile "Anna's Tangled Destiny," Ursula Obst uses the present tense to describe the setting, action, and appearance of bag lady Anna Podobna:

> Winter and summer, she wears a black coat, so carefully darned in places that it appears embroidered; her thin, red hands protruding from its too-short sleeves are usually encumbered by white plastic shopping bags. She is impeccably groomed, and she walks with a determined step that is only occasionally halted by a suffocating cough. Her bed is the street at times, but mostly she confines herself to a small, barren room in a dilapidated hotel. There is only a handful of people she chooses to acknowledge, always with a smile and a courtly bow, as she paces out her daily routine within the four blocks of Broadway she considers home.

In the middle of the work, Obst switches to the past tense and a *then* moment to chronicle and document Podobna's life:

> I met Anna Podobna ten years ago when she was less guarded and reserved than now. She bowed as we were introduced, greeted me formally in her native Polish, then sat down erect, her head held high. Her feet, strapped in delicate white sandals, were grotesquely swollen, yet she managed to cross her ankles gracefully as she smoothed her skirt over her knees.

In her open ending, echoing the theme of "uncompromising pride," Obst allows readers to glimpse the bag lady one last time at the setting foreshadowed in the introduction, switching to the *now* moment and employing the pushed present tense:

> It is 5 p.m. I watch her come down the street toward me, stopping on the median strip in the center of Broadway where a group of elderly loiterers are overcrowding the bench as usual; intent on the traffic, she does not acknowledge them. With a determined step she crosses the street and heads north. I follow her cautiously and wait outside as she disappears into a fresh produce store that spills its wares onto the sidewalk. A few minutes later I see a hand in a black sleeve placing a banana on the grocer's scale. Walking out, she stops between the fruit stands, holding up her white plastic bag with the handles spread apart as if she expects someone to drop something inside. She stands for about a minute, a vacant half-smile on her face, her eyes darting between the apples and the cashier inside. Then, slowly, she closes up her bag and walks south. On the next corner, she stops outside the window of a lingerie store. She stares at the nightgowns, she leans forward then back, cocking her head to one side then the other, as if the display contained some enchanting and wondrous things. She slowly walks on, surveying each shop window. She reaches the corner and stops short. I see her body begin to shake. She turns, her face is contorted—eyes open wide, cheeks blown out, lips trembling. Her very thin, very

red hand protruding from the short coat sleeve clutches at the air spasmodically. She is paralyzed in her progress by a suffocating cough. She stands there for a long time battling with it until the shaking ceases. Then she resumes walking, back in the direction she came from. As she passes close by me I notice that the cloth of her coat has worn through at the shoulder and has been intricately mended with many tiny stitches. I follow her to Sloan's Supermarket and through the plate glass window I watch her in an exchange with an elderly woman. The woman hands her money. She bows deeply several times, a smile widens her face. The woman walks away but Anna remains, and the smile spreads. Her face is a child's face, its expression a child's delight. She unfolds the bill with two hands, and then folds it slowly and places it into her plastic bag. Then she takes hold of a shopping cart and disappears from view. Perhaps fifteen minutes pass, a long time, it seems. She pulls in line for a check-out counter, in her cart are four bottles of Coca-Cola. She stands by the window ledge, smoking a cigarette and watching the goings-on in the gathering dusk outside with an expression of intense interest. She stands there smoking and staring for a half hour. Finally, encumbered by two white plastic bags, one in each hand, she heads north. Two blocks up, she enters the Red Apple Supermarket, where she buys tissues and a small container of milk. Twenty minutes she stands at the window smoking. She walks out to the street; outside, on Amsterdam Avenue, the kids from the projects have spilled onto the sidewalk and are circling under the corner streetlights like fireflies. Slowly, laboriously, she struggles up the hill toward home.

You are heading to The Craft Shop to learn about endings from esteemed critic and writer Dana Gioia. Then you will check out The Newsstand to determine types of endings in your target publications. At The Keyboard, you will finish outlines and write endings for each developing story idea in your project files. Finally, you get to choose one story idea for your first draft.

T H E   C R A F T   S H O P

On Endings

Dana Gioia, Freelance Writer and Literary Critic

The only thing harder than beginning a piece of prose is finishing it properly. Finding the best way to start a review, memoir, or essay may be difficult, but once the right departure point is discovered, the energy of the initial inspiration carries the author a considerable distance. If my experience is any measure, once a writer gets going, it often feels as if one could continue forever. And that, of course, eventually becomes the problem—knowing when and how to stop. A writer must not only avoid the danger of going on too long; he or she must also find a way to end the piece as meaningfully and arrestingly as it began.

Playwrights and theatrical composers know that a dramatic work must pick up speed as it continues. The second half of a play or opera almost inevitably is shorter than the first. Likewise, in most novels, the slow and detailed work of exposition occurs at the beginning. Even in poetry, a work usually builds momentum as it continues. The Italian-style sonnet, for instance, does not divide its fourteen lines into two equal parts. The sonnet opens with an eight-line stanza and concludes with a shorter unit of six lines. The English-style sonnet is even more lopsided—with the opening twelve lines followed by a snappy two-line conclusion.

Many nonfiction writers, however, have a tendency to slow their pace toward the end of a piece. They feel the need to repeat or summarize what has gone on before. There are, of course, some circumstances that require authors to recapitulate particularly complex arguments. Elucidation is fine, but repetition always comes at a risk. Undue repetition suggests that an author doesn't entirely trust an audience's intelligence or attention. Good writers resist the temptation to end a piece by telling readers something they already know.

Once you start looking for redundant endings, you will be surprised at how often they turn up. You can skip the last paragraph of most newspaper articles without missing anything essential. Even in more ostensibly literary writing like essays and reviews, the final paragraph too often only reiterates observations already made to better effect earlier in the piece. You feel the author's imaginative energy running down—and the reader's engagement starts to sag as well. In contrast, when a writer concludes with an unexpected but appropriate flourish, the reader finishes the work fully engaged and alert.

A good ending should provide some tangible sense of closure. It will also usually introduce something new—a fact, an image, an incident—in combination with elements already familiar from the body of the work. While the reader must feel a sense of closure, it is often more effective to make that sense implicit rather than explicit. As in a poem or short story, nonfiction prose will end most effectively if the final moment allows readers to use their imaginations. A defining anecdote, a revealing quotation, or even a single provocative image is almost always worth more than an abstract summary of what has gone before.

Having pronounced so definitively my view on writing a good ending, I now find myself in the awkward situation of having to conclude this piece in a razzle-dazzle manner worthy of my own theory. But can this little note really bear the weight of a grand finale? Like a cartoon character busily sawing off the branch he sits on, I will simply pause a moment to survey my own handiwork, smile sheepishly, and drop quickly out of sight.

THE NEWSSTAND

Endings and Audiences

1. Check out the most recent issue of each publication targeted in your project files. Consider all columns, features, and articles, noting:

   - Do they end openly by *echoing* topic or theme or in a closed manner, *resolving* topic or theme?

   - Do they employ common beginning-ending strategies (the pivotal anecdote, the answered argument, the humorous allusion, the resurrected symbol, and the bookend moment)?

2. Now compare the ending and/or beginning-ending strategy with the *type* of story in the magazine. (Typically, you find open endings, echoing topic or theme, in pieces employing the *now* moment of narration or using other time elements in travel, cuisine, romance, supernatural, suspense, horror, humor, satire, outdoor, and adventure pieces. Likewise, you should find closed endings, resolving topic or theme, in pieces employing the *then* moment of narration or using other time elements in detective, science, religious, business, medical, psychological, news-oriented, service, consumer, and inspirational articles.)

3. Each time you find an ending relating to the type of story you are envisioning and outlining in each of your target publications, photocopy and include it in your Story Sample file.

T H E   K E Y B O A R D

Nailing Your Endings

1. In each project file, you should have an introduction based on The Keyboard assignments in Chapter 7. The introduction represents the beginning of your journey, according to the map illustrated in Magazine Story Structure discussed earlier in this chapter. Ask yourself: When I end my story, what impression or resolution do I want to leave my readers with? That's your destination. Now write an ending aligned with the introduction for each of your story ideas, based on data in The Newsstand exercises concerning open versus closed endings for specific types of stories. Make sure your ending:

   - Echoes or answers the introduction, fulfilling the contract promised in the title of your work

   - Has been prepared for, or foreshadowed, via at least one preceding thematic statement

   - Is the last and most memorable segment of time line in a work employing the *now* moment of narration; the most memorable segment or significant comment in a work in the *now and then* moment; or the most significant comment in a work in the *then* moment

   - Contains your final epiphany or peak experience for take-away value

2. Now decide whether any of the common beginning-ending strategies might better serve your objectives for each of your developing story ideas. If so, rewrite the introduction and ending with a common beginning-ending strategy, according to methods discussed earlier in this chapter.

3. By now, you should have a clear vision of the distance you must travel to reach the final destination for each of your developing story ideas. Now you need to finalize outlines in each of your project files, garnering enough insight or research to compose the middle of your work. Ask yourself:

   - Have I contemplated my theme to generate enough statements to lead readers to my epiphany or peak experience?

- Have I done enough library or field research to execute the middle of my manuscript, establishing an authority base so that my readers will trust my perceptions or assertions?

If not, do so now and enhance your outlines for each story idea in your project files.

4. After finishing each outline, you should know which ones are likely to produce publishable columns, features, or articles. These are stories that you should envision clearly and are itching to write. Select one to compose according to methods described in the *next* chapter.

The Writing Process

Preparing to Write

Congratulations. If you have understood the tools, techniques, and concepts discussed in previous chapters, and have done your assignments at The Newsstand and The Keyboard, you are now a natural-*re*born writer. You may have begun as a wanna-be, making the difficult decision to become a novice who writes for an audience (rather than for his or her ego). You may have struggled with the demands placed on you in this book, as you encountered each magazine component. But you have traveled this far without learning writing tips such as How to Create a Snappy Lead or How to Compose Effective Transitions. All that should come naturally now because you have been learning techniques from top authors, reading magazines as a writer (rather than consumer), researching your topic and theme, and enhancing your story ideas with basic components like moment, voice, viewpoint, and ending. More importantly, you have been outlining a story based on an item from your highs, lows, and turning points. You can commit to copy like that, willing to do legwork to share your truths with readers who hold the same truths or who can benefit from yours. So there is little left to discuss about the writing process, except how to sharpen your vision of the first draft.

To do that, you need to align your topic, occasion, theme, title, voice, moment, and ending. Those components provide a snapshot of your first draft so that you can determine if any are out of alignment or inappropriate for your target audience. Make adjustments now before you write one word. (Otherwise, your words may be wasted.) Because you already have aligned your introduction and ending, all that remains is the middle, which you should have researched or prepared for according to the exercises in the last chapter.

To show how you make a *snapshot* outline of basic components, let's return to that mock manuscript about divorce and renewal, discussed in earlier chapters and targeted at *New Woman*. You align basic elements for such a piece like this:

> *Topic:* Divorce
> > *Theme:* Renewal
> > *Title:* Descriptive
> > *Approach:* Anecdotal
> > *Length:* Article
> > *Voice*: Informational, upbeat, conversational
> > *Moment:* *Then,* to provide comment
> > *Ending:* Closed, to resolve theme

As you may recall, you also learned how to do research and make a source box for this article. You might imagine that the file for this piece should be brimming with interviews and information for the middle segment of the manuscript. In the previous chapter, you envisioned the flow and requirements of the middle segment, depicted in Figure 8.2, Magazine Story Structure, linking the introduction and ending via grounding, thematic statements, voice, viewpoint, research, moment, and epiphany or peak experience. With all that data in a project file marked Divorce and Renewal, a beginning writer might forget the basics, violate voice and viewpoint, neglect to ground or foreshadow, or commit moment lapses. That's why the snapshot outline is essential when you are writing your first draft. It continually reminds you that components have to harmonize or else problems will occur later.

You should be able to cipher some problems in this snapshot for the same divorce story, with components out of alignment:

> *Topic:* Divorce
> > *Theme:* Renewal
> > *Title:* Label
> > *Approach:* Personal experience
> > *Length:* Article
> > *Voice*: Informational, bitter, conversational
> > *Moment:* *Now,* to show drama of divorce
> > *Ending:* Open, to echo topic

That's a prescription for failure at *New Woman*. It wouldn't matter one whit how many times you polish that piece or how many writing tips you employ to revise it, you are never, *ever* going to place it at that target market. First of all, the title will be too cryptic for your theme. The approach is wrong, too. You would have to have experienced an incredibly bizarre divorce—committing an ax murder rather than an infidelity—to justify an article-length piece. True, even ex-spouses who experience renewal may have survived bitter phases of their divorce. But you can't use a bitter tone to convey theme in a magazine whose concept is based, in part, on self-discovery. And how will you incorporate informational and conversational tones in a moment set in the *now* to show the drama of a divorce? Worse, why would you echo the topic in an open ending—*New Woman* readers *know* about the topic—rather than resolve the theme in a closed ending, inspiring the audience?

You are not going to commit such flagrant errors. If you followed advice presented in earlier chapters and did all the assignments at The Newsstand and The Keyboard, your snapshot already should be in alignment. Use that mini-outline every page or so to check the progress of your piece in the middle segment, making sure that you stay within the boundaries of your basic components.

When writing, ask yourself:

- Am I clearly distinguishing my topic from theme via grounding and foreshadowing?
- Is my approach still effective after the introduction? Does it harmonize with my topic and theme? Is it powerful enough to lead me to my epiphany or peak experience? Do I need more or less information to execute the approach?
- Is the estimated length of my piece going to be violated, decreasing my chances of publication, because of problems with my approach?
- Am I straying from my voice tones, especially when I am quoting sources or inserting research?
- Is my moment of narration affecting the approach, indicating that I should change one or the other to reach my epiphany or peak experience? Is my moment of narration affecting my voice in any way, indicating that one or both elements are out of alignment?
- As I continue toward epiphany or peak experience, am I foreshadowing the type of ending that my snapshot predicts, or some other ending requiring me to change previous foreshadowings and thematic statements?

Most natural-born writers are thinking about these things—whether they admit it or not—as they "discover" their stories at the keyboard. That's why they eschew outlines, claiming that they hinder creativity. Baloney. There's no mystery to this business of magazine journalism. These natural types are following a subconscious snapshot that helps them envision their destinations as they compose, making small adjustments here, altering course there, to reach an open or closed ending they know by heart—that's the much-heralded "discovery" process.

You're going to reach your destination, too. To inspire you to do so, Table 9.1 presents 18 snapshot outlines by top-name writers whose work has

T A B L E   9 . 1   Snapshots of the Pros

TITLE	OCCASION	TOPIC	THEME	VOICE	MOMENT	ENDING
1. Lady Borton, column, "A Forgiving Land," _The New York Times Magazine_						
Suspense	A visit	Viet Nam	Forgiveness	Descriptive Reportorial Compassionate	Now	Closed
2. Molly Peacock, column, "Where You'll Find Me, _Mirabella_						
Suspense	A visit	Garden	Grace	Descriptive Intelligent Introspective	Then	Closed
3. Bill Brohaugh, column, "Talking to the River," _Writer's Digest_						
Suspense	Meeting a deadline	A stream	Control	Confidant Conversational Overwhelmed	Then, _pushed_	Open
4. Patricia Raybon, column, "Too Close for Comfort," _USA Today_						
Suspense	A confrontation	Stereotypes	Pride	Experienced Emphatic Reportorial	Now and Then	Closed
5. Bethany Matsko, column, "it happened to me," _Sassy_						
Standing title	None	Parents' marriage	Values	Chatty Witty Informed	Then	Closed
6. George Plimpton, column, "Bonding with the Grateful Dead," _Esquire_						
Descriptive	Concert	Grateful Dead	Bonding with children	Self-effacing Sophisticated Observant	Multiple	Open

7. Carol Muske Dukes, feature profile, "Farrah Fawcett Up Close," House and Garden

Descriptive	A visit to a celebrity's home	Farrah Fawcett	Magical transformation	Descriptive Enchanting Conversational	Now and Then	Closed

8. Kelly Cherry, feature profile, "Mr. Allen Dewey Spooner," The Chattahoochee Review

Descriptive	A hurricane	Grandfather	Loving memory	Compassionate Intelligent Historical	Now and Then, with *moment shifts*	Closed

9. Dana Gioia, article profile, "Meeting Mr. Cheever," The Hudson Review

Descriptive	Meeting a famous writer	None	Surprising impressions	Sophisticated Observant Gracious	Then	Open

10. Ursula Obst, article profile, "Anna's Tangled Destiny," New York Woman

Suspense	Observing a bag lady	A Polish immigrant	Uncompromising pride	Informed Observant Compassionate	Multiple	Open

11. Bruce Woods, opinion feature, "The Hunting Problem," BackHome

Descriptive	None	Hunting	Truth	Informed Open Contemplative	Then	Closed

12. Kevin Bezner, interview, "Right Work: An Interview with Gary Synder," Left Bank

Descriptive	An interview	Famous poet	Work	Informed Conversational Philosophical	Then	Closed

13. George Plimpton, interview feature, "How to Face a Firing Squad," Esquire

Descriptive	Doing lunch	Firing squads	Morbid curiosity	Self-effacing Sophisticated Observant	Multiple	Open

TITLE	OCCASION	TOPIC	THEME	VOICE	MOMENT	ENDING
14. David Lazar, literary essay, "The Coat," *Mississippi Valley Review*						
Label	Shopping at secondhand stores	A coat	Appearances	Intelligent Aloof Descriptive	Now and Then	Open
15. Catherine Johnson, personal experience article, "The Broken Child," *New Woman*						
Suspense	Birth of twins	Autism	Mother-love	Conversational Experienced Anecdotal	Then	Closed
16. Amy Hudson, personal essay, "Invictus under Glass," *Writer's Digest*						
Suspense	None	Anorexia nervosa	Control	Anecdotal Intelligent Introspective	Now and Then	Closed
17. Karin Horgan Sullivan, article, "Do You Really Want to Eat This?" *Vegetarian Times*						
Suspense	Visiting a pie shop	Sugar consumption	Obsession	Informational Savvy Skeptical	Then	Closed
18. Patricia Westfall, personal essay, "An American Dream," *Esquire*						
Suspense	Buying a farm	Marriage	Perception	Observant Plaintive Introspective	Now and Then	Open

been featured in previous sections of this book. You can see from the snapshot outlines that one cannot easily switch components of work by top writers and still publish in target magazines. You can envision that, too. Take components from each outline and exchange them so you can see how misalignment dooms the writing of celebrated authors. In magazine journalism, mastery of language is a *given*. The emphasis ought to be placed on *harmonizing* elements.

The misalignments in Table 9.2 are flagrant but not extreme. For a bizarre example, try switching components of George Plimpton's "How to Face a Firing Squad" with Lady Borton's "A Forgiving Land." What a mess. This quagmire of concept, full of sound and fury, signifies nothing—at least nothing easy to envision. You, however, will be on terra firma when writing your first draft, as long as your refer to your alignment frequently. Otherwise, you may encounter serious problems later when you try to revise your manuscript.

Preparing to Revise

The best way to introduce the revising process is to show you a typical first draft containing common errors. Knowing them in advance, you will be less likely to commit them when writing *your* first draft. More importantly, you will learn how to fix such mistakes by employing tools such as grounding and research, to distinguish topic from theme; techniques such as transitions and thematic statements, to propel readers toward your epiphany; and other concepts discussed in this book, including the importance of endings.

The following column was composed by Robin Rauzi, a member of a graduate student workshop at Ohio University. She envisioned her piece the same way you are, targeting hers at the *New York Times Magazine*. She aligned her occasion, theme, title, voice, time elements, and ending the same way you are doing in assignments at The Keyboard. And her first draft contained the same type of mistakes that you might make, bracketed and explained below in smaller boldfaced type:

Bury My Map at Wounded Knee   [Confusing title resulting in a mixed metaphor alluding to Dee Brown's *Bury My Heart at Wounded Knee*.]

I studied the menu hanging on the wall and quickly rejected the idea of buffalo meat on my pizza, doubting I would get much argument from Beth. We ordered a medium with pineapple, and I sat down to wait while she used the

T A B L E 9 . 2 Doomed Misalignments

TITLE	OCCASION	TOPIC	THEME	VOICE	MOMENT	ENDING
1. Patricia Westfall, personal essay, "Sister Soldiers," *Esquire*						
Suspense	Buying a farm	Grandfather	Dissatisfaction	Reportorial Introspective Skeptical	Now and Then	Open
2. Kelly Cherry, feature profile, "Too Close for Comfort," *The Chattahoochee Review*						
Suspense	A hurricane	Marriage	Pride	Experienced Emphatic Contemplative	Now and Then	Closed
3. Patricia Raybon, column, "Mr. Allen Dewey Spooner," *USA Today*						
Descriptive	A confrontation	Feminism	Perception	Compassionate Intelligent Reportorial	Now and Then, with *moment shifts*	Closed

only phone, back in the kitchen, to call the boyfriend she'd left behind in Los Angeles.

"Where in the hell am I?" I thought as I sat down at one of the three tables in the double-wide trailer. {Narrative beginning without any grounding in the *now and then* moment.} An old TV with poor reception was broadcasting the Judds' farewell concert for anyone listening, which was only me. Through the window I could see about a dozen teenagers—all of whom I figured to be Sioux Indian {Insufficient research or grounding resulting in English rather than tribal name.} —playing volleyball. The sun was setting and the game was breaking up as it got too dark to play, but no one came inside. The one woman who'd taken our order had disappeared into the kitchen with Beth.

I strained to pick up Beth's voice over the TV, but all I heard was the crackle of a radio scanner. Did the woman hear us on the CBs as we'd pulled up to the trailer with the giant letters PIZZA painted on its side? Did she hear me say, "Well, what do you think?" or Beth respond, flatly, "I think I'm hungry."

It didn't matter, I decided. The woman knew we didn't belong there, even if she didn't figure we were lost. {Occasion occurring too late in the introduction, compounding problem of lack of grounding.} After all, it is difficult to wind up in the middle of the Pine Ridge reservation by accident. Beth and I had done it only with the help of a map from AAA marked in orange highlighter by someone who knew less about the Oglala Sioux than even I did.

Beth and I were a week into our cross-country journey. {Grounding occurring too late in the introduction.} After nearly five years in Los Angeles, I was headed to graduate school in Ohio; she was en route to culinary school in Philadelphia. This stretch through South Dakota was the end of our western adventure. In the last seven days we'd driven through Nevada, Utah, Idaho, Wyoming, and Montana. But from here our the trip would be city-hopping: Minneapolis to Madison to Chicago to my hometown of Mount Vernon, Ohio.

There was something about this place, something that made me restless. I wanted to shut off Naomi and Wynonna, but the concept of silence made me apprehensive, probably for the same reason that I had kept tapes blaring in my car since we left Mount Rushmore.

Mount Rushmore was a disappointment after the natural wonder of Devil's Tower, which stood out from the plains like a signpost placed there by God. But Mount Rushmore was different—a kitschy, over-done facade of a frontier town leading up to endless parking lots and four 60-foot heads carved into stone. It's not that the feat wasn't impressive; the setting was bad. These were not the "purple mountains majesty" of "America the Beautiful"; these were the Black Hills of South Dakota. Washington, Lincoln, Jefferson and Teddy Roosevelt had less defense for being in the Black Hills than I had for being in this Pizzeria in Pine Ridge. We, after all, weren't trying to stamp our identity on this place; we were just hungry.

We'd eaten at a Perkins Pancakes in Rapid City before the Rushmore letdown. Then, 55 miles of road construction—light on road and heavy on construction—ground our pace to a three-hour second-gear crawl. By the time we stopped in Hot Springs, Beth wanted to go running so badly that I could see the signs of endorphin withdrawal in her eyes. {Lack of grounding explaining why Beth needs to go running.} After that we drove 60 miles to the next sign of humanity, which read "PIZZA, 3 miles," with an arrow to the right.

So now it was dark and we were at least 100 miles from Interstate 90. If I'd shot a rifle due south, the bullet would've landed in Nebraska. I'd suggested a detour through Nebraska earlier. "No way is this Jew going into Nebraska" was Beth's reply. "All those neo-Nazi, white supremacist groups are based in Nebraska." {Unanticipated tangent without grounding or research to support claim.} I didn't know if that was true or not; my AAA map didn't tell me. {Vague thematic statement, calling attention to lack of thematic focus, compounding earlier grounding problems, so that topic is not clearly distinguished from theme.} Of course, there was no indication that this was an Indian reservation, either, save the marking for the Wounded Knee National Historical Site.

One of the young men finally came inside from the volleyball game. Then, he too disappeared into the back of the trailer. As a USC {Confusing abbreviation for national audience; spell out or use generic term "college student."} student living in South-Central Los Angeles, I was used to tactile hostility. Or at least to a hostility I understood. {Lack of grounding to explain vague reference to "hostility."} His indifference to my presence was even more isolating.

Beth returned a short while later, and about the time the Judds sang "Love Will Build a Bridge," our pizza was ready. I remember it as the best pizza I have ever eaten, though I was, admittedly, ravenous. Eventually we paid, left a generous tip, and left. Not surprising, there was no invitation to come back soon. {Lack of authority base inasmuch as earlier reference gave no indication of the pizza woman's indifference to customers.}

We drove 15 miles or so in the dark before we realized that we'd missed State Route 27, which was to take us north through the Badlands back to the Interstate. My CB had a short and was blinking out, so I couldn't even tell Beth who was behind me. {Lack of grounding interrupting narrative inasmuch as there was no clear earlier reference that the women were traveling in two vehicles.} Periodically, old American sedans packed with teen-age boys would tear up the road, passing us, and disappear.

It was Beth's turn to ask directions when we spotted a gas station. She walked fearlessly up to the store while I watched the teenagers who'd passed us do doughnuts in the gravel parking lot. As they sped back out onto the highway, they looked back at me sitting in my Honda, fair-skinned and freckle-faced. {Dangling modifer, indicating the Honda is fair skinned and freckled.}

I couldn't pass for any kind of Indian, let alone Sioux. {Lack of grounding becomes confusing, especially when followed by data about Native American heritage in the rest of the paragraph.} I remembered a poem my mother wrote about being taught to count the five "greats" on her fingers to get to the grandmother who was a Cherokee. My mother had wanted to retrieve that native identity, and at that moment, so did I. {No space break necessary because thematic focus is weak at this point in the narrative.}

The words Pine Ridge meant nothing to me. I was 3 years old in 1973 when two American Indian Movement warriors were killed during the "Second Battle of Wounded Knee." I was 5 when Leonard Peltier killed two FBI agents on this Sioux reservation. {Lack of research inasmuch as many people question Peltier's guilty verdict; moreover, if implied author was 5 years old at time of the killings, Peltier at that point was "charged" with murder.} The Battle of Wounded Knee and the 153 Miniconjou Sioux killed there was something glossed over in my American history class between Custer's last stand and Teddy Roosevelt's presidency. {Lack of transition and thematic statement leading out of flashback, momentarily jarring the reader.}

Beth came back with the map and the route to the nearest town with a hotel. {Lack of thematic focus, though "map" seems to be the second level of meaning in the piece.} The final 46 miles to Kadoka were marked by an eerie stillness after the demise of my CB. The parching Utah desert, the Mormon enclave of Paris, Idaho, the endless big sky country of Montana—no place on this trip unsettled me like this region of South Dakota. Not even Los Angeles, when it burned on every side of my apartment, sent such a direct message to my soul. {Lack of grounding resulting in a confusing reference to 1992 L.A. riot.}

"This land is not yours," it said. "You do not belong here."

My map didn't warn me of this, the way it told me where there were no gas stations or family restaurants. A map tells you how to get from A to B with the least mileage to your car, not your conscience. By what is printed on them, maps give you an indication of space; by what they omit, though, they give you a sense of time. {Lack of thematic statements throughout the work weakens otherwise enlightening epiphanies about maps.} My map, circa 1993, comes from a time when most Americans believe that no frontiers remain. {Lack of grounding resulting in a vague reference in what appears to be a closed ending meant to resolve theme.} I know differently. {Weak ending comment with no thematic take-away value for audience.}

These are common first-draft problems. In Rauzi's case, she made 10 grounding-based errors, 6 thematic-based ones, 2 research miscalculations, 2 voice-related lapses, 1 authority-base oversight, and 1 grammatical error. These are easily fixed with "brushstrokes" in subsequent drafts. As in painting, a *brushstroke* is a small change that produces significant improvement. Too often, beginners revise from top to bottom when errors similar to ones Rauzi made are pointed out in a workshop or editorial critique. The typical workshop leader or editor can overemphasize small missteps, giving the impression that an entire manuscript is doomed.

Actually, entire write-throughs are rare if you envision your work according to methods discussed in this book. (Natural-born writers know this, of course, and brushstroke without fear.) Now you're a natural-born writer, too. You know that magazine journalism should have at least two levels of narration: topic and theme. If you blow one, you end up revising about half of your manuscript. You should have three voice tones. If you muff one, you usually rewrite one-third of your piece. You have three viewpoint options: narrator, persona with viewpoint source, and persona with no viewpoint. If you choose the wrong one, you have to refocus statements in each paragraph—typically one-fourth of your manuscript. If you pick the wrong ending, you rewrite your foreshadowings and final paragraphs. Assuming you know spelling, grammar, and punctuation, the only time you need to do a top-to-bottom rewrite is if you pick the opposite moment of narration (*then* instead of *now,* or vice versa). As you can see, envisioning your work not only sidesteps the hit-and-miss strategies of typical writing workshops but it also saves you scads of time during the revising process.

Despite 22 problems in Rauzi's first draft, mostly concerning grounding and theme, her column had strong potential. Rauzi was a serious writer, too, eager for constructive criticism. During the revising process, she addressed each comment given and deftly wove her changes into her narrative. Analyze her brushstrokes in her final draft, again bracketed to explain the improvements:

Shape of the Human Heart   {Good suspense title echoing theme and foreshadowing content.}

I looked at the list of pizza toppings posted on the wall and quickly
rejected the buffalo meat, sure I'd get no argument from Beth. We settled on
a medium with pineapple, and I sat down to wait while she used the only
phone—back in the kitchen—to call Los Angeles and tell her boyfriend we had
made it safely to South Dakota.

Beth and I were a week into our cross-country journey. {Grounding occurs
early, distinguishing occasion from theme.} After five years in Los Angeles, I was
headed to graduate school in Ohio. She was en route to culinary school in
Philadelphia. So far, we'd driven 2,000 miles, our two cars connected only
by cheap Radio Shack CBs. {Good grounding, clearing up the issue of narrator and
Beth driving *two* cars, while foreshadowing the CB radios, important in a later scene—
accomplished in 10 words.} This stretch of South Dakota marked the end of
our western adventure through Nevada, Utah, Idaho, Wyoming and
Montana.

"Where in the hell am I?" I thought as I sat down at one of the three
tables in the doublewide trailer. A PBS {More grounding, enhancing authority

base.} broadcast of the Judds' farewell concert was blaring from a TV with poor reception. Through the window I could see about a dozen teenagers— whom I figured to be Oglala Lakota (Sioux) {More research, enhancing authority base.} —playing volleyball. The sun was setting and the game was breaking up, but no one came inside. The woman who'd taken our order had disappeared into the kitchen.

I strained to listen to Beth's voice over the Judds, but heard only the crackle of a radio scanner. Had the woman heard us on the CBs as we'd pulled up to the trailer with the giant letters PIZZA painted on its side? Did she hear me say, cautiously, "Well, what do you think?" or Beth flatly respond, "I think I'm hungry."

It didn't matter. The woman could tell we didn't belong there, even if she didn't suspect that we were lost. {Occasion clear now because of grounding in second paragraph.} It is, after all, difficult to wind up in the middle of the Pine Ridge reservation by accident. Beth and I had done it only with the help of an Auto Club map marked with orange highlighter by someone who knew more about Mount Rushmore than Pine Ridge.

Mount Rushmore was a disappointment. We'd started the day at Devil's Tower, a natural stone wonder that stood out from the plains like God's own signpost. But Mount Rushmore was different—a kitschy, over-done facade of a frontier town leading up to endless parking lots and four 60-foot heads carved into stone. It's not that the feat wasn't impressive; the setting was bad. These weren't "purple mountains majesty"; these were the Black Hills of South Dakota.

You can't tell from looking at a map, but pictures from space show that the Black Hills mirror the shape of a human heart. {Thematic foreshadowing, echoing title and focusing readers toward epiphany.} In the Lakota language, they are called *Wamaka Og'naka Icante*—"the heart of everything that is." {More research enhances authority base.} This was the place where the Lakota tribe, according to legend, was expelled from the center of the planet and emerged through the caves in the Black Hills. {More research enhances authority base.} Washington, Lincoln, Jefferson and Roosevelt seemed out of place. But for that matter, so did Beth and I. The difference was we weren't trying to stamp our identity on the landscape; we were just passing through, looking for a place to get dinner.

We hadn't eaten since Rapid City, before the Rushmore let-down. Then, 55 miles of road construction—light on road and heavy on construction—ground our pace to a three-hour, second-gear crawl. By the time we stopped in Hot Springs, Beth—a runner since age 15 {More grounding clearing up earlier confusion.} needed exercise so badly that I could see the signs of endorphin withdrawal in her eyes. After her hour-long run we drove 60 miles to the next sign of humanity, which read "PIZZA, 3 miles" with an arrow to the right.

My map, which dutifully showed the location of gas stations, AAA offices and KOA campgrounds, gave me no indication that we were in the middle of the Pine Ridge reservation. {Thematic statement replacing earlier unanticipated tangent about Nebraska Nazis.} There was only a tiny tan spot marked "Wounded Knee National Historical Monument." And while the map may have told us where to find this historical marker, it didn't tell us how to experience it. Maps can give only a sense of space, not place. They reflect the geographic myth of the twentieth century, that we "Americans" have clear title to everything from sea to shining sea, pizzeria to greasy pizzeria. {Three thematic statements, establishing second level of meaning and ending with a transitional phrase—"pizzeria to greasy pizzeria"—returning to the narrative moment.}

One of the young men finally came into the trailer from the volleyball game. Then, he too disappeared into the back. As a college student {Grounding clears up earlier USC reference for national audience.} living in South-Central Los Angeles, I got used to the palpable hostility that came from trespassing on African-American or Latino territory. {Grounding clears up earlier confusion about meaning of "hostility."} That was a hostility I understood. This rural indifference to my presence was more chilling, more isolating. I couldn't wait for Beth to finish her phone conversation.

She returned a short while later, and about the time the Judds sang "Love Will Build a Bridge," our pizza was ready. It was about 14 inches in diameter, not big enough for two ravenous travelers. {More data enhances authority base.} But I remember it as the best pizza I have ever eaten. As we departed, the woman who made the pizza told us, perhaps as a reflex, to come again. {Grounding clears up earlier confusing reference about pizza woman's indifference.} The suggestion seemed so infelicitous that we didn't respond, probably seeming rude.

We drove 15 miles or so in the dark before I realized that we'd missed State Route 27, which was to take us north through the Badlands to Interstate 90. {More grounding enhances authority base.} My CB had a short and was blinking out, so I couldn't tell Beth, who was behind me. I sped along in this dark vacuum, alone, looking for a highway to take us north. Periodically, old American sedans packed with Lakotan teenage boys would tear up the road, pass us and disappear.

It was Beth's turn to ask directions when we found a gas station. She walked fearlessly up to the store while I watched the boys who'd passed us do doughnuts in the gravel parking lot, their long, dark hair dancing wildly out the window. {More sensory data enhances viewpoint.} As they sped back out onto the highway, they looked back at me, slender with a fair, freckled face and short, reddish hair. {More sensory data enhances viewpoint and eliminates earlier dangling modifer concerning Honda.}

Despite my distant Native American heritage, I couldn't pass for any kind of Indian, let alone Lakota. {Grounding clarifies earlier confusion about narrator's heritage.} I remembered a poem my mother wrote about counting five "greats" on her fingers to get to the grandmother who was a Cherokee. My mother always wanted to retrieve that identity, and at that moment, so did I.

{Earlier space break omitted.}

The words Pine Ridge meant nothing to me. I was 3 years old in 1973 when two American Indian Movement activists were killed during the "Second Battle of Wounded Knee." I was 5 when Leonard Peltier was charged with killing two FBI agents. {More research enhances authority base.} I didn't know about the violated Treaty of Fort Laramie, or how the Lakota tribes refused a $191 million settlement for the theft of the Black Hills. {More research enhances authority base.} The Battle of Wounded Knee and the 153 Miniconjou Lakota killed there were glossed over in my American history class between Custer's last stand and Teddy Roosevelt's presidency. Neither Beth nor I had any sense of the history of this place; we were lost in the heartland—not the American one—but the Lakotan. {Thematic statement clears up earlier flashback lapse and provides transition back to the main narrative.}

Beth returned with the map and the route to the nearest town with a hotel, and we sped off. The final 46 miles to Kadoka were marked by an eerie stillness, with my CB on the blink. Even when I knew we were on the right road, I searched for reassuring mile markers. There were none. {Thematic foreshadowing, focusing readers toward epiphany.}

The parching Utah desert, the Mormon enclaves in Idaho, the big sky country of Montana—no place on this trip unsettled me like this corner of South Dakota. Not even Los Angeles, when it burned on every side of my apartment in April 1992 {More grounding clears up earlier confusing reference about L.A. riot.}, sent a message so directly to my soul.

"This land is not yours," it said. "You do not belong here."

The next day, Beth and I did not stop for lunch until we'd driven 250 miles to the Minnesota border. We didn't sleep until we'd crossed the Mississippi River. While the urban grids of Minneapolis and Chicago were comforting for the next few days, they weren't enough to erase the anxiety inscribed by South Dakota. {Grounding and thematic statements help set up epiphany.} Even when I approached home, the map of Ohio, whose highways I know like the creases in my own palm, seemed untrustworthy. {Epiphany sets up closed ending resolving theme.} And still, when I glide down the exit ramp of an interstate highway, my heart pounds a little harder, faster, as if synchronized by my sojourn in the Black Hills. {Closed ending resolves theme, focusing readers on narrator's "heart" and fulfilling the contract promised in the title bearing the same word.}

Robin Rauzi cut a few passages in her revision and added more grounding, foreshadowing, and research. But in her final version, she changed only 10 percent of her first draft, adding a total of 175 words. The revisions may look simple when you see them on paper, but the word count doesn't reflect the effort of *mind* and *heart* that is showcased here. The word *revision* literally means to envision again—in keeping with the concept of this book. In Rauzi's case, the key was distinguishing her occasion (a road trip) from her theme (meaning of maps). "I recall the whole writing process of this as an educational experience," says Rauzi, now a reporter for the *Los Angeles*

Times. "I'd been fascinated by the idea of maps, especially after that trip across the country and a similar road trip from Virginia to Massachusetts the following winter. Even after driving back to California again—with the same car and the same cheap CB radio—I am fascinated by the idea that we think we know something about an area by drawing lines around it and labeling its parts." That observation led to Rauzi's epiphany. But her focus also involved additional research. In other words, Rauzi wasn't awed by her ability to write creatively. She was willing to do legwork. When a student in her workshop mentioned that from outer space, the Black Hills resemble the shape of the human heart, she headed straight to the campus library. "I researched that and the history of the Sioux tribes to write the later drafts of this piece. The [envisioning] process not only improved the article, but helped me understand the nature of my experience in South Dakota."

You are going to envision, compose, and revise your first draft at The Keyboard. But first, you'll head to The Craft Shop for more information about envisioning and revising manuscripts, and then to The Newsstand to get ready to write.

THE CRAFT SHOP

The Re-*Visioning* Process

Lady Borton, Freelance Writer

It was as devastating an editorial conference as any I've had. This was in 1990. I'd gone to the Bennington Writers' Conference to meet with Joyce, the editor who had worked on my first book, *Sensing the Enemy: An American Woman among the Boat People of Viet Nam* (Dial/Doubleday, 1984). This editor (and a good many others) had already turned down the proposal for *After Sorrow,* a book about the ordinary Vietnamese who had fought against the Americans.

In 1990, *After Sorrow* was still sodden with research; I didn't know how to lighten its weight. I've always been good friends with my editors, perhaps because I'm careful not to ask for favors. However, as a participant at Bennington, I could seek Joyce's suggestions without imposing on our friendship.

Our manuscript conference was on a crisp, sunny day in August. We sat on the grass in front of a white frame New England farm house. Nearby pines spread their fragrance all about us. Joyce pulled my manuscript from a stack of manila envelopes, then tossed it onto the grass.

"I don't want to read any more of this," she said. "It's dull."

Clouds scudded across the sun. I felt as if my seven years of research and writing (and accumulated rejections) had collapsed into a pile of cinders all about me. Even the grass turned gray. I reminded myself that I'd come to Bennington precisely because I valued Joyce's honesty; and I remembered the lesson implied in our editorial sessions on *Sensing the Enemy:* Revision is **RE**-vision; **EACH** re-vision must take the writer all the way, **ALL THE WAY**, back to the beginning.

From my tote bag, I removed the manuscript for "A Forgiving Land," which drew on material from *After Sorrow*. I'd sent the article to the "Hers" column at the *New York Times Magazine* but had received no response. The manuscript had gone through dozens of re-visions in an effort to convey the dignity, humor, pain, and pathos that I'd absorbed from Second Treasure, a Viet Cong woman who had once been our enemy.

In 1990, I was still the only foreigner whom the Vietnamese government allowed to live among ordinary Vietnamese; I was haunted by a need to re-create these former enemies as people whom we Americans might now even come to love.

"Would you look at these few pages?" I asked Joyce, handing her "A Forgiving Land."

As Joyce read, a breeze rustled the pine branches. The long, slim needles whispered with spirit voices like those I'd heard among the iron pines edging the Chau Thanh Cemetery for War Martyrs, where Second Treasure and I had lit pungent sticks of incense and poked them into the urn at the foot of her mother's grave.

I turned away from this memory when Joyce looked up from her reading. This time, she set the manuscript gently in her lap. "This is it," she said. "This piece has voice."

That same afternoon, I received a phone call from the *Times* accepting "A Forgiving Land." For the next five years, I held those few pages before me as I worked on *After Sorrow,* which Viking published in 1995.

I wanted to take readers to a place no American had ever visited. This required a voice rich with sensory detail. Since I was asking American readers to join me on a journey that would at best make them wary, I could not stoop to "lessons." I wanted the reader to be moved by the experiences among our former enemies just as I had been moved by their forgiveness and acceptance. To create that effect, I realized, I must always subjugate my research to emotion and my ego to the simple, disarming voice of a storyteller.

THE NEWSSTAND

Psyching Up to Write

1. Go to a real newsstand. Take in the bustle at a busy one, the smell of coffee, the ring of the register—whatever catches your attention. *You will be writing for a magazine sold here.* Casually observe readers paging through or purchasing specific titles—especially your target publication. *You will be writing for consumers like these.*

2. Buy the most recent issue of your target publication. Take in the flash of the cover; smell any perfume and cologne ads; touch the glossy or pulp paper stock; feel the heft of the magazine; page through and listen to the rustle of pages; and imagine tasting the food in any food ads, recipes, or restaurant spreads. *This is the aura of magazine journalism that writers like you help create.*

3. Read the contents of the most recent issue of your target publication. *Imagine your byline between the covers of this book.* Scan stories to psyche yourself up, along with ones in your Story Sample file.

THE KEYBOARD

First to Final Draft

1. Align the basic elements (topic, theme, title, approach, length, voice, moment, and ending) of your selection, as shown earlier in this chapter. Before writing your first draft, photocopy the Magazine Writing Checklist shown in Figure 9.1, reviewing the basic components of a publishable manuscript.

2. After you have finished your first draft, wait a week before revising it. You want to come to the piece fresh. Fill out the preliminary information, including the date and draft, in your photocopy of the Magazine Writing Checklist, following revision guidelines in that document.

3. Wait another week, after finishing your second draft. Fill out the date and draft in your photocopy of the Magazine Writing Checklist, following revision guidelines again.

F I G U R E   9 . 1   Magazine Writing Checklist

Target audience:
Preferred submission: ___ **Query** ___ **Manuscript**
Name of specific editor:
Address of magazine:
Title of your work:

_____ _____   _____ _____   _____ _____
Draft One   Date   Draft Two   Date   Final Draft Date

1. Is the topic of your article appropriate for the intended audience? If not, scan a year's worth of back issues of the specific magazine and revise accordingly.
2. Does the title constitute a contract with the reader, clearly foreshadowing material to come? If not, create such a title. Do you need a descriptive subtitle to state theme or clarify a suspense main title? Do you need subheads to parcel information? If so, compose an appropriate subtitle/subheads.
3. Does the introduction play off the title or subtitle? Does it present a problem, issue, or intriguing situation to capture the audience's interest? If not, isolate where in the manuscript you focus on such a problem, issue, or situation and revise so that it is highlighted from the start of your piece.
4. Is the theme evident and developed throughout the draft? If not, mark specific passages in your draft where a thematic statement might be inserted.
5. Is the piece grounded so that the reader understands the topic and theme from the very start? If not, mark passages where such grounding can be added and revise accordingly.
6. Use three adjectives to describe the voice you hear on the page. Are those tones appropriate for the topic? The intended audience? If not, suggest other tones and revise your manuscript.
7. Are you funneling your facts through a narrator (first-person structure, *I* or *we*) or persona (third-person structure, *he, she,* or *they*)? Is your viewpoint properly aligned with voice so that the tones on the page and perspectives *throughout the piece* are associated with the narrator? The storyteller? If not, isolate troublesome lapses and unify them.
8. Circle facts, quotations, citations, or other evidence of research in your draft. Is the amount of research appropriate for the topic? The audience? If not, revise the draft so it is ___less ___more personal or informational.
9. Analyze the moment of narration (*now, now and then, then*) and determine whether your manuscript needs more drama/tension or comment/perspective. If you need more drama/ tension, move the moment closer to the *now* and revise accordingly. If you need more comment/perspective, move the moment closer to the *then* and revise accordingly.
10. Do you end in an open manner, echoing theme or topic, or in a closed manner, resolving topic and theme? Do you need a beginning-ending strategy to sharpen focus? Does your ending contain take-away value? If not, what kind of message should you leave the audience with?

Reminder: *Have you done a fact check? A spelling check? A grammar check?*

4. Recalling information presented earlier in this book, type or print your final draft according to the standard manuscript format. Write a cover or query letter, and then mail and market your manuscript.

CHAPTER TEN

The Freelance Process

Standard Manuscript Format

Many manuscripts are rejected on sight because they appear amateurish. Before you send your work to an editor, you should type or print it in standard format. Use 20-pound 25 percent cotton white stock. Do not use onionskin, colored, or erasable paper. Always use black ink, even if you have a color laser printer. Do not print via poor-quality dot matrix. If using a typewriter, clean the font keys, balls, or daisy wheels and buy a new ribbon before preparing your final copy. Do not pencil in corrections; use correction fluid or correction ribbon to fix typographical errors. Some editors allow clean photocopies, others do not. It depends on the publication, so check your writer's guidelines to see if photocopies are permitted. Most editors still like the crisp feel of good bond paper.

Use a serif font that is easy to read, such as the font of this textbook. (*Serifs* are those little hooks and slants on each letter.) Standard ones are Courier New or Times New Roman. Avoid display fonts without serifs such as Arial or Avant Garde, better suited to advertising. Do not use fancy fonts such as GALLERIA or Broadway.

Your font height should be 10 to 12 points. If you are using a computer or word processor, you can print titles boldface in larger point size, usually 18 points, with subtitles in 16 and subheads in 14. If using a typewriter, type all your titles in uppercase to distinguish them from the text.

Set the margins on your typewriter or the page setup on your computer so that you have one-inch margins, top and bottom, left and right. Always double-space your text, with the exception of your single-spaced name and address on the first page. (The style of epigraphs and footnotes varies from magazine to magazine, so consult writer's guidelines if you are unsure.)

Your name and address should appear at the upper left corner of the first page. Pertinent telephone numbers and/or e-mail addresses should appear at the right corner, in this manner:

Michael J. Bugeja   Office: (614) 555-5555
E. W. Scripps Hall   Home: (614) 555-4444
Ohio University   Fax: (614) 555-3333
Athens, Ohio 45701   e-mail: bugeja@test.com

Drop down six to eight lines and boldface your title and subtitle, preferably in the style of your target publication. Separate the title from the subtitle (and the subtitle from the first paragraph) with an extra line of white space. Here is how to print a title and subtitle on a manuscript targeted at *Writer's Digest:*

The Essential Elements of a Great Article

**All articles rely on these elements so that writers
can connect with readers. Here's a refresher course
to help you *sell, sell, sell.***

Drop an extra line and write your first paragraph. Indent all paragraphs three to five spaces rather than setting them flush left with an extra line of white space between paragraphs (a newspaper format). Always paginate your manuscript, typically on the bottom center of your paper. Do not italicize your copy for the sake of slanted type; italicize only if you mean to *emphasize* a word. (A few editors still prefer underlined type to indicate italics, and you should underline if your typewriter does not have an italics function; however, most editors use popular word-processing software and prefer italics so that they can send copy on disk to the composing department—without changing underlines to italics.) Figure 10.1 shows how the text of the manuscript for "The Essential Elements of a Great Article" appeared below the writer's name, address, title, and subtitle.

As you continue from the first to subsequent pages of your manuscript, you should keep a few pointers in mind. First, you can adopt a typing style that always begins a new paragraph on the subsequent page. (In other words, if you can't fit the whole paragraph at the bottom of a page, you'll begin that paragraph at the top of the next page.) This style avoids *widows*— a printing term used to identify the last word or two of a paragraph that appears alone at the top of the next page. If you're using a computer, you can format this via the *text flow* function on your word-processing software. Typically, however, most editors do not care about widows on manuscripts—only on their published pages.

F I G U R E   1 0 . 1   Sample of Manuscript Prepared for Submission

---

Michael J. Bugeja   Office: (614) 555-5555
E. W. Scripps Hall   Home: (614) 555-4444
Ohio University   Fax: (614) 555-3333
Athens, Ohio 45701   e-mail: bugeja@test.com

[6 lines of white space]

The Essential Elements of a Great Article
[Extra line white space]
**All articles rely on these elements so that writers
can connect with readers. Here's a refresher course
to help you *sell, sell, sell.***
[Extra line white space]
Articles in magazines have them. Articles in SASEs don't. I'm talking about such basics as topic, theme, title, voice, viewpoint, moment, and ending.

You may or may not know those terms, so here's a quick review:

■ *Topic.* An obvious term, meaning "the person, group, place, thing, incident, or issue in an article." Yet I have seen rambling, incoherent manuscripts that lack a topic and force me to ask: "What is this about anyway?"

If an editor asks this, you haven't got a chance.

■ *Theme.* Call this "a second layer of meaning." If you forget this, you'll end up writing hard news. The next time you read a newspaper article, ask: "What is the *real* meaning of this report?" You won't find any. A story about war is really about war. A story about Congress is really about Congress. That's why Ben Franklin and Andrew Bradford invented the magazine. They had a distinct slant on life.

So do I on writing. Theme here is clear-cut: *publication.* Learn these elements, and publish. Piece of cake.

1

Second, you need to type your name in the upper left corner and your title in the upper right corner of all subsequent pages:

Michael Bugeja   "The Essential Elements of a Great Article"

Then drop down four to six lines and continue the text.

Subheads and breaks require special typing guidelines. Drop four lines before inserting a subhead to separate sections of an article. Subheads usually are typed flush left, boldface, in 14-point type and may appear anywhere on a new page:

I'll explain these concepts fully, showing how beginners in my magazine workshop apply them and often publish their first attempts at magazine nonfiction.

Topic

You may think you have a topic when you actually don't. Heather Paige Preston thought everyone would know what she was writing about in this introduction.

An asterisk break should not appear as a widow at the top of a new page (or else it looks like a typo or a stray mark). After an asterisk break, drop down four lines and center the asterisk between paragraphs, like this:

I'll explain these concepts fully, showing how beginners in my magazine workshop apply them and often publish their first attempts at magazine nonfiction.

*

You may think you have a topic when you actually don't. Heather Paige Preston thought everyone would know what she was writing about in this introduction.

Drop four lines between sections if you're using a space break. Space breaks that fall at the top of a page are trickier, however, because some editors might mistake the extra white space as paragraph spacing. You indicate a space break at the top of a page like this:

Michael Bugeja   "The Essential Elements of a Great Article"
(break)

You may think you have a topic when you actually don't. Heather
Paige Preston thought everyone would know what she was writing
about in this introduction.

Drop-letter breaks follow the same format as space breaks, with a typographical enhancement of the first letter in the *entrance sentence* (the one
that immediately follows the white space). The first letter should be cast in a
larger point size than appears in the text (about 48 points):

I'll explain these concepts fully, showing how beginners in my
magazine workshop apply them and often publish their first attempts
at magazine nonfiction.

Y ou may think you have a topic when you actually don't. Heather
Paige Preston thought everyone would know what she was writing
about in this introduction.

You can execute drop-letter breaks only via a computer with a compat-
ible word-processing program. If you lack those—using a typewriter, for instance—remember that drop-letter breaks simply represent a combination
of space and asterisk breaks. As such, use the appropriate combination of
space and asterisk breaks to suit your particular manuscript.

A clean manuscript never guarantees an acceptance, of course. It *does*
indicate that the writer has respect for the submitted work. Most editors will
honor that with a close reading, increasing the chances of publication.

Cover and Query Letters

Writer's guidelines and standard directories explain a magazine's policy on accepting an entire manuscript for submission. If the magazine
does accept full manuscripts, send a cover letter with the manuscript.
If not, write a query letter asking an editor to consider the manuscript. Do
not send the manuscript, but do include a SASE.

A *cover letter* is a specific type of business correspondence that makes a
brief, first impression on editors concerning the writer's ability to craft an
acceptable story. Here's how to put one together: In a direct, friendly, and

professional voice, introduce your submission and, if possible, the section of the magazine at which it is targeted. (For example, in the freelance magazine *Writer's Digest*, the *standing column section* is called "Chronicle"; the *short-article/news section* is called "The Writing Life"; and the *filler section* is referred to as "Tip Sheet." Most magazines have similar sections that do not require query letters, unlike features and articles at most publications.)

Your first paragraph should specify basic information about the title of your piece, the section of the magazine at which it is targeted, and a brief summary statement about its contents:

> Please consider the enclosed narrative "Angels in the Smoke" for the Chronicle section of *Writer's Digest*. The essay discusses a former student who had a near-death experience, "seeing" her late uncle in the aisle of a jet about to crash. The jet didn't crash, but the "angel" encounter—a real or psychological response—taught my student, and eventually me, the power of the imagination.

In the body of the letter, describe your piece in more detail and relate it to the target reader:

> The manuscript is just under 2,000 words in keeping with your guidelines. Because of the delicate subject matter, I have told this angel story in a straightforward voice. My student, an aspiring writer at the time, like thousands of your readers, taught me that we not only should "write about what we know"—a common cliché—but *research* what we do not know, empowering the muse.

Finally, list your writing credentials, and if appropriate, add information about yourself:

> I've published personal essays in these writing magazines: *Journalism Educator, Editor & Publisher*, and *Quill*. I teach magazine journalism at Ohio University and am a subscriber of your magazine.
> Thank you for your time and consideration.

The procedure for compiling a cover letter is the same for a student as well as a new writer with few previous publications. In such case, discuss any hobby, skill, or interest that relates to the magazine or the manuscript. If you have published in newspapers or worked in journalism, mention that, too. Figure 10.2 shows a sample cover letter by a college student.

FIGURE 10.2   Sample Cover Letter by a College Student

000 Main Street
Athens, Ohio 00000

May 1, 1997

Paul Worthington, Senior Editor
Mac Home Journal
612 Howard Street, Sixth Floor
San Francisco, California 94105

Dear Paul Worthington:

Please consider the enclosed manuscript "Give Your Mac an
Interface-Lift" for publication in *Mac Home Journal's* "Short Takes"
department. The piece provides the average Mac user an easy way
to improve the aesthetic quality of the interface on his or her computer by installing seven simple control panels and extensions from
on-line shareware libraries.

I wrote the feature for my Advanced Magazine Feature Writing
Class at Ohio University. I am a student journalist and have
published several pieces in the independent student newspaper
here, as well as in other various university publications.

Thank you for your consideration. I have enclosed a self-addressed
stamped envelope and look forward to your response.

Sincerely,

Keith Johns

Keith Johns
(555) 555-5555

A *query letter* is a specific type of business letter correspondence that solicits an assignment from an editor. The letter should be composed in standard business form with appropriate opening and closing salutations. In addition, a query requires research into back issues to see if the magazine has published something similar in the past two years. If the magazine has not published a similar piece, then you should pitch the idea to a specific editor. If your submission is targeted at a specific department, send the manuscript to the appropriate editor listed on the *masthead* (the page that lists a magazine's editors and their names).

In the voice of your proposed article, introduce your topic and/or theme, highlighting your research or slant:

> Children in one out of every five families in southeastern Ohio go to bed hungry, a number that has increased more than 15 percent in the past decade. Behind each number is a face and behind that, the memory of a disenfranchised childhood.
>
> My sources tell me that social problems arising out of hunger will cost the state some $15 billion in aid to children in the next five years. Moreover, they say, lack of adequate nutrition is one of the leading causes of educational dysfunction, requiring more tax money to hire remedial teachers.

In the body of your letter, help the editor visualize your piece:

> I would like to send you a 2,000-word article, "The Face of Hunger in Ohio," for your "Other Voices" department. A check of two-years' back issues indicates that you have not carried information on this topic, and in the interim, much as occurred, including a new federal study that puts Ohio in the top ten crisis states.
>
> I plan to interview state and local officials for background and political overtones, setting the stage for more pertinent research: interviews with five or more families whose food aid this year has been cut. I want to make the statistics real, putting the children in question on your readers' doorsteps.

In the last paragraph, list your credentials, so the editor can determine whether you have the ability to execute the proposed article:

I was reared in southeastern Ohio, the area of the state that has the highest incidence of child hunger. I have published features regularly in area newspapers and have placed three articles in the past two years in *Appalachian Heritage, Southeastern Ohio,* and *Ohio Magazine.* (I've enclosed two of those magazine clips.)

Thank you for your time and consideration. I've attached a business-sized SASE for your reply.

If you have published similar magazine pieces, photocopy a few of those and enclose them with your manuscript. Figure 10.3 shows a sample query letter by a new magazine writer.

Here are some general rules about cover and query letters:

- Single-space all business correspondence.
- Do not guess at courtesy titles (*Mr., Miss, Mrs., or Ms.*) or appear informal by using first names (*Dear Jane*); rather, use the full name (*Dear Jane Doe*).
- The cover letter should be no longer than 125 words; the query letter should be no longer than one page.
- In any correspondence with an editor, include a self-addressed stamped envelope (SASE) large enough for the returned manuscript or reply. (See Mailing and Marketing.)

Mailing and Marketing

After you have composed your cover or query letter, you need to mail it in the standard way. Invest in a postal scale so that you know how much your manuscript weighs. (That saves a trip to the post office.)

If you are sending a cover letter with your article, you need two 9½ × 12½ manila envelopes. Write, type, or label one envelope with the name and address of the magazine editor. Write, type, or label the other envelope with your own name and address. Now weigh the two envelopes along with your manuscript and cover letter. Check the scale to note how many first-class stamps you will need to mail those four items to an editor. Then remove from the scale the envelope addressed to the editor and note the new weight. The second figure is the number of first-class stamps required on the envelope addressed to you so an editor can return your manuscript with a rejection or rewrite letter.

FIGURE 10.3 Sample Query Letter by a New Magazine Writer

0000 Main Street
Athens, Ohio 00000

April 17, 1997

Jean P. Kelly, Editor
Ohio Magazine
62 E. Broad Street
Columbus, Ohio 43215-3522

Dear Jean Kelly:

One of the most successful environmental efforts in the last 25 years has been the miraculous restoration of Lake Erie. In 1972 some scientists believed that the effects of massive pollution and intensive commercial shoreline development upon the lake were irreversible.

Scientists in a Toledo-based research group are optimistic that people are learning to make reasonable tradeoffs between their need to develop the lake shoreline and maintain the lake's ecological integrity. An unlikely combination of luck, governmental support, public awareness and scientific ingenuity has rescued the lake.

I would like to send you a 2,000-word article, "The Miracle of Lake Erie," for your "Environment" department. As this is the 25th anniversary of the lake's cleanup, I plan to show how far the lake has come and its prognosis for the next 10 to 15 years.

I am a writer with more than 10 years' experience in public relations and journalism. I am working toward a master's degree in journalism at Ohio University.

I look forward to hearing from you and have enclosed a stamped, self-addressed envelope for your reply.

Sincerely,

Les Roka

Les Roka
(555)555-5555

Affix the correct postage on each envelope. Fold in half the envelope addressed to you and paperclip your letter to it. Paperclip your manuscript, too. Most editors dislike staples. Put both paperclipped items in the envelope addressed to the editor and seal the envelope. Your submission is ready to mail.

If you are sending a query, address one No. 10 business envelope to the editor and one No. 9 business envelope to yourself. If you are not sending clips of previously published material, simply put one first-class stamp on each envelope, fold your query letter in thirds, and put it and the No. 9 envelope in the one addressed to the editor. Seal that envelope, and it is ready to mail.

If you are sending previously published material, you will need to weigh those clips on your postal scale along with your two envelopes and query letter. That's how much postage you need to mail all your items to an editor. Now take off the No. 10 envelope. That's how much postage you need for an editor to return your materials with his or her reply. Affix those stamps to both envelopes. You may staple clips, by the way; to do so, fold them in thirds, and place them aside. Now fold your query in thirds and place it on top of your clips. Take both items and your SASE and place them in the envelope addressed to the editor. Again, you're ready to mail.

If you are sending copies of long articles with your query, you may need to replace your No. 10 and No. 9 envelopes with 9½ × 12½ manila ones. Otherwise, your clips won't fit in business-sized envelopes. (Most editors hate to stuff material in SASEs.) Simply follow the procedure outlined for cover letters, thinking of your clips as a manuscript.

Finally, when you mail a manuscript or query, you need to log the submission in a business file. There are any number of ways to make a log. You can use a computer file and print it out, you can use a 3 × 5 file card system in a box on your desk, or you can log submissions in long hand in a personal notebook. Do what works best for you. Dedicate a file, card, or notebook page to each manuscript or query. Note the title of your piece or contents of your query, along with the name of the editor, the magazine, and the date sent. When an editor reports back to you, note the date of the rejection, acceptance, or rewrite request.

For more information about marketing and etiquette with editors, see the business sections of standard directories such as *Writer's Market*.

Always act professionally when dealing with editors. Do not send nasty notes or e-mail when they reject you and do not annoy them with requests about the status of your article or query. (Check writer's guidelines or directory listings to see how long the editorial process takes at each magazine.) Generally, if you have not heard back from an editor in six months, you should send a brief letter, with a SASE, inquiring if the manuscript or query is still under consideration. If you don't hear back in another two months, send a postcard withdrawing the manuscript or query from consideration.

Send your magazine to a new market. Do not get discouraged by rejection. Some veteran writers send out a manuscript 20 or more times before an editor accepts it. In any case, do not send your manuscript or query out to a new magazine until the first one responds. Most editors do not appreciate *simultaneous submissions* (sending one manuscript out to two or more publications). Again, editors who do allow this practice state so in writer's guidelines or directory listings.

Do not send more than one manuscript to the *same* editor or magazine until you receive a response about your first submission. Sending several manuscripts in this manner is known as *multiple submissions,* and it usually irks editors.

Editors are busy people who can help establish your freelance writing career. Treat them with respect and learn from them whenever the opportunity arises. As Catherine Johnson, contributing editor for *New Woman,* says, "I have learned over the years that writing for magazines is a more collaborative art than writers sometimes realize. One piece of advice I would give to new writers is to value and protect the relationships they develop with editors along the way.

"Good editors make good writers better," she adds.

Good luck.

THE CRAFT SHOP

awright, here's what i learned . . .

Bethany Matsko, Assistant Editor, *JazzTimes*

I had a hard time choosing which version of my *Sassy* article to send for inclusion in this book because I am the perfect person in my own little world and those who edited my piece are not. I would have loved to argue with my editor, Diane, for hours over the changes she made to the piece. What was wrong with it? It was the story of *my* life, not hers. The facts were correct (after all, hadn't I lived them?) and the grammar was just as I'd planned. It read well, was quick to get through, and the voice was perfect for the *Sassy* audience. I should know, I'd been reading the magazine since its birth, and the thoughts trucking through my head each day were always in that voice. I all but worshipped the publication—it was a real person to me. I knew the vocab, parlayed the slang, breathed its language.

After several heart-breaking edits and radically different drafts of my piece, it slapped me in the face that learning a voice, adopting it as my own and mastering it were not as simple as I'd led my somewhat arrogant self to believe. Although I still adhere to a somewhat simply structured writing style and voice (á la *Sassy*), writing this piece for actual publication brought about some startlingly painful discoveries about said voice. (And editors.)

I wrote the column for Michael Bugeja's Magazine Feature Writing class during my junior year of college. I was 21, and felt as if I'd lived a thousand lives; I had easily written that many columns junior year alone. It was easy. So I set out once again on a linguistic journey, this time armed with a few new tactics I picked up from Bugeja. I picked my occasion of narration, located the moment of narration, chose to wrap it up with a closed ending, and assigned what I thought would be the strongest and most dire part of the story: a narrator, my point of view, and an interior monologue. This would make the column pure *me*. I knew my writing voice better than I knew the constellation of freckles on my nose, and the only writing strategies that would bring out my best was to tell the story from a personal point of view in an authoritative, hip narration mimicking the voice in my own head. I'd been taught that once a writer develops his or her own voice, it becomes relatively simple to adapt to the voice of a particular magazine.

Ha.

At this point, not only had I perfected my own voice, but I had, through studying every agate line in *Sassy*, become fluent in *Sassy*-speak. I fit the word-puzzle together, wrote the piece, and submitted it for publication a couple months later.

It takes a good editor to knock the wind out of someone's sails—gently. Which is exactly what Diane did to me. Here I was, an extremely self-adoring 21-year-old magazine wanna-be, standing next to the fax machine, impatiently waiting for the first proof pages. Two days later, I was back again, waiting for the second edit. And the third, and it goes on. You see, the points we discussed and which were bored into our heads in Bugeja's class were of utmost importance, and through our workshop setting, I had arranged them all correctly. I completed the puzzle as I mentioned, added my own panache, and Diane was telling me through her edits that I had not hit the mark. At all.

The column was written like this: a savvy 21-year-old chickadee related a story to her friend's 15-year-old sister while they made their way across Manhattan. In my head, the two were shopping in the Village, crossing busy intersections boldly in hard-soled shoes, and inhaling the black air with vigor. They weren't completely carefree—they had growing pains on their minds, and the story relieved the pressure. It was gently authoritative and possessed enough "big words" to make the young girl feel like an equal: despite their educational and experiential differences, they could communicate effectively. The older one didn't feel pressured to "step down" a level, and that was important. That was *Sassy*. And what made the publication the best one out there for teenage girls was that it respected them through its voice.

Inadvertently, I had incorrectly interpreted the voice. I was not your average *Sassy* reader. I was too old. When I read the magazine, I was reliving my early teen years, experiencing nostalgia, and I needed to figure that out. Diane beat me to it. Once I saw my copy in print and read how baby-ish it sounded, I was furious with myself for not realizing what I'd done wrong. Once Diane shaved about six years off my voice (basically changing my narrator), the piece was finally right. It was supposed to sound like a 15-year-old talking to another 15-year-old (possibly younger), in the same setting I had imagined—but perhaps shopping for notebooks and hot pink mechanical pencils rather than low-slung belts.

Editors. Professors. Ahhhh . . . what to say about them? Professors warn of editors and editors warn writers to unlearn. Bugeja warned me—and everyone else in his magazine writing classes—that just because I thought it was a good piece, it wasn't necessarily so in the eyes of an editor. He taught me to fit the pieces together, which I had, but that an editor might hand you a new puzzle and five minutes to complete it.

Anyway, I had the choice to submit my graded piece and the one that ran in the magazine to be excerpted in this book. I sent Bugeja the published version, which I chose because I realize I am not perfect, and neither was my piece. This edited version of my voice (the sum of narrator, monologue, and point of view) may not be the cat's meow to me, but in Diane's eyes it was close enough for publication, and once I saw my story in print, Diane's view was all that mattered. I was published. In *Sassy*, no less.

The sum of Bugeja's six rhetorical terms are all relative, obviously—*New Woman* would never run this piece—but each are important and should be assigned wisely (sometimes without pride). Like a well-written magazine piece, each magazine possesses its own occasion and moment of narration, narrative persona, point of view, monologue, and ending. Writing for magazines requires that you uncover each element and adhere to it. This is an incredible process, and is why discovering the voice between the glossy sheets is my absolute favorite part of reading magazines. A good writer will know when this happens—the magazine's personality will suddenly extend its hand warmly and say, "Nice to meetcha."

THE   NEWSSTAND

Final Preparations

1. Return to the magazine rack of your local or college library. Check the masthead of the most recent issue of each of your target magazines, recording the name of the editor responsible for the section or department where you intend to send your manuscript or query letter. You will need the name and address to write a cover or query letter to this editor at The Keyboard.

2. While you are at the library, locate three new magazines that you would like to write for in the near future. Turn to the masthead of each publication and record the name of the managing editor so that you can request writer's guidelines.

3. Follow the procedures listed in The Newsstand exercise from Chapter 1 and envision your new target audiences. Develop new story ideas and project files according to the assignments outlined at The Newsstand and at The Keyboard from Chapters 2 through 9. This ensures that you will have a steady supply of manuscripts to create, revise, and market, earning the title of *freelance writer.*

THE   KEYBOARD

Preparing Your Submission

1. Type or print your manuscript according to the procedures outlined in this chapter.

2. Read the writer's guidelines of your target market to determine whether you can send an entire manuscript or whether you should query first. (A word about queries: Although working freelance writers

always query before writing first drafts, unlike novices, they also have published clips that can win contracts with kill fees. You need to place a few manuscripts, and the best way to do so is to compose them first, as you learned to do in this book.)

3. Depending on editorial policies of your target market, write a cover letter or a query letter by following the procedures given in this chapter.

4. Prepare your submission and make a business log according to the procedures outlined in this chapter.

Readings in Magazine Nonfiction

Guide to Readings

The following anthology includes a selection of the most frequently published genres of magazine journalism: columns, profiles, opinion and interview features, and essays and articles. Within these main formats are subcategories: personal, inspirational, public affairs, teen and literary columns; consumer, personal, literary, and investigative profiles; exposé, outdoor, small-press, and political opinion and interview pieces; and informal, personal experience, research, small-press, literary, and natural history essays and articles. The selected manuscripts originally were published in a wide array of consumer, men's and women's general-interest, teen, public affairs, house and garden, trade, Sunday supplement, newspaper magazine, small-press, literary, and other mass market publications. Some of the authors are well known (George Plimpton, Molly Peacock, and Carol Muske Dukes); some are also editors (Bill Brohaugh, Ursula Obst, Bruce Woods, Karin Horgan Sullivan, Bethany Matsko, and Catherine Johnson); some are educators (Kevin Bezner, Patricia Raybon, Kelly Cherry, David Lazar, and Patricia Westfall); and some are full-time writers (Dana Gioia and Molly Peacock). One contributor, Amy Hudson, is a freelance writer and a staff psychologist at a federal prison in Oklahoma, and another, Lady Borton, is a freelance writer and school bus driver.

Despite the diversity of selections and authors, these readings do not purport to represent all nonfiction styles and publications. They were chosen because they illustrate the techniques discussed in earlier chapters of this book, from titles to endings. Excerpts of them already have been presented to showcase specific lessons, but now you need to read the complete manuscript to see how each writer aligns basic elements of nonfiction to create a publishable work. Although individual formats, voice tones, and truths represented here differ greatly, the elements of nonfiction do not, combining to empower each piece.

In the Editor's Note that precedes each piece, you will learn more about these elements and authors. Also added are discussion questions that you can address in a personal journal, workshop, or class. As you go through the anthology, identify basic formats—column, profile, opinion, interview, essay, or article—that appeal to you. Scan the pieces for specific voice tones that motivate you and that might meld with your own topics and themes. Note how each writer expresses his or her personal truths to target readers, and determine which strategy might harmonize with your own epiphanies and peak experiences.

Finally, as you have been encouraged in the exercises at the end of each chapter, keep reading a wide array of consumer, trade, regional, small-press, and literary magazines. You'll discover authors and outlets not included here that will inspire and educate you as you embark on a fulfilling career as a writer and observer of this life.

Columns

E D I T O R ' S   N O T E

Lady Borton, former field director for the American Friends Service Committee, worked for that Quaker organization during the Viet Nam War. In subsequent years, she lived in Hanoi and elsewhere in Viet Nam. That experience inspired two books, *After Sorrow: An American among the Vietnamese* (Viking) and *Sensing the Enemy* (Dial/Doubleday).

Borton also publishes children's books, poetry, and newspaper columns on a regular basis. When she is not writing, she tends a cattle farm in southeast Ohio and drives a school bus.

In the "Hers" column that follows, which originally appeared in the *New York Times Magazine,* Borton discusses returning to Viet Nam and living among the people who were once enemies to all Americans. As you read her piece, ask yourself:

- Do you feel as if you have visited Viet Nam? If so, determine any passages of sensory data.
- How does the moment of narration affect voice and depict action?
- How are quotations presented, capturing distinct voice tones?

Note these elements as well: The occasion is a visit to a former Viet Cong stronghold. The topic is Viet Nam and the theme is stated in Borton's suspense title: forgiveness. She transports readers to Ban Long by combining a descriptive, reportorial, and compassionate voice with a moment of narration close to the action, so that we experience what she does in land graced by milk trees and rice paddies. Aside from a few paragraphs of grounding, Borton cannot comment much because the moment is in the *now*. When she allows herself to speak, she expresses an epiphany related to theme. In her closed ending, Borton quotes Second Treasure, a former Viet Cong woman who commanded 100 guerillas in the war, graciously giving her the last word.

A Forgiving Land

Lady Borton

"Hands up, American!" Second Treasure said in Vietnamese. She poked my ribs. "You're under arrest!" I lifted my sandals over my head. In the moonlight, the tiger cactuses along the rice paddy loomed like phantoms with prickly limbs.

"Forward!" Second Treasure said in a teasing voice. She was leading me into Ban Long, a village of 4,000 people in the Mekong delta southwest of Ho Chi Minh City. Throughout the war, Ban Long had been a Viet Cong base. American B-52's had bombed the village, turning houses into craters, families into corpses. Agent Orange had stripped the earth of green.

Now, 15 years after the war, foliage obscured the moon. Milk trees hung heavy with fruit. Frogs chortled. Frangipani flowers like tiny trumpets broadcast their insistent perfume.

Amazing, I thought: The earth has forgiven us.

During the war, I'd worked in Viet Nam with the Quakers as a health administrator. Ten years later, in 1980, I lived in Malaysia's largest refugee camp for Boat People who'd fled Viet Nam. Now, I wanted to know Vietnamese who had chosen to stay.

"We'll stop at my father's," Second Treasure said. She pointed to a wooden house in a grove of breadfruit trees. I balked. Between me and the house stood a creek with a "monkey bridge"—a single palm trunk. Muddy footprints greased the palm's bark.

"Dead already," I muttered in Vietnamese.

Second Treasure stepped onto the bridge. Her face was open, like a lotus at midday. She reached for my hand. In the darkness, braced by this former Viet Cong woman, I edged across.

This trip, earlier this year, was my fourth visit to Ban Long since the war. I remained the only foreign writer whom the Vietnamese allowed to live with peasants in the countryside. I was watched by the curious villagers. Unbearably so. I was the circus come to town.

"A giant!" the kids announced. Wherever I went, they stepped on my heels, petted my arms. "She's furry like a monkey!" "Look," they whispered, surprised that hair could be curly, "it's like dead vines."

"The giant is timid, like a toddler," they said whenever I teetered across a "monkey bridge."

These children had never seen an American. Even teenagers couldn't remember the war. In contrast, during his 80 years, Second Treasure's father had known only 15 years of peace.

I called Second Treasure's father Senior Uncle, the same title the Vietnamese had given Ho Chi Minh. Uncle was a tiny man with huge hands. He could swing among the waterapple trees, gathering the dimpled fruit as nimbly as his grandsons. His mind was equally keen. Yet with me, Uncle repeated himself, as if to make up for the years he had missed knowing me.

"Child," Uncle said each evening as we rinsed our bowls in the creek, "always save rice for tomorrow. Who knows? Tomorrow you may have nothing to eat. Never drink from the creek. Drink from the rain-water crock under the eaves . . ."

"Father . . . ," Second Treasure said. She worried I might find Uncle boring. Second Treasure hovered, tending me as if I belonged to an endangered species.

During the war, Second Treasure had commanded 100 Viet Cong guerrillas. She would load her canoe with weapons, concealing the contraband with leaves. Then she'd slip along sluices and creeks. When helicopters appeared, she'd jump overboard.

"Always keep these two holes above water," she said, touching her nostrils.

"We were rats," her father said. "We lived underground, in tunnels. Slept by day, prowled at night. Our feet knew the way. But we were different from rats." He chuckled. "We were smarter."

During the war, Uncle had organized Ban Long's literacy campaign. To his lifetime treasures—a Confucian primer, a book on Lenin, a volume of Ho Chi Minh's poetry—he now added the photo book of New Jersey my father had sent with me. Uncle showed the photographs to every neighbor who visited.

"Do you have a water buffalo on your farm in Ohio?" one woman asked.

"Do you eat watermelon?" a second said.

"Do you fish in a bomb crater?" Fifth Brother asked.

"You don't grow rice?" his mother, Third Sister, exclaimed. She'd lost three sons during the war. Toothless, she mashed her betel nut in an American shell casing. "Then how do you eat?"

One day, Third Sister laughed so hard she couldn't finish her betel nut. Eight women had come to visit. Middle-aged, they looked like a bridal party posing for a silver anniversary photo. All wore overblouses in varying hues and the traditional loose, black trousers. They asked about American bridal dress.

What?" Third Sister said at my description. "No trousers?" The women rollicked at this immodest thought.

As with everything else, the villagers watched me harvest. Second Treasure, standing among them, chuckled as I stepped off the paddy dike.

"Please!" said an old woman bent like a walking cane. "Don't take your pretty white legs into the paddy muck."

I sank to midcalf in mud. I slogged toward the row of women harvesting. The mud sucked me off balance.

"Did she drink rice wine?" the old woman asked.

The harvesters cut the tall rice with sickles. They set the grasses aside on the stubble. They cut and set, cut and set, moving together in a long line, as if choreographed. Sickle in hand, I joined them.

"Hold the grass farther down," Second Treasure yelled.

I slid my left hand down.

"No! Five plants at once."

I sliced the grass.

"No, no, farther up."

I set the grasses aside.

"Lay the stems even!"

I felt like a dancing bear. I'd had days of this. I was tired of Second Treasure telling me when to wash my feet, how many bowls of rice to eat, when to shake out my grass mat. I stood up, sickle in hand, fuming.

"Didn't Uncle Ho say, 'Eat with the people, live with them, work with them?'"

"Yes."

"When did Uncle Ho say, 'Stand on the dike, give orders'?"

Second Treasure looked dismayed. Her face wilted.

I was horrified. I'd been insensitive. Rude. "Forgive me," I said in Vietnamese.

"Hello?" Second Treasure said in English. To get me to smile, she tried all the phrases I'd taught her. "O.K.? Thank you?" Then she herded the watchers down the paddy dike, her laughter reaching back across the mud and stubble.

My last evening, the harvesters came to visit. They brought milk fruit, waterapples, breadfruit and dried tamarind. "Please," they said, "take these gifts to the women in America."

After they left, Uncle approached me. In his palms he cradled a tiny photograph. He pressed it into my hands. "This is the only picture of me young. Give it to your father. Tell him to come live with me in Ban Long. I'll take care of him in his old age."

It's even more amazing, I thought: the people have forgiven us.

Later that evening, Second Treasure and I swung together in the hammock. She worried about her teen-age son, who ran with a fast crowd in town. She couldn't keep him in bicycle brakes. She worried about her father alone in the countryside. Recently he'd fallen from a waterapple tree.

"Older Sister," I asked when the conversation lulled, "are you a Communist?"

Her fingers fluttered in the southern Vietnamese gesture, No.

"Uncle?"

"No, no! Father fought the French rulers 30 years before he heard of Communists."

Second Treasure nodded toward her father's house under the breadfruit trees. The fragrance of ripe fruit tinged the air. In the distance, an owl called out, "*cu, cu,*" sounding its Vietnamese name.

"Don't you understand, Little Sister?" Second Treasure said. "This is all we wanted."

Molly Peacock is one of the country's leading poets, with several books to her credit, including the celebrated collection *Original Love* (W. W. Norton). She has received numerous awards and fellowships, including ones from the Ingram Merrill Foundation and the National Endowment for the Arts. She is also an essayist and magazine journalist, publishing mostly in the literary press.

The following piece originally appeared in the "State of Grace" standing column in *Mirabella*, a women's general-interest magazine. As you read Peacock's prose, ask yourself:

- Which passages relate to topic and which to theme?
- Which passages showcase especially rich voice tones?
- Which passages would appeal to an audience of "intelligent, cultured, affluent, secure, curious and confident" women (as described in *Mirabella's* media kit)?

Note how Peacock sustains her descriptive, intelligent, introspective voice, from first to last sentence. The topic is a garden, and the theme is grace. The moment of narration is pushed toward the *then,* allowing Peacock to comment and focusing acute attention on her elegant voice tones. Perhaps the most important element is her archetypal symbolism, from garden to *Lilac Fairy Book* to journeys—real and universal ones. In her closed imagistic ending, Peacock addresses *Mirabella* readers directly, explaining how they, too, can evoke a state of grace.

Where You'll Find Me

As a Child, the Writer Felt at Peace among Her Grandmother's Poppies and Apple Trees. She Still Does.

Molly Peacock

Orange poppies lolled in a great pride, like lionesses, beside the apple trees. Huge and real, they leapt to life from a book I had stowed in my suitcase that summer, the *Lilac Fairy Book*. I'd finally come to visit my grandmother by myself, old enough to be sent the mere hundred miles that separated my prim suburbia from her ramshackle house. She'd placed the perennial beds in a remnant of an apple orchard that still had a few gnarled trees, just to make her garden even more of a fairy tale. Forces I felt responsible for but did not understand were the cause of my prolonged visit: the death throes of my parents' marriage, and my grandmother's insistence that I go to summer Bible school. But the religion she gave me was her garden.

It was a place of grace, a sanctuary I spent hours in, where flowers had personalities, including the queen, a recalcitrant French lilac who had gotten her seasons turned around and insisted on producing blossoms in September. In my parents' house I was never free of the tasks that helplessly fell to me as their lives disintegrated: the care of the house and meals and my younger sister. I had two selves, really: a robot self to dispense my obligations, and a true self that was dangerously buried or, as gardeners say, "caught in the bulb." But in that garden, where I was able to act dreamy, my true self was released.

A Buddhist might call it mindfulness. A Quaker might call it connecting with the light inside you. To be able to look an orange poppy in its chartreuse eye and simply be doing nothing other than looking at that blowzy-headed flower, feeling only one experience without competing subsidiary ones, is my idea of grace. To be fully inside the looking moment is to be fully in your true self, not the one you have created for others' demands. This grace is a kind of blooming.

Because the garden is do deeply connected with the true self, it is also deeply sensual, and intensely so for women because flowers, so shockingly sexual, are identified with women.

That summer I became a seed-catalog junkie, entranced with pictures of flowers. I was riveted and embarrassed by the close-ups of orchids. Each orchid was me, it was every girl, turned inside out for all to see.

My grandmother's poppies and apple trees are long gone, but just the way we sometimes feel that someone whom we loved and lost is not gone entirely, but transformed somehow into another type of energy, that garden is inside me. It has become a portable state of grace.

And I need it, because I live a portable life. Having lost each other for decades, my highschool boyfriend and I met again and married. Since we both had well-established lives in two countries, we decided not to dismantle them, but to enlarge—and complicate—our lives by keeping both. Now we live in London, Ontario, full of stately trees and tiny backyard gardens; and in New York City, where the flowers are in tin buckets at the fruit markets and in the unexpected gardens one discovers inside stately buildings like the Frick Mansion.

Although I don't always feel it, I carry that dreamy flower state within me as I lug my suitcases through customs. Tucked inside, like the *Lilac Fairy Book* in my first suitcase, it insists on its presence, just like the Lilac Queen in my grandmother's garden, who bloomed when she wanted to, turning everybody else's fall into her spring. My attention to a flower can help me rediscover my true self, the self I lose to forces I'm responsible for but often do not completely understand. That centered staring helps erase the robot self of Lists, Calls, Chores, Duties, Dampened Desires.

The frailest of nature's objects, these most female emblems, have staying power. Staying power has healing power, too. You can stand in front of flowers and look them in their many eyes and see *just them*, and for a moment you are doing only one thing fully, being in the presence of their tart soil and tender personalities, and connecting with the tart and tender within yourself.

E D I T O R ' S   N O T E

Bill Brohaugh, editorial director of *Writer's Digest* and Betterway Books, is author of *Write Tight* and *Professional Etiquette for Writers* (both by WD Books). From 1982 to 1990, Brohaugh edited *Writer's Digest Magazine,* which originally published the inspirational column that follows, titled "Talking to the River." As you read it, ask yourself:

- Which passages especially appeal to an audience of aspiring writers?
- Which passages ground the topic, distinguishing it from theme?
- How does the author's use of verb tense affect voice?

Though column length, Brohaugh's piece has the clout of a full-length article. Basic elements harmonize beautifully. For instance, Brohaugh uses a suspense title that forebodes passages in the work, and he heralds his topic (stream) and theme (control) in the subtitle, establishing a contract with readers. His confidant's voice has two other tones: conversational and overwhelmed. His narrator knows the audience intimately and speaks directly to readers, confiding shared experiences about the writing process. Most distinctive is his use of moment—toward the *then,* allowing comment—but cast in a pushed present tense, adding a confessional element. In his well-foreboded open ending, his epiphany is poetic: Words are rocks to be moved and to move readers.

Talking to the River

Sometimes Moving a River Is Easier Than Writing Well

Bill Brohaugh

Halfway into the biggest writing project I have ever tackled, I decided to change the course of a river.

The poetically correct would call it a river, anyway. The real-estate agent who sold us the six acres two years back had called it a stream, and indeed by each mid-summer, it settles down to a trickled rivulet over the rock bed it has bared over the years. But in its annual spring resurrection, the "stream" rain-swells to about 25 feet across, rushing downstream to take its assured time in eating away the base of the hill where construction has begun on our house.

I'll finish writing *The Chronology of the English Language* in that eventually existent house. The book was begun a year before the bulldozer touched topsoil, and will be done, if my projections are right, six months after we step over the finished threshold. I conceived *Chronology* as a fun project, a couple hundred pages long and a few months in the compilation. A reference book chronicling the approximate dates of words' entry into the language, a fun project? I soon found out just how crazy I was: Now, a full year after I started *Chronology,* and about a month before my original deadline to have the book completed, I find myself only halfway through the research.

So much writing work to do, and yet I stand at the side of the stream, about to ask it to move. I will be polite and undemanding. I don't want to send the stream up hills. I don't want it to do loops in the air, or watery half-gainers as it sweeps down over a falls. I just want to move it a few feet to the left. As if it were a couch.

I begin the project in April. The idea seems simple. A bank of sand and sediment has developed on the left side (as I look downstream). It was deposited there as the river, over time, meandered to the right, digging into the hillside. I'll divert water by moving rocks from the left bank to the right, allowing the stream to wash away the sediment and expose more rocks for me to chuck across the river. Eventually, the relocated rocks will trap new sediment, this time where I want it, forming a cushioning bank at the foot of the hill that holds the house.

I toss the first rock.

There are a lot of rocks.

That night I close my eyes in bed and see quicksilver geology in front of me. All the rocks I picked up, pried up, dug up, then chunked to the other side of the stream: I see images of all those rocks piled together, swirling, rearranging themselves, stifling then creating gnawing eddies of water. Such imaging is familiar to me. After a few hours playing computer games, I'll close my eyes and watch aliens and their spaceships exploring my mental darkness and asking me why I killed the electron streams that gave them life. After I've completed a long night drive, closing my eyes launches a flow of white lines stabbing me in the left shoulder.

I don't recall ever closing my eyes after a long day at the keyboard and seeing words trotting in left to right, caroming off each other, roiling and mixing like the rocks I visioned that evening.

If anyone were to interrupt my rock-tossing to ask me what I was doing, I would say, "I am talking to the river."

My work, I would explain, is a negotiation. I can't tell water what to do. The word *inexorable* was created for water. I can only talk to the river: Bribe it with paths of least resistance. Give it reason to flow in this direction instead of that.

But no one is around to ask me what I am doing; I tell no one that I am talking to the river. I am disappointed that this beautiful phrase I've come up with goes unheard except in seemingly unending mental repetition as I struggle to extract rocks with sucking sounds from the muck of this shore and chuck them to that. The phrase replays in my head because it is unused. Should it eventually find an audience, I will release it; then I will struggle to extract other words with sucking sounds from the muck of my head and form beautiful shores with them.

My wife does not tell me I am crazy for wanting to change the course of a sometimes river. She sits on the hillside I am trying to preserve and watches. Not me, but the sky and the trees around me. "I can see the progress," she says when later I sit, exhausted, beside her.

I think she is very kind.

She sometimes tells me I'm crazy for tackling two-year-long book projects.

I think she is very right.

I wonder if I would have tackled the river if I hadn't learned the necessity of the long haul while working on the book. Each day at the keyboard, the words clatter across other words as I toss them over flowing waters, and eventually the work gets done.

The lesson taught me by the book suddenly frightens me.

I see the river changing course faster than the book digs its own.

A couple of weeks into my negotiations with the river, I have made far more progress than I could have expected. The river has stirred, about to roll over in its sleep. Roll over just a few feet to the left, please.

I realize this progress one May Saturday before noon, after putting in a few hours' labor, as I stand in my ancient-and-therefore-soakable Reeboks in the middle of the stream, feeling the cool erosive against my ankles the way I'm asking the bank on the left to feel it. The inexorable splashes/eddies against the rocks I haven't yet conquered.

I am sore from my work; this is something a 40-year-old with occasional back problems shouldn't be doing. My fingers sport scratches no computer keyboard could inflict. My butt, well exercised at my desk, is the only part of me that doesn't hurt. I shouldn't be doing it—I shouldn't be succeeding. Yet, I can now stand with weary pride at a shortened shore; the streamwater and I have pushed one bank as much as a foot to the left. Not a couch-width, but a start.

I've moved the stream a foot.

More important, I have moved the stream.

I watch crayfish dart backwards through quiet pools. Clouds dart through the waters of the sky even more quickly, casting me and the crayfish in shadow, bathing us in sunlight, dim/bright, dim/bright. For some reason, I close my eyes. This time, I do not see rocks. I see nothing, but I know what the nothing is.

I write well that night: triple my daily quota on *The Chronology of the English Language Meets Godzilla*. Two pages of notes on my next project. And for my dessert: I write many of the words you read now.

I saw nothing and knew what the nothing was. Rather, I saw nothing that stood out as being unusual. I was seeing things, yes, but things happily invisible to me, the way that your own breath is mostly unbearable. That's why I've never had night visions of words. The words indeed revisit me after long sessions at the keyboard as I lie in bed, but they pass by unnoticed, familiar and welcome, expected and unnoted. The rocks/the river are a brief obsession. The computer games, a hobby. The long drives, an every-so-often chore.

But the words—the words are always there, not standing out in the night of my unconscious because they are my unconscious. I don't see the words because they take the form not of aftervisions of the day's work at the keyboard, but of premonitions of what those words will create—the stories, images of things that are quite unrocklike in the fact that they don't exist, except there in my mind and, with luck and a bit of rock-tossing, eventually on paper.

The next weekend out on the river, shortly after winning a wrestling match in three falls with a slab of stone as wide as me and half as tall, I see/don't see a story.

The story is about those who don't understand us. It has a cast of characters that is one character: the man at the party afraid to let liquor go to waste; the investigative neighbor who is sure of your shoe size even though you aren't; a well-meaning friend who asks you questions about your craft and reacts to your answers as if yearning that your exploits could be more glamorous. It could be any of those, but let's say it is the man with the vodka sour in his hand.

"So you're a writer," he says, not disparagingly but neither with particular respect. He takes another swig. "I've had a pretty interesting life. I could write a novel if I wanted to."

You smile politely. "I'll tell you what," you say. "You go out and find yourself a river. Then . . . move the river. After you do that, come and talk to me. Because," you will say, "moving a river is easier than writing well."

He will reel a bit, and vodka will have nothing to do with it. You will smile politely still. You say: "And when you have moved yourself a river, close your eyes and tell me what you don't see."

Now in the water of his eyes you see the crayfish streak away, the sun flicker in, out. "Close your eyes," you will say, "and if you are able to first see and then describe what you don't see because words have become so integral to who you are, maybe you could write that novel after all."

You leave so you can return to your work. He stays so he can continue his.

And the next time you and I sit at our respective keyboards, we feel the rushing cool of the words against our ankles, vowels splashing/eddying against rock consonants, moving a little to the left, rising.

E D I T O R ' S   N O T E

Patricia Raybon, author and educator, teaches magazine writing and other journalism courses at the University of Colorado. Her work has appeared in such publications as the *New York Times Magazine, Newsweek, USA Today,* and *Guideposts,* among others. Her first book, *My First White Friend* (Viking Penguin), is a collection of long narrative essays on racial forgiveness.

The following column, "Too Close for Comfort," reprinted from the Sunday newspaper supplement *USA Weekend,* is about race relations. As you analyze it, you should ask:

- Which passages express truth or epiphany?
- Which passages contain resurrected clichés?
- Which passages concern topic, occasion, and theme, respectively?

Raybon handles basic elements deftly. The topic of racial stereotyping combines with the occasion of a confrontation, both of which are distinguished from the theme of pride. Note, too, the resurrected cliché conveyed via the suspense title, and the subtitle that heralds topic and theme. Raybon's voice is emphatic, experienced, and reportorial. She employs a moment between the *then* and *now* to comment on and then describe a tense encounter between neighbors. Her closed ending, a personal plea, opens doors.

Too Close for Comfort

A Racial Stereotype Ruined Their First Meeting.
Now Stubborn Pride Keeps Neighbors Apart.

Patricia Raybon

I am not the maid. My family understands that. One of my neighbors doesn't. But it isn't her fault. She's just a student of time and place and circumstance, and she has been well taught.

So, when she rang my front doorbell one day last winter, she did what comes naturally when somebody who looks like me answers the door in her neighborhood.

She looked startled. Then she coldly issued an order. "Would you get the lady of the house, please?" Her question left me anxious and breathless, too angry to shout a reply.

I am not the maid.

But my occupation wasn't the point; I don't have anything against maids. I was angry and hurt, because the young woman standing on my porch couldn't see me as I see myself. The image and identity that are so clear to me were murky to her. It was a standoff. We let a few foolish words seal our fate.

Some would call this a race problem. And that's part of it. But we weren't just two racial icons at an impasse. We were neighbors unsure what comes after hello. She let a racial stereotype rule her responses. I let weariness and history rule mine. Instead, we should have laughed and moved on. But we couldn't. We didn't know how.

So she stood on my porch, this woman who lives a few dozen yards from my back door, and we remained strangers.

It went very badly, this encounter. It went so badly that I am embarrassed to tell about it.

"I'm your neighbor behind you," she finally said, understanding now that I was the homeowner, not the hired help. She tried to smile, but it seemed too late, and we knew it. "And this is my son." She gestured to a child in a stroller.

On a good day, in good times, I would have fussed over the cute little boy, perhaps invited them in for tea.

But this was a bad day now, a moment of tension and regret that in that instant summarized all that has gone wrong with America. In short, we don't know each other. We don't trust each other. And we don't know how to fix it. It is sad, and we are in trouble. Adrift and at odds.

"What did you want?" I asked. My tone was cool and blank. I didn't seem to have the guts, or maybe the will, to change it.

She explained the purpose of her visit, but in the end her story didn't matter as much as our differences, or our failure to find some common ground.

In fact, she had come to lodge a complaint. The security light in my back yard was angled in such a way that its beam shone directly into her back yard, making her family feel as if they were under surveillance in their family room. I apologized. We'll move it, I said.

She said OK. She turned to go. But then the bad moment got worse. She turned back and lectured me, threatening to call "the authorities" if the problem wasn't fixed, "and I mean right away."

Something made my neighbor say that. Maybe it was the worst in her, or the look in me. But it was a turning point. We were now far gone, past the point where people can recapture a lost opportunity to fix something gone wrong.

That is why people divorce, I suppose. It's why friendships break up. Why strangers shoot at one another on the freeway. Why some police officers suspect the innocent, especially if they are black. Why some black people distrust the innocent, especially if they are white. It's why neighbors live next to each other for years and never speak, barely even wave, hardly even realize that in their estrangement something precious, invaluable, is lost: their humanity.

A few months later, at our neighborhood block party, I thought I recognized this young woman and her baby. I waited for her to speak, and maybe she was doing the same.

But in the end neither of us made the overture, leaving us both without a back-fence friend or, at least, a happy ending.

If our story is to earn another chapter, it will take bravery and forgiveness on my part, justice and intelligence on hers. Certainly big hearts, not stubborn pride, are in order, even if we seem uncertain how to use them. Until then, we live as close as thieves but as far apart as enemies. The geography of difference is the map of our existence, a landscape both familiar and daunting. Do I cross it? Try harder? Aim higher?

A fence reminds me that I must. Somebody lives on the other side. God help us both to cross over.

EDITOR'S NOTE

Bethany Matsko was editor of *The Post,* the campus newspaper at Ohio University, when she wrote this column in Michael Bugeja's magazine workshop. Matsko describes the writing and editing process concerning this column in her earlier sidebar "awright, here's what i learned" in Chapter 10. Upon graduation, Matsko became a production associate at *JazzTimes,* a music publication based in Washington, DC.

The following piece appeared in *Sassy,* under the standing title "it happened to me." As you read it, ask yourself:

- What words, phrases, and passages would appeal to a teen audience?
- What facts do you think the writer had to look up or verify before sending a manuscript to a magazine?
- What images or sensory data help readers envision the author's parents?

The theme of values enhances Matsko's nostalgic topic: her parents' marriage. A moment close to the *then* allows her to comment and focuses our attention on her voice: chatty, witty, and informed. Her final two paragraphs contain epiphanies about stereotypes—something every teen reader is concerned about—and set up a nifty closed ending that harkens the magazine's standing column title.

it happened to me

Bethany Matsko

I sometimes tell my friends that I remember my mom's 21st birthday. I had just turned six years old, and we drove to my great-grandmother's quaint little green house with the davenport in the living room. My aunts and grandparents had decorated the apple tree outside with brightly colored balloons.

Mom was 15 and Dad was 19 when I was born. They had met two years earlier the way most teenagers meet. Mom and a friend were walking through the gas station that my dad was working at, and he flirted with her. Mom didn't like him at first. It was the '60s, and his hair wasn't long enough, she says. But Dad won her over, and they started dating soon after.

Becoming parents at such a young age wasn't an easy decision for my mom and dad. I estimate that I was conceived sometime in November 1971. There was a lot of pressure on both of my parents. *Roe v. Wade* hadn't been decided yet, so abortion wasn't really an option. Friends and relatives tried to convince my parents to give me up to an older, more responsible couple who could raise me in a soft and comfy atmosphere. But they didn't listen. They got married in March 1972 in a courthouse. Mom wore an orange and blue flowered polyester dress, which she gave away about eight years later. (I'm still mad at her for that.) Dad wore a dark suit and platform shoes. I was born five months later in Cleveland, and they named me after a character on a soap opera my mom watched.

My mom always tells me stories about what my childhood was like. Before I was even born, she says, she stuffed her body (and mine, because she was eating for two!) with Big Boy hamburgers almost every night for dinner. She and Dad couldn't wait to buy me blue jeans, the kind that snap and have a real zipper, and little suede moccasins, instead of the typical baby clothes and those ugly flat white walking shoes that babies are supposed to wear. I have my own special memories too. Like how every Christmas when I was little, Santa would drop two old-fashioned wooden Yankee Clipper sleds under the Christmas tree—one for me and the other for my sister Aimee, who was born two and half years after me. We would put on our winter clothes and take our sleds to the hill behind McDonald's.

Mom and Dad sledded too. They loved going down the hill just as much as we did.

I really appreciate my parents for everything they did and how they raised me. My favorite picture of us was taken at a family reunion in July 1973. Mom's white blond hair is flowing all around her face, and she's cuddling me in her lap. She's wearing gingham polyester bell-bottoms and a tiny blouse to match. Both of us are smiling.

Still, there were a lot of rough times for my family. Mom didn't get a chance to finish high school, and Dad barely made enough money to support us. We were on welfare a lot. I remember never wanting to go to the grocery store because people would see that my mom had to use food stamps. In school, I was ridiculed about my parents' ages. When I was in the sixth grade, one girl told me that my mom wasn't really my mom. She said my "real" mom ran away because my dad was an alcoholic. Though the teasing hurt, it never bothered me to have such young parents. I never had a baby-sitter, because wherever my parents went, I went. I always hung out with their crazy teenage friends.

Because I've had so many great times with my parents, a lot of people think that they must have been pretty lenient with me. Actually, they were kind of strict. As a teenager I wasn't allowed to ride in cars with people who were younger than 21, even if they had licenses. It was just one of my father's rules. Once in high school I was in a car with some of my friends. When we pulled into the parking lot of a convenience store, my dad saw me in the car. He followed us for miles until we drove into the high school parking lot. That's when he got out of his car and demanded that I come home with him. Also, I could only go out one night each weekend. My dad told me to pick either Friday or Saturday to hang out. Not both. Mom and Dad wanted me to focus on my grades so that I could go to college.

So many of my friends click their tongues and say, "Oh, I can't imagine doing what your mother did. I wouldn't have enough to give a child." That's not the way my mom and dad thought about it. With the right amount of parental love, encouragement and guidance, I was able to step over the cracks and begin to achieve more than what they were able to. Their youth enriched me more than financial stability ever could have, because they showed me the importance of love.

Despite their naiveté and relative inexperience with life, my parents have managed to stay together (they just celebrated 21 years of marriage) and raise four great kids. The classic argument is that young parents—mothers especially—who aren't financially secure will fall into poverty, giving birth to children who will eventually do the same, creating a vicious cycle. In my case, this is wrong. I'm a senior in college who's putting herself through school by working two jobs. I get good grades too, and scholarships. My goal is to become a fashion editor of a magazine. It could happen. I know it will.

EDITOR'S NOTE

George Plimpton—author, actor, editor—is a consummate magazine journalist, known in literary circles as editor of *Paris Review*. However, he has been an associate or contributing editor for other mass-market publications, including *Sports Illustrated, Harper's,* and *Food and Wine.* Plimpton mastered the art of "participatory journalism," appearing as a guest conductor of the Cincinnati Symphony and as a pitcher in a postseason all-stars game at Yankee Stadium. Perhaps his most famous stint was an exhibition game as third-string quarterback for the Detroit Lions, which led to his 1966 sports writing classic, *Paper Lion* (Harper). His essays and columns, including the one reprinted here—"Bonding with the Grateful Dead"—appear regularly in *Esquire*. As you read it, ask yourself:

- Which passages showcase the author's trademark voice?
- What images or symbols relate to "fashion sense," of interest to *Esquire* readers?
- Which passages in the first six paragraphs relate to grounding, foreshadowing, and theme, setting up the structure for the rest of the piece?

The following literary column is classic Plimpton. The topic (rock concert) and theme (bonding) are heralded in the snappy title. The moment begins in the *then,* showcasing Plimpton's witty voice: self-effacing, sophisticated, and observant. The moment gradually moves toward the *now* as concert time approaches with an italicized epiphany occurring at its height. Then comes the open ending focusing on fashion—prepared for via foreboding—beginning with the son's Deadhead garb and continuing with references to old sneakers, Paul Newman's tasseled oxfords, and finally an ironic Jerry Garcia tie, a literal and metaphorical bonding symbol.

Bonding with the Grateful Dead

George Plimpton

Years ago, practicing participatory journalism, I made a halfhearted attempt to join a rock group as a tambourine thumper or whatever to get a brief sense of what that world was about: the travel, the fans, what it was like to gyrate on the stage with a sea of faces out front . . . Three Dog Night, Led Zeppelin, the Rolling Stones. The Grateful Dead—Jerry Garcia, Bob Weir, Pigpen, et al.—were on the list. None of them had been anxious to take on a part-time tambourine player. Perhaps it was just as well.

I remembered that one of the Dead, in the clarity of an overdose, had seen great lobster claws in the sky and pterodactyls in the garden. I went on to try other professions.

The Grateful Dead came back into my life recently, largely because of my children's interest. My daughter has been *associated* with the group—I find it difficult to apply the common description of a fan as a Deadhead—since she was fifteen. Her school band, the Cosmic Country Sound, was patterned after the Grateful Dead; she was its lead singer and tambourine player.

I had no idea that my son, four years younger, had any interest in the group. His room is decorated with posters of Boris Becker and Albert Einstein. But then a year ago he let his hair grow into a mane, started wearing beaded necklaces and rope wristlets, and, sure enough, turned up one day at my study door to announce, "Dad, there's this concert I'd like to go to. . . ."

I have persuaded myself that this is a phase—that one day my son will come back from school clipped and shorn and politely ask for one of my ties and enough money for standing room at the Metropolitan Opera.

Both of my children have urged me to go to a Grateful Dead concert. I hadn't taken them up on the offer until this summer, when by chance I met someone way up in the band's hierarchy who gave me not only some tickets to a concert at the Meadowlands in New Jersey but also a backstage pass. I told my son. His eyes widened at the news. He invited three of his friends. His sister, with a job on the West Coast, was devastated that she couldn't be on hand.

My son's friends arrived at the apartment a couple of hours early (just to be sure they wouldn't be left behind)—sartorial look-alikes with wild hair, tie-dye T-shirts, bandannas, and faded jeans that had been rubbed, my daughter once told me, with No. 5 sandpaper. I picked out what I thought was appropriate to wear—a safari jacket, fatigues, and an old pair of sneakers. We drove out to the Meadowlands in my station wagon. On the rear window, a few summers before, my daughter had affixed a Grateful Dead sticker—a row of marching skeletons. In the back, the boys played Dead songs—bootlegged tapes of extraordinary poor quality but desirable nonetheless because they had been recorded on the scene rather than in a studio. At the wheel, I felt socially correct. We were missing only the famous bumper sticker of the Sixties: I BRAKE FOR HALLUCINATIONS.

At the Meadowlands, the laminated pass—a design of a clutch of red roses—got us waved through the checkpoints and finally down a ramp into the overhang of the stadium itself. I sensed a rising respect from my carload, especially when the door was opened by a security person who referred to me by name and led our little group through a series of curtain-hung alcoves serving as temporary dressing rooms. We passed a stoutish, bushy-haired man with a white beard who recognized me and stopped to shake hands before moving on. Consternation in my little group. "Who was that?" I asked. "Oh, my God!" my son exclaimed. "That was Jerry Garcia!" He stared after him and then turned back, his face full of wonder . . . very likely because I had not known who the gentleman was.

We were ushered into an alcove—sofas, a coffee table, potted palms in tubs. The rest of the Dead—Bob Weir, Phil Lesh, Mickey Hart, and Bill Kreutzmann—were sitting there, and we were introduced. To my surprise, Paul Newman was in the alcove, but the boys seemed to take no interest in him. They stood in a small, nervous knot, staring at the Dead as if to imprison the sight in their minds forever.

I was asked to sit. The talk was about environmental matters, a particular concern of Bob Weir's. That was one of the reasons Paul Newman was there: His daughter is working on conservation efforts in the Pacific Northwest. The actor was elegantly outfitted in a tailored jump suit and highly polished and tasseled oxfords. (A toe had worked through one of my sneakers, and I tried to disguise it by resting one foot on top of the other.)

I asked Weir if the Grateful Dead had ever performed songs about environment. "No," he said to my surprise. They were into things more "mystical . . . spiritual." He turned his head slightly to hear the questions better, as if the steady thunder of the music over the years had impaired his hearing.

We chatted until Weir and the others drifted out to prepare for their set. The kids left for the field. Behind the stage I ran into Jerry Garcia. This time prompted by my son's identification, I greeted him warmly.

"Hey, Jerry!"

He took me up on the stage to show me around, keeping to the shadows so the sight of him wouldn't set off a furor in the crowd out front. We sat for a while in a cubbyhole he set up—chairs and pillows just behind the great clifflike bank of amplifiers.

Garcia remembered when I had asked to join the group in the Sixties. They were on the rise, and publicity always helped. He said they had a meeting about it . . . and had turned me down because things were wilder back then, and perhaps I wouldn't survive to write the story. Or perhaps I'd get too Presbyterian and write disapproving copy.

When I grinned and said yes, I might have written about pterodactyls in the garden, great lobster claws . . . he looked slightly startled.

When the concert started, Garcia let me watch from backstage, behind the drums, so that I could see what the players looked out on—a vast, convoluted tumult of faces and arms. After a while, awed, I went out onto the field to search for my youngster and his friends, moving slowly down the crowded aisles. On either side, a long line of Deadheads stretched out toward the distant confines of the stadium. Standing on their chairs, they gazed at the stage or, more likely, at the huge twin screens showing close-ups of the musicians and, on occasion, the twirls of psychedelic designs. Everyone moved to the beat in a curious vertical hop—about all one could do on a metal-chair top. The only seated person I passed was a young mother nursing a child whose ears were blocked against the pulsing sound with Band-Aids. The music was incessant, pounding from one number to the next without stop, the shift apparent to my uneducated ear only when the crowd roared its approval upon recognizing a new song. From where I stood I could see, back in the stadium entryways, the so-called spinners—Deadhead faithfuls who twirl like dervishes in the corridors. I could smell the patchouli, the perfume sold outside that permeates the concerts. "It's supposed to be organic," my daughter once told me. "I hate it—earth and body odor."

I was offered some acid. I demurred politely, saying inaccurately that I'd already had some. I saw very little evidence of that sort of thing. The few miscreants were being held in a detention room back in the corridors, which I had happened by. Seated on benches, looking scared and chastened, they were being questioned by the security people, perhaps not questioned as much as scolded for whatever they'd done. Those in charge were acting not in the grim manner of enforcement officers but rather in the guise of parents. "What were you thinking of?" I heard a burly officer shout at a youngster. "Use your head!" It was obvious the kid was about to be let loose back into familiar waters.

I finally found my son's contingent—standing on a row of chairs. My son's hair bounced on his back. I thought, *What a curious bonding experience we are going through*—in which any exchange of words was impossible because of the torrents of sound.

The boys couldn't get enough of the music. On the way back to the city, they played their bootlegged, scratchy cassettes and asked, rather nervously, what I thought of the concert. I told them that I had been pleasantly surprised at the almost religious fervor, the lack of violence, the politeness, the sense of a huge extended family, the feeling that everyone was sharing a kind of wonderful secret. They were pleased. I looked back and grinned at my son. I said I didn't mean I was going to start wearing string necklaces and releasing patchouli perfume in the house.

A few days ago, just before my son left for school, my wife gave him a going-away present in the familiarly shaped box that almost inevitably contains a tie. He looked at it woefully. Sure enough, a tie emerged from its wrappings, a deep green outlined with a pattern of small frogs: a conservative tie at best. "Oh, wow!" my son said politely but weakly, trying to disguise his disappointment at being given a symbol of such propriety.

"Take a look at the label," my wife said.

He turned it over and gasped. The designer was Jerry Garcia of the Dead!

My son wore the tie that night at dinner and the next afternoon to visit his grandparents; I half expected him to be wearing it when he came in to say goodbye before leaving for school. I know it's in his backpack. Now if the Dead only had a line of blazers, gray flannels, button-down shirts, and tasseled oxford shoes. . . .

Profiles

EDITOR'S NOTE

Poet and writer Carol Muske Dukes has placed work in such publications as *New Yorker*, the *New York Times*, and the *Los Angeles Times*. She is a professor in the English department at the University of Southern California and has published five books of poetry, a collection of essays, and two acclaimed novels—*Dear Digby* and *Saving St. German*, both by Viking. Muske Dukes lives in Los Angeles with her daughter Annie and actor-husband David Dukes.

The following profile, "Farrah Fawcett Up Close," originally appeared in *House and Garden*. It differs in structure from the more formal literary work that has distinguished Muske Dukes as a top creative writer. However, because she appreciates specific audiences, she is able to write for a mass audience. As you read her prose, ask yourself:

- Which passages contain vivid word pictures, allowing the reader to envision the celebrity's house?
- How are quotations processed—punctuation, attribution, and so on— while still sustaining voice and maintaining paragraph structure?
- What facts in the profile do you think the author had to research?

As you will see, the author profiles Farrah Fawcett and her house with a theme geared to audience: magical transformation. The *now and then* moment enhances Muske Duke's enchanting, descriptive voice; she can comment on and invite us personally into Farrah Fawcett's home. She even allows the actor to have the last word in a closed-quotation ending—"The time has come for all of us to settle down"—in keeping with the target magazine's concept.

Farrah Fawcett Up Close

Carol Muske Dukes

There's a ruckus outside in the hall. A worried little boy with platinum hair and zebra-striped pants hurries into the living room, gesturing and murmuring to himself like the White Rabbit. He's lost his wand, he tells the room at large, then throws himself disconsolately into his mother's lap. She whispers in his ear, he nods and trots off happy—she turns back to me, magically transformed from Mom to Farrah Fawcett.

The house, which Farrah shares with actor Ryan O'Neal and their five-year-old son, Redmond, appears to be the product of a wand with an enlightened personal touch. Outside, it is a deceptively conventional California ranch-style spread, circa 1950. Inside, it's another matter entirely. From its hilltop vantage, the house commands panoramic views of the San Fernando Valley and the city of Los Angeles on either side and has, apart from these dramatic bids for attention, an interior that could have gone in almost any decorating direction. Its meandering series of rooms includes a library, a racquetball court where Ryan and Farrah have daily matches, a formal dining room, a built-in recreation room, and a delicate boudoir overlooking a rose garden. Some of the spaces feel cozy and small, others larger than life. In them, familiar objects mix with relics of fame filtered through Farrah's strong politics (there is a poster of her controversial TV movie *The Burning Bed,* a spectacular photo of her in another TV movie as the photojournalist Margaret Bourke-White, and a still from *Extremities,* the powerful feminist play adapted into a movie).

In the living room a big Warhol hangs over the fireplace—all blond flying hair and cheekbones. The Warhol is hard to ignore, but then so is Farrah, even dressed for what looks like a big night at home playing Nintendo with Redmond, who returns from his bedroom triumphant, wand in hand. The results of her domestic magic make Farrah smile, and her sweat suit, black flats, and red barrettes don't diminish the kliegish radiance of her looks: the famous angles and planes of her face and the familiar tumble of Burne-Jones hair.

She shares an ivory sofa with her decorator, Sylvia Longoria Dorsey, as we chat about my husband, whom she recently worked with on a film, and our kids. Her decorator is an old friend from her University of Texas days and Farrah trusts her implicitly. ("I considered a few others who will be nameless.") The room we're sitting in, done in alternating shades of creamy white, sandy brown, and darker earth tones (except for the jewel box Warhol), reflects Farrah's love of eloquent restraint: clean lines, simple statements. A delicately curving Japanese roof tile reclines on a shelf-like maverick haiku; there is a Byzantine crucifix on a table, an El Grecoesque bust by the fire.

Farrah thinks of the house, which she purchased in 1976, as a work in progress. Its structural eccentricities seemed to require a slow approach, which suited Farrah fine because she admits to having an aversion to shopping for furniture and art. "I get impatient and hungry. Once in a gallery I felt so frantically ravenous I dipped into a bowl of biscuits sitting on a counter. The owner looked at me strangely and I asked him if was all right if I ate one. 'Sure,' he said, 'if you like dog biscuits.'" Her leisurely approach has given rise to a homey ongoing eclecticism, nurtured by Dorsey, a fearless shopper who picks out things she thinks Farrah will like and brings them to her for approval. The system works smoothly because, as Dorsey says, she's become completely attuned to her friend's visual sense, which is indeed acute. A little-known fact: Farrah Fawcett is an artist, and a skilled one at that.

She studied painting and sculpting at the University of Texas with Charles Umlauf, whose influence is still pronounced in her work (hence her preference for painting "nudes and religious subjects, rarely anything in between"). The El Grecoesque bust, which looks like bronze, turns out to be an example of her metallic-glazed ceramic sculpture. It is a head of Jesus—an arrogant grandeeish Jesus—thrusting out his beard. Propped against a livingroom table leg is a deftly executed painting of a nude torso, also by Farrah. She shows me a pastel drawing—two heads sharing a face, a little cubist cameo—which she did "in a matter of hours" on a movie set. Other examples of art Farrah holds in high esteem are scattered throughout the house. There's an Umlauf Madonna and child in the skylighted entryway, a cluster of primitive santo-like crucifixes in the master bedroom, a partially restored eighteenth-century canvas of a bacchante by the English painter John Opie in the dining room and, on an end table in the livingroom, a mystery drawing of a sleepwalking man (possibly an unsigned Chagall) that "Ryan and I picked up on a side street in Rome." This is not high-powered museum-quality art. There are no Dubuffets or Calders on the lawn near the Zen-like rose garden, no Schnabels in the study. Instead this is a collection of lovingly chosen devotional objects—art as amulet. This house, too, is a refuge, a sanctuary for a woman weary of cliché and the camera's reductive eye.

Farrah and Ryan are currently facing the cameras together, shooting a new television show, *Good Sports*, which airs this season. Farrah describes it as a comedy, but the move to make the series reaffirms their serious commitment to their home base in Los Angeles—and to Redmond. "He's traveled all over the world," says Farrah. "But now he's in school and needs a regular routine. The time has come for all of us to settle down."

EDITOR'S NOTE

Writer and poet Kelly Cherry has published 19 books, including the acclaimed nonfiction work *Writing the World* (Missouri). Her stories have appeared in *Mademoiselle, Redbook,* and *McCall's* and in such prestigious literary journals as *The Georgia Review, North American Review,* and *Iowa Review.* Cherry is a distinguished professor at the University of Wisconsin–Madison.

In the following piece, which originally appeared in the literary journal *The Chattahoochee Review,* Cherry profiles her mother's father, Allen Dewey Spooner, and in doing so retraces roots of her own identity. As you read it, ask yourself:

- Which passages contain sensory images or descriptions?
- What symbols or images enhance the author's epiphany?
- What facts do you think the author had to research?

Time plays a crucial role in Cherry's profile. She uses the occasion of a hurricane and the theme of loving memory to generate tension via multiple moments. The work begins in the *then,* allowing Cherry to comment compassionately, intelligently, and historically. Wind is a symbol of memory and an element of hurricanes; it blows throughout the piece, foreshadowing the closed ending wherein memory is cast in new light of a candle.

Mr. Allen Dewey Spooner

Kelly Cherry

I can barely remember him, but I will never forget him. He was my mother's father. He died when I was seven. He died in Gulfport, Mississippi, at one end of the country, while I was a child in upstate New York at the far other end. We lived in a railway flat in a tenement apartment three flights above a grocery store on a busy, dirty street. My mother typed dissertations for Cornell students at a nickel a page. When she heard the news, she "sat down and typed for forty-eight hours straight," she told me, "just as if my heart had not been broken forever."

He was descended from Pilgrims. The first Spooner in America landed at Plymouth Rock in 1637. Allen Dewey Spooner was born in 1872 in Rensselaer Falls, New York, and grew up there, but his family moved south, and at twenty-three he was working for a lumber company in Lake Charles, Louisiana, where he met my grandmother Hattie, who called him "Allie." They were married—after some spectacular arguments between redheaded Hattie and her Grandma LaBesse, who needed to be persuaded that a Yankee could be an acceptable suitor—and eventually my mother appeared on the scene, the youngest of three daughters, each of them so different from the other two that Hattie and Allen must have thought, sometimes, that random selection would have resulted in more comparability. Perhaps the first one had scared Allen a little; fathers seem to be nervously cautious about their first daughters, unsure what to do with an appealing but undeniably alien creature. The second was a hellraiser, destined from the day she was born to be a flapper in short skirts and long beads. My mother, of course, was his favorite. She was shy and smart and loved music and sent notes to him that read, "Would you like to have lunch with your daughter Mary?" He always wrote back, "It would be very fine indeed to have lunch with my daughter Mary." He was a saw filer, keeping the teeth of the giant saw impressively and precisely sharp, and they ate lunch on a tablecloth Mary spread over a broad, flat rock near the mill. He was the foremost filer in the business, it was said in that part of the country. This was a strange and beautiful part of the country, where huge cypresses immodestly revealed their roots, and hanging moss swayed back and forth like silent wind chimes, and a heavy aroma of sulphur lay on top of the still day, smothering it, clinging to people's throats like a scarf. . . .

My mother had just been released from six weeks' quarantine in an upstairs bedroom that Hattie was now fumigating, to rid it of scarlet fever germs. It was Sunday, and there were always callers on Sunday afternoon. Allen was in his Sunday suit, having played the organ prelude at First Presbyterian. After a midday dinner of crab gumbo and pot roast he would step into the parlor to select an afternoon's worth of symphonies from a stack of quarter-inch-thick Edison records that lay next to the only phonograph in Gulfport. Despite Hattie's protestations, he remained convinced that intelligent visitors would rather listen to good music than make small talk, and he refused to give up this conviction even after he drove them out to the sun porch with his record of the entirely shocking new piece *Sacre du Printemps*.

This day there was an uneasiness to the afternoon that even my five-year-old mother could sense. Everyone seemed on edge. There were rumors that a hurricane had devastated Grand Isle and might be headed for Lake Charles. For once, Allen did not object when Hattie asked him to turn off the phonograph. The sister who was going to be a flapper in just a few more years but was still in pinafore and pigtails peered out the parlor window. "Come look at the funny clouds," she begged everyone. Allen examined the barometer on the parlor wall. "She's falling, all right," he reported. "Better get ready for a little blow."

The conversation in the parlor turned to the war. It was 1917, and the day before, a trainload of soldiers from nearby Gertsner Field had pulled out of town to the accompaniment of cheers and waving banners, and the town band in which Allen played clarinet. Grandma LaBesse expressed displeasure with the neighborhood children for mocking poor old Professor Schultz and shouting "German spy! German spy!" as he shuffled along the sidewalk. Flags draped front porches; women rolled bandages for the Red Cross; and Mr. Cloony, the choir director, organized community "sings," flailing his arms enthusiastically while belting out the words to "It's a Long, Long Way to Tipperary" and "I'm Forever Blowing Bubbles." Everyone ridiculed the Kaiser and boasted of self-imposed privations. Mrs. Beardsley told the assemblage in the parlor how she had carried a case of railroad salvage pork and beans all the way from the depot to the house in South Ryan Street, and Hattie explained, to their daughters' lasting horror, that the "scrambled eggs" they had eaten for supper the night before had really been brains.

After the guests left, the family went into the kitchen for a supper of peanut butter and jelly sandwiches. Hattie didn't cook on Sunday nights. She would have liked to keep the entire Sabbath holy, but that was clearly impossible. Instead she managed, by getting up at five a.m., to free Sunday afternoons and evenings. From five a.m. until time to leave for church, she bustled about the kitchen, striving so zealously toward her half day of rest that God, one must believe, forgave her those few sinful hours of industry.

Just before dark the rain began to fall.

By morning, frenzied gusts of wind were slinging rain against the windows so hard that the panes shuddered and threatened to collapse. My mother crept downstairs to the kitchen, where oatmeal had been steaming all night in the "fireless cooker"—a double-welled cabinet with hot round slabs of stone at the bottoms of the wells. Allen motioned for her to sit down at the breakfast table while he read the scripture aloud, as he did every morning. Then Hattie read a prayer from a familiar booklet titled *Our Daily Bread*. It didn't matter that my mother didn't fully understand the scripture passages: Just the fact that her parents were seated there, so inseparable in their faith, lent stability to her small world.

But today, the ritual seemed somehow perfunctory, as if her parents were really thinking about something else. There was an impatience, an urgency in the room. As soon as she finished reading the prayer, Hattie told her daughter that she was not to go to school that day, and then she resumed a discussion with Allen that had obviously been going on before Mary had entered the room. She was pleading with him not to venture out in the boat—his only way of getting to the sawmill. "I have to go, Hattie," he said. "I have to warn Eddie and Jack to board up their houses and get to higher ground."

Eddie and Jack were Allen's helpers in the filing room. Jack, as Hattie now pointed out, could take care of himself (and if not, she said his tattoos were a kind of false advertising). But as much as she wanted her husband to stay home, she had to admit that the younger and more imaginative Eddie seemed a bit uncertain about how to deal with the real world, though he did his best. One Christmas, when Eddie went to the commissary to buy six monogrammed handkerchiefs for his boss—"Mr. Allen Dewey Spooner," he announced proudly—and discovered that the *S's* were all sold out, he bought 3 *A's* and 3 *D's*.

After Allen left for the mill, Hattie paced the floor and watched the barometer. The wind had gotten worse. The top blew off the rabbit coop, and little Mary, naturally concerned for her pet rabbits, sent up a howl that could be heard above the roar of the storm. Clinging to the fence and clothesline poles, her red hair flying in the wind like a cardinal on the wing, Hattie made her way to the coop, wrestled the top back on, and latched it securely. Mary calmed down.

And then the wind got *worse.*

Windows were blown in as easily as if they'd been made of cellophane, the chimney crumpled as if it had been made of tissue paper, and the servants' house in the back yard toppled over. The mailman, conscientiously trying to make his rounds in the horse-drawn cart that had a little step on the back, where he stood, gave up just has he reached the Spooner residence. He brought his pouch into the parlor, spread the wet letters all over the imitation Persian rug, and carefully patted them dry. Every time a window blew in, Hattie and her daughters and the mailman would push a heavy piece of furniture up against the opening. Just when Hattie determined that they should all make a dash for the school building, a tin roof came hurtling past the house and she decided they'd better stay where they were.

Allen had designed and built his boat, *The Flick,* by himself. Her hull was finest mahogany, her hardware solid brass, and the varnished canvas that covered her prow was smooth and tight. (*The Flick* frequently took top honors in exciting boat races at twenty-one miles an hour.) The route to the mill might have been considered by some to be hazardous even in good weather. Large and deep, Lake Charles was rough and gray and white-capped in stormy weather. From Lake Charles, Allen's route led him a short distance up Calcasieu River and then through a cut-off that provided a cross-over to Prien Lake. The cut-off was like a miniature bayou, manmade, the water blackened by the shadows of dense overhanging vines and moss-covered trees whose branches dripped fat cream-colored snakes. Prien was dotted with islets, most of them nothing more than a few cypress trees surrounded by tall marsh grass and cattails. Herons stalked the shallows around the islets, searching, with dignified deliberation, for minnows, and kingfishers and sandpipers skittered along the edges. Prien appeared at first glance to be a navigator's nightmare, but its treacherous "stumps" invariably turned out to be alligator snouts that sank slowly and mysteriously out of sight when *The Flick* approached. From Prien, Allen would have to travel a short distance up yet another river to Lockport.

Despite the choppy water and rising wind, Allen made it safely to the mill. He moored *The Flick* in the boathouse and, drenched and bent double against the wind, walked up to the mill. An outside stairway led to the filing room on the second floor. Eddie and Jack were there, but of course working had been out of the question; it was all they could do to move the machine tools away from the windows as the panes shattered on the filing room floor. Sawdust, made amazingly painful by the force of wind, whirled through the air like a sandstorm and stung the men and lodged in their eyes and nostrils as they struggled with the heavy machinery.

Hurricanes usually dissipated fairly soon over land. Eddie and Jack had not really thought that this "squall" would turn out to be a full-fledged storm. Allen ordered them to leave at once. "You must tell the Cajun laborers to go home and protect their wives and children," he explained. The men left gratefully. In those days, storm warnings could reach the bayous only by word of mouth; there were no radios or newspapers in remote areas.

Behind the sawmill was a slag heap—a great pile of burning wood scraps and sawdust that rose almost to the level of the mill's roof. It smouldered night and day, giving off an eerie glow and occasionally sending up showers of sparks and hissing snake-tongues of flames when the wind touched it. Even the rain from the storm could not put out the fire that was deep within it, as alive and red as a heart. Suddenly a tremendous gust, a mighty rogue rush, ripped the smouldering heap apart and carried blazing debris to the mill, igniting the roof. The fire, whipped about by the wind, shot up to the sky. The rickety wooden building, its timbers parched by summer temperatures, flared up almost in one spontaneous burst of flame. Then the sparks leaped to the adjacent lumberyard, where stacks of rich pine boards glistened with amber beads of resin drawn out of the wood by the intense heat. Raindrops sputtered and fizzled, powerless against the fire. Allen—he could not say how he found the strength—picked up his heavy chest of treasured hand tools and flung it through a window. Then he ran down the wooden steps, reaching the ground as the flames roared up behind him to engulf the stairway. Dragging his tool box, he made his way slowly to the boathouse. As he looked back over his shoulder at the mill burning to the ground, he thanked God that he had sent Eddie and Jack away.

Once in the boat, his tool chest stowed securely in the back seat, Allen didn't know whether to start for home or sit it out. The storm had apparently reached its height and the wind seemed now to be dying down. He recognized this as the eye of the hurricane and made up his mind to head for home in the hope of getting there before the eye could pass over and the storm regain its impetus. But in his eagerness he backed out of his shelter a few minutes too soon, and as he sped down river to Prien Lake, a flying piece of timber struck *The Flick* and punched a gaping hole in her side just above the water line. Only his intimate knowledge of the waters through which he passed enabled him to make the trip home. As he reached the front door, which had been knocked askew and given a permanently crazy look by winds that hit 150 miles per hour, Hattie flung it open and cried "Oh, Allie!", throwing herself joyfully into his arms.

Allen and Hattie worked hard all their lives and never missed a single Sunday at church, but they also loved dancing to Strauss waltzes. Allen enjoyed photography and fishing, and after he bought his first automobile, a Model-T Ford, he took his family on trips to see the sulphur mountain and the red-pepper fields and the tropical-bird sanctuary and the sugarcane fields. They visited a salt mine, and a plantation that had survived the War Between the States.

When he was seventy-four and Hattie was sixty-eight, he drove her from Gulfport to upstate New York. He was already dying of cancer, but this was their "honeymoon"—better late than never. They even went to Niagara Falls. That summer, we were staying in a dilapidated house on Lake Rosseau in Canada, where chipmunks actually scampered around the kitchen. (Chipmunks! Scampering! In the kitchen!) Allen and Hattie drove to Canada, bringing gifts for the grandchildren. While my mother, now a beautiful young woman and professional violinist, was chatting away with her mother, the elderly gentleman we'd been told to call "Grandpa" set the toys down on the floor in front of us and watched us from a straight-back chair. In front of me was a sizeable glass fire truck filled with tiny, brilliantly colored candies. I was four, and had never seen such an entrancing thing as this fire truck.

What I remember about him, that elderly gentleman sitting so straightly on the ladder-back chair, is how his shadow seemed to fold itself around me, like the wings of a watchful angel. What I remember is how my mother, whose life, finally, did not turn out as happily as she might have wished, could always be made happier by the thought of her parents, but especially the thought of her father. Her face, when she had become old in her own turn and reminisced about her parents, but especially about her father, seemed to light up, like a candle one lights in loving memory.

E D I T O R ' S   N O T E

Poet, translator, and writer, Dana Gioia has published several books, among them the critically praised nonfiction work, *Can Poetry Matter?* (Graywolf). Gioia, a former executive for General Foods, quit the corporate world in the early 1990s to devote all his energies to writing. His work appears frequently in such publications as the *New York Times, New Yorker,* and *The Hudson*

Review, which originally published Gioia's profile of the great fiction writer John Cheever. As you read it, ask yourself:

- Which passages contain truths about writing?
- Which passages denote the theme of "surprising impressions"?
- What special qualities or images appeal to you in the ending?

Note, too, that the occasion of the piece is stated in its title. Theme permeates the piece, often heralded by words such as *surprised* and *astonished.* Although Gioia does resurrect specific scenes involving Cheever—at a residence hall, a reading, and finally at a library—the moment is pushed toward the *then* so that Gioia can share his research and impressions in a sophisticated, observant, and gracious voice. His open ending is elegant. (For more information, see Gioia's sidebar "On Endings" in Chapter 8.) Via a series of images in his final paragraph, Gioia suggests that a great writer has left the literary scene too early and is dearly missed.

Meeting Mr. Cheever

Dana Gioia

I was supposed to meet John Cheever in the fall of 1974 when I was a graduate student at Harvard and a tutor at Radcliffe's North House. Among my modest duties at the house was helping run a weekly literary table for undergraduates. Every Wednesday we would read work by a contemporary author and discuss it over dinner, and, if the arguments got lively, continue later over drinks in the nearby apartment of our obliging faculty sponsors. The notion of a planned literary table may sound unbearably stuffy, but in practice it usually provided interesting conversations about good books. It also gave this otherwise remote house, located almost a mile from the heart of Harvard, an excuse to invite local writers to dinner.

That fall John Cheever had begun teaching in the Boston University writing program, the most active and well-publicized graduate program in the area, whose faculty also included Anne Sexton, John Malcolm Brinnin, and George Starbuck. I knew a girl in the program, and whenever we met I would quiz her about her courses and teachers, especially Cheever, whose work I had admired for years. To my surprise she said that Cheever seemed lost and lonely in Boston and suggested that I invite him to North House for dinner. She even offered to make the arrangements. A few days later she called to confirm the time and place for Cheever's visit, adding, "Make sure you have something to drink." I immediately went out and bought three bottles of a good red wine to ease his arrival.

A flier announcing the visit went out to North House students, and the members of the literary table were assigned "The Enormous Radio," "The Swimmer," and a few other stories to prepare for the evening. I called his apartment over near Kenmore Square a few times to see if he needed directions, but no one ever answered. "Don't worry," my friend at B.U. told me. "It's all set up."

Attendance the night of Cheever's visit was excellent. Every regular member of the group was there plus a few new faces. One student even wore a tie. Sitting in North House's fanciest common room with three open but untasted bottles of red wine, we all waited for our guest of honor. Half an hour passed. Then an hour. Finally just as the dinner service was about to close, we scooped up the bottles and rushed into the dining room to secure some food—including an extra tray for our guest, who never appeared.

I tried calling my friend to ask what had gone wrong, but I couldn't reach her at first. By the time I did a week later another terrifying event took precedence. Answering the phone, she told me that Anne Sexton had just killed herself. My friend was frantic and confused, and by comparison Cheever's non-appearance seemed negligible. I never mentioned it. Not until a few months later when Cheever suddenly left Boston University because of a drinking problem did I guess what might have happened the night of our invitation.

A little over a year later I had left Harvard's Comparative Literature program for the Stanford Business School. German, French and English literature had been replaced by Finance, Accounting and Statistics, but some things remained constant. I was still living as an advisor in an undergraduate dormitory and still running a literary table, though this time more quixotically among the decidedly unintellectual denizens of Florence Moore Hall (or "Flo Mo" as it was universally known), a dour complex of concrete-block dormitories in the postwar institutional style sometimes referred to by Californians as "early Gestapo."

One day in mid-January 1976 I stopped by the Flo Mo office to check my message box. The secretary told me there was a writer coming the next day who would be staying in the guest room for a week. The housemaster wanted me to show him around.

"What's his name?" I asked unenthusiastically. She looked at her reservation card and read, "John Cheever." For a moment I forgave the house-master all of his interminable staff meetings.

Intoxicated by the news of Cheever's visit, I mentioned it to some undergraduates, but soon learned that none of them knew who he was. Undismayed, I decided I would show them and went off to the university bookstore only to discover that all but one of his books were out of print. Determined to get some of his work in circulation among the students before his arrival, I made the rounds of the local used bookstores where, one by one, I picked up about a dozen copies, including some remaindered hard-cover editions of *The World of Apples,* stamped with large blurry red H's on the flyleaf and priced at 99 cents. I passed these books out to some of the more pliable freshmen with firm instructions to read the stories checked in pencil (such precise directions were needed since none of them could be trusted to read an entire volume). Meanwhile, remembering my friend's advice from Boston, I also bought some wine.

January 1976 marked the nadir of Cheever's literary reputation. His last novel, *Bullet Park* (1969), had received poor reviews, and *The World of Apples* (1973) with its mere handful of stories published in the last decade seemed meager compared to Cheever's previously generous collection. His work had stopped appearing in *New Yorker* and now surfaced at the rate of about one story per year only in magazines like *The Saturday Evening Post* and *Playboy,* which were known to pay well for inferior work by famous authors. His critical reputation had never gained the stature of his most notable contemporaries like Updike, Bellow, Mailer, Pynchon or Barth. He was not so much discussed as routinely dismissed as a dated suburban satirist, and he had become a sort of ceremonial scapegoat for all the real and imagined sins of *New Yorker.* He was credited with a few ingenious stories of middle-class *Angst,* but his novels were considered messy amalgamations of short stories. Without the support of critics or teachers and with little new work to call attention to himself, Cheever had lost the younger generation of readers. They were reading his contemporaries, sometimes even as class assignments, but his work was now largely unknown. Even if they wanted to try one of his books, it would have been difficult since they were mainly out of print. And nowhere was his reputation lower than among the radical chic of Northern California who did not spare him their most obscene epithets—elitist, Eastern, suburban and (their lips tightening to a sneer) unabashedly middle class.

The next morning the house secretary phoned me to say that Cheever had arrived. She asked me to go over and show him around the campus, adding in a quiet tone, which seemed to bespeak all of history's lost causes, "He wants to eat in the dorm." Sensing that here indeed was a man in need of guidance, I hurried over.

The Florence Moore guest room was a tiny concrete-block cubicle set on ground level at the end of a dormitory hallway. Rarely used except by visiting parents in distress and a few relatives of foreign students who didn't know better, its stark walls and low ceiling contained a steel bed, a small desk, a dresser and a closet-sized bathroom. Everything but the furniture was painted a pale institutional green.

Not surprisingly, Cheever was pleased even to see me. I apologized for the sparseness of the room, but he immediately replied with the chivalrous generosity, which would characterize his stay, that it was absolutely perfect.

The room had a desk and windows, he pointed out, as if these were rare appurtenances in the world of accommodations. His compliments seemed so sincere that momentarily I felt I had done that obviously splendid suite an injustice.

Although Cheever looked almost exactly like his many dust jacket photographs, I was initially surprised by three things about him. First, he was so small. For some reason, probably not unconnected with my mental images of his fictional protagonists, I had expected a magisterially tall Yankee gentleman instead of this slight, almost boyish man who stood only a few inches over five feet. Second, Cheever was the most perfectly poised man I had ever met. Every gesture was so gracefully conceived and executed that he scarcely seemed part of the clumsy everyday world. Even the way he sat still seemed as carefully composed as a professional portrait. Not that his presence was domineering or dramatic; just the opposite was true. His manner was relaxed, understated, and self-assured, but he nevertheless had a style that captivated one's attention the way a great actor can steal a scene on stage without speaking a word. Finally, I was stunned by his voice. Cheever spoke a brand of patrician Massachusetts English which I now suspect he invented, for I have never heard anyone else speak quite like it. Nevertheless, he used this suave, fictional dialect so convincingly that in his mouth it seemed to have the force of ancient authority, as if he were some New England Homer standing at the apex of a long oral tradition.

I had talked to men funnier or wiser than Cheever, more inventive or intelligent, more perceptive or likeable, but I had never met anyone who exhibited these qualities so generously in such deft balance. His wasn't the pedestrian balance of an earnest earthbound mind but the arduous equilibrium of an acrobat. His conversation was the natural extension of his physical poise. He never said anything merely for effect, but virtually everything he said was phrased effectively. Almost every sentence boasted some unusual detail that made both the thought and the language seem remarkable. Yet there wasn't anything pretentious about his conversation, if only because he never stopped paying attention to his listeners. He was not a brilliant monologuist repeating the same anecdotes verbatim into the footlights, but a consummately engaging conversationalist. One had the feeling he watched his listeners' every response and tailored even the oldest story to their special requirements. The freshmen, who largely did not care much about literature, appreciated this attention which was one reason why they always joined him at meals (whereas usually they dreaded sitting with visiting faculty). His conversation never excluded them. It was intelligent without being intellectual, informed but not pedantic. And he was very funny. After all, as he once said, "You can't expect to communicate with anyone if you're a bore."

We talked in the guest room for quite a while because Cheever asked that we wait for his son, Fred (or Federico to give his full Christian name, which his father enjoyed using). They had arrived together, but Fred would be staying with some friends from Andover elsewhere on campus.

The ostensible object of Cheever's visit to Stanford was to see what kind of school it would be for his son. Indeed, both as we waited that morning and over the next week, he quizzed me repeatedly about the school, the faculty, the area, even the sports teams. Likewise he enjoyed discussing the relative merits of Stanford versus other schools with the Flo Mo freshmen who were delighted to be treated as authorities on something. But I couldn't help thinking that these efforts were done more for his own edification than Fred's. He talked constantly about his son, but in an oddly formal way for a father. He seemed very consciously trying to play the role of the perfect father—especially around the freshmen—but his performance had a certain studied air that betrayed it as the sincere effort of a man who had difficulty in showing his love for his children.

When Fred finally appeared it was obvious he needed no paternal assistance in sizing up Stanford. Having made sure that his father was safely ensconced at Flo Mo, he quickly left to rejoin his friends from Andover with whom he spent the rest of the week. Until he and his father returned East a week later, I saw them together again only once. Yet neither of them seemed to mind.

Fred looked a great deal like his father, though he was slightly taller and more handsome. But father and son were dressed identically in the not-yet-fashionable preppy style—tweed sports coats, crew neck sweaters over long-sleeved shirts, slacks and penny loafers. While this was not especially remarkable for Fred, who after all was a preppy, it was hardly usual for a sixty-three-year-old man. But rather than seeming odd, Cheever's clothes suited him perfectly. He had never bothered to grow old. He still seemed a brilliant young man, not a sagacious patriarch. No one who met him that week would have put him much older than fifty.

As his staff host, I expected to see very little of Cheever after taking him to lunch that day. To my astonishment, I spent most of the next week with him. He had arrived at Stanford with the best of intentions but the vaguest of plans. Since Fred was busy following his own agenda, his father had nothing to do except wait for a class visit and the English Department reading toward the end of his stay. Cheever knew no one at Stanford, and the people who might have sought him out were largely unaware he was on campus. Unconcerned by this lack of attention, he just hung around Flo Mo, treating this large, spider-shaped complex like a resort hotel. He would linger over meals until the last student left and then go off to sit in one of the run-down and usually deserted lounges. Whenever I returned from classes, I would invariably find him sitting by himself smoking in one of the huge Naugahyde chairs. He agreed to almost any suggestion I made—a walk, a drive, a visit. Eventually I gave him a key to my room so he could borrow books or listen to my record player when I was in class.

It is impossible to summarize that week of conversations, spoken in dining halls against the clatter of trays and silverware, in meandering walks through campus, in an old car winding through January-green hills to the Pacific. Now ten years after the fact, the exact words are lost, and with John the exact words were always much of the magic. Still, some of his ideas have stuck with me. But since so much of what one remembers is not what was said but that part of it which one was prepared to hear, I must apologize in advance for these fragments which scarcely do justice to the man they try to evoke.

First, I remember his modesty as a writer, which did not come from any lack of self-esteem but rather from his intense conviction about the importance and difficulty of the writer's vocation. Having already met too many self-absorbed literary mediocrities, I found John's humility before his calling surprisingly pure and unaffected. He was proud of what he had written but without any pretension. He was unconcerned with posterity, which he claimed would take no note of him, for posterity meant less to John than the letters he received from *New Yorker* readers, those "estimable men and women," who wrote to say how much they enjoyed reading one of his stories. What mattered was literature as an act of shared discovery between the writer and the reader. Fiction, he insisted, was innovative, not by technical experimentation but by being "constantly and profoundly questioning."

I was also impressed by John's candid explanation of his own religious impulses. He told me he went to church and communion every Sunday morning, sitting quietly for the better part of an hour, because this was one place where he could in a small but genuine way become spiritually refreshed. He claimed to believe in God but in an evanescent way impossible to describe adequately to anyone else. Despite his loyal high Episcopalian church-going, he was less a Christian than a deist, but one who felt most comfortable worshipping with familiar liturgy in a traditional church. I think religion also had an important social and cultural function for him. In his own heretical version of the Communion of the Saints it was a way to affirm his connection with other people—both living and dead. It also was a means of keeping faith with the past which was at least one reason why he could respond only to traditional liturgy like the Cranmer prayerbook and even the Latin Mass (though he was decidedly not a Catholic). Like literature, great liturgy with its superb language helped cement the past and present. Cheever's religious sense was therefore inseparable from his vocation as a writer, though critics rarely noticed this connection. He was not primarily a satirist of suburban mores but an essentially religious writer whose subject was how contemporary man came to terms with his own mortality against the infinitely beautiful backdrop of the natural world. Was it the unusual surface brilliance of Cheever's work that so often fixated critics on its most literal level?

Finally, I was struck by John's belief that a real writer could and indeed should lead an ordinary life. Genius didn't need to be rootless, disenfranchised or alienated. A writer could have a family, a job and even live in a suburb. His marriage, his children, his home were all immensely important to him. Talking about them, he proselytized in a way he never did about religion. I could feel his passionate concern for these modest human values—indeed I was somewhat dazzled by his talk which could make a mortgage or a report card shimmer divinely like some sacred script. What I did not realize then was how bitterly won these quotidian consolations had been for him.

His insistence on viewing the writer as a whole man colored his judgements on the many authors he had known. We talked, no doubt at my eager prompting, about many of his famous literary friends—Edmund Wilson, John Dos Passos, James Agee, John Updike, and others. But the writer he spoke of most fondly was E. E. Cummings, who had been a sort of literary foster-father for him in his early New York days. Cummings' energy, intelligence, and dedication made a profound impression on Cheever, and Estlin, as he called him to my wonderment (how astonished I was back then to hear writers referred to by their first names as if they were not also human beings), had become a model for the kind of writer Cheever liked to consider himself. Later that week he summed up Cummings' importance to him in a characteristically Cheeveresque way saying that the older writer made it clear "that one could be a writer and also remain highly intelligent, totally independent, and be married to one of the most beautiful women in the world."

John also made an odd little comment about his work that has stuck with me. We were talking about some fine point of prose style when he announced, "I have never used italics. Never! If I am tempted to underline my meaning in that crude way, I go back instead and revise the sentence." Almost at once I began noticing how superfluous and heavy-handed most use of italics was. Soon considering them a vulgar typographical trick, I revised them out of my own work, and when one crept in despite my vigilance, I blushed to see it in print. Surely the audience recognized this blunder as a sign of my poor literary breeding. Luckily my typographic puritanism was tempered years later when I came across three italicized words in one paragraph of a Cheever sketch. Granted, it was an uncollected piece, but it comforted me to know that even Homer nods.

During this week at Stanford John had a particular radiance that he had already lost by the time I next saw him two years later. He gave off that almost visible aura of joy and serenity that people have just after they have experienced a genuine religious conversion or suddenly recovered from a long life-threatening illness. It was the joy of having been resurrected from the dead. In John's case it was a resurrection from alcohol. When I offered him some wine the first night of his visit, I was embarrassed by his frankness in discussing his drinking problem. But I soon realized that this victory over alcohol was the base for all of his present happiness. Only a few months out of an alcoholic rehabilitation center, he had no romantic delusions that drinking was fate's price for his poetic soul. It was a destructive addiction he had very painfully overcome.

The night of his reading some of the freshmen decided they wanted to take John out to dinner. We chose a modest French restaurant in Menlo Park, and a dozen of us came along including the friend who had originally introduced me to Cheever's work. Delighted that the waiter didn't ask for I.D.'s, the freshmen all ordered wine and kept offering it to John who smiled avuncularly and kept to his club soda. He entertained us with stories about teaching creative writing at B.U. and Sing-Sing, claiming that his students at Sing-Sing had shown more aptitude. At the end of the meal as the freshmen searched drunkenly through their wallets, several of them discovered they didn't have enough money to pay their share of dinner. With consummate politeness John quickly took the bill and the inadequate cash at hand and made up the difference from his own pocket, refusing to let either my friend or me chip in more than our share. Not only did John not mind this embarrassing situation, he honestly seemed to enjoy being cast in the role of parent getting his kids out of a jam.

Scheduled at short notice, the reading took place in Bishop Auditorium at the Graduate School of Business, which was the only empty hall on campus. In the car over from the restaurant, John began coughing violently. Arriving at the Business School, we found him a water fountain, but it barely helped. "This isn't nerves," he told us firmly.

Bishop Auditorium was virtually full with about two hundred people, almost all of whom were middle-aged or older. Few students had come and only a fraction of the English faculty. John was introduced by Richard Scowcroft, the head of the Creative Writing Program, who was genuinely excited by Cheever's visit. While his guest of honor hacked away beside him, Scowcroft gave a warmly nostalgic introduction about reading Cheever's stories as a young man. The elegiac tone of Scowcroft's remarks revealed a tacit assumption probably shared by most of the audience that night a year before the publication of *Falconer*. They thought Cheever was now at the end of his career and had long ago written his best work.

John appeared to improvise his program, but actually his first two selections that evening were a set program from which I never subsequently heard him depart. He began with "The Death of Justina," one of his best but least celebrated stories, followed by "The Swimmer" (introduced with anecdotes about its filming in Hollywood), and ended with a brief sketch he called "The Death of the Short Story" (it was actually the conclusion to "A Miscellany of Characters That Will Not Appear") which suffered in comparison with its two bewitching predecessors.

That night he began badly, coughing his way through "Justina" and chopping its exquisite opening to bits. But gradually his throat cleared up, and by the time he reached "The Swimmer" his suave storyteller's voice had returned. For the next twenty minutes the audience was mesmerized. Hearing this famous story again, they knew it was a small masterpiece. The spell, however, was quickly broken by the brittle humor of his concluding sketch which seemed small and cold by comparison. Though it was actually an old piece, its minor elegance seemed to confirm rumors of his recent decline. To make matters worse, John also began rushing through the text, perhaps sensing that it was not coming across well. But afterwards the audience applauded generously.

We left John to manage the Creative Writing Department's reception on his own. Outside on the Business School steps we noticed a writing instructor smoking a cigarette. He was telling an undergraduate that Cheever's talent was exhausted.

Cheever's reading was his one public moment at Stanford. Earlier in the week he had had little opportunity to enjoy the special status of a visiting literary celebrity because his arrival had been upstaged by another last-minute visitor, Saul Bellow. Bellow's unexpected sojourn had also been occasioned by a family matter. His new wife was interviewing in the Mathematics Department, and he had accompanied her to tease the University with the prospect of a package deal. The Administration exhibited no hesitation in swallowing the bait.

If Cheever's literary star was in decline that January, Bellow's was indisputably ascendant. His last novel, *Mr. Sammler's Planet,* had won the National Book Award making him the first author ever to win that prestigious prize three times, and his new book, *Humboldt's Gift,* which eventually would win the Pulitzer Prize, had been rapturously received, and his photograph had recently smiled from the cover of several national magazines. Moreover, he was widely—and, as it happened, correctly—rumored to be in consideration for a Nobel Prize. An author who never cultivated publicity, he had become an international literary celebrity. The English Department and the Administration waxed ecstatic. One saw a classic author, the other a classy acquisition.

One reason Cheever was left alone during most of his stay was that his hosts were busy courting Bellow. John neither begrudged nor envied Bellow his royal reception for it was obvious, even to an outsider, that like Queen Elizabeth's endless inspections of expanded hospital wings, new army barracks, and improved bridge crossings this tour would offer little enjoyment to the visiting monarch. The Administration had eagerly crammed Bellow's short stay with meetings, parties, speeches, and public appearances.

Bellow bridled at some of the more ludicrous engagements such as speaking in a dormitory to a restless group of students who only vaguely knew who he was, but he generally followed his official schedule with a weary air of obligation. He deceived no one, however, into thinking he was enjoying himself. Administrators wrung their hands, and John, half diplomat/half palace gossip, quietly pointed out each embarrassing academic *faux pas.*

Bellow certainly looked regal. Although like John he was very short and graceful, their similarity ended there. John always seemed amiably relaxed and informal whereas Bellow projected unapproachable dignity and reserve. Entering a room, he appeared intimidatingly confident. At sixty he was still trim and handsome. His well-tanned skin was unwrinkled. His thin grey hair brushed into deceptive thickness. And a king's haberdashery would not have surpassed his wardrobe. His tight, expensively-tailored suits and handsewn shirts stood aloof from the crowds of crumpled tweed and corduroy around him.

On his last evening Bellow agreed to give a short reading, but he requested that the University allow no publicity whatever beforehand. He also asked that to keep it small and informal the reading be held in a student residence. The Administration, anxious to end his visit nicely, planned to preface the reading with a fancy cocktail party and dinner. By coincidence, the reading was planned for Mirlo, the section of Florence Moore Hall where I served as resident advisor. For this reason I was invited to the preliminary festivities.

Being young and callow, I assumed that writers enjoyed talking with strangers about literature. After all, I did. So at the cocktail party, while Wallace Stegner chatted with Donald Davie and Cheever caught up with Bruce Bliven, I innocently tried to engage Bellow in literary conversation. He winced at each of my eager questions before making his pointedly terse reply. Posterity, alas, will be denied a complete record of our *tête-à-tête* because I have blocked out all but one of the exchanges made before I slinked off in defeat. I only remember asking what contemporary fiction Bellow most admired. "Literature is not a competitive sport," he retorted. Unaware I had asked for a game score, I was about to reply, but suddenly he rattled off what I assume was the first-inning batting order for his own literary All-

Stars Game: "Wright Morris, J. F. Powers, and a man standing in this room," he paused for effect, ". . . John Cheever."

Bellow's admiration was returned by John who viewed him as his most gifted contemporary. But while John respected Bellow's writing, he was not above gossiping about the novelist's life, and he would entertain me with extraordinary stories about Bellow's life in Chicago and New York. At the cocktail party he assured me *sotto voce* that Bellow was considering a job at Stanford mainly to get away from his ex-wife in Chicago. As he described the unusual ways this prodigious harridan plagued her ex-husband, I began to wonder for the first time if all of John's suspiciously detailed stories were true.

After dinner our group wandered into the Mirlo lounge which was already filling up with people. John and I grabbed front row seats. I noticed then that Bellow was carrying neither a book nor manuscript. A few minutes before the reading was to begin he walked over to his host, the Director of Residential Education, and said, "I need a copy of *Humboldt's Gift*." The director turned pale. How could he find a copy of a new novel available only in hardcover at the last minute in a freshman dorm? He rushed off to search the audience for a copy. Overhearing the conversation, I ran to my room to retrieve what was probably the only *Humboldt's Gift* within half a mile (and which I possessed only by accident). Just as the director was returning to Bellow after having frantically searched the crowd in vain, I handed him my book. Bellow accepted it without a word.

The hall was now overflowing. Seeing two old women desperately eyeing the packed room, John got up and led them with great panache over to our seats, and we then moved to the floor in front of them. Bellow walked over to us, bent down, and said, "John, you'll pardon me if I make a fool of myself, won't you?" With John's advance absolution, he walked up to the microphones, and began a powerful reading of two long passages from *Humboldt's Gift*. Making almost no introductory comments, he plunged into the heart of the novel. Most of the audience were soon lost, but to those who had read the new book, his fluent reading was intellectually and emotionally dazzling. Or at least the sound of his voice was. The audience could barely see him behind the three large microphones placed to amplify and record the event. John leaned over to me and whispered, "I can hear Saul, but all I see are a shiny pair of reading glasses peeking over the microphones."

Finishing the second passage, Bellow looked up and snapped the book shut. The audience exploded in applause. Smiling stiffly, he quickly walked in front of the microphones and the moment the applause ceased, he held out my book. Since he wasn't looking at me, I didn't immediately realize that this was my signal to fetch the volume, but in a moment I got up and retrieved it. By then people were beginning to walk to the front of the room, but Bellow was too quick for them. As soon as I took the novel from his outstretched hand, he disappeared out the side door, thus ending his visit to Stanford.

On his last day John agreed to sit for an interview to be published in *Sequoia,* the Stanford literary magazine. I drove him up through Stanford's sumptuous "faculty ghetto" to the house of a professor who had generously loaned us his living room. Michael Stillman, who had been recording Bellow and Cheever all week, set up his equipment in the huge glass-walled room which commanded a 120° hilltop view of the Stanford campus and nearby foothills. Millicent Dillon, who freelanced at that time for the Stanford News and Publication Service, asked at the last minute to join us and was invited along.

Most of Cheever's published interviews reflect his uneasy and defensive attitude towards critics (among whom he counted interviewers). He often viewed his interlocutor competitively, and his answers were sharp and aggressive. Determined not to be misunderstood, he often rejected, redefined or even ridiculed questions until the embattled interviewer raised concerns he felt deserved a serious response.

By comparison our long afternoon conversation with John was relaxed and amiable. He took an immediate liking to Mike and Millicent. After a few preliminary pleasantries, he leaned back on the large couch and talked for nearly three hours. Much of the conversation eventually appeared in *Sequoia.* John wrote me that he found the printed version "splendid" and claimed that it was the only successful taped interview he had ever done. I suspect he was pleased at the way the interview caught the fanciful quality of his conversation.

The published version of the interview, however, contained only a fraction of the conversation. The editor cut thirty-five single-spaced pages of transcript down to the six published pages, and at least as much interesting material vanished as finally appeared. Some of John's best remarks, however, disappeared by prior agreement. Several times during the interview he told us he was now speaking "off the record." Many of these private remarks concerned his experiences in the Soviet Union, but there were also some devastating appraisals of a few contemporaries. For example, John described one celebrated novelist by saying, "his principal gift was the ability to describe bilgewater, rotting wood, and the smell of wet hemp."

At the end of the interview I drove him back to his room. We talked a few minutes, then Fred arrived. They had to leave for the airport presently, so we made our quick farewells.

We exchanged a few short letters, and I occasionally saw John at readings after moving to New York in 1977, but I never pursued our friendship.

The week at Stanford had been a special situation, which one could not repeat. By that time, too, not only had he recouped his critical fortunes with *Falconer*, but he had also achieved a greater public celebrity than ever before. This success made me especially reluctant to presume on his generosity. I felt more comfortable seeing him beaming from the cover of *Newsweek* or chatting with Dick Cavett on television.

The last time I saw John was by accident. In late September 1981 my wife and I went to hear Eudora Welty speak at the Katonah Library. It was a crisp autumn day when the leaves in Westchester were just beginning to turn, the sort of day John so frequently celebrated in his work. Outside the library a long, noisy line of people waited for the doors to open. Walking to the end of the line, we passed Robert Penn Warren, William Maxwell, and, my old teacher, Robert Fitzgerald. Everyone seemed hale and happy. A waterfall of conversations filled the air. Then suddenly I saw John and his wife, Mary, standing quietly near the end of the line. He looked thin, ashen, and painfully frail next to her. When he coughed, he shook with pain. That afternoon he seemed half a century older than the quick, boyish man I had met only six years before. I stopped to say hello, but as we talked, he sounded so tired that I quickly excused myself. After the reading Mary led him gently through the packed room towards the door, and I watched them over the bobbing heads and shoulders of the crowd until his tiny, shuffling frame disappeared into the early evening.

E D I T O R ' S   N O T E

Ursula Obst, journalist and editor, is a former columnist for the *Philadelphia Daily News*. She edits books now, primarily for Simon & Schuster, and remarks, "Oddly enough, in 1989, I was asked to finish a book because the author had died. He was Harold T. P. Hayes and the book was *The Dark Romance of Dian Fossey*, which was made into a movie, *Gorillas in the Mist.*"

"Anna's Tangled Destiny," reprinted here from the premiere issue of *New York Woman*, is a meticulously researched portrait of a Polish woman who suffered greatly during the Nazi occupation of her country. (For more information about the writing of this piece, see Obst's "Research and Commitment" in Chapter 4.) As you read it, ask yourself:

- What role do space breaks play in this piece, with respect to foreshadowing?
- How do direct and indirect quotations characterize sources?
- Which passages provide transition from time element (chronological, literary, grammatical) to another?

As for structure, the voice here is informed, observant, and compassionate. The moment allows Obst to share her research in the body of the piece as we accompany her on various interviews. A moment shift toward the *now* occurs to dramatize the open ending, foreshadowed in the introduction. The theme of this profile—uncompromising pride—is stated in the subtitle characterizing Anna Podobna, whose life Obst has captured in her penetrating profile.

Anna's Tangled Destiny

A Woman's Uncompromising Pride
Defines Her Own Harsh Existence

Ursula Obst

Winter and summer, she wears a black coat, so carefully darned in places that it appears embroidered; her thin, red hands protruding from its too-short sleeves are usually encumbered by white plastic shopping bags. She is impeccably groomed, and she walks with a determined step that is only occasionally halted by a suffocating cough. Her bed is the street at times, but mostly she confines herself to a small, barren room in a dilapidated hotel. There is only a handful of people she chooses to acknowledge, always with a smile and a courtly bow, as she paces out her daily routine within the four blocks of Broadway she considers home.

I met Anna Podobna ten years ago when she was less guarded and reserved than now. She bowed as we were introduced, greeted me formally in her native Polish, then sat down erect, her head held high. Her feet, strapped in delicate white sandals, were grotesquely swollen, yet she managed to cross her ankles gracefully as she smoothed her skirt over her knees.

I could see the network of bluish veins through the skin of her bony hands. Her arms were twigs. Above the neckline of her blouse, the collar bones stuck out sharply. Her gray hair was swept back neatly and coiled at the back of her head. Her face was pale and drawn—eye sockets defined by dark circles, prominent cheekbones, concave cheeks, flesh collapsing into a toothless mouth. The corners of her lips frequently curled into a half-smile as she talked, responding with shy courtesy to my polite remarks, while her eyes studied me with intense interest.

Anna was then fifty-two. She had been living in New York since 1960, when, at age thirty-six, she had come from Poland to America to be married. The marriage never took place, but, because she left Poland without the necessary permits, she could not go back. She had no choice; she stayed.

I was once shown a photograph of her taken shortly before her arrival in New York. It was a shock to see it. There was the same gentle smile, the same large eyes, hair pushed back and piled high the same way, but the face was round and smooth. Illuminated softly by the photographer's lights, it was the face of a fresh, beautiful, hopeful woman. I assumed at first that the photograph had to have been taken in the 1940s and that the trauma of the war years had ruined her beauty. Much later I learned it was New York.

A fragile psyche cannot survive here. Yet, I discovered through the people who knew her over the years (by the time I undertook this search for her past she would not talk with me anymore) that, at whatever cost, she has saved her sense of self. Battered by life, repeatedly caught up in events beyond her control, she has managed to retain her independence and her pride.

Born May 27, 1923, Anna was the youngest (her sister Lesia was seven years older, her brother Stanislaw, now deceased, eleven) in a Catholic family that had endured many hardships. From the time Anna was three, when her father, Jan, a train conductor, died, the family had lived on his small pension and on what Marianna, her mother, could eke out of a hectare of land behind the small house they owned in Grodzisk (a town located about fifty kilometers from the city of Poznan). The house on Polwiejska street, number 4, near the railroad, was modest. Stuccoed gray like many country houses, it contained only two rooms, one in front and one in back, with a shed added on for a kitchen and an outhouse in the yard.

The year the Nazis occupied Poland, Anna—a proud and spirited but level-headed girl—was barely sixteen and was still in school. Her education was interrupted, and, like all Poles, she had to go to work for the Germans. Grodzisk, along with a large portion of western Poland, had become part of the Third Reich. But life, so long full of hardships, was not unbearable, according to her sister Lesia. It all changed on an autumn morning in 1940.

Lesia, Anna, and their friend Irena, were walking to work. "It was before eight o'clock," Lesia remembers. "I had my breakfast with me, just a couple of little sandwiches. My sister didn't bring breakfast. We were walking near the railroad, and the Nazis, two Nazi guards, were leading a column of prisoners, about thirty of them."

The prisoners—Lesia thinks they were French—were a half-starved, ragged lot being led to forced labor at the railroad yard. As best they could, the men made efforts to attract the attention of the three young women.

"They were stretching their hands to us, asking for bread. I was afraid, but she, my sister, she was courageous. She took my little parcel with my breakfast and she threw it to them. My friend did the same with her breakfast."

The guards didn't notice, but a German looking out a window had seen them and informed.

"We were at work for about two hours when they came for us," Lesia said. "They said we threw pieces of paper with information, forbidden information, to the prisoners. There was a long interrogation. We denied that we did anything like that. It was only an act of kindness. They wrote everything down. A few weeks later there was a trial. My mother had to be present because my sister was a minor. I was let go, but my sister got four weeks in prison and my friend Irena, because she was over twenty-one, got a six-week sentence.

"Irena told me that they were not kept in the same cell, but they worked together. They had to work very hard. They had to make rope. They were given soup, but it was made from moldy turnips, and it wasn't edible. All they ate was black bread with black coffee. It was very, very cold that winter, and they were in prison in January. When they went out in the yard the snow was up to their knees, and they had to walk through it. It was very cold inside the prison. They had to wash floors on their knees and it was so cold their hands would get frozen to the rags. When Anna came back from prison, she looked exhausted and so thin. She seemed lifeless, she didn't talk much. We all cried."

The way Anna dealt with her imprisonment—hard labor bound to break the spirit of a young girl—shaped the way she would approach tragedies and heartbreaks in her life. She did it alone and she did not talk about it.

Plagued by the informant, who thought she got off too lightly, Anna decided to get out of town; and a few months after her release, she went to Krakow.

One of Poland's most historic and picturesque cities, with steep, red-tiled roofs, quaint cobblestone alleys weaving under magnificent archways, Krakow was then a city of rigidly enforced curfews, of bloody executions on street corners, of *lapanki,* indiscriminate round-ups of young people—in the middle of Sunday afternoon, all those seen on certain streets might be caught, packed into trucks, and shipped off to labor camps. Food was expensive and scarce, more so. Anna scavenged the best she could.

"She once told me that she always tried oatmeal," recalls Melania Kulil, a friend Anna made in America. "She said she knew oatmeal was very important, because she had observed a horse, how a horse eats oats and can work very hard and doesn't get sick. And he looks good! That's what she said."

Alone, a seventeen-year-old girl needed friends, protectors. Options were few; many like her became prostitutes. How Anna coped no one knows precisely. The family heard very little from her. She wrote occasionally, saying she was homesick, and when her mother died in November of 1943, she managed to obtain a permit to come home for the funeral, but she arrived too late and missed it.

"She had to go back right away," Lesia recalls. "She did not say very much of what happened to her in Krakow. But when she came home for her mother's funeral, she showed me the scars on her legs. I saw them with my own eyes. She said she had a job in a laboratory, and they were attaching boxes there and lice, that there were lice in those boxes. She didn't say much more about it. I thought she was embarrassed."

The laboratory, on Czysta Street, number 18, was part of a network of Nazi laboratories in several European cities which manufactured typhus vaccine badly needed by the troops at the Russian front. The typhus vaccine the Nazis used was produced by injecting bacteria into the rectum of a louse; once the bacteria multiplied in the louse's intestines, the louse was sliced open and the intestines removed. Three doses of the vaccine, requiring 175 louse intestines, had to be administered for immunization.

Lice have to drink human blood to live and breed, and for this purpose small metal boxes were covered with silk through which the lice could bite human flesh but not escape. These boxes were attached to the thighs of the persons on whose blood the lice fed. Millions of lice were needed to supply the vaccine and hundreds of people were needed to feed the lice.

The Krakow laboratory employed some 200 feeders, according to Dr. Zdzislaw Przybylkiewicz, a Pole who worked there directly under the Nazi overseer, Dozent Hermann Eyer. The feeders were required to come twice a day; each feeder was given forty boxes containing 500 lice to feed during the course of a given day. A feeder lost ten cubic centimeters of blood daily, he says. And, yes, there would be scars.

The war ended; at the same time that Anna came home, Lesia married and moved away. Her brother Stanislaw opened a restaurant in Poznan and gave Anna a small room in the back. She worked as a secretary in a slaughterhouse and moonlighted during the summers on the staff of the Poznan International Trade Fair. There she met a visiting Polish-American from Chicago and fell in love.

Stanislaw, as the head of the family, objected when Anna announced her plan to follow her lover to America to be married. Anna would not be discouraged. She went to Munich, purportedly to visit an elderly aunt. There, in a few months, she managed to obtain an entry visa to the U.S., but when she arrived in New York on December 12, 1960—scarcely two weeks before Christmas—it was only to learn that she would be attending a funeral, not a wedding. Her fiancé had been killed in a car accident.

A lawyer who had helped her get to the U.S. got her a job at a Polish newspaper, and she worked there, in the payroll department, until she repaid her debt to him. Then she had a job in a door factory, which she quit because the place was too cold, and she also worked in a doughnut shop.

She lived in Harlem, rooming with Janina Gorska, a Polish writer who had a large apartment at 136th and Broadway.

A slight, wrinkled woman with steel gray hair, Janina Gorska now runs a rooming house at the New Jersey shore. She is soft-spoken, but her manner is direct and she confronts my questions about Anna with a sharp stare. "Oh yes, I remember her, she caused me a great deal of trouble, a great deal of pain.

"She was very clean, very neat, more so than I. She was very polite, so polite that something in her manner demanded a return in kind, but I didn't pay much attention to her. She lived with me a year, and I didn't suspect anything. Then one day she said to me that she was certain she saw one of the other roomers putting poison in her food. And then we started to notice that when she sat at the table with us she never ate anything. So I decided it was better that she not live with me anymore, and I asked her to move out. She left, but that wasn't the end of it. For five years she kept coming around with her problems.

"I tried to help her. I gave her food, I gave her money. She didn't have warm clothes. I bought her a coat on sale. She left it outdoors. 'Why?' I asked her. Do you know what she told me? 'Someone else may be as cold as I am.' She had many jobs—where I don't know.

"Then she had an accident. She was standing someplace on a street corner and a man offered her a ride. I figured this out later. He gave her a ride, took her somewhere, and he must have invited her in. How naive could she have been? He started to make advances, and she must have made excuses. So he got angry. What did she expect? So he raped her. It happened. He simply raped her. It affected her very badly. She wouldn't talk to men after that. She would just turn and look at the wall. Before this, she didn't have any trouble with men, only she didn't really seem to have a way with them; she was very attractive, but they left her alone. The accident affected her very badly.

"Yes, she had unfortunate experiences. But, you know, this couldn't happen to you or me. It's a matter of free will. Each person has a free will. She can help herself. But there are people who don't want to, and they indulge themselves. Anna is a bum. I feel sorry for her. Still, Anna is nothing but a bum. I have written many stories, but I wouldn't write about Anna."

Sometime after Anna left Janina Gorska, she moved to Seventy-fifth and Broadway to the Millburn, an 800-room single-room occupancy hotel that, though no longer there, is well remembered by police.

"We called it the Milky Way," Officer Moran of the 20th Precinct tells me. "You could get anything there—dope, women. You wanted somebody knocked off, go to the Milky Way. Something for everybody. We had a raid there every night. It was a big place."

Anna had been robbed several times while living there and lost the few small things she owned—a watch, a radio, even her shoes. It was while she lived there that New York welfare officials recorded, in June of 1973, the "onset" of her "disability." Two years later, cut off from welfare and unable to pay the rent, she was thrown out. For a time, she was allowed to sleep at the 20th Precinct, until one day she shocked a female employee who found her taking a sponge bath in the ladies' room and her privileges at the police station ended. She began sleeping on the street, occasionally taken in by a shopkeeper. That's when Melania Kulik and her husband Boni found her. They had met her brother on a visit to Poland, and he gave them a photograph and an address, asking them to check if she was still alive.

"We went there to that address, that hotel," Boni recalls. "The manager of the hotel, Weinberg, said she was there, but no longer. He said he knew all about her. She had come there soon after she left that Mrs. Gorska in Harlem. So he knew her a long time. And when she had money it was all right, and when she didn't he threw her out. What was he to do? He had to throw her out.

"In the course of the conversation Weinberg told us he knew where she was," Boni continues the story, "and he would go with us because we would never recognize her, because it is night and day, the difference from the photograph we had from her brother. So we walked with him about ten blocks north on Broadway. She was there, in a space between buildings, but he told us to wait, he said he would talk with her first.

"She was sitting on a box. In a little niche between buildings." Boni tries to remember the details: "She was wearing a black coat . . . white blouse and a skirt, silk, checkered red . . . and shoes with little wedge heels. Her legs were swollen, but she was clean, very clean."

"When Weinberg told her who we were, when he told her she should talk with us, she started to cry. She was embarrassed that she was in this situation," Melania explains. "She said: 'Why did you do this to me?' That's what she said. She must have wanted to hide it. We pretended there was nothing unusual."

"Later," Boni recalls, "when we asked her how long she had lived on the street, she said from the seventh of May, and we found her on the twenty-ninth of June."

The Kuliks took Anna home, thinking that a job and an income would fix her problems, but it proved not so simple. The job they found her as a housekeeper for a wealthy woman did not work out; she quit after three days, complaining the employer's house was too cold.

Melania said that Anna had a pleasant disposition, and she never spoke ill of anyone. She was uncommonly neat and clean. She was willing to work and was helpful. Her only vice, as far as Melania could tell, was chain smoking. Yet, she also exhibited eccentricities Melania found hard to overlook. She would not sign the few simple forms the Social Security bureaucracy required for disability benefits. She refused to see a doctor about a hacking cough which plagued her. She would wear only the white blouse and red skirt she had worn when they found her. Boni, a tailor, had gone to considerable trouble to alter an entire wardrobe of secondhand clothes for her, but she would not touch it. He persevered. Because she would not wear the good *gray* wool coat he altered for her, insisting on her battered black one, Boni found a good *black* wool coat. She gave it away "to the poor," and kept on wearing the one she always wore.

Her departure from the Kuliks' home was provoked by their insistence she quit smoking, which, she maintained, was her sole pleasure in life. When she disappeared, they knew where she went, and there they found her living on the street again. They didn't have the heart to leave her without a roof over her head. Weinberg wouldn't take her back—the place was to be converted shortly to luxury apartments—and he sent her instead ten blocks uptown to another hotel. Through the winter, Boni paid the $95 a month for her room there, until he lost all patience with her and gave up, but she stayed around, and Beacon Hall is where she still lives.

When Anna first moved to Beacon Hall, the manager Joe Caplan, a Polish-Jew and concentration camp survivor, became her friend. Joe can still recall when he first noticed Anna: "She would talk to nobody in the building. I tried to find out her name and a little bit about her. I tried to talk in Polish. At first she wouldn't talk to me. But, after a while, I got her to talk. I bribe her, like with candy, you deal with her like a child. I got her a cup of coffee and kept talking to her. I lost my whole family in Poland during the war. I'm a survivor myself. I told her: 'Trust me. As long as I'm here you're going to have a roof over your head.'"

Born in the coal-mining town of Bedzin, Joe speaks English with a thick Polish accent. The instant impression I get is that Joe is a serious man, and in the course of three long meetings, he smiles only once. Each time we meet he insists on buying me a meal and, as we eat, won't let up until I share in the food on his plate. He is in his late fifties and looks more Slavic than Jewish with his round and wide face made wider by a receding hairline, except for the large, sad brown eyes that stare intently from behind thick lenses in black frames.

Joe says he understands Anna. "Listen, I know, I know. She is very frightened. As soon as I met her, I knew right away she is afraid."

Memories can cause suffering and be a trap from which there is no escape, Joe says. He has seen it all too often in fellow camp survivors. Anna, he says, "lives in the past, and she is afraid. In New York, in Warsaw, in any city, there are people who survived like she did. There were thousands, hundreds of thousands of girls like her. They made them into prostitutes, they did experiments on them. Our friend, she never had a good dream. Even if she did, it never came true. Always there is a *plama*, you know what that means in Polish, a black spot. There is always a black spot."

I think it is not so simple—a spot. *Plama* can mean an indelible stain.

Anna refused Joe's offers of help, he tells me. She would not take his advice to see a doctor, and he could not get her to sign her name on those Social Security papers. Joe thought for a time he could circumvent the bureaucracy on Anna's behalf, but he hit a stone wall. "I explained to them this woman has been tortured, she can't work. But they go by number, by Social Security number. The rich, the bureaucrats, they will never understand. They have very little patience. Many times, years back, a field worker would come out and interview in person and see for themselves. Now they've laid people off and cut this out. Now it's numbers on a sheet. Are we no more than numbers in Washington? No matter. It's the same thing, in a concentration camp they put a number over here (he points to his shoulder), or over here (he points to his arm). People don't want to know. People don't want to hear bad news."

Looking for help anywhere he could find it, Joe involved the Reverend Laura Jacobs, a minister from a nearby Presbyterian church.

"She was suspicious of me," Laura tells me in our first of many meetings. Tall, slender, and blonde, Laura has perfectly symmetrical features and translucent skin, only her face shows deep lines when she does not smile, and her eyes have the dark circles of someone who never gets enough sleep. "She wouldn't open the door to her room. I went to see her many times, then I told Joe he had to speak to her and tell her she could trust me."

At that time Laura had an office in the church building with a window that faced out on a squalid alleyway and the back wall of Beacon Hall. "As it happened, when I sat at my desk I looked into her window. It was usually open, and so I would watch her.

"I could see very well into her room. There was a table near the window, the sink was to the left, the bureau next to it. There was a hot plate on the bureau and an aluminum pan, you know, one of those sauce pans. She covered everything with white cloths. The bed was on the right, always made in a very flat way, very tight, like a hospital bed. She had such a routine. I would watch her . . . I would watch her fold things, move things, go to the sink and come back, always smoking, always smoking. She made coffee. I thought she made hot oatmeal, but I never saw milk. She could have made it with hot water. She took sponge baths at the sink. A lot of grooming, a lot of time on her lipstick and on her hair, combing it carefully, slowly for a long time. It would take hours in the morning—walking back and forth, picking up and moving one thing at a time. Always smoking nonfiltered cigarettes, down to the very last."

In her first few encounters with Anna, Laura tried to resolve her financial problems. Boni Kulik, had, by then, stopped paying for her room. "Joe and the people at Beacon Hall, much to their credit, never forced her out, but I think she felt she had no right to the room. She would stay out on the street and come in at odd hours to wash up and leave again. She had a key and they never changed the lock. I suppose she thought they didn't know she was still using the room, but of course they did."

Despite Laura's efforts, Anna would not sign the Social Security disability application. Perhaps it was pride, perhaps she would not admit to being disabled, Laura is not sure.

It took a long time for Anna to trust Laura enough to admit her into her room, but once she did, she welcomed Laura's visits. On one such visit Laura asked her about the war. "Joe told me he believed she must have been in a concentration camp, so I was kind of on the lookout for something that created this way she coped with life." Laura had wanted more information, but when Anna began to talk about it she was unprepared—shocked and moved, she could not ask for details. "She told me there were boxes, I didn't understand about the lice. She showed me a scar. She pulled back her skirt and there it was on the inside of her right thigh. That conversation was clearly the most intimate moment we shared."

Their relationship changed after Laura, frustrated over another fruitless attempt to get Anna to sign, lost her temper and spoke harshly to her. "It seems to me, after that, she didn't give me access to her room or to her thoughts. I think I hurt her pride."

Eventually, Anna did sign. On a freezing night in January she showed up unexpectedly at the Kuliks' doorstep and agreed to everything.

Laura arranged an appointment with Social Security officials and Melania made sure Anna kept it. "I remember this," Melania tells the story, "we were given an address and told she must go to the Social Security doctor. He was going to decide whether she was disabled, whether she would get the check or not. All this was happening in January in the worst freeze, it was very, very cold. And we couldn't get a cab in the snow, and we walked from the hotel all the way to the Social Security office. We stood and we stood, and we waited, and there were no buses or cabs. The office was in the Fifties. We walked thirty-six blocks. She had a hat then, a white wool hat and mittens. And she tied herself—you know her coat, it has a tent shape—she cut off a piece of plastic from the top of a garbage bag, the green kind, and she tied the coat with that. So, we went to the doctor. At first he called me in and he said she should go to the hospital, and I said she won't do it. She does not regard herself as sick. She is very clean, I told him, and she can take care of herself. And then he called her in, and the first words she said to him were: 'Mister Doctor, help me get the check. Without the check, I cannot live.' And the doctor told her something I didn't hear. I left the room. And after the visit to the doctor she got the check."

She decided then that she would go back to Poland; regimes had changed, and there was no longer a barrier to her return. Lesia recalls receiving a letter from Anna about that time saying she was coming home. Several packages followed, containing items Lesia understood she was to hold for Anna's return—there were coffee mugs and other small kitchen utensils, three pillows and two quilts, and nightgowns and underwear, sewn by hand with tiny stitches and trimmed with delicate lace.

The Kuliks remember when Anna sent those packages. They remember her plans to return to Poland in style. "For years she got nothing, for two years she had been cut off from welfare and she got nothing from the government, so she was sure when she signed that they owed her a great deal of money. It was her intention, when she got this big backlog, to go back to Poland," Melania tells me.

The big check never came for Anna. She kept hoping nevertheless. She insisted to the Kuliks that she was entitled to it. "She wrote to the president," says Boni. "She wrote to President Ford when Carter was already president. She wrote 'President Ford, White Home.' Ford was no longer there, so they sent the letter back. The manager told me this."

She wrote the president several times. What she said in those letters nobody knows, but after a while she stopped talking of the big check. She accepted life such as it was. And she was not without friends.

To George Stavros, the gentle Greek who owns the restaurant she frequents, and to his employees, Anna has been a special customer, and object of curiosity. They had speculated about her past and had come to call her "our famous lady."

Anna had been coming into his restaurant for about nine years, George figures. "She don't change much. Still the same, but she lost some weight. Much more skinny, I think. The only thing she eat is soup, soup and coffee, and once in a while rice pudding. Very rare, she eat eggs, once a month maybe. All the time, chicken soup and coffee. Sometime she stand outside for hours, not move. All the time she ask: 'Can I please sit in the back?' There, in the back there is an empty corner. Sometime, she sleep there."

George, Melania has told me, bears a strong resemblance to Anna's brother Stanislaw. A broad-shouldered meaty man of about forty, he is almost bald, but his remaining hair is jet black. Stanislaw too was a big dark-haired man.

When she first started coming into the restaurant, Anna wrote him notes asking to borrow money. The notes were carefully composed, written in fine penmanship. "I think she feels embarrassed to ask for money, and she write what she want to say," George says.

"She don't bother nobody. She is very polite, very clean, very nice. 'Hello Mister George'" (he takes a deep bow imitating Anna), "when she see you on the street. Many times she ask for two dollar, five dollar. When she get check. She pay back."

"At the beginning she never talked to me at all," says Johnny Rodriguez, the current caretaker of Beacon Hall. "But, after Joe Caplan was gone, she opened up to me, but only me."

Johnny is Anna's friend at Beacon Hall. A native of Puerto Rico, Johnny has lived at Beacon Hall for twenty-four years and has worked there the last seventeen. He has a pockmarked face, greasy black hair which he is fond of smoothing back with the palm of his hand, and a ready smile that reveals a broken and stained set of mismatched teeth. I figure that it is his gentlemanly manners that must appeal to Anna—he is quick to push forward a chair, open a door, offer a cup of coffee.

"When she needs something taken care of, something fixed, she comes to me. And she always specifies the day and the hour when she wants the work done. She is like that. Par-ti-cu-lar."

"One thing I never understood why she goes out and stays on the street." Johnny wrinkles his brow. "I recall this one time I saw the police talking to her out there on the corner where she always sits. They wanted to take her to a hospital. But I told them she has a home here. She is afraid of going to the hospital.

"A few months ago, we had a problem," Johnny continues. "She didn't get her check. They held it up for three months. She didn't pay her rent, she borrowed here and there a little, here and there a little. But when the check came, when I added up what she owed us, she pulled out a piece of paper and her figure was exactly the same. Exactly. We don't consider her a mental case. She is very smart that lady. Everyone knows that. Believe me, all the guys out there know her, they wouldn't bother her," he gestures out to the street where I had seen Anna walking past hoodlums and drug dealers.

It is 5 p.m. I watch her come down the street toward me, stopping on the median strip in the center of Broadway where a group of elderly loiterers are overcrowding the bench as usual; intent on the traffic, she does not acknowledge them. With a determined step she crosses the street and heads north. I follow her cautiously and wait outside as she disappears into a fresh produce store that spills its wares onto the sidewalk. A few minutes later I see a hand in a black sleeve placing a banana on the grocer's scale. Walking out, she stops between the fruit stands, holding up her white plastic bag with the handles spread apart as if she expects someone to drop something inside. She stands for about a minute, a vacant half-smile on her face, her eyes darting between the apples and the cashier inside. Then, slowly, she closes up her bag and walks south. On the next corner, she stops outside the window of a lingerie store. She stares at the nightgowns, she leans forward then back, cocking her head to one side then the other, as if the display contained some enchanting and wondrous things. She slowly walks on, surveying each shop window. She reaches the corner and stops short. I see her body begin to shake. She turns, her face is contorted—eyes open wide, cheeks blown out, lips trembling. Her very thin, very red hand protruding from the short coat sleeve clutches at the air spasmodically. She is paralyzed in her progress by a suffocating cough. She stands there for a long time battling with it until the shaking ceases. Then she resumes walking, back in the direction she came from. As she passes close by me I notice that the cloth of her coat has worn through at the shoulder and has been intricately mended with many tiny stitches. I follow her to Sloan's Supermarket and through the plate glass window I watch her in an exchange with an elderly woman. The woman hands her money. She bows deeply several times, a smile widens her face. The woman walks away but Anna remains, and the smile spreads. Her face is a child's face, its expression a child's delight. She unfolds the bill with two hands, and then folds it slowly and places it into her plastic bag. Then she takes hold of a shopping cart and disappears from view. Perhaps fifteen minutes pass, a long time, it seems. She pulls in line for a check-out counter, in her cart are four bottles of Coca-Cola. She stands by the window ledge, smoking a cigarette and watching the goings-on in the gathering dusk outside with an expression of intense interest. She stands there smoking and staring for a half hour. Finally, encumbered by two white plastic bags, one in each hand, she heads north. Two blocks up, she enters the Red Apple Supermarket, where she buys tissues and a small container of milk. Twenty minutes she stands at the window smoking. She walks out to the street; outside, on Amsterdam Avenue, the kids from the projects have spilled onto the sidewalk and are circling under the corner streetlights like fireflies. Slowly, laboriously, she struggles up the hill toward home.

Opinions and Interviews

EDITOR'S NOTE

Bruce Woods, former editor of both *Mother Earth News* and *Writer's Digest*, has authored three books, including *Chui! A Guide to the African Leopard* (Trophy Room Books), *The Birdhouse Book,* and *Whirligigs and Weathervanes* (both from Sterling/Lark).

The opinion piece that follows, originally published in *BackHome,* takes a controversial subject in some circles—hunting—and explains it with strong emphasis on viewpoint. As you read the piece, ask yourself:

- What role does voice play in conveying beliefs about hunting to readers who may disagree with the author's viewpoint?
- Which passages contain epiphanies or peak experiences?
- If research does not play a key role in this piece, then what other basic magazine elements are at work to make a strong argument?

Woods announces the topic with a descriptive title. Appropriately, he uses a moment pushed toward the *then* to convey his viewpoint to target readers. His voice is open, informed, and contemplative, expressing the theme of truth in a series of epiphanies and peak experiences in the final 10 paragraphs of his feature.

The Hunting Problem

Bruce Woods

The beauty of hunting lies in the fact that it is always problematic.
　　　　　　　　　　　　　　　　　—Jose Ortega y Gasset

The killing bothers me.

Oh, I haven't stopped hunting. Killing is, after all, the only way to make meat, and I enjoy meat. Raising grain kills, too. Every additional acre in cultivation is an acre not available as wildlife habitat, an acre lost to indigenous flora, an acre that loads another chamber in humanity's slow game of pesticide roulette.

But that's the stuff of rationalization, of apologia; I'm after more elusive game here. If the killing bothers me, what exactly is there about hunting that I like (or need) enough to cause me to tolerate the resulting deaths? What return do I get for my discomfort?

How, too, am I reimbursed for the hundreds of hours I spend each year on rifle practice and on preparing, component by component, the most accurate ammunition I'm capable of; on working out with bow and arrow, computing and extending the maximum distance at which I can *invariably* put an arrow into a circle the size of a deer's heart/lung area; on the constant exercising of my ability to estimate ranges, something that I practice almost subconsciously whenever I walk anywhere; or on scouting the woods before and after hunting season, attempting to reconstruct the activity of animals from the tiny clues left behind by creatures that owe their lives to their elusiveness?

There are a few relatively easy answers. I hunt, despite the killing, because it puts me in the outdoors, most often alone, during its most beautiful seasons. I hunt for the chance to observe truly wild animals without contaminating their activities by making them aware that they're being observed. And I see many, many animals while hunting that I don't, for one reason or another, attempt to kill. (In the past year of bow hunting, for example, I've released one arrow; the results are in my freezer, which is emptying week by week, an hour glass to the upcoming deer season.)

I hunt, and force myself through the training that I feel any hunter must have, because hunting reminds me that I *do* have a home in this world. One of my favorite of Gary Snyder's poems, "By Frazier Creek Falls," includes a line that says we can live on earth without clothes or tools. Gary reminds me that we were *designed,* by God, evolution, whatever, to survive and thrive upon the wilds of this planet. And hunting allows me to make use of those aspects of my design. Because I hunt, I know what my local whitetails are likely to be feeding on with each change in season; I know how to read tracks and picture each footstep of the animal at the end of them, to learn something of its size and condition through tell-tale strands of hair or fur rubbed into rough bark, to decipher the daily diary of feces and—yes—to translate the bright dribbles and spews of a blood trail.

Because, you see, the real answers to the hunting problem aren't easy.

It has been said that we don't hunt to kill, but kill to have hunted. That's true, as far as it goes. The philosopher Ortega y Gasset speculated that "the only adequate response to a being that lives obsessed with avoiding capture is to try to catch it." There's some truth in that, too.

But neither these nor the other reasons cited above are enough to justify the killing. To do that, I have to follow the trail into the swamp, to the place where Hemingway said things become tragic.

Because beyond the quest for healthful meat, and culminating the pursuit and the always sudden and magical appearance of the animal, I think the core of my love of, my need for, hunting is found in the primitive, by which I mean ancestral, ecstasy felt at two moments.

I mentioned before that many animals are passed up by hunters. The reasons for this are varied. The shot might be too difficult to bring off with confidence; the hunter could decide to wait for a larger, older animal, or for an antlered male; or the hunter might simply not be emotionally ready, at the time that the animal shows, to take the irreversible step of deciding to attempt a killing.

But when I am ready, when the range and position of the animal presenting itself are correct, when I'm sufficiently confident of my equipment and abilities, when all of this is as it should be, that moment of decision, marked by the sudden knowledge that I am going to attempt to kill, is overwhelming and even addicting.

We often say that, in the grip of great emotion, we "forget everything." From the decision to shoot until the collapse of the trigger, until the freeing of the arrow, I am truly not aware of the frustrations of my daily job, my hopes and fears for my family or even the familiar aches and awkwardness of my body. Consciousness becomes concentrated into a laser-focused bond between the eye and the animal. At such moments I am as pure a creature as I'll ever be, involved in an act of monumental seriousness. It has little to do with sport, and it sure as hell isn't a game. It combines the delicious, fearful anticipation of shouldering a great responsibility with the euphoria of discovering that you can, for however brief a moment, bear its weight.

And then I also hunt for the moment after the shot. Because, and I must face this, too, there is a primitive sort of triumph in having killed; the hand reaches out beyond the body to touch with terrible magic, to *make food.* The war of celebration and regret that defines such moments leaves me awash with emotion, hyper-aware of colors and scents and feeling physically lighter, as after extraordinary sex or a purging cry.

So now we must turn our attention to the event in between these defining moments. The success of the hunt demands that it, the *killing,* be gotten over with as quickly as possible. That's the reason for the scouting and study of natural history, the regular, disciplined physical and mental *training.* Because killing to eat is ugly, and if poorly done it can forever poison the moment of anticipation with doubt, and replace triumph with self disgust.

Killing to eat is too ugly an act, in fact, to leave to others all of the time. That would be a shirking of responsibility akin to, in my mind, forcing a subordinate to tackle a firing that's your responsibility, or using the telephone to tell a lover you have a venereal disease.

You might say that the ugliness of the killing, and the dipping of my hands into the hot, reeking, slippery-organed soup of it, is the price I pay to remain, as I choose to be and as my body's design directs me to be, an omnivore.

Sure the killing bothers me.

It's supposed to.

And if it ever stops bothering me I pray I'll be big enough to let go of hunting forever. Because to hunt and not despise the killing would be to become not an animal, but a form of human that I shudder to even imagine.

EDITOR'S NOTE

Kevin Bezner's literary interviews have appeared in *American Poetry Review, Denver Quarterly, Mississippi Valley Review,* and *Sonora Review.* He is coeditor of *The Wilderness of Vision: On the Poetry of John Haines* (Story Line Press) and author of *About Water* (Drycrik Press). Bezner teaches English at Livingstone College in Salisbury, North Carolina.

In his interview with the famous poet and environmentalist Gary Snyder, originally published in the small-press magazine *Left Bank,* Bezner uses a question-and-answer format. As you read his piece, ask yourself:

- Which questions by Bezner are meant to solicit a thematic response?
- Which answers by Snyder provide the response and change direction, prompting Bezner to make a follow-up question?
- Which comments or questions by Bezner provide transition from one aspect of the interview to another?

As in all profiles, the topic is the interviewee; the theme, however, is foreboded in the suspense title "Right Work." Bezner explains the work theme in a research introduction that incorporates Snyder's "environmental and philosophical concerns." The moment is in the *then,* because participants are sharing opinions. Nonetheless, note how Bezner's questions elicit thematic responses. His last one, appropriately, contains an epiphany and a closed ending.

Right Work: An Interview with Gary Snyder

Kevin Bezner

Gary Snyder was born in San Francisco in 1930. He grew up in Oregon, was a student at Portland's Lincoln High, and in 1951 graduated from Reed College. Snyder then studied anthropology in graduate school; worked as a member of a Yosemite trail crew in the fifties; associated with Kerouac, Ginsberg, and others as part of the San Francisco Renaissance of the fifties; studied Zen Buddhism in

Japan; and traveled in India, the Japan Sea, and California from 1956 to 1968. During these years, Snyder held a wide variety of jobs. In addition to working on a trail crew, he was a forest-fire lookout, a ship's hand, and a logger. Throughout the years, his poetry and essays have concerned such work.

In 1970, Snyder built a house in the Sierra Nevada of Northern California, and he has lived at what he calls Kitkitdizze ever since. In 1990, Snyder and a group of his neighbors—people such as furniture maker Bob Erickson and carpenter Lenny Brackett—established the Yuba Watershed Institute, which its occasional journal Tree Rings *describes as "a nonprofit organization . . . dedicated to discovery, research, and dissemination of information on the Yuba Watershed and to assisting in the management of the Inimim Forest."*

At Kitkitdizze in the Yuba Watershed, Snyder carries on what he calls "the real work." This means knowing where your food and water come from so that you can actively participate in the decisions that affect the region in which you live; it requires hands-on work and living interdependently with the natural world. While Snyder teaches at the University of California at Davis and gives lectures and poetry readings to earn a wage, his aim is to avoid what he has called (in an interview with Peter Barry Chowkra in The Real Work*) the "triple alienation" of contemporary life—alienation from energy and resources, the body, and the mind. This is why he is involved in all aspects of work at his home, why all members of his family are engaged in such work, why he has taught his daughter how to change the oil on the generators at Kitkitdizze, and why he has a deep love and respect for tools and knowing when to use the right tool. This is why, too, he respects men such as John Dofflemeyer, a California cattle rancher (and poet) working to maintain a traditional way of life on the land tempered with a sense of how to work in harmony with it.*

Since the publication of his first book, Riprap, *Snyder has explored these ideas in eight collections of poetry, including* The Back Country, *the Pulitzer Prize-winning* Turtle Island, *and* No Nature: New and Selected Poems, *published in 1992. A collection of essays,* The Practice of the Wild, *addresses environmental and philosophical concerns.*

Kevin Bezner: How do you define the word "work," which in our culture seems to have taken on the definition of something you do to do something else?

Gary Snyder: You mean like "work" as occupation. That you have to do to support yourself. Yeah. That's actually called wage work, or wage earning, and as Ivan Illich points out in his very useful book called *Shadow Work,* working for wages is a very recent thing in history, and it's part of the rise of industrialism, the destruction of rural agriculture, and the creation of a working class. And in earlier times there's no work as defined in that way. One's life is one's subsistence is one's play is one's work. And it is not done in even a personal or individual way, it's done as part of what you do with your family and with other people, so that life is actually a family enterprise, or a household enterprise.

KB: That's what you have in your own life?

GS: Not entirely. Since we all live in a money economy, all of us in our household do some things that help bring money in. And some of what we do could be called wage earning. Some of what I do as a teacher at Davis could be wage earning, but the greater part of what I do could be called some kind of hunting and gathering. And as a writer it's very hard to draw the line between what's work, what's play, what's daily life in what you do in getting your material, seeing your world, being mindful, leading up to writing something. So that's more like the older sense that everything you do in life is done with an eye to subsistence. When you go for a walk, you watch for mushrooms. You come back with a couple of sticks of firewood. Is that work or is that play?

KB: One of your poems that I admire the most is "The Bath." What you're doing there, in that poem, is the real work of showing your son Kai how one cleans oneself and how one lives in a family.

GS: Well, that's what you have to do with your kids no matter what. If you don't prove a leader to your own children and take time to show them each of the little things they have to do, and then take time out to help them learn to cook or help them learn to handle tools and involve them in the things that you do around the place, how are they ever going to learn? I'm teaching my little nine-year-old step-daughter how to change the oil on the generator right now.

KB: How is she doing?

GS: She's perfect. If you take her through a procedure, she doesn't forget it. And she knows where the tools are. She's going to be dynamite when she's a little older. I'll have her fixing the cars.

KB: You have a family enterprise where you take people through the procedure, but you—and the people around you—seem to have moved into a way of taking the community through a procedure. In a sense, what you're doing with the Yuba Watershed Institute is showing people how they can live in the wild.

GS: What we're trying to do is learn how to do it ourselves first. In a sense, we're learning and showing at the same time. It's not exactly in the wilds, not in the wilds in the sense of protecting or preserved. It's primarily forest landscape—with some manzanita brush fields and a little bit of grazing and agricultural lands—in which we're all in the process of trying to learn to live and make some use of it, and at the same time enhance it. Some of that's public land, some of it's private land.

KB: Within this structure is a place for a Bob Erickson, who makes fine furniture and uses materials from the forest, and at the same time, there's a place for people who are attempting to preserve those forests.

GS: Bob does both himself. That's an example, it's one of the better examples that we have. Someone like Bob is able to make some use of the local hardwoods. And someone like Lenny Brackett, who is a fine carpenter and designs and builds traditional Japanese houses, is really tuned in to what's available locally. Like when it came to his attention that a very, very large old-growth sugar pine had died the next ridge over from a beetle kill, he was right over there on it and had it tagged by the Forest Service. He bought that dead tree and got it down on the ground and had that sawed up for lumber before the stain could get into it, because it was precious. In the lumber business as a whole, who's going to go out there for one snag? Lenny knew just what he wanted.

KB: The lumber business tends not to be local as well, and what you're talking about is a local economy.

GS: Right. That's very much part of it. The local economy can and will make it possible to precisely use one dead snag.

KB: How are we going to be able to find a way to bring out local economy values in a system that attempts to destroy or prevent that?

GS: It's extremely difficult. Obviously many people are not in a position to be able to even try. How do we keep family farms going? How do we keep a sustainable logging industry going that will be truly sustainable and at the same time make logging communities and logging culture viable? How do we have a sustainable ranching economy and ranching culture? Can the ranching culture have any place in the future? That's what John Dofflemeyer is working on. And maybe in a slightly larger picture is there any place for real skill, real craft in the working class at all, anywhere? Is there any place for a good carpenter? So much of our economy rewards you for being hasty and sloppy, and taking shortcuts, and even cheating. But it doesn't reward you for doing a good job. Or it only rewards you for doing a good job if you can sell your product to lawyers and doctors who will pay $3,000 for something unique. But not the economy at large.

KB: We're so rooted in a money economy that many people who have been exploited by companies and made dependent on an industry can't separate themselves out.

GS: We're seeing before our eyes right now the true face of this kind of capitalism. It talks a good line when it wants to, but when it's ready to pull out and move on and fire a bunch of people, it does it without a second thought. And what our current economic situation is doing—and maybe this isn't bad, maybe it's one of the good things—is that it's throwing people back on community and family resources. Young people in their twenties cannot afford often to rent a place on their own, an apartment or a house in the city. They come back and share in the family household, and families find themselves forced to try to make a family economy around the fact that they need more to live together; they need more to find ways to work together to make the family one of the bases of the economy. I see that happening more rather than less. And there's nothing shameful in that. It's only an American kind of vision of total fragmented independence, an individualism that gives people the idea that children should go away from home, everybody should live apart from each other, grandparents one place, aunts and uncles another place, children in another place. Yeah, we finally got the nuclear family. Whereas it's more normal and certainly more cost-effective to block out what we do together, like say the way an old Japanese farm family does. The slowing down of mobility in the United States, the fact that we have come to the limits of "boundless resources," and the fact that we are becoming more clearly aware that we need community as well as individual freedom—and that it's not impossible in some way to have the two together—is gradually making, as you would expect, American society slowly turn toward being more like a traditional society. There's good reason for it.

KB: By traditional, you mean?

GS: Larger families, family economies, the willingness to work together more. That becomes more of a possibility again now, I think, at least in some parts of American society. There are some parts that are alienated and fragmented, of course.

KB: So the conditions that are occurring now are prompting us to alter the larger view we have?

GS: Yeah. The older American view, which is the view of limitless resources, limitless opportunities, and "strike out on your own, young man, and go West," or whatever. That ceases to be a viable possibility. There's no West to strike out for. You can't afford an apartment in San Francisco, like I could in 1952. I came into San Francisco, got an entry-level laborer's job on the docks. With what I earned, I could afford to rent a small apartment on Telegraph Hill. A lot of younger people did that. Nobody can go to San Francisco, get an entry-level job, and afford to rent an apartment in the city any more.

KB: So much of this has to do with place, and making a commitment to place, and making a commitment to a community rather than the idea that we move about and shift places. Many in our culture, myself included, have moved where the work is.

GS: I appreciate that, certainly. I would like to say as a little caution against my own enthusiasms, though, that I don't think that "place" is automatically essential to this. It does happen more easily in place, but place can be a neighborhood in the city. It means just being someplace long enough to get some roots down and do something together. So it's as important that neighborhoods and the green city movement make cities more livable. That's really critical. And I might add, just to go back a little bit, somebody might say to us, "Why, you guys are talking about family values." Well, yeah, we are talking about family values, and these are much more profound than the Republican Party's rhetoric, which simply refers to a few right-wing Christian moral principles and not to the idea about cooperation, or to the idea of community, of sharing. So when the Clinton campaign says the Republicans talk about family values but they don't do anything about it, it's right on.

KB: So we need to change our government as well?

GS: I would like to see the policies changed in corporations and in government hiring that require people to keep moving or they won't move up on the company ladder. There's built-in obligatory mobility in a lot of higher-level jobs in government and industry. Sometimes it makes some sense, a lot of time it's probably not necessary. So that destroys a sense of place for such people. That keeps some of the most talented people from being rooted in any community.

KB: Do you think that if we approach a corporation with the right spirit and sensibility we can create a community there that will not negatively affect others within the larger community of our national culture?

GS: We have no choice but to try. Companies and corporations are here to stay, at least for quite some time. There are few companies that have tried out very creative, worthy practices. I'm thinking of

Ben & Jerry's in Vermont that I understand is voluntarily paying the local dairy milk suppliers for their business a peg higher than the price standards set by the federal government; they recognize it cost the dairymen more than they would be paying them. They're voluntarily giving them more, and so they've made a choice to support their whole community economically. The Patagonia Corporation has incorporated child care and kindergartens right into the workplace, so that mothers bring their preschool children to work. Imagine a communitarian and somewhat more libertarian corporate culture. The next step is also to realize corporations can have a kind of culture, and they revel in it sometimes, but they lack place and they generally tend to bust place. They say, "Well, let's move this plant to Texas. All you guys go to Texas or you get docked." It would be incredible to see a corporation make a commitment to really stay in the place and become a part of the neighborhood. When we do that, we'll be beginning to make a big step towards healing America. I don't know many companies yet that have said, "We won't move from here." Truly bioregional companies. Although there might be some, I haven't heard of them.

KB: In summary, would you say the writer bears a specific responsibility, or any responsibility that goes beyond what the average citizen might have?

GS: Well, first of all, I would turn it the other way. Writers have the same responsibilities that other citizens have and they shouldn't forget it. In addition to that, they are the caretakers of the language and have a profound responsibility to tell the truth. Or the third Buddhist precept, "Do not abuse language." And that means a lot.

EDITOR'S NOTE

Among George Plimpton's many publications is a book series titled *Writers at Work: The Paris Review Interviews,* which he has edited since 1957. He is a master interviewer able to elicit answers from sources that somehow augment his chosen themes.

In the interview with artist Larry Rivers, originally published in *Esquire,* Plimpton bones up on firing squads (topic) and presents his research in his trademark voice. Plimpton tells readers of *Guide to Writing Magazine Nonfiction:* "I have always looked for the light touch, or the twist, a bit of levity, the surprise . . . but one has to have luck to find such ingredients and to know how and when to use them." As you read Plimpton's piece, ask yourself:

- Which passages funnel research through voice, mixing facts with author comment?
- Which comments provide transition from paragraph to paragraph, propelling the piece forward?
- How do Plimpton's quotations depict Larry Rivers's character and/or sustain theme?

Certainly, Plimpton has done library research—he even mentions that in his piece—to prepare for his interview. He devotes the first third of his essay to research, retelling anecdotes to augment theme (morbid curiosity). Note, too, the subtle foreshadowings as the moment shifts from the *then* to the *now,* allowing readers to do "lunch" with Larry Rivers, whose near execution was sparked by dining at a Nigerian restaurant during civil unrest in that country. Rivers looks over his plate and tells Plimpton how his life flashed before his eyes—all because of a sandwich. The final touch occurs in the open ending when Plimpton recycles a bit of research and allows Rivers, appropriately, to have the last word.

How to Face a Firing Squad

George Plimpton

In the early hours of December 22, 1849, Fyodor Dostoyevsky was led out to the Semyonovsky parade ground in St. Petersburg to be executed by a firing squad. He was twenty-seven at the time. The crime he had committed was the "attempt to disseminate writings against the government by means of a hand printing press." Twenty others—poets, teachers, officers, journalists had been sentenced with him. The procedure was that they would die in groups of three. Dostoyevsky was in the second group.

It was a monstrous hoax, of course, initiated by Nicholas I, known with good reason as the Iron Czar. Just as the adjutant in charge of the firing squad was to lower his saber and shout "Fire!" one of the czar's aides-de-camp galloped across the parade ground and handed the officer a sealed packet that contained commutations of sentence. According to a historian friend of mine, these were read out at agonizing length by an officer known as the worst stutterer in the Russian army. Dostoyevsky was sentenced to four years of penal servitude.

I looked all this up the other day because I had a luncheon date with Larry Rivers, the well-known painter, who during the civil unrest in Nigeria some time ago went through a similar, if not quite as dramatic, experience. How often does one have lunch with a man who has survived the firing squad?

I admit to a morbid curiosity about this sort of thing, especially about what runs through people's minds at such times. In his novel *The Idiot*, Dostoyevsky uses the character Prince Myshkin to describe what he himself felt, staring at a church roof reflecting sunbeams (it was 8:00 in the morning) and realizing that in a short while he would somehow merge with them.

This kind of fatalistic serenity is not uncommon. One thinks of Anne Boleyn, who remarked, "I hear the executioner is very good, and I have a little neck." Or of Sir Thomas More, who rearranged his long beard on the executioner's block so the ax wouldn't cut it, explaining, "My beard has never committed any treason." Or more recently, Fred Wood, the so-called Jericho Turnpike murderer, whose last words before he went to the chair in Sing Sing in 1963 were (according to the chaplain): "I'm goin' to prove conclusively that wood conducts electricity."

Perhaps the most collected of gallows remarks was made by a member of the revolutionary Decembrist movement, formed after the death of Alexander I, in 1825. On the scaffold the rope broke under the weight of the condemned man, who turned to the officials and commented loudly: "They can't even *hang* you properly in this country. Now you can see why we revolted!"

Some last-minute comments turn out to be rather wistful. Guillaume Brune, a marshal of France and one of Napoleon's top generals, was heard complaining just before being lynched by a mob in 1815: "To live through a hundred battles, and to die hanging from a lantern in Provence!"

And then there were the great gestures. I had always heard that Mata Hari, the famous courtesan-turned-spy, had bared her breast before the firing squad, causing no end of tumult. Not so, apparently. I looked it up. She wore a corset, a pale-gray dress, a large tricorne, a blue coat, long gloves, and, as the memoirs report, "very elegant shoes." Not easy to slip out of this ensemble to bare a breast! However, not only did she decline to wear a blindfold, she refused to be tied to the stake, which allowed her at the last to blow a kiss to the firing squad. One of them fainted and was subsequently carried off on a stretcher. Mata Hari's biographer, Russell Warren Howe, suggests that he fainted not because of her beauty (she was forty-one at the time and in the Sûreté mug shot looks remarkably like Colonel Noriega), but because of her fame. In more contemporary terms, what was done—guilt aside—would be the equivalent of putting Mae West before a firing squad. As it was a considerable amount of weeping went on afterward.

Of course, many didn't behave this way at all. Serenity is not that easy to come by. Edith Cavell, Mata Hari's counterpart on the German side, fell in a heap at the sight of the firing squad, which was then obliged to move forward and fire into her inert body. Madame du Barry howled until the ax stopped her.

All of this was mildly on my mind as I went downtown for my lunch with Larry Rivers. He lives on Manhattan's Lower East Side. His studio is enormous. It has room for a raised bandstand—piano, chairs, music stands. He has a considerable reputation as a jazz musician, having played saxophone in sets with Chet Baker, Charlie Parker, and Gerry Mulligan, among others. His paintings hang in the Tate and the Whitney. At the moment he is writing an autobiography, tentatively titled *The Unauthorized Biography of Larry Rivers*. It contains a remarkable description of an adolescent love affair with an overstuffed blue armchair. Rivers has recently done a large painting of this unnatural coupling, which may do for overstuffed armchairs what Philip Roth's *Portnoy's Complaint* did for liver.

Larry is loquacious, his monologues rich with detail. What follows is merely the gist of a two-hour description of his experience. It begins in East Africa, where he had gone with Pierre Gaisseau, an award-winning French documentary producer, to make a film titled *Africa and I*.

"We never really discussed what the movie was about," Larry told me. "Pierre wanted to make a traditional documentary, visiting tribes and so on. I thought that kind of film was over. So there was constant tension."

"What sort of scenes did you want to do?" I asked.

"I got some people to carry a stuffed lion through the streets of Nairobi. Pierre did a lot of groaning about this."

Larry imitated a Frenchman's groan.

"We got so desperate for interesting footage, I'd get out of the Land Rover and walk up on the animals—lions or whatever—so at least we'd get shots of me running through the bush. Pierre wanted to sit with the Masai in their huts, but when we looked at the footage back in New York it looked like a lot of people wearing costumes. It didn't add up to much. So Pierre and I decided to go back—this time to Nigeria, in west Africa. We went to Benin City, one hundred fifty miles east of Lagos."

At one point, as they were filming in a palace, an official came up and said, "Would you come with us?"

"It always starts with something simple like that," Larry said. "At headquarters we were questioned by an English-speaking hipster, a graduate of Ohio State. 'Yeah, man, you blew with Charlie Parker?' They let us go, but later we were picked up again. 'Would you come with us?' This time we were taken to police headquarters on the outskirts of town. Lots of questions. They were distant but polite. 'Ever been a member of the Communist party?' And so on. I felt during all this that since I was a liberal Jew, Africans would be able to read my face, how human I'd been to them all my life. *Hmmm.*"

"Things went wrong?"

"Well, not right away. It was obvious we were going to spend the night in the police station—as guests more than prisoners. Evening came. We were asked what we wanted to eat. I said, 'A sandwich, something like that.' Pierre says, 'A sandwich? I don't want to eat a sandwich.' Just like a Frenchman. He asks if there's a restaurant nearby. The police tell us there is a restaurant down the road, good food, but they warn us that at night it's difficult. The civil war is going on some miles to the south. The army controls everything after sundown. So I said we should stay in the compound under the jurisdiction of the police. No; Pierre didn't want a sandwich. So the police gave us two Nigerian bodyguards—huge guys, almost seven feet tall—and we drove to the restaurant. I was sort of glad we went at first—interesting place. But in the middle of the meal this officer suddenly appeared. He had a riding crop tucked under his arm. He made a considerable impression—the kitchen staff peering around corners, then ducking back when he looked their way. He came over to our table."

"He could speak English?" I asked.

"Impeccable. Did I say he was drunk? He was. He spoke slowly but perfectly. He asked what we were doing there. When we told him, he motioned to the door and a group of soldiers in battle fatigues appeared and dragged off our two Nigerian bodyguards. We could hear them being beaten up outside. I tried to explain. I said we were making a movie. I had a real interest in Nigeria. I studied history. I had a map. Man, was *that* a mistake. 'A map! You have a map!' It was in my passport—a little hand-drawn sketch hat showed where Lagos and Benin City were. He looked at it, 'These men are spies!' he said. He pulled out a gun. 'Stand up!' We stood up. I said we weren't doing anything . . . just trying to make a movie. 'You're a liar!' he said, and he punched me in the face. 'Put your hands up!' We put our hands up. He called in some more soldiers and ordered, 'Take them to the wall!' The wall! They marched us outside. I was crying. I told Pierre, who was walking alongside with his hands in the air, 'A sandwich. You couldn't eat a sandwich back there in jail, and because of that we're being taken to the wall to be killed.'"

"How was he reacting?" I asked.

"Pierre? He was very agitated. He told them we weren't doing anything, and a soldier came over and hit him in the face."

"He didn't take up the sandwich issue with you."

Larry looked at me over his plate. "I don't know what was on Pierre's mind, but I can tell you that I felt I was in some sort of crazy production of

Alfred Jarry's *Ubu Roi*. It made no sense. I didn't see my life flash before me. I didn't have any compulsion to see my kids. I felt the irony that I was crazy about black people, played music with them all my life, and now they were going to shoot me."

"What happened when they got you to the wall?" I asked.

"Just before we got there," Larry replied, "some officers came up the road and asked what was going on. They talked it over for about twenty minutes. The two Nigerian bodyguards were brought, and we were all marched down the road with our hands up. I thought they were going to shoot us in the back."

"Did you yell over your shoulder that you'd blown with Chet Baker? Something must have worked," I said. "Here you are."

"Who knows," he said. "They must have decided we weren't spies. They pushed us all into a car and we got back to the police compound."

I couldn't resist it. "If you'd gone to the wall, did you have any last-minute statements or gestures in mind?"

"Like what?"

"Like blowing a kiss to the firing squad." I told him about Mata Hari.

"No, nothing like that."

He must have sensed my disappointment.

"Well, maybe next time," Larry said.

Essays and Articles

EDITOR'S NOTE

David Lazar is director of creative writing at Ohio University and associate editor of *The Ohio Review.* His essays have appeared in *Southwest Review, Aperture, Denver Quarterly,* and the *Houston Chronicle.* His essays often appear in annual *Best American Essays* anthologies, the 1993 edition of which reprinted the following essay after it was published in *Mississippi Valley Review.* As you read Lazar's piece, ask yourself:

- Does the risk Lazar take at the end of piece succeed? Why or why not?
- Which passages contain sensory data, putting the reader in a specific place?
- What role does the primary symbol, a coat, play with respect to occasion and theme?

The occasion of the piece is heralded in the title: buying a secondhand coat. The theme is appearances, which takes on an ominous meaning in the final paragraphs when Lazar breaks several basic nonfiction rules. (Read his explanation in The Craft Shop in Chapter 6.) Lazar uses an aloof, intelligent, descriptive voice through most of his essay set in Dublin and funnels his voice through a moment between the *now and then,* allowing him to comment and tell a story. Toward the end of that narrative, which closes openly, a tragic incident occurs, prompting the implied author to emerge with an appropriate voice shift: candid and tense. Typically, the implied author should remain hidden throughout a publishable work. Typically, the writer should sustain voice tones throughout the work as well. But Lazar is not a typical essayist whose contribution here is to show that rules are mastered first and broken later.

The Coat

David Lazar

I made my song a coat
Covered with embroideries
Out of old mythologies
From heel to throat
      —Yeats, "A Coat"

Cool Sligo, grey Sligo, promising cold and promising night. Buying a coat seemed reasonable, seemed practically sensible. Of course, I owned coats, but two were in London hanging in a hanging closet, and two were in

Houston, gathering dust in storage. I thought . . . "a green raincoat with heavy lining . . . a bloated blue down . . . a triple-folded peacoat . . . a brown car-coat . . ." but these thoughts did not warm me. The temperature was dropping or my imagination was faltering, or, an ominous thought, both. A shiver was the signal of sudden determination. For years now, however, I have had trouble spending more than ten or twenty dollars at a time on clothing. I like buying clothes; I like new clothes. But years of shopping at second-hand stores have made me queasy when it comes to shelling out for my shell. I remember my pleasure at my parents' horror when I would proudly announce that some shirt or sportcoat they admired had cost three dollars at Goodwill. Over time, as my ventures into the once, twice, thrice-used became more frequent, my pleasure in shock value turned to pride in real value. Nothing pleased me more than driving home with the new-old, thin, silk, dark-colored, appealingly worn-in tie, which cost seventy-five cents and had been overlooked for days, weeks, or years by the less discriminating, or more indigent shopper. And the prospect of such pleasure in another country is multiplied, for it isn't just any bargain shirt, tie, or coat one finds, but a London shirt, a Dublin scarf, or a Sligo coat, worn originally by a cousin of Yeats, a twentieth generation member of the gentry fallen on hard times, or a visionary, though never-published poet. I do not despair what limbs these fabrics have touched. Nor do I dwell on the possibility of leprous old men, or young men felled by mysterious methuselean bacteria. On this day, which could be well-described as an "overcoat day," nothing could have attracted me more than a rundown second-hand shop on a side street, coats hanging in the doorway (next to a butcher shop, where other hanging shapes served up a surreal echo), that is, nothing more than a second-hand shop with no name. Nameless places tend to have a kind of prestigious mystique, a mystique summoned by the very lack of necessity for a name. In the States we call such places the "No Name Bar," or the "No Name Restaurant," appellations implying a kind of generic superiority. However, no one would have presumed to call this shop anything, not even the "No Name Place." It was too homely even for that. But the coats and the cold beckoned.

Seated behind an old high table piled with indistinct clumps of clothes, the old proprietor had burrowed out a hole through which he talked to an undoubtedly old friend, and seemed surprised if not quite delighted by my presence; he treated my request for permission to try on some coats almost pleasantly, as an irrelevancy. I put on a sumptuous black cashmere coat, which made my head look like a pea. My legs, and fingers barely protruding from the sleeves, looked like dissevered doll parts; I took off the coat in record time. On the small side, I am not unused to such discrepancies, but neither do I relish the occasional Tod Browning vision of myself in the mirror. After the first coat, the second, an indistinct pattern in a mohair blend, seemed like a gift. It seemed to fit nicely, always a surprise. But the sudden contrast lured me into fatal error: I looked into the slanted mirror on the floor, and lo, liked what I saw. The Irish, I would learn, can beguile even the wary, the experienced, and slanted mirrors are notorious. They can make any garment which is within three sizes too small or large look like it has been custom tailored. And the dim light of the shop: residents of Sligo must be well-aware of tricks of the light in the land where Yeats wandered, conjuring faeries and fancies, Aengus chasing ethereal spirit in the dimlight, the witchlight of Hazelwood days. I also failed to pay attention to the streaks on the mirror, preventing a clear view, dimming the contours of the coat. I bought the coat, paid the modest fifteen pounds delightedly, wore the coat for what was left of the late afternoon, the evening, and then hung it in the closet of my B and B (the weather warmed, conspiring with the mirror, with the light) until I returned to Dublin two days later on my way back to London. My conspiracy theory is abetted by the way the mistress of my Sligo lodging responded to my coat; she assured me that it was "lovely." That beautiful Irish word, "lovely," can be as dangerous as a slanted mirror. I was callow; I was unaware. I did not know that the word is frequently a nonresponse, a neutral response. The Irish can respond with one "lovely," or several in a row to pronouncements of fine weather, plans for the future, funeral arrangements, the purchase of a new coat. . . .

Cold Dublin, grey with no shadings. A cold fog hung over it; life seemed impossible. I donned my Sligocoat at Connelly Station, checked my bag, but kept my burgeoning pack, and ventured out for a long final tour of the city; I had eight hours to kill before the bus was to leave the train station for the ferry to Holyhead and the train to London. Though dreary, the city was not as cold as it looked. My shirt/sweater/sportcoat/Sligocoat combination, along with the fifteen pounds on my back, made the time run in beads of sweat. My back began to ache. A mile or so from the station I realized the pack would never do. I trudged back to the station, looking like an Irish Quasimodo with a green monkey on his back. They checked my burden, and the relief was immense, but the ache would not oblige by staying behind as well. I returned to the National Gallery for another viewing of the Jack Yeats and Emile Nolde watercolors; I bore the impossible crowd at its satisfying restaurant and settled for a seat in the courtyard, dining quickly in a brisk wind, which would have been impossible without my coat. I then walked south to Stephens' Green, Dublin's central park: a charming little St. James. Walking past a shop window, I caught a glimpse that caused me to shudder: a fleeting image of myself as a dumpy man in a frumpy coat. Trick of the light, I thought; the coat looked fine in Sligo.

I sat on a bench in the central circle of the green. The soft light of the afternoon subdued the over-ripe leaves into pastel. Few people out. Still life. No chill, but a perfect cool. I felt unusually calm. Yet reveries, spells, are made to be broken. Mine was punctured by an old man who sidled up to me on the bench. Face a sagging mass of wrinkles leading to a smooth double-chin, breath laborious, wearing a formless green corduroy coat and lavender pants, he edged closer to me until he was a fraction of a coat-length away. I bolted.

Despite the disruption of my wool-gathering, I wandered happily, if sluggishly, through Dublin. But the disturbing image I had glimpsed an hour earlier started appearing with an alarming, a confirming frequency. I took off the coat and examined it; it looked fine, the same handsome blend I had bought. But it was a coat removed from its native environs: the landscape of myths. A changeling coat? I dismissed the idea as quickly as I had handed over fifteen pounds. I found myself on the west side of central Dublin. Second-hand clothing stores started materializing out of the encroaching darkness and mist. I walked into one aptly, almost elegantly called "Second Hand," which offered a cornucopia of tweed jackets in small sizes. It also had a mirror, clean and vertically hung, in which a small man wearing a woolen tent stood with a look of desperation. Lo, he was unlovely.

I was seized with the urge to dump what had once been a find, something to take home. I offered to trade my fifteen-pound coat for a nine-pound jacket, "even up" as we used to say in Brooklyn. My cashier genially shook his head. I offered the coat and three pounds (furrows on the brow of the freak in the mirror started pulsing nervously). He explained that in the absence of the proprietor he could make no deals. I pleaded; he apologized. I left. I tried an outdoor stall down the road. It was owned by the same absentee clothes merchant. She evidently inspired great fear in her employees since my offer of the coat for a vest and two ties was also summarily refused. Time was running down. I felt the danger of missing the first domino of the journey back to my transient home. If I missed the bus, my first connection, I would have to fall back on the night in Dublin, for which I was eminently unprepared financially. I hated my coat more than I've ever disliked a piece of clothing. I tried one more shop: "Rose's" (second-hand implied). Their specialty was clearly coats; they had a dazzling array. In addition, there was a floor mirror, but it was standing upright. A middle-aged man with a sagging face full of flagging hope flared out of it from an unlovely wonderland. I tried on a black cashmere: too long. Then a salt and pepper wool and acrylic: the sleeves would have hit China if they hadn't been stopped by the linoleum floor. On the third try came luck, buyer's kismet: a blue calf-length coat of coarse material, perfect sleeves, and it hung loosely, but fashionably, like a cape. It cost seventeen pounds. The figure in the mirror, a dashing modern highwayman, turned to the man at the cash register: I'll give you twelve pounds and this—

Thirty minutes ago I was about to type the word "coat." I looked up from my desk and saw a child on a bicycle slammed into by a mail truck. He or she flew fifteen, maybe twenty feet. He or she started spinning around, shrieking in pain, a wounded banshee. I ran out. There were already half a dozen people there. Two boys were running to the news agent's to call for help, running with commitment and care in their speed. I didn't need to get closer, did not need to look at a broken child. I have the twisted little thing firmly in mind. The ambulance just arrived. The crowd is larger, flashing blue lights. The familiar European siren sound changes its pitch as it approaches.

I wonder about writing this, if whoever reads it will feel tricked, annoyed by the intrusion. I wonder if I should just say "coat." I didn't have much more to say. I left the store with two coats. I was going to say that no self-respecting person should be caught dead with two coats, that that made me more self-conscious than before, that a couple of women smiled broadly at me on my way back to Connelly Station and at first I felt my sense of attractiveness regenerate, followed by the frightening possibility that they were laughing with the divined knowledge that my new coat was worse than the old coat, which pulled me up short. I was going to say (the ambulance has gone and there is only a police car with smaller flashing lights) that I was determined to rid myself of that albatross of a coat, that I wanted to give it to a beggar, a busker, in a saintly gesture, a convenient self-apotheosis, but I didn't see any, a feat in Dublin. I left the coat hanging in a toilet stall in Connelly Station. And though I'm sure some poor unknowing soul has claimed it, not knowing what he was getting into, I think of it there, a desultory image. I was going to comment about my vanity.

Some men are pointing to the spot where the child landed. It is very close to the Chalk Farm tube station, and I'm hoping there will not be an outline in chalk. How heavy that coincidence would seem. But things just come together that way sometimes; they clash, they collide, creating new intersections. This intrusion wasn't my intention. I may have ruined the rhythm of a story, but at times it can be desperately hard to care. I have nothing else to say except that the street has resumed its normal, sullen flux.

E D I T O R ' S   N O T E

Catherine Johnson, a contributing editor at *New Woman,* has published articles in such magazines as *Redbook, Cosmopolitan,* and *Working Woman.* She also is the author of *When to Say Goodbye to Your Therapist* (Simon & Schuster) and *Lucky in Love: The Secrets of Happy Couples and How Their Marriages Thrive* (Viking/Penguin).

The following article originally appeared in *New Woman.* As you read it, ask yourself:

- Which comments sustain theme, gearing the piece to audience?
- What role do quotations play in grounding topic or foreshadowing theme?
- Which passages contain interior monologue—the author speaking to herself—and what function do they play in propelling the story, anecdote by anecdote?

Again, note how basic magazine elements harmonize in this article. The topic is autism, and its theme is mother-love. Johnson's voice is conversational, experienced, and anecdotal; her piece employs a moment close to the *then* so that she can comment about autism and parental concerns. Well-foreshadowed epiphanies precede the closed ending as Johnson's "broken" child becomes, momentarily, "whole."

The Broken Child

*A True Story about Loving and Living
with an Autistic Son*

Catherine Johnson

For years before I became pregnant with my second child I heard the story about the new baby: bringing a new baby home and expecting your older child to love it, people say, would be just like having your husband bring home a pretty new wife and expecting you to love her. "What fun we'll all have together!" says the husband.

I always loved this story; to me it perfectly captured the fall from grace suffered by the big boy or girl who, suddenly, will never be his or her mother's baby again. But until I had my own new baby (babies, in my case; my second pregnancy brought twins) I never realized how much this story would have to say not only about my older child and his feelings, but about me and mine. For this is not just a story about a child displaced. It is also a story about a parent's love displaced: it is a story about a grown-up who has fallen in love with someone new.

For me the dawning of new baby love was complicated by the fact of my older child's handicap. My 7-year-old, Jimmy, is autistic. And I do mean autistic; you will notice that I haven't called him a "child with autism," as I am supposed to do. That would be politically correct, but it would be wrong. In my house—let's be honest—it's pretty much autism wall-to-wall; there's very little child visible apart from the disability. Jimmy is always, always autistic; we do not get a break, and neither does he.

And autism is not a particularly lovable condition. With autism you have a child who is spinning and flapping and hooting away at the top of his lungs; a child making eye contact only to demand food; an enraged child biting and scratching his parents or himself; a child whose idea of play is to pull out a pitcher of juice from the refrigerator and dump it out on the living room carpet. It's the bottle of shampoo dumped on the sofa; the bucket of green paint dumped in the hot tub. It is hundreds of dollars spent each month replacing and repairing the latest toll of household destruction.

And the Kodak moments are few and far between, not least because an autistic child will refuse—violently refuse—to pose for a snapshot: with autism you have a child who doesn't comprehend Christmas, or birthday parties, or toys; a child who is impervious to the "magic" of childhood; a child who doesn't sing songs or draw pictures; a child who, at age 7, has yet to have his first conversation with his parents, except in our dreams at night.

And yet . . . and yet . . . my seven years as Jimmy's mom and no one else's are now years that I miss. Because despite his disability, Jimmy and I, we were a team. We had that Oedipal magic of mother and son alone together, with no other children to get in the way. I worked part-time, and at home, so when the bus pulled up after school I was all his, and he was all mine. We baked bread together, we tooled around in the car, we ran errands, we got lollipops at the dry cleaner. We had a life. And having no other children to compare him with, I often experienced his disability as being not that . . . different.

The new babies changed all that. Apart from the fact that the twins, appearing as they did after years of infertility, were tiny miracles in a way Jimmy had not been, the little boys could not help but highlight all that was wrong with Jimmy. "Starting over" with two new babies, we relived the agony we had experienced as we watched Jimmy, perfect at birth and for months afterward, slowly but surely fall off the developmental track in his second year of life.

As for Jimmy, he did not make things easier. When the babies first arrived, he was fine. He was so happy to have me home (I had spent the last four weeks of my pregnancy in the hospital) that he didn't care about the babies. I was back; that was what mattered.

But within weeks his attitude changed. He was angry, he was agitated, he was obsessive to a degree that was, simply, unbearable. Jimmy now refused to do the two things he had once been able to do independently: he would not watch his beloved Disney videos, and he would not swim in the hot tub. If you tried to make him do one of these things, he would scream, tantrum, writhe.

His one obsession in life now became the chronic demand that we, his exhausted parents, take him bye-bye in the car. "Bye-bye-in-the-car-to-get-me" he would keen, in his singsong voice, over and over and over again until my nerves had shattered. We would have both babies screaming; we would have me trying to breast-feed two infants at once; we would have the kitchen a chaos of things that needed picking up, putting away, cooking . . . and there Jimmy would be, shouting "bye-bye-in-the-car-to-get-me" at the top of his lungs, directly in my face. Pulling my arm, clutching his ears, screaming, screaming, screaming.

And he was a menace to the babies. Big and strong and quick, 75 pounds of boy compared with their four and five pounds of preemie, he would dart up to them, span their tiny heads with his big, wide hand (his beautiful child's hand a perfect miniature of his father's), and squeeze. This from a boy who, whatever his other deficits, knows perfectly well how to bite, scratch, and hit. But now, with the babies, he went for their heads. Of course, for my husband and me, terrified as we were by the prospect of more children with brain damage, heads-squeezing was the one behavior certain to send us into orbit.

I remember one day, early on, we got our wires crossed: my husband thought I was watching the one twin who was awake and I thought he was, and the upshot was that the baby was left alone in a room with Jimmy for some minutes. When I discovered what had happened, I was heartsick and scared to death. The baby seemed fine, but there was no real way to know whether Jimmy had hurt the baby or not. And I could not stop thinking about it. *We left the baby alone with Jimmy, we left the baby alone with Jimmy . . .*

It was a nightmare, and suddenly we found ourselves hating Jimmy's handicap. Hating it, and wishing it away. And, inevitably, wishing him away. We would be walking down the street, pushing the carriage holding our two sweet babies, and Jimmy would be chanting and keening and tantruming and I would think: *He could live somewhere else. He could be placed.*

If we had been living in my parents' generation, he probably would have been. In the 1950s children like Jimmy were sent to institutions, or to special boarding schools. One time my mother-in-law observed, with an air of concern, that back when she was raising her children no one had a boy like Jimmy. You could see she was trying to parse the situation, trying to fathom just how uniquely unlucky we had been. And it threw me into confusion because, when I thought about it, I didn't know any families with boys like Jimmy back then, either.

And then it came to me: in those days autistic children didn't live at home. I said this, and her face changed; yes, she said, there had been a family down the street whose child had not lived with them. I could see it was one of those moments that give pause, suddenly coming face to face with all those other people's grandchildren who had been sent away.

And suddenly coming face to face with the fact that, when it comes to a situation like ours, *there is a way out.*

Until the babies came, keeping Jimmy at home did not feel like a decision, per se; he was our child, and he lived with us. But with two new children, the "placement" option took on a different cast. Now we had more than enough children (according to my husband we had one too many) and, though we tried not to think about this, Jimmy was not the child we had wanted.

And in his heart, he knew it. He must have. How else to explain the obsession with squeezing their heads? I would see Jimmy go for a baby head and I would think: *He knows. He knows what's wrong with him, where it's wrong. He knows the babies' heads are better.*

I'm not sure, looking back, whether Jimmy was ever in any real danger of losing his home with us. I am certain that, during those early months my commitment to being his full-time, on-site mother wavered. There were times when I longed, and I know that my husband longed, for Jimmy to be someone else's problem.

Because at that point living with Jimmy was like living in a fire station. I remember going into the babies' room one day to discover a bottle of Benadryl, which had been completely full, now completely empty (we couldn't know whether he'd dumped it or drunk it, because he couldn't tell us); I remember another day Jimmy coming into the house with his whole body covered in the thick white liquid we use to scrub the hot tub clean (again, no way of knowing whether he'd drunk any, or if so, how much); I remember a trip to the vet's, where Jimmy shot away from me, snatched a squeeze bottle of chlorine bleach from off the veterinarian's shelf, and gulped down a big squirt of it. We were having one near-poisoning incident a week, it seemed; I was making so many calls to Poison Control I was expecting to be turned in to Protective Services at any moment. And each time it was a guessing game: take him to the emergency room and have his stomach pumped or wait and see?

Always, we chose to wait at home, looking for signs. And each time Jimmy turned out to be fine. Maybe he hadn't drunk any of the stuff; maybe he'd dumped it all instead. He likes to dump. Or maybe his system tolerated the amounts that he did drink before he dumped the rest. We will never know.

I know this sounds irresponsible and incompetent on my part. And it was. But I was no longer in the awake-and-aware state I needed to be in to function as Jimmy's mother. I was tired beyond belief, one baby was getting up seven times a night; the other, three times. I was tired in a way the word *tired* does not convey; I was tired in a sick way, a flat-on-your-back-with-the-flu way, not a stayed-up-too-late-watching-television way. I was weak, I was confused, and I had no memory left at all. I just couldn't remember—

I physically could not remember—whether I had done something, like put the Benadryl back in the lockbox, or not.

My writing partner, a Boston psychiatrist, told me the problem was that severe sleep deprivation shuts down your frontal lobes (he and his friends, he told me, always used to say that new parents have had "frontal lobectomies"). This sounded about right. Jimmy had gone on his rampage at the very moment that my brain was no longer functioning. He was looking for trouble; he was crazed. Our lives were out of control.

Things came to a head somewhere in the fourth month after the babies' birth. It was dinnertime, and my husband was sitting at the kitchen table, playing with one of the babies. Unnoticed, Jimmy went off to our bedroom. At some point I experienced that maternal sixth sense, that hair-on-the-back-of-the-neck sensation that all is not well. I stood up and walked to our bedroom. Our newly built, newly decorated master bedroom.

I was walking straight into the worst scene of our autistic lives. Before I saw it I smelled it. The room reeked of human excrement; it was like walking into an outhouse the size of a barn and closing the door behind you. There I saw it. *Fecal smearing.* I'd read about it in books; now here it was, the real thing. Shit (and *shit* is the only word for what I saw, and for how I felt about what I saw) smeared everywhere: shit on our new carpet, shit on our new bedspread, shit on our new paint. Shit all over my son.

I felt a terrible pressure inside my skull, a physical force pounding my brain. Yet I didn't shout at Jimmy. I didn't spank him. I couldn't. I hated him so much at that moment that the only possible expression of my rage would have been to beat him within an inch of his life. To slam him against walls, strike him, pound the autism out of him once and for all. Because at that moment I needed the autism to be gone.

I think we came close to making a change that night. I called my mother, told her what had happened, screamed into the phone that Jimmy was "retarded" and "horribly damaged" and "never going to be better." She listened, then went through her housekeeping books and found the formula (1 tablespoon ammonia + ½ teaspoon liquid detergent + 1 quart H_2O) for removing poop from fabric. My husband did all the work; he spent hours in his exhausted state blotting and damping while I stood by, dazed and in despair.

The next day my mother called to say, quietly, that it was time for us to think of finding a place for Jimmy. He could be with other children like him during the week, then come home on weekends.

I just listened, reassured, I think, to have someone, namely my mother, tell me I wasn't going to be an evil person if I went down that path.

But life went on, and Jimmy stayed put. He was awful, the babies were impossible, the house was a mess, and there was no sleep for anyone. Then one day there was a glimmer of change.

We all were sitting in the kitchen together—babies, Jimmy, Martine the nanny, and me. I was dutifully rehearsing Jimmy on his speech, saying, "Jimmy, how many babies do we have?"

He'd been able to answer this query correctly once before: "Two," he'd said. In the midst of all the misery, his and mine, it had been a happy moment, since whether or not Jimmy will ever be able to learn numbers is, at this point, an open question.

So I was saying, in my loud and cheery pay-attention-to-me voice, "Jimmy, how many babies do we have?"

No answer. I did get some eye contact, which, for me, always sparks hope; I always assume when Jimmy looks at me as I speak that he's trying.

Of course, I could be wrong.

Nevertheless, right or wrong, I gave Jimmy his "prompt": "Jimmy, how many babies do we have? *We have . . .*"

Again, no answer. Now he was looking back down at his snack.

So I went back to the prompt, extending it this time. "Jimmy, how many babies do we have? We have t—" Exaggerating the *t*.

By now I was just going through the motions, not expecting much more than an autistic echo: "we-have-two-babies" intoned lifelessly, expressionlessly, when suddenly Jimmy looked me in the eye and came out with it: "We have too many babies." *That* was a Moment! Jimmy was transcending the autism, was breaking through, telling me exactly what he thought. I looked across the table at him, and I felt my heart stir; if I had fallen out of love with Jimmy after the babies, suddenly, here and now, I remembered the passion that had held me fast to my son and his future for so long.

The moment passed, to be sure; shortly after Thanksgiving he started sneaking off to far corners of the house to poop in his pants; this was his latest thing. So I was expecting another fecal smearing incident any day. And I was not happy about it.

But there wasn't going to be another incident. Exactly five months after the babies came home, Jimmy *got it*. His psychiatrist had told us that an autistic child could be either worse about new babies than normal children, because autistic children loathe change, or he could be better, because the new babies would simply become part of the expected way for things to be. And now, five months in, Jimmy's new attitude seemed to be, "Oh, right. We have babies." We have babies, we have *always* had babies. Now whenever Jimmy came across a baby he'd grasp its little head firmly in his big hand, bend down, and kiss him. He learned their names, and within a couple of months he learned which name went with which baby. Jimmy had bonded.

For us, this was good enough; it was all we needed to be happy again. Watching Jimmy learn to love two new babies, we figured that this is as good as life gets.

But it wasn't. Life was changing all around us still, bringing us gifts of happiness we hadn't expected. I first noticed a difference one harried day, when I took Jimmy, the dog, and one of the babies for a visit to the vet. Things went fine until I was paying the bill, when suddenly, along with having to wrangle baby, dog, and autistic 7-year-old, I had a huge amount of stuff to carry: vet's bill, flea spray, dog medicine, you name it. Of course, in a normal family the 7-year-old would do the carrying. But Jimmy had never successfully carried anything for me, ever. Yes, you could put a bag of groceries in his hand and he would walk away with it, but halfway to the house he would drop it to the ground the way an infant drops a rattle. And there it would lie.

But now I was so overwhelmed with baby, dog, child, and stuff that I didn't stop to think. I loaded Jimmy up, handing him every piece of dog paraphernalia I had and then, for good measure, hanging my purse around his neck. "Jimmy, carry this stuff," I said firmly, and we set out for the car.

The amazing thing is, we got there. We walked fast, my theory being, Let's get as far as we possibly can before we drop everything on the ground. So there we were, speed-walking up the veterinarian's driveway to the parking lot behind, and I looked down at Jimmy and saw a boy holding on tight to all the items I'd given him, taking care not to drop a thing! Amazing.

But when we got in the car suddenly all the stuff had disappeared. I instantly assumed the worst: "Jimmy!" I said in a thoroughly annoyed tone. *"Where's the stuff?"* I said this even though until that moment Jimmy had never responded to such a query. With Jimmy, once something is gone, it's gone. He can't find it. Moreover, he doesn't seem to possess the fundamental social concept of "showing" something to someone else; Jimmy has never used his index finger to point. Never.

But now Jimmy responded to my question at once, bending over to retrieve all the various dog items from beneath my purse where he'd put them. Bending over to *show me.* And suddenly I registered this for the miracle that it was. "Jimmy!" I burst out happily. "Thank you! *Thank you so much!"* But my burst of gratitude didn't seem to make much of an impression on Jimmy, who was acting as if this kind of helpful behavior happened every day.

So we drove home. There things took a turn for the worse, as my husband had to work late and both babies chose that evening to melt down. I was trying to get everyone dinner, breast-feed, jiggle two screaming babies, give the dog his medicine, with no help at all . . . it was hell. I was in a state of meltdown myself when Jimmy came bolting in from the hot tub (he had started going into the tub again, another sign of his recovery from the shock of new babies) crying out, "Put the top on, Daddy! Put the top on, Daddy! Put the top on, Daddy!"—his stock phrase for asking that the hot tub cover be put back on, regardless of whom he is *actually* addressing.

It was autistic perseveration to the max, and I was in no mood. For Jimmy, certain things have to be done, and they have to be done now. Putting the hot tub lid back on after he's done swimming is one of them, and for Jimmy, getting that hot tub lid on carries the exact same urgency that, say, dialing 911 would carry for me if one of the babies were choking to death on a marble. I understand this, and usually I drop everything I'm doing and drag my dog-tired, mom-of-twins body out to the hot tub where I wrestle the enormously heavy hot tub lid back on. I do this all day long, because it makes Jimmy feel better.

But that night there was no force on earth that could make me drop two screaming babies in order to go out and restore the hot tub to its rightful state of coveredness. "Jimmy!" I said sharply. "I'm *very* busy with the babies, and I'm *not going to put the lid on!* Daddy will do it when he gets home."

I didn't actually expect Jimmy to listen. What I expected to happen, what normally would have happened, was an autism standoff. Jimmy dancing around me in a state of near panic, fixating on the word-string Put-the-top-on-Daddy while I struggled to "extinguish" the behavior by ignoring it, as I've been taught. (Extinguishing a behavior by "not reinforcing it with attention" is a technique, I might add, that, while the favorite of behaviorists everywhere, in actual practice will cause a mother's head to explode.)

But tonight there was to be no head exploding. Instead, Jimmy looked at me and seemed to hear.

Miraculously, he did not ask again. Instead, he did something so sweet: he sat down beside me and the crying babies and softly chanted the words "Daddy's coming home soon, Daddy's coming home soon" to himself. I looked at Jimmy, and I could not believe what was happening. He was talking sense to himself, calming himself down. For once in his life, Jimmy was choosing not to be the crazy one. He was giving me a break.

As frayed as I was, a happy emotion crept over me: a feeling of deep love for Jimmy. A feeling of pride. I started to think: *Jimmy is helping.*

I should probably explain that helpful behavior is not something you expect to see in an autistic child. It is often said that autistic people lack empathy, that they don't see inside others; autistic people who can communicate will tell you this themselves.

But now, I began to believe my eyes. Jimmy *looked* like he was trying to help. I decided to give it a test.

By that point both babies had pretty much lost their minds; I had one baby up in my arms being jiggled for all he was worth, but the other baby was flat on his back on the bed, screaming bloody murder. Jimmy, still clad in his swimsuit, was taking all this in. So I said, "Jimmy, the baby is crying. Can you help the baby stop crying?"

Galvanized by my words, Jimmy jumped up on the bed and kissed the baby smack on the head.

The baby just lay there, screaming away while I jiggled, jiggled, jiggled his brother.

Thwarted, Jimmy moved on to Plan B. He looked the baby in the eye, then pressed his own forehead gently up against the baby's forehead and held it there. Two brothers eyeball to eyeball.

The baby screamed on. So Jimmy sat back up and frowned at the wailing baby, thinking. Finally he took hold of the baby's thighs and delicately manipulated them through the air. Who knows what he thought this would accomplish, but frankly, it was as good a try as any; nothing I was doing was working. It was a shot.

Frayed at the edges and dog-tired, I watched this scene, and suddenly I felt awash with love. Surrounded by babies, Jimmy had finally grown to his rightful age; he had learned how to be an autistic 7-year-old instead of the autistic baby of the family he had been for all of his life. Jimmy had become, at long last, a big boy. My big boy, my beloved firstborn.

When I think about all we've gone through to get to where we are today, the image that always comes to me is a scene from last spring. It is a beautiful day; everyone is relaxing. Martine, the nanny, and Kim (a psychology major who is Jimmy's therapeutic companion) and Jimmy and I are all sitting around the kitchen table while the babies nap, talking about—what else?—our bottoms and how enormously big they are.

We've gotten pretty carried away with this topic when Kim says she has been watching a music video on MTV all about women's bottoms: it is a rap song with a line "I like big butts and I cannot lie."

I *burst* into laughter. I find this so funny I am actually borderline hysterical with laughter. An entire life's worth of female ridiculousness has just been summed up for me in a rap song that says "I like big butts and I cannot lie." Twenty years spent obsessing over my perfectly unremarkable bottom *for nothing,* I think. All those years I thought my worst problem was the size of my bottom, when what was coming at me down the pike was autism and infertility and God knows what else is still out there, lurking just around the corner. . . .

Then I notice Jimmy, sitting at the other end of the table from me, a tentative little smile on his face. He is studying me intently, trying to figure out what the joke is; he wants to be in on it, too.

And suddenly, he gets it: "Mama *waughs* at me!" he exclaims, beaming with pride. In his little-boy mind, his little-boy-mind-with-autism, he is the source of all this fun.

I look at him in astonishment. How can he be coming up with this completely original, completely nonechoed and nonmemorized sentence? A perfect sentence; the only thing missing, the *I.* Of course, he has the meaning of the scene all wrong . . . but the *sentence!* It is priceless.

And I have to conclude that this is one of those small miracles that happen while we're busy doing other things. As I sit there in the quiet kitchen in the spring light, my heart floods with mother-love for Jimmy, new babies or no. And I feel some small measure of forgiveness for myself, too. Because whatever my failings as Jimmy's mother, whatever my faltering will, I have raised a boy who thinks, when he sees me cracking up in laughter on a sunny day, that he is the source of his mother's joy.

And that much, he has just right.

EDITOR'S NOTE

Amy Hudson, Ph.D., is a staff psychologist working in the Federal Bureau of Prisons in Oklahoma. She is a published poet and former editorial assistant at *The Saturday Evening Post.*

She wrote the following essay in my feature writing workshop and published it in *Writer's Digest.* As you read it, ask yourself:

- Why, exactly, should an audience of aspiring freelance writers be interested in the narrator's personal experience with illness?
- Which passages feature voice tones that establish empathy in readers?
- Which transitions allow the author to move freely through chronological time or to pivot from topic to theme?

The topic is anorexia nervosa and the theme is control. The *now and then* moment allows the author to comment and tell a story about her illness in an anecdotal, intelligent, and introspective voice. Epiphanies in the final paragraphs are directed at writers, resolve the theme, and set up the climatic and closed ending.

Invictus under Glass

A Writer Discovers Her Own Balance of Life and Art
through Her Battle with a Modern-Day Disorder of Control

Amy Hudson

I was born five and six years behind my sisters and three years before my brother, into a middle-class family in a rural Oklahoma town. We were not a family of academics or writers. Our lives revolved around a gargantuan family-owned general store created by my great-great-grandfather during the town's coal boom days. Seventy years later, most of the county was economically depressed and the store did much of its business through credit. My parents were pillars of the Wednesday-night prayer group and the Monday-night bridge club. My mom, though she wouldn't admit it, was a recognized local source of advice on elegance, gentility and taste; my dad was everybody's friend and the financial savior of many. They were loved and admired. Also resented.

My folks worried that the store and all it symbolized in the community might alienate their children. From the beginning, we understood that we were no "better" than our neighbors, regardless of how they might treat us. But drawing the line between accepting our identity and apologizing for it was our own conundrum. It was the difference between honest self-appreciation and creation of a persona for the consumption of others. My siblings leaned toward self-acceptance; I tilted the other way.

At age 4, I often played school with an older sister, and before long she had actually taught me to read. At home the activity drew praise and attention. But when first grade started, it went over like a lead balloon. I took the primers home at night and enjoyed them after bedtime by the hall light; when my turn came in the reading circle, I was inevitably daydreaming or off on another page. Every day I took a spanking in front of the class for not paying attention. The message in Miss File's Fly-Back paddle stuck: Forget about the self. *Give people what they want.*

Ironically, the same experience taught me that words could be a refuge. I skipped over the intimidation children can feel in grappling with verbal skills and moved straight to appreciation for the security and escape reading offers. And I took up writing, partly due to my perception that it fits the image of a child who likes to read, and partly out of genuine enjoyment in playing with words. Making up poems and rhymes was, on the one hand, an honest kind of construction and, on the other, manipulation.

The family gave encouragement and support.

Once I lugged a copy of *The Life and Times of Adolph Hitler* into my room to copy the charcoal sketch of the evil-looking man on the cover, and gradually became aware that the family assumed I was reading the mammoth book. Another time I copied a poem I liked from a children's book, only to have my mother discover it and think it was my own. I didn't try to correct the misconceptions. They brought approval, and I wanted them to be true. While other kids explored their real horizons, I perfected a passive deception.

My siblings grew up with different interests and talents. My parents fostered that. We were a basic All-American happy family. We were also well-fed, so watching weight was an everyday practice. Nothing extreme. Sweet 'n Low in the cabinet alongside the sugar and 2% milk instead of whole. I was a sedentary kid who played with words instead of jump ropes, and by adolescence I was chubby. My mom suggested we attend Weight Watchers together. At that age, my weight came off quickly. Juggling the calories and meals was sort of fun, like playing with words in poems. Grownups reacted to my change in appearance approvingly, and at school I gained a more respectable spot in the playground team-choosing pecking order. I lost weight and then some: my appetite. My mom took me to the doctor, who informed me that if I didn't eat enough, among other things, my hair would fall out. I promptly lost interest in counting calories and settled into an average, healthy diet.

I almost forgot about the weight-loss phase completely, until a couple years later when my cousin ran across an article on anorexia nervosa in *Seventeen* magazine. We were 14 and just becoming figure-conscious. We had never heard of the disorder. "That's what you had," she said, adding that it would be nice to have just a little anorexia, so you could get real skinny for a while and eat whatever you wanted. I agreed. But the article's main focus, as with most of the anorexia literature then, was on ballerinas and gymnasts who placed high priority on thinness. My image was more literary. The whole thing just didn't apply.

Years rolled by. I attended the local high school; it was small, and secure. There were activities, friends, good times. I wrote mostly for fun— poems for family birthday dinners and a diary of crushes, school events, summer carnivals. Yet, I was still aware of the pigeonholing process that children experience, and in my eyes my slot was that of a literary type who would somehow grow up to be extraordinary. How, I had no idea. I waited for the scenario to write itself.

My senior year started. Changes loomed ahead. College. This must be the transition, the point at which I should start being extraordinary. I wasn't.

Confidence ebbed; the answer, as in the past, seemed to be to get organized. I started to structure patterns—a study schedule, an exercise plan, a diet regimen—and clung to them. It felt good, like turning control over to some higher part of the psyche, some auto-pilot function in the brain. My family was impressed with the new-found responsible attitudes. But for me, dependence on this new mechanism just brought anxiety that the machine might break down. And underlying that, as always, was the hollow fear that this wasn't really me anyway, just another artifice, and that any day I'd be exposed as an inept, incapable creature.

Literary talent was the real key, what I thought was really expected of me, and deep down, what I wanted. It was time to find out, one way or another, if I had it. I set my sights on two goals. One was a patriotic essay contest sponsored by local VFW clubs. The other was a two-week summer arts institute.

The contest was held in fall. The trophy was a gold microphone replica that looked like a corncob. By my own standards, I worked hard on my entry and waved the flag with as much eloquence as I could muster. I didn't even place. My perceptive cousin did, along with an El Salvadoran exchange student and a guy who wanted to be a Baptist minister. In the context of four years of other high school activities, it really meant nothing. But to me, it symbolized realization of my worst fears. I wasn't what people expected, what they wanted, what *I* wanted.

But everyone around still seemed to expect the extraordinary. I forged on; my attitude was determined and strange. I'd give it my absolute best shot and fail; that would prove them wrong, and prove it to me, too. I'd be a nobody, and we'd all finally learn to accept it.

I focused on the poetry portfolio. I had no real education in the discipline, so I read up on it voraciously. As always, I didn't trust my own freedom, so I grasped at forms; every one I read about, I tried. I tried all three kinds of sonnets; the theme was burning down to the essence of the self and finding nothing of value. I tried rhyming couplets about a soldier who wasn't what he seemed. I tried pantoums, sestinas, villanelles, acrostics whose line lengths equaled different multiples of their syllabic feet.

I took a crash course in great poets, from Wordsworth to Eliot to Whitman. I liked Whitman's imagery; I couldn't understand his joy. I wrote my senior composition paper on Byron, Shelley and Keats, but never came close to grasping the defiant self-awareness of Romanticism. Keats wanted to glean the full ripen'd grain of his talents; I was pretty sure my fields would be fallow. I felt more like the embodiment of William Ernest Henley's ubiquitous contribution to hoary English verse anthologies: "Invictus," unconquered, master of my fate, captain of my soul. Nothing wrong with the airtight structure; but the content was an unconvincing farce.

Still it was the structure, the routine, that held things together. I ate three perfectly balanced meals every day, comprising the same amounts of the same foods. I ran five miles at the same time every day without fail. Obsession with self-control often leads to fear of wasting time. I developed an almost comical drive for perpetual productivity. One caesura might undermine the whole system of controls, which, I knew, was constantly in danger anyway, as I wasn't really capable of maintaining it. I not only stopped watching television; I wouldn't even look at a set that was turned off lest the temptation strike. Over meals, I studied. I ate standing up for more exercise. In the shower, I did deep knee bends. While running, I worked on poems in my head. While driving the car, I learned to play the harmonica. If all else failed, I grabbed a needlepoint project out of my purse for a quick productivity fix.

But it was all joyless. How I felt came out in one of my half-finished verses, with its subject "crabbing away at a desk in a small, musty night-room." Writing was no longer fun word-juggling, or even cathartic self-expression. It was a chore, a duty. A penance.

In the next months, I ran more, rounding the farthest corners of every street, and if I cut one I ran the whole course over later. I studied harder, later into the night. And ever so gradually I started cutting back on meals. Half a banana for breakfast became a quarter, and that became a fraction. I consumed the shrinking portions agonizingly slowly. I broke things into tiny pieces and chewed them, sucked on them, waited for them to melt. I wouldn't take another bite till my mouth was completely empty, and I stuck to the routines with the precision of a timer on a bomb. I wouldn't even drink water except at prescribed times. I castigated myself for feeling hunger, and responded by picking up a pen or a book and going back to work. I took no pride or happiness in any of it.

My weight dropped. I hardly noticed. I rarely looked in the mirror anyway, because any attention to self was a reminder of self's inability to achieve. My family noticed, and by Christmas they became alarmed. I couldn't explain the situation, even to myself, and I couldn't sympathize with their concerns; the paralyzing inner fears had numbed all other feelings. I had developed a passive and emotionless facade.

Since September I had dropped 15 pounds. Over winter the lack of fat in my diet caused the skin of my hands and feet to dry and crack all over; I slept with them slathered in lotion and covered with gym socks. My hair was dry and frizzy. I started to develop the downy covering of body and facial hair that grows on an undernourished body to keep it warm.

My mother read up on anorexia and grew convinced that was the problem. I shrugged the idea off. I reasoned that the weight loss wasn't intentional and would correct itself. My dad agreed. My weight kept dropping. Rifts developed in the family; everyone wanted to help, but no one knew how. They reasoned, cajoled, pleaded with me. Meanwhile, I increased my running, took an independent studies college course in Latin, and rigged the self-propelled lawn mower so it would be harder to push. The poetry application had long since been sent off, but I kept writing anyway, out of force of habit, convinced that it was all drivel, yet unable to stop.

I became acquainted with Sylvia Plath, the American poet who had taken her life the year before I was born. She had shown in correspondence to friends and family an anxiety about living up to expectations. As a teenager, Plath also structured her writing in preconceived forms. Later in life she surpassed the formal patterns, but her work focused increasingly on bleak, stark images of the darker abstractions—pain, despair, death. My attempts at this point spoke more and more of drowning, fading out, dying away. But the despair was a little different. In Plath's literary persona it was complete and whole. In my attempts it wasn't quite.

That spring I wrote in my journal, "life is essentially a search for an escape from loneliness. We are nuclei of atoms, filling the shells around us with families. We generate activity—we give of ourselves, our time, our love, our efforts, only in search of companionship, only to be less lonely, only to feel more alive." And still, I spun madly in my own perverse orbit, creating a force specifically to ward off others, keep them outside the busy shell that I perceived had some semblance of worth in the world, away from the hopeless, incomprehensible individual at the center.

One Sunday when everyone was home, my brother wandered through the house after another confrontation at the dinner table. My mother was in the back bedroom having what we know now was an anxiety attack, shaking all over as my father held her. The oldest sister paced back and forth, at a loss. The other was in the utility room bewildered, folding dirty laundry. I sat at the kitchen table in front of my full plate, calmly, impassively reading. My brother just stared at me. "I love you, Amy," he said after a while. "But why don't you go live someplace else?"

We tried several therapists. The consensus was that I should go into a special clinic for extensive therapy. I didn't buy it. I had been accepted into the arts camp, I reasoned, and now I had to go. But the real reason I rejected counseling was that the problem, I thought, was not my structured world; it was the very prospect of losing it. It was like an intricate, deranged sestina I had trapped myself in; I wasn't happy in it, but if I changed it—even one element of it—the whole thing might fall apart.

One afternoon I stood in the office waiting for my mother to schedule the next appointment with my Oklahoma City psychiatrist; considering that I was undergoing therapy for my folks' benefit, not mine, I let them handle the particulars. A girl, about my age, sat next to me in the lobby, dressed in surgical scrubs, like I often wore because they were loose-fitting. Her hair was in a French braid, the style I adopted when my hair got so dry that it was unmanageable. She wore running shoes. She looked like a normal-weight version of me on any given day. She looked up and spoke.

"How much do you weigh?"

I was startled. "Excuse me?"

She repeated the question slowly, as if speaking to a mildly retarded child.

I told her 90 pounds, padding it by 15 or so.

"I used to weigh less than you," she said, "but I started gaining and now I can't stop." She was talking fast, in a secretive voice, but urgent. "I wish I could get back down. I keep trying, but I can't stop gaining. I just can't."

What a weird girl, I thought.

I went to the arts camp, convinced it was a mistake and I'd probably wind up being sent home. The young writers there were all different, and all talented—some dramatic, some shy, some serious and some exuberant. It was a chance to interact with other people like me, maybe with similar apprehensions and aspirations, and to learn from them and befriend them. But I didn't consider myself one of them—a real writer. I didn't even feel worthy of admitting my desire to be one. So I passed the two weeks in a haze, grinding away in my own little sphere of anxiety, agonizing over my own work, missing out on the whole joy of writing as spontaneous creation and of sharing that act with others.

After the camp, I kept writing, but aimlessly—mostly autobiographical stuff about confusion and aloneness. I had no big activities left for the summer except preparing for college, so my parents laid down an ultimatum. I would go into the psych ward of an Oklahoma City hospital for ten days of testing, evaluation and observation. "This is ridiculous," I wailed to the therapist in a family session. "I don't belong here. These people are crazy." The room was silent, all eyes on me and my emaciated, frantic body. I felt a chill. And then I went to the hospital.

It made me angry, the first crack in the emotionless barricade. Control started to splinter. Weary of regimens, starting to see that they didn't matter that much, that I still wasn't extraordinary in any sense of the word, I began to give in to urges—to sit and do nothing, to waste time, to slack off on exercise, and to eat. But the normal appetite mechanisms were all twisted. Now, once I started on food, some part of me grabbed hold and wouldn't stop. I binged. The binges were comparatively small because I couldn't take in much at once, but they could last hours, mostly at night in the psych ward snack bar or in my room, often most of the night. When they happened I had absolutely no control. All I could do was fast as long as possible and exercise as hard as I could between them. Food wasn't part of my structured system anymore; it was the absolute enemy. And the shell wasn't just the facade of a cool, capable person hiding a frightened fool. Bingeing was disgusting, shameful. Now I really had something to hide.

My parents knew about the change. At that point they were only glad I was eating. They let me start college; my therapist told them I had a 50:50 chance of working everything out. Things got worse. The bingeing mentality was there; I couldn't stop it. The dorm cafeteria was a nightmare where I could spend hours once I got started. I dealt with it by fasting all day and creeping back to my room at night to eat food I stored there. But buli-

mics don't want to know how much they eat, so they get food in unortho-
dox, immeasurable ways. They steal it from others. And they scavenge for it
in dorm waste cans—pizza crusts, half-full boxes of cookies, and so on. I fell
into the habit and was absolutely terrified. I saw other girls do it late at
night—dark, secretive creatures, horrified at themselves, watching each
other down halls, pretending to be totally unaware of the common bond between them.

Over two years in college, my weight increased two and a half times.
My study habits faltered. My grades went down. I wanted to give up. As a
writer, as a person. There was no more shell; I was exposed as a failure. My
weight, my grades, the lack of any accomplishments that qualified as extraordinary—the worst of all possible outcomes had happened. I was bared to
the world once and for all in my ineptitude and banality.

Suicide surfaced as the next logical step. I could never regain the quality of self-control I had before, but I could take a kind of ultimate power
over my destiny in one violent step, albeit a choiceless one that led to a preconceived outcome. I was still writing—mostly self-absorbed litanies on the
meaninglessness of life, or at least of my own. I reacquainted myself with
Sylvia Plath, like countless other young girls have done, fingering the pages
of her books with a mixture of awe and dread because *she had really done it.*

One night I sat up late, reading the familiar words about a woman who
disappoints others and is perfect only in death. Her body, Plath wrote, dons
a smile of accomplishment.

She understood, I thought. Then, *Not really. I disappoint myself.* There
was a difference between the poet and me, based on factors even deeper
than her superior intellect and literary prowess. What was it? A longing?
One that ribboned through the past months like a refrain; the days and days
of work, trapped inside dozens of empty, senseless rituals; the nights
hinging, scavenging, alternately hiding from myself or watching in disgust;
trying so hard to deserve something, never reaching it. And the people, the
faces of family and friends who looked on not understanding but still loving
the real person they believed they knew, despite the passive shell, despite
the bizarre behavior, always offering her the one thing she most wanted.
And then I saw, maybe unlike Plath, that this was the key. In their acceptance of me was the potential for my own.

Four summers after the onset of anorexia, my weight was higher than
ever. It bothered me. I went to a diet clinic and was shocked to see how
much I really had gained. I received a diet and exercise plan and a small supply of different-colored appetite suppressants to help me get started. In the
parking lot, I rolled them over in my hand. These things alone weren't
going to make me what I wanted to be. Weight or lack of it wouldn't do the
trick; nor would iron will; nor could I make a front to hide behind—in the
end, they all turn out to be transparent.

The answers would have to be in the constant, intricate interplay of all the forces in life. And they would be in life itself, which, like art, isn't really made at all, but grows from within us. It occurred to me as I stood in the hot Oklahoma parking lot that I had a great deal of growing to do. I'd probably have to divert some of all that energy spent constructing, engineering, manipulating, creating myself for the people I cared about while simultaneously separating myself from them.

The change didn't happen overnight; with luck, it's still occurring. But it started then. That year I wrote my favorite of my efforts at poetry so far. It was about the death of an infant in my neighborhood and what that meant to a 12-year-old girl on a warm, small-town summer day. Like my previous attempts, it had a sad theme. It was self-absorbed. But it was an honest look inside, and an attempt to honestly express the grief that family and friends all felt over Brent's death.

> That a month went by was the thing
> we all hated, clinging to possibilities
> that hung by the straight thread
> of a silent brain scan.
>
> They told me that blue July morning you were gone,
> Brent. Your mother came home to start again
> somehow. That was the day
>
> My bicycle chain broke. I kicked it hard on the grass.
> It's funny, as I walked home
> past your yard I saw your mother had
> washed your favorite overalls and hung them on a line.

Writing, for the first time in my life, was liberation. It had become a chance to see the real self inside the shell. And more important, it had become an answer to loneliness, rather than the source of loneliness. Once, writing was a barrier I built between me and a world I thought shouldn't accept me because I couldn't accept myself. Now it had become a channel through which to reach and share those feelings and experiences that are common to all of us, that bring us out of isolation if we choose to come.

Because the fact is, we are bound, inextricably, to the nature that produced us all, to all humanity, to the very human capacity to love and accept. The only separation for me was in the persona I had contrived out of fear and doubt. And it was gone, released by some part of the self that was apparently wiser than the conscious mind. Frost makes flowers, Plath wrote in "Death & Co.," and dew makes stars. Her poem concludes that somebody is done for.

This time it didn't look like it was going to be me.

Karin Horgan Sullivan, senior editor at *Vegetarian Times,* says she usually avoids using personal anecdotes to validate research. "I tend to shy away from using myself in articles," she notes, "but for this one I thought I had compelling anecdotes that a lot of readers would be able to relate to." As you read her piece, ask yourself:

- Which passages contain research and author comment and how do they work in tandem to funnel information to readers?
- Which passages contain voice tones that would appeal especially to readers of this specialized magazine?
- Which passages contain insights that build up to and then complete the theme?

The topic is sugar, but the obsession theme empowers the piece, sending the writer on a quest to research her craving for sweets. "That was the first article I did that required a lot of scientific research," Sullivan says. "When I look at it, I can't help think of all the sources I know now that I didn't know then, and I wish that I'd talked to them." That's always a concern of food writers such as Sullivan who want to give readers as many facts as possible about nutrition. To do so here, she uses a savvy, informational, skeptical voice. The moment is in the *then* so that she can share research with the audience. Foreboding is a factor here, too; the pie shop in the first paragraph reappears in her closed ending.

Do You Really Want to Eat This?

A Sugar Lover's Quest for the Truth about Her Habit

Karin Horgan Sullivan

Of all the editors at *Vegetarian Times,* I was the obvious choice to write an article on sugar. This is not a fact I'm proud of, mind you, but one that's hard to deny, given the well-trodden path between my desk and the pie shop conveniently located across the street from the *VT* office. My lusty affair with simple carbohydrates has a long history. I remember being soundly chastised at a Brownie troop meeting when I interrupted the goodbye speech of our junior leader to ask if it was time to eat yet. Mrs. Snell, the troop leader, didn't appreciate that I was merely trying to move things along to more important business, namely the fudge brownies I knew we were having for our snack.

Or there was the time when I was about 10, when my family had lunch at the home of some family friends. For dessert we kids got King Dons, a packaged, cream-filled cake treat that we never had at home and one with which I instantly wanted to pursue a more intimate relationship. I spent the afternoon hounding Stephanie, the daughter who was my age, to ask her mom for more King Dons, until my mom caught on and gave me a stern talking-to.

I'm sorry to say that these are not isolated memories, and that my fondness for sweets was not limited to my childhood. Though my diet has become pretty healthful over the course of seven years as a vegetarian, I still occasionally have moments—okay, days—of incredible weakness. Last summer I attended a three-day nutrition conference in Washington, D.C., at which there was nary a sweet to be had. By the end of the conference, I was obsessed with finding a dessert. Within 45 minutes of the closing remarks, I had found an ice cream parlor and had downed a double-dip cone. Still feeling deprived, I ate a donut the next morning; lunchtime found me peering into the bottom of a hot-fudge sundae dish at a Smithsonian cafeteria and sadly shaking my head. "You read *reams* of nutrition information every week," I berated myself. "You know how terrible this stuff is for you. You've got to get this sugar thing under control."

Thus, I welcomed the chance to delve into the scientific literature on sugar, to see for myself the havoc my habit was wreaking on my body, to come face to face with irrefutable evidence that I Must Change My Ways. Turns out it's not that simple.

In the first place, the health-oriented media and nutrition researchers are not in harmony on the issue of why people consume so much sugar. Though popular diet and nutrition literature are rife with references to overcoming "sugar addiction," all the experts I spoke with agree that consuming even excessive amounts of sugar does not truly qualify as an addiction. Unlike heroin or caffeine addicts, someone with a penchant for sweet stuff doesn't develop a tolerance to sugar that requires increasing amounts to achieve the same level of satisfaction; nor does a withdrawal syndrome of physical side effects arise when one attempts to kick a sugar habit.

"Using the word 'addiction' that way weakens the term," says taste researcher Gary Beauchamp, Ph.D., of the Monell Chemical Senses Center in Philadelphia. Beauchamp's research indicates that humans are born with a preference for the taste of sugar. He has studied the responses of both premature and full-term infants to sweet substances, and in both types of studies, says Beauchamp, the babies showed "an immediate and profound preference for sweetness."

Though difficult to document, says Beauchamp, the presumption is that this preference for sweetness is the result of natural selection. Plant parts that are safe to eat and rich in nutrients generally are sweet; the poisonous parts usually are bitter. Throughout history, those with an inborn yen for the sweet survived while those with a bitter taste in their mouths often perished.

Somewhere along the way, though, this inborn preference becomes an out-of-control habit for a lot of folks, including me. Seems like the inner child just won't let go. According to a 1986 report from the U.S. Food and Drug Administration's Sugars Task Force, a panel convened to interpret the scientific literature on the health effects of sugar, sugar consumption is at a high. In the United States, the average per-capita intake of added sugars (as opposed to naturally occurring sugar, such as that in fruit) is 53 grams per day—which equals 48 pounds per year—or 11 percent of daily caloric intake. Now, admittedly, some of us are making up for others who eat only a fraction of that average, but the fact remains that as a whole, Americans eat an awful lot of sugar. Why do we have such a desire to belly up to the sugar bowl?

Judith Wurtman, Ph.D., a nutrition researcher with the Massachusetts Institute of Technology in Cambridge and author of *The Carbohydrate Craver's Diet* (Houghton Mifflin, 1983), says that our propensity to indulge in sugary foods is driven by our moods. According to Wurtman's research, eating carbohydrates—which she says includes everything from cookies and cake to more nutritionally correct staples such as bread, cereal and potatoes—stimulates production of the brain chemical serotonin, which creates a calming, soothing effect. Wurtman maintains that virtually the only time a person craves sweets is when he or she is under emotional stress and is driven to reduce that stress with the drug-like effects of serotonin. (Personally, I'm not sure *I* buy this argument; I can recall craving an ultra-rich, extremely-hard-to-come-by piece of cake while very happily tripping the dusty roads of India. Then again, not being able to find cake made me feel stressed.)

The reason people think they're addicted to carbohydrates, says Wurtman, is that "99 percent of people don't know the proper dose and form of carbohydrates to alter their mood." Most people go for carbohydrates accompanied by a lot of fat. And fat, says Wurtman, can triple the time for the serotonin release to take effect; in the meantime, a person keeps eating more of the food in an effort to achieve satisfaction and ends up feeling like a junkie. Also a critical factor is whether the carbohydrate is consumed with a high-protein food, such as tofu or cheese, which Wurtman says completely blocks the serotonin effect. "The body doesn't even know you're eating a carbohydrate," she says. She maintains that eating one or two ounces of fat-free, starchy carbohydrate by itself—such as a bagel—will lead to a serotonin release and the end of the craving within an hour or so.

I decided to try Wurtman's suggestion to satisfy one of my sweet cravings with a nonfat, nonprotein carbohydrate, in this case a piece of dry toast. Emotional status at the time: anxious to finish this story. Level of satisfaction one hour later: not much.

Other research indicates that it isn't sugar we want at all, but fat. This idea makes sense to anyone who's tried to appease a sugar craving with a practically nonfat sweet, like jelly beans; they're just not as satisfying as a piece of pie. Adam Drewnowski, Ph.D., director of the Program in Human Nutrition at the University of Michigan, is the leading expert on what he calls the "fat tooth." He and his colleagues studied the responses of both normal-weight and overweight women to the fat-sugar ratios in a variety of milkshake-type drinks. They found that normal-weight women preferred a mixture of 20 percent fat by weight and 10 percent sugar, while the overweight women preferred a mixture of 33 percent fat and 4 percent sugar. Based on such evidence, Drewnowski concludes that what we overindulge in is fat, not sugar; the reason we gravitate toward cakes and pies is because they're full of fat—a little sugar simply makes the fat taste better.

The mechanism behind these findings isn't yet understood; Drewnowski currently is looking at whether a particular fat-sugar ratio stimulates the release of endorphins, the body's natural painkillers. Regardless of the mechanism, says Drewnowski, it's important to recognize that much of what Wurtman calls carbohydrates—especially cakes and cookies—are in fact sweet-tasting, highfat foods. "It's a misnomer to call them carbohydrates," Drewnowski says.

So, I think, I'm a fat addict—or, rather, a fat *craver*. And I like my fat with sugar. Score a point for accuracy. The question remains, though, what is my fat/sweet tooth doing to my health?

This question has been asked before, of course. It was a hot topic about 20 years ago, when a book convinced thousands of Americans that sugar was the sole source of all their ailments. In *Sugar Blues* (Chilton Book Co., 1975), journalist William Dufty blamed refined white sugar for myriad medical evils, from the bubonic plague that swept London in 1665 to increased rates of mental illness in the 20th century. Although Dufty's book is an entertaining read on the history of sugar, he cites very little scientific evidence to back his medical assertions, leaving the reader to take it—or leave it—on faith.

The major reviews of epidemiological and clinical studies on sugar consumption have failed to find a direct link between sugar and any health problem except for dental caries (otherwise known as cavities). Two massive scientific tomes, *The Surgeon General's Report on Nutrition and Health* (U.S.

Dept. of Health and Human Services, 1988) and the *National Research Council's Diet and Health* (National Academy Press, 1989), both maintain that there is no truth to the rampant belief that sugar is the direct cause of obesity, diabetes, hypoglycemia or hyperactivity. And according to the Sugars Task Force report, "Other than the contribution to dental caries, there is no conclusive evidence that demonstrates a hazard to the general public when sugars are consumed at the levels that are now current and in the manner now practiced."

Noted vegan author and nutrition expert John McDougall, M.D., begs to differ. Although he agrees that sugar doesn't directly cause diabetes or hypoglycemia, he points out that large amounts of sugar can raise triglyceride, or blood fat, levels in some people, which in turn may aggravate diabetes, hypoglycemia, heart disease and problems associated with poor circulation. Also, says McDougall, sugar's concentrated calories add up quickly—before someone eating sweets feels full—and can indeed contribute to obesity.

Nevertheless, says McDougall, "Sugar is not the evil demon people make it out to be. When used judiciously, sugar can give an awful lot of pleasure with a minimum amount of destruction." McDougall says it's fine to eat up to three teaspoons—10.5 grams—of sugar a day. He recommends that we place added sugar on top of food, where the smallest amount will be most easily tasted. "This may make a difference in whether or not someone eats their oatmeal," he says.

Furthermore, says Michael Armstrong, Ph.D., chair of the biochemistry department at National College of Chiropractic in Lombard, Ill., the popular wisdom that sugar "leaches" B vitamins from the body is in error. True, sugar doesn't provide any B vitamins, some of which are necessary to metabolize food; to convert sugar to energy, the body must borrow the required vitamins from other foods. But this borrowing is the same as what the body does to metabolize other foods that don't provide adequate amounts of the necessary B vitamins.

Just as I was beginning to feel that my love for sugar wasn't such a bad thing, I came across some research that gave me pause. The November 1973 *American Journal of Clinical Nutrition* published a small study that examined the effects of sugar on the phagocyte index. Phagocytes are white blood cells that eat up harmful bacteria; the higher the phagocyte index, the stronger the immune system. The researchers—who, incidentally, were from Loma Linda University, a longtime leader in the study of vegetarian nutrition—found that ingesting 100 grams of sucrose, glucose, fructose, honey or orange juice all led to a significant drop in the phagocyte index. (According to my calculations, 100 grams of sugar is about what you'd find in two pieces of a devil's food layer cake.) At its lowest point, two hours after ingestion, the index had dropped from an average baseline of 15.9 to an average of 9.6

for all the sugars. Five hours later, the index was still down at an average of 13.1.

According to Albert Sanchez, R.D., Ph.D., program coordinator for the Pacific Health Education Center, in Bakersfield, Calif., and lead researcher in the study, sugar can decrease the protective functions of the body. "Our interpretation was that eating large amounts of sugar, particularly on an empty stomach—which is the way most Americans eat it, between meals—has a profound effect on the body's capacity to resist infection," Sanchez says. Though it would be inappropriate to blow out of proportion the results of this one study, Sanchez does say he is not aware of any follow-up studies on sugar's effect on immunity, and he stresses that we still don't know how smaller, more typically consumed amounts of sugar affect the immune system. Also unknown is how a temporary reduction in immune system functioning affects health in the long run.

What's interesting about this study is that white table sugar, honey and fruit juice all had the same effect, once again proving the point that sugar is sugar. So-called "natural" sweeteners may be somewhat less processed than white sugar, but with the exception of blackstrap molasses (which contains calcium and iron), these sugars are no better for your health.

Another, seemingly serious problem has been raised recently in the popular press: that sugar can accelerate aging by damaging collagen, the body's main structural protein, which forms an important part of tendons, bones and connective tissues. This concern, however, is based on animal research; no one has conclusively researched how sugar affects the aging process in humans.

How convincing you consider the immunity and aging studies is probably more a function of your personal sugar philosophy than of your scientific acumen. But whether you believe that sugar is perfectly harmless or that it is the bane of human existence, one fact cannot be denied: Sugar doesn't bring anything to the party except calories—no vitamins, no minerals, no fiber. All agree that consuming too many high-sugar (and usually, by default, high-fat) foods in place of nutritious foods—as I did after the nutrition conference last summer—is not good dietary practice.

In the course of doing this story, I realized that all too often what I eat to satisfy a sweet craving is something awfully high in fat. I'm trying to be more disciplined about jettisoning such junk food from my diet—but I refuse to spurn my old love. On those days when I've eaten at least five fruits and vegetables, kept my fat intake low and still feel a desire for dessert, I reflect on the perspective of George Blackburn, M.D., head of the Center to Study Nutrition and Medicine at New England Deaconess Hospital in Boston: "The belief that sugar is bad is based on our Puritan background, that we're not put here to enjoy life, that something must be a sin to taste so good. Sugar eaten in moderation is okay." I find this excellent food for thought on my way to the pie shop.

EDITOR'S NOTE

Patricia Westfall teaches magazine writing, editing, and information gathering at the E. W. Scripps School of Journalism, Ohio University. Among her several books are a writing/editing text *Beyond Intuition* (Longman) and *Real Farm* (New Chapter Press). A former contributing editor for *Savvy,* Westfall has published articles in *Country Journal, Midwest Living, Folio,* and *Esquire,* in which the following piece originally appeared. As you read it, ask yourself:

- What role does the meaning/lyric graph in the introduction play, with respect to theme?
- Which passages contain sensory data and how do they relate to theme?
- Which symbols or images recur through the piece, leading to epiphanies?

As the subtitle indicates, the occasion in "An American Dream" is the purchase of a farm in Iowa. But the theme here is perception, which Westfall illustrates with numerous statements and foreshadowings. Pay particular attention to the latter. Note, for instance, how her name is used in the introduction and last paragraph. The moment falls in the *now and then* zone, allowing Westfall to comment as she narrates her story in an observant, plaintive, and introspective voice.

An American Dream

Everyone Dreams of Packing It in and Moving
to the Country with Someone He Loves.
Here's a True Story of Two People Who Tried It.

Patricia Westfall

I used to ask to be called Patricia. To me, Patricia was a pretty word, unlike Pat, which seemed abrupt, or Patty, which seemed too silly and girlish for a woman nearly six feet tall. Of course I asked Jeff, shortly after we met, to call me Patricia, and to my surprise he firmly refused. No friend had ever refused this harmless request before, but he argued that names are external, something others use, something my parents and friends choose for me. To attempt to control my name was to block intimacy, because, in part, it is through the names we give one another that we carve paths to one another. Those were not his words, I'm sure—he always spoke in a rapid avalanche of metaphor that I find impossible to capture or mimic—but those were the ideas. Over the years he called me many names, even the dreaded Patty. In fact, in the word Patty especially there were many doors.

We met at a picnic, a company picnic of all things. I had just returned to the company, a publishing firm in Tennessee, after a dark six months away sorting out my life. Jeff had joined the company in my absence as a gatherer-of-facts-by-phone. He'd taken the job to see him through while he waited for a teaching job. The school board had hired him and then told him, after he'd spent his savings moving to town, that there was a funding snag. He was in a foul mood most of the time, including at this picnic.

The powers that be had intended the picnic as a retreat, so each of us was required to speak briefly about the most important thing in his life right then. I said most important to me was getting my four-hundred-pound couch out of the kitchen of my new apartment, where the carpet layers had left it. Jeff, who sat opposite me, said most important in his life was poetry and the greatest influence on his life had been a poet with wedgewood-blue eyes.

Later I sat on a rock, saw him standing by a tree, and asked would he like to share my rock. Someone took a picture of us on the rock and later gave it to us as a wedding present; it's the only picture of him I've kept. On that rock we had, I felt, a magical conversation, which began when he challenged something I was saying. I can't imagine what now, but I'm sure it was an all-things-are-relative sort of remark. He retorted with a quote from William Blake's "Marriage of Heaven and Hell": "Truth is such that it cannot be perceived and not be believed." I countered; I said perception could not be absolute. He said with effort it could be. I said perhaps, but there were so many approaches to perception it was hard to know which approach to apply to which event or truth. He didn't follow, so I offered to draw him a map of perception. I said it was also a map of the universe. My map was like this:

MEANING ——————————————————————— LYRIC

A poetry professor of mine once had argued that all writing could be placed on an axis with meaning and lyric the extremes. The more lyrical a piece of writing, the more it resembled pure poetry and the more absurd it was to read it for message or meaning. Meaning was prose.

I had liked that axis. It seemed to describe reality as well as poetry. The more spontaneous and spirited an event, the more absurd it was to try to explain it. On the other hand, why look for joie de vivre in an annual report? It's inappropriate.

Jeff still disagreed. He did not think meaning and lyric were opposite equals. As we argued I began placing dots on the line, writing names of people next to them. I put one with my name to the lyrical side of center, then handed him the pencil. "Where do you put yourself?" I said.

Jeff became strangely agitated: "It doesn't . . . this can't . . . I . . . I'm here. He had placed a dot off the line, above and beyond the lyric. Off the line.

I had played this game many times and never before had anyone violated the axis. Not questioning my universe, people would place themselves on the line. Not Jeff; my axis didn't hold, which made me unbearably curious about him.

Sunday he arrived with a bottle of wine and a book of prose poems by W. S. Merwin. The wine was too dry and the book incomprehensible. I served a salad with celery and a casserole with eggplant. There were only two vegetables in the universe he hated: celery and eggplant. We moved the couch in a sputter of polite but lousy teamwork, so lousy we almost failed. We stood on the apartment balcony, he straining to be taller, me leaning to be shorter. And we talked. He did live in a world of poetry; it affected everything he did and thought. Two poems from that awkward celery/couch evening I remember in particular. One was James Wright's "A Blessing," which ends with lines about a man stepping out of his body into blossom. The other was William Carlos Williams's famous lyric, "The Red Wheelbarrow," about so much depending on a rain-glazed wheelbarrow beside white chickens.

We were married the following Thanksgiving, which that year also happened to be William Blake's birthday. And for Jeff's birthday the next year I gave him a red wheel barrow. The chickens would follow a few years later, after we bought a small farm in Iowa.

A farm was the only lyrical option, of course, though it took us several houses and gardens to become convinced of that because nothing in Jeff's experience had prepared him for either. He was born in Brooklyn and had lived in apartments. When he was six his parents divorced and his father disappeared. To support Jeff, his mother lied her way into a secretarial job by having a friend give a phony reference. She also arranged a singing audition for Jeff at a boarding school. He passed, and so lived thereafter at the school on a music scholarship. He would shuttle between dormitory and apartment for the rest of his childhood. He never lived in a house until we rented one shortly after we married. This house awed him. Windows on four sides seemed more freedom than life deserved. But the garden was even more awesome. His mother couldn't be bothered to keep even a cactus, so all of it was utterly new to him, the feel of the soil, its color, its smell; the unfolding of leaves; the shapes of seeds. Seeds intimidated him; if the envelope said plant a quarter-inch deep, he felt that meant as measured by a ruler. I told him seeds had been evolving for million of years and were just glad enough to touch dirt; they weren't all that particular about inches and centimeters. He wasn't convinced. He measured.

He read anything he could find, ransacked the libraries and extension offices, buttonholed neighbors and friends for advice, and hounded me with questions about things I'd never thought about: soil tilth, mulching, organic pest control, companion planting. My parents had gardened, but they were from the put-it-in-the-ground-and-see-if-it-grows school. Jeff made me be more serious. He didn't want just a few seeds thrown out the door; he wanted an accomplishment. And the more he experienced, the more he wanted. When the leaf lettuce was ready, he marveled at the different colors, tastes, and crispness and decided he wanted no more store lettuce—which set him dreaming of a greenhouse. When he tasted our first young carrots, he wanted a root cellar. When we shared the first tomato—we had watched it ripen for days; I wouldn't let him pick it too early—he wanted us to someday grow enough to make our own sauces.

Then came the corn. The wait for the corn had been agonizing. The silks had to be brown and the ears had to look full, I'd told him. One evening we checked and I said they were ready; he reached to pick one.

"Not yet," I said. "First we put water on to boil."

"What?" he said.

When the water was boiling, I ran to the corn patch; he walked behind me. I tore off several ears and frantically shucked them. Jeff was moving too slowly.

"Hurry," I said. "It's important to move as fast as you can."

I ran toward the kitchen. He didn't, so I yelled to him, "I'm serious. Run. You must run."

He was puzzled, but he ran. Into the boiling pot, wait five minutes, no more, and hand him an ear, no plates, no table. I'd looked forward to this for months. The sugar in corn kernels is short-lived, at its peak only at ripening; the instant an ear is picked, the sugar begins to change to starch. Ear corn from the supermarket picked last week is good; ear corn from a roadside stand picked that morning is excellent. But nothing can compare with garden corn eaten minutes after picking while the sugar is intact. Gardeners wait all year for this secret moment; other folks never suspect the moment is possible. Jeff laughed, he was so pleased; he wandered to and fro in the kitchen, tasting, exclaiming, tasting again. At the window he paused to look at the garden. "We will always live in a house," he said. "We will always have a garden."

The next house we rented was in the country, with space for a truly large garden, including potatoes. In early July I put a pot of water on to boil. Jeff looked about the kitchen but saw nothing ready to go in the pot.

"The corn can't be ready," he said.

"It isn't, but the new potatoes are," I said.

By this time we were living in Iowa, where Jeff was working on a Ph.D. in literature and teaching part-time in the English department. I also was teaching at the university, also part-time, but for the journalism department. I continued to edit and write for the Tennessee company as well. It was a time of numbing contentment for us. We had money, leisure, and good friends in Iowa. In fact, we had enough money to begin looking at country houses. We first saw the farm we were later to buy when we were guests of the owner, one of Jeff's professors. My only memory of that evening is of snow outside the door and of some coat hooks in the kitchen. About then Jeff had been writing a poem I liked very much about owls that had recently begun perching on our roof. The poem described how in the stillness that follows making love one discovers the stillness of winter, the stillness of night, and the haunting soft stillness of the owls' intimate *whooing* above us. Just from curiosity Jeff checked the library to learn the symbolism of owls and came home disturbed, having found that in several folklore the owl was a symbol of death. Jeff's professor died that December.

His widow decided to sell almost immediately after, and so we offered to look. We spent a long afternoon tramping through woods and snow, seeing what twenty acres can be. The land was steep, too hilly for crops, and had a severe erosion problem. The woods had been overgrazed, so most of the trees were under stress. The house was cozy but too small. The barn roof had buckled and its foundation was crumbling. The shed leaked. The garage was on the verge of collapse. But there was a working windmill; it actually pumped the farm's water. It was the windmill that won us. We bought the farm for the windmill.

The windmill was a lyrical detail in the classic sense of the word—that is, exuberant, almost pure sound. The windmill had a marvelous sound whenever it pumped, not quite like a cricket, not quite like a heartbeat. It was distinctive, and it set the tone—very literally—for us in the months that followed the move. Jeff instinctively understood the importance of sound—or seemed to. He bought me a wind chime for the porch, but a very special one, tuned to a Grecian tonal scale, he said. It was beautiful, producing rich notes and pure melody in endlessly intriguing variety. I never tired of it and thought it an exceptionally appropriate gift for the farm because, of course, the discovery process in this place would be sensory and sound should be dominant.

In spring, for example, there would be a night when all at once all the frogs began bellowing; it would sound as if there were more frogs on the pond than stars above it. And yet the sound of a single whippoorwill, which always followed a few nights later, was more strident than the noise of those millions. The call was a mixture of surprise and urgency, made strange by the fact that it came at night, so rare among birds. Decoding the sounds became a major adventure for us, both still basically city kids despite the gardens behind us. Our training taught us to distinguish bus from dump truck, not oriole from goldfinch. We learned most sounds simply by freezing in place in woods or pasture, hoping for a glimpse of the bird or animal that made the noise. We also mastered farm sounds, such as the cry of a sheep separated from the flock (it was infuriating how the flock never answered the lost one) or the screams of hogs being loaded into trucks for the one-way trip to market. One sound defied decoding by us for a long time. It was a sound cattle made, a roar of rage or pain, similar to the screams of hogs but always from one animal at a time. Then Bird, one of our goats, kidded for the first time. Her bellows were different, but even so the connection was clear. We felt foolish not to have realized sooner we were hearing cows calving.

Most people think sight is the sense of discovery; they think what is lyrical must be something seen, but that is not true. Seeing was very difficult in this place; too many distractions, too many changes.

Once we saw a blue heron in the swamp just over our north fence. It stayed for days, preening itself and watching us watch it. Once I saw a flicker in the grass, focused on it, saw it was only a frog and then, before I lost focus, that the frog's head was inside the mouth of a huge painted snake, six feet long and as thick as my wrist. I had nearly stepped on it. The snake was eyeing me and its eye was trying to reason with me, telling me how long it had been since it had anything to eat, let alone a good frog, and if I would just keep my distance it could keep its frog. I fought down my panic and stood watching for a long time. Such prolonged glimpses were rare.

One spring, our second spring on the farm, we bought two thousand tree seedlings to fill in our woods and recruited a small army of friends to help us. We began work on planting day, all of us chatting, but as the rhythm of the work took hold of each person he fell silent. Soon the only sound was a thumping as we closed each planting slit. I found myself working alone as again and again I sank a shovel, rocked it, slipped in a seedling, closed the slit. It took only seconds per seedling, but I did it over and over and over. The rhythm of fixing slits for trees set my thoughts wandering for a time. Then the rhythm emptied my mind entirely so there was only the work of it, so simple, but over and over and over. Then in the rhythm I began seeing the ground. There were ferns curled in whorls, wild flowers emerging, tiny may-apples, miniature goldenrod, tiny Virginia creeper—hundreds of things I seemed able to see only when they were large and unavoidably evident. I stopped work to look, the ground became invisible again, still late-winter brown. But if I kept the rhythm going, I saw unmerged things in their April beginnings. This had become our woods; we owned it, walked it, cut firewood from it, made payments on it, fixed fences around it, lived by it; how little of it we saw. That night neither aspirin nor brandy would relieve the soreness I felt from planting, but neither would the soreness cloud the pleasant clarity planting our woods had brought me. This is the only moment of vision I can claim here, though. Because vision was so rare, Jeff and I rarely discussed sights, but we found words for sounds.

The idea that we plant those two thousand trees was the forester's. In fact, the forester thought we should become tree farmers. And he had sketched us a map, charted symbols, filled out forms, and mailed off "our" forestry plan to the state nursery before either of us could contemplate what the forester was, or think about what his impact upon us might be. The issue would not be trees, of course, but perception. Jeff had not changed since the day on the rock; he still saw perception as absolute; I was willing to allow for some confusion. Even if our perceptions on sounds and sights were the same, we would discover through the forester, that our shared sense of lyric did not extend to actions or people. Jeff saw the forester as the embodiment of the lyrical life-style. I did not. I saw him as a living myth.

I knew we were headed for trouble when Jeff remarked to me that the forester and his wife reminded him of a couple we'd known in Asheville, North Carolina. I'd had the same thought. The Asheville husband was a motorcycle repairman who had learned his skills from *Zen and the Art of Motorcycle Maintenance*. The wife was a weaver. They were organic gardeners, and organic carpenters and organic vegetarians, with a perfectly mannered organic baby just learning to crawl. She knew healing through foot massage. He created their furniture. They had exquisite taste in music, cheese, and wine. They read books. They had no television. They had a friend named Ed.

Ed, they told us, had built a log cabin out of trees he'd cut and shaped himself with tools he'd made himself out of metal he may have dug and forged himself, drove nails with his fingertips, trapped raccoons with baling twine, they said. This all made me very nervous. Living myths have always made me nervous. Not so Jeff. Jeff loved the Asheville couple and kept writing them letters they never answered. He felt betrayed by them, but I felt vindicated to learn later via channels that the Asheville man had quit repairing Zencycles and was now selling sunglasses from a Toyota. The forester was building a house himself with some tools he'd invented himself, after a design he'd done himself. Solar, of course. The forester made me very nervous. This is not to say that I didn't appreciate all we learned from the forester. This is just to say that he made me nervous. Not so Jeff. Jeff idolized him.

The forester did not look like the embodiment of a lyric or myth. He was not seven feet tall or muscled enough to fell a tree with one swipe of an ax. He was short, potbellied, with glasses, and had a beard so dense it was impossible to tell if his face was handsome or homely. He drove an ordinary two-door car, and his voice was thin.

He was cautious. He visited us shortly after the move and began by asking us broad questions to probe how we felt about the land, what we wanted to do with it. Jeff said our goal was to use the land well, to produce income without abusing it.

"Do you want livestock?" the forester asked.

"Perhaps a few meat animals and a dairy cow," Jeff said.

"Are you interested in wildlife habitat?"

"Definitely," Jeff said.

The forester sorted this out silently, sizing us up. It was impossible to guess what he might be thinking behind that massive beard. Abruptly he suggested we go for a walk.

We had barely stepped out the kitchen door when he bent down and plucked a lawn weed, the ubiquitous one with oval leaves, parallel veins, and an unmowable center stalk. "Plantain," he said. "In the spring the leaves are terrific in salads or cooked as greens." Jeff's eyes opened wide. That a weed had a use was a new idea to him.

Just past the garden gate the forester stopped again. "Taste this," he said, handing us a pale-green clump of cloverlike leaves. "Suck on the leaves, don't chew." It was sour, like sucking on a lemon, but sweet too, fresh-tasting. "This is wood sorrel," he said. "It has more vitamin C than most plants you can name, including the lemon it tastes like." Jeff bent over to gather a handful. "Don't use too much," the forester cautioned. "Too much over time can cause your bones to weaken; it interferes with calcium absorption." Jeff drew back as if it were thistles.

The forester continued in this manner, alert for plants. The grass in the fields was a mixture of timothy and brome. The weeds in front of the barn were spearmint, an excellent tea or flavoring for jellies. Queen Anne's lace was wild carrot; common mullein, a tea; day lilies, an asparagus; even nettles were edible. Every plant he saw seemed to have food potential. I raced ahead of them to find a spot I'd discovered a few days earlier. A nondescript spot in spring, it had suddenly exploded into color in summer. It contained occasional stands of purple aster, surrounded by broad sweeps of a calf-high plant with whorled yellow flowers and lacy leaves. The color was butter-rich, reminiscent of a field of daffodils, but more intense, thicker. These plants rustled in the breeze like cellophane and grew unended, unplanted, unseen mostly; because this spot was hidden. "What is this?" I asked the forester.

"Partridge pea."

"What can it be used for?"

"Nothing."

"Nothing?"

"Even goats won't eat it."

"A useless plant?"

"Well, it's a legume; it's a good soil builder."

"He's saying there's no such thing as a useless plant," Jeff said.

"Poison ivy is pretty useless," the forester corrected. His thin voice took on a sudden wry edge, which made me look at him with a start. I immediately suspected he never ate wild vegetables himself. I became sure of it. This was a man who liked his beans domesticated. Here he'd made Jeff so excited by wild edibles I was sure I'd be peeling thistles and boiling roots the next day. The forester was just setting us up, I thought.

Jeff thought the forester was the most interesting person he'd ever met. It wasn't just that he was clever. Jeff admired his values too. They made him lonely in some ways. Jeff liked that. Once the forester had gone door to door asking the farmers in the county not to be neat in their mowing but to leave weeds growing here and there for wildlife habitat.

"And?" said Jeff.

"And they about laughed me into the ground," the forester said.

No wonder the man was cautious. And no wonder he liked us. Our fields and ditches were a mess. Jeff didn't mention the fact that this was because we were so inept with machines we couldn't keep a mower running. So I mentioned it. "Don't think we're wildlife nuts," I said. "We're messy because we're incompetent."

The forester said he could tell that. I had to acknowledge he had a sense of humor, something rare among living myths. But he still made me nervous.

He collected his household water from the roof; Jeff wanted us to catch rainwater too. He dug his garden with a hog; Jeff wanted us to hog-plow too. He heated his home with a passive solar system; Jeff wanted us to put in a solar system too. He watered his garden with "graywater," spent bathwater collected in a tank; Jeff wanted us to save bathwater too. He had a composting toilet; Jeff wanted that too. I balked at all this. We both worked, our finances were limited, our skills were even more limited, and we had other projects to finish first. None of the forester's things were necessary, to my mind. There were symbols of a life-style, so they could wait for a more convenient time, when we knew more.

It became a pattern; whenever the forester suggested something, Jeff would be immediately enthusiastic and I would have immediate reservations. One Saturday the forester showed up so early at our house that I hadn't yet fully grasped it was Saturday. He wanted Jeff to go with him because he had found a collapsing barn with a stone foundation from which the owner had agreed to let him salvage stone. He wanted stone for a hearth. Jeff wanted stone to put around the deep beds he'd been digging in the garden. It was all a blur of activity, so I wasn't sure what they were up to, only that they had just given me some time alone with the place—what was left of it. Every room in the house had been disturbed by our wood stove installation. We were tearing out a wall to make room for the stove. I was becoming convinced we were destroying the house in the process.

I sat down at my desk, still in my bathrobe, still nursing my first cup of coffee. The scene outside the window was as chaotic as that inside the house. Normally the view was an anchor for me. When working, I could steal glances out the window to renew my link with woods and garden. But this morning the garden was, as it had been for many mornings, a distressing riot of trenches. Jeff was digging deep beds.

The deep beds were another of the forester's ideas and another thing I felt we didn't need. Beds were for people with limited garden space and no tiller. We had space and a tiller; why bother? But Jeff liked the idea, whether we needed them or not. He dug. The usual method of digging a bed is called bastard trenching. Essentially, a fork-depth strip underneath can be disturbed, not dug, by plunging in a fork and waggling it. This technique loosens soil down to about twenty inches. I've done bastard trenching. It's easy; it takes about two hours for a twenty-by-four-foot bed.

Jeff, however, interpreted bastard trenching to mean lazy trenching. To him, laziness was expediency and expediency was lack of commitment. Somewhere he also got the idea that the beds should be three feet deep. So he decided he would take three feet of soil completely out of the each bed and mix the layers. I said I didn't think soil should be disturbed so much. He said he'd read this somewhere. But there's clay under there, I said. He said he was sure this was right. He dug. He created a splendid disorder beneath my study window until finally the forester noticed what he was doing.

Soil is a fragile ecosystem, the forester said. Disturbing the layers could wreck the microorganism communities in it. In fact, it could be years before the soil recovered from the damage Jeff had already done.

The forester told Jeff this as gently as possible, perhaps too gently. Jeff kept on digging, but now the idea fueling his effort was that the beds would never have to be redug. They would be loosened forever. The forester told me normal action of wind and rain packed soil. Deep beds have to be loosened each year, just like any other garden. But neither of us had the heart to tell Jeff.

Jeff finally stopped digging at twenty six inches—six inches deeper than the bastard method called for, true, but ten inches shy of his goal. He had dug some admirable holes; they awed me, but troubled me too. I thought they'd never be refilled because Jeff seemed to be discouraged. He saw those splendid holes as a failure. I studied the mounds from my window and considered the digger. What was happening to him? Why had he assumed the hard way was the better commitment? I finally figured out where the three-feet idea had come from. Having read that plant roots can grow to that depth, he assumed that that meant digging that deeply was necessary.

Most bewildering in the deep-bed project was the way Jeff began to blame the forester for his own misinformation. I could have accepted this if it was only information he was upset about. But his anger was in terms of trust. When the forester suggested we use herbicides to control weeds on our steeper slopes, Jeff reacted as if he'd been betrayed. He saw it not as a suggestion that he could accept or reject but as a heresy. The man who had asked farmers not to cut their weeds could not turn around and recommend a weedkiller and still be trusted, to Jeff's mind. I began thinking about a strange outburst from the forester a few days earlier. He had stopped by to check on our progress with the wood stove installation and had made a suggestion, a good one. I'd complimented him on how much he knew.

"Do I? Do I? I only wish I knew as much as people think I do."

I was shocked at his tone; tense, angry. I wondered who had been angry with him recently to make him defensive. My sense of him changed suddenly. Perhaps he wasn't a living myth at all but something else, an applied scientist, maybe. The herbicides recommendation made me think this. Like a scientist, he was curious, interested in knowledge even if what he learned warred with his values. No living myth could be curious for curiosity's sake, as the forester was. Living myths look for something to believe in; they would search not for information but for truth. I wondered suddenly what had happened to the Asheville couple. Why had they totally turned on their dream and returned to the suburbs? Sunglasses? A crises of faith? Did confusing the practical problems of country living with faith make compromise impossible?

I was beginning to understand why the Asheville couple made me so uncomfortable. Jeff was right; trust was the issue. I didn't trust them. I had thought their tendency to convert me rather than convince me, to put their ideas in terms of values not facts, had been what bothered me. But I should have been able to ignore this. Why was my caution bordering on fear? Was it because there's no compromising faith? One believes or does not. A living myth would rather quit than compromise and so cannot be trusted to endure the inevitable contradictions with you. This is what must have happened to the forester. Someone had believed in him too much. Someone had been angry at a contradiction. The forester must have a great deal of confusion about him, I thought. He wasn't what he seemed to be.

When Jeff and the forester returned with the stone, it was obvious Jeff was upset about something. But there were other people about, strangers to me. Several trucks were in our yard, and with them a great deal of uproar, so it was hours before I could ask him what was wrong.

"I'd never realized what a lazy guy the forester is," Jeff said. In Jeff's lexicon that was a serious charge. Lazy means expedient means lack of commitment means lack of faith.

"How so?" I asked.

Jeff said that man kept taking breaks, and while he was really careful at picking his own stone, he was not so careful picking Jeff's. I said the forester was ten years older than Jeff so probably needed more breaks, and stone for a hearth was different from stone for a garden, and then I asked him, "What are you really mad about?"

"I was talking to another man there who said he had a small tractor for sale, so I'm getting interested and the forester jumps in and says he thinks maybe he wants to buy it."

There Jeff is trying to be coolly interested to keep the price down and suddenly his friend whom he trusts becomes a bidding rival. That betrayal was the final incident for Jeff. Odd how both of us had changed our perceptions of the man. Jeff's revision meant the end of a friendship, however. I was sorry. I was just beginning to like the forester.

Though I was sorry, I was relieved too. I thought now there would be less pressure from Jeff to do so many projects. We would repair the damage we had done to house and garden; we would go back to reasonable tasks; we would return to simpler goals; we would develop our skills slowly. My professional work had been suffering; too much money had been spent. We would rest.

"You haven't started the solar-greenhouse research yet, have you?" he asked me a few nights later.

"No." I had decided weeks ago that with a wood stove and a well-insulated house we did not need a solar greenhouse. I also felt we needed some time to recover from the expense of the stove before we tackled another expensive project. But I had promised to at least start the library research, although I knew I didn't have time or energy for even that. I was coping by ignoring the project.

He looked at me as though suddenly perceiving this. "You're not going to, are you?" he said.

I started to begin my litany of objections again: we don't have the time; we don't have the money; we don't have the skills. But I stopped myself before I said anything.

I was realizing at last that none of these were at issue. The issue was quite simply that he wanted to be a living myth. And I didn't.

He repeated the question. Perhaps he thought I hadn't heard. Time. Money. Skill. And pleasure in accomplishment; we had failed at nothing. Lyric and myth were not the same in my mind. Lyric is small and takes pleasure in all accomplishment. Only by mythic standards was anything we had done less than ideal.

Couldn't we enjoy what we had and not measure it against a dream? Wasn't simple activity enough?

He was staring at me. It wasn't like me to be silent, ever. I felt if I said I would do the research I'd destroy myself, because I was truly exhausted. Life here had become untenable chaos. If we did not pause to recover, I would break. But if I said I'd not do the research, I'd destroy his vision of me. He would begin to see me as expedient, not committed, perhaps not lyrical. Lyric and myth seemed to be the same to him. His perception of me would change, perhaps slowly, perhaps quickly. I would become something silent and songless in his mind, a dot firmly attached to a line that measures realities like time, money and skill. I wouldn't be what I seemed to be.

"Patty?" he said. He sounded frightened too. The night was filled with its usual sounds, the windmill, the wind chimes, the crickets, the frogs, and a sound new to this house, the soft sound of owls whooing on the roof.

INDEX

pp. 85–86: "What J-Profs Should Be Teaching You" by Andrea Tortora is reprinted with permission of the author.

pp. 99–100: "The Power of a Title" by Audrey Chapman is reprinted with permission of the author.

pp. 105, 266–270: "How to Face a Firing Squad" by George Plimpton is reprinted with permission of the author.

pp. 107, 109–110, 139, 152, 276–285: "The Broken Child" by Catherine Johnson is reprinted with permission of the author.

p. 110: "Tradition" by Ellen J. Gerl is reprinted with permission of the author.

p. 112: "And Then I Met Matthew" by Anna Szymanski is reprinted wiht permission of the author.

pp. 112, 118–119: "Covering the Rape of a Child" by Megan Lane is reprinted with permission of the author.

p. 114: "Jorma Kaukonen's Organic Odyssey" by Peggy Dillon is reprinted with permission of the author.

p. 116: "Hurricane Journal" by Erika Firm is reprinted with permission of the author.

pp. 120, 271–275: "The Coat" by David Lazar is reprinted with permission of the author.

pp. 127, 153–154: "The Superman Syndrome" by Daniel Horn is reprinted with permission of the author.

p. 128: "Dangerous Games" by Amy Zaruca is reprinted with permission of the author.

pp. 135–136: "Yearbooks and Friendships" by Laura E. Churchill is reprinted with permission of the author.

pp. 142, 218–221: "Bonding with the Grateful Dead" by George Plimpton is reprinted with permission of the author.

pp. 144–145: "First-Love Breakups" by Cathy Twining is reprinted with permission of the author.

pp. 158–160: "On Endings" by Dana Gioia is reprinted with permission of the author.

pp. 169, 171–174, 175–180: "Shape of the Human Heart" by Robin Rauzi is reprinted with permission of the author.

pp. 180–181: "The Re-*Visioning* Process" by Lady Borton is reprinted with permission of the author.

p. 194 (Figure 10.3): Sample query letter by Les Roka is reprinted with permission of the author.

pp. 196–199: "awright, here's what i learned . . ." by Bethany Matsko is reprinted with permission of the author.